Springs
~in the~
VALLEY

Books by Mrs. Charles E. Cowman

Streams in the Desert, Zondervan Classics Edition

Streams in the Desert: An Updated Edition in Today's Language (L.B. Cowman, edited by James Reimann)

Zondervan Classics

Springs
~in the~
VALLEY

Mrs. Charles E. Cowman

ZondervanPublishingHouse

Grand Rapids, Michigan

A Division of HarperCollinsPublishers

Foreword
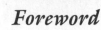

The first edition of *Springs in the Valley* was produced in 1939. Because of the tremendous success of its predecessor, *Streams in the Desert*, it was felt that another collection of thoughts, quotations, and spiritual inspiration from the pen and files of Mrs. Charles E. Cowman would be welcomed by the reading public. Thus was born *Springs in the Valley*.

The enthusiastic response accorded this devotional collection has more than justified the publishers' decision. *Springs in the Valley* has proved itself a worthy companion volume to the classic *Streams in the Desert*. The same spiritual insight and sensitivity to the deepest needs of people went into the selection of the devotional gems in this book. And the same kind of blessing and inspiration has been reported by those whose hearts have been warmed by this more recent collection.

It gives us great pleasure and deep satisfaction to issue this newest edition of *Springs in the Valley* with the prayer that it may continue its ministry of blessing and inspiration.

The Publishers

He sendeth the springs into the valleys,
which run among the hills. (Ps. 104:10)

January 1

*For the L*ORD *thy God bringeth thee into a good land, a land of brooks of water, of fountains and depths that spring out of valleys and hills; A land of wheat, and barley, and vines, and fig trees, and pomegranates; a land of olive oil, and honey; A land wherein thou shalt eat bread without scarceness, thou shalt not lack any thing in it; a land whose stones are iron, and out of whose hills thou mayest dig brass. When thou hast eaten and art full, then thou shalt bless the L*ORD *thy God for the good land which he hath given thee.* (Deut. 8:7–10)

We are entering upon a new year—surely we cannot but believe, a new age. If we have rightly learned the lessons of the past, there lies before us a heritage of unspeakable blessing, which none of these vivid metaphors can too strongly describe; infinite sources of blessing, for the fountains and waterbrooks are but the figures of God's illimitable grace. For *with Him* is the fountain of life.

A Fountain Fed by Eternal Springs!

They tell us of boundless supply: "Bread without scarceness," the olive oil that speaks of the Holy Ghost, the honey that tells of the sweetness of His love, and the pomegranates that are the seed fruit which speak of a life that reproduces itself in the blessing of others.

They tell of the "nether springs" which flow from the depths of sorrow, in the hard places, in the desert places, in the lone places, in the common places which seem farthest from all that is sacred and Divine.

How delightful it is to have His gladness in the low places of sorrow, and to be able to *glory even in tribulation also.*

They tell us of pleasures that come out of the very heart of trial, treasures wrung from the grasp of the enemy.

How precious the springs that flow into the places of temptation, for there is nothing in life so trying as the touch of Satan's hand, and the breath of the destroyer. Oh, how sweet it is, *even there,* to find that the light is as deep as the shadow, and heaven is nearest when we are hard by the gates of hell, so that we can *count it all joy when we fall into diverse temptations,* and can say, "Blessed is the man that endureth temptation: for when he is tried, he shall receive the crown of life, which the Lord hath promised to them that love him."

How blessed to drink from the springs of health, and find our strength renewed day by day, and the life of God flowing into even our physical organs and functions!

"All my fresh *springs are in thee!"*

Beloved, God has for us these springs, and we need them every day. Let us drink of the living waters. Nay, let us receive them into our very hearts, so that we shall carry the fountain with us wherever we go. A. B. SIMPSON

We shall never be "springs" until God comes to us. We shall never be fresh, or fruitful, or useful to others till God comes to us. If we do not have constant visitations of God, we shall soon cease to be "springs," and shall go back to the old dry and barren days. HELENA GARRATT

Let us claim our inheritance in these coming days, and find the hardest places of life's experience God's greatest opportunities and faith's mightiest challenge.

Springs in the valley are very unusual; but He will give us both the upper and the nether springs!

January 2

Jesus himself drew near, and went with them. (Luke 24:15)

A night in Spring ... and two men walking the Emmaus road—saddened by their master's death—bowed down beneath their load, when suddenly *Another* overtakes them as they walk. A *Stranger* falls in step with them, and earnestly they talk—of what is in their hearts—moved by a warm soul-stirring glow—and when they reach Emmaus they are loath to let Him go; and so they bid Him stay awhile and share their simple board. And as He breaks the bread ... *they know.* They know it is the Lord.

Oh, may He *overtake* us as the Path of Life we tread! Along our way of sorrow may His radiant Light be shed.... Oh, may He come to warm the heart and ease the heavy load—and walk with us as long ago He walked the Emmaus Road.

Take the road ... the lonely road—courageous, unafraid; ready for the journey when the twilight shadows fade.... God whose Love is Omnipresent—will He fail us then?—or forget the covenant that He has made with men? PATIENCE STRONG

Jesus never sends a man ahead alone. He blazes a clear way through every thicket and woods, and then softly calls, "Follow me. Let's go on together, you and I." He has been everywhere that we are called to go. His feet have trodden down smooth a path through every experience that comes to us. He knows each road, and knows it well: the valley road of disappointment with its dark shadows; the steep path of temptation down through the rocky ravines and slippery gullies; the narrow path of pain, with the brambly thornbushes so close on each side, with their slash and sting; the dizzy road along the heights of victory; the old beaten road of commonplace daily routine. *Everyday paths He has trodden and glorified, and will walk anew with each of us. The only safe way to travel is with Him alongside and in control.* S. D. GORDON 🐝

> *Come, share the road with Me, My own,*
> *Through good and evil weather;*
> *Two better speed than one alone,*
> *So let us go together.*
>
> *Come, share the road with Me, My own,*
> *You know I'll never fail you,*
> *And doubts and fears of the unknown*
> *Shall never more assail you.*
>
> *Come, share the road with Me, My own,*
> *I'll share your joys and sorrows.*
> *And hand in hand we'll seek the throne*
> *And God's great glad tomorrows.*
>
> *Come, share the road with Me, My own,*
> *And where the black clouds gather,*
> *I'll share thy load with thee, My son,*
> *And we'll press on together.*
>
> *And as we go we'll share also*
> *With all who travel on it.*
> *For all who share the road with Me*
> *Must share with all upon it.*
>
> *So make we—all one company,*
> *Love's golden cord our tether,*
> *And, come what may, we'll climb the way*
> *Together—aye, together!*
>   ROADMATES, BY JOHN OXENHAM 🐝

After a long trying march over perilous Antarctic mountains and glaciers a South Pole explorer said to his leader, "I had a curious feeling on the march that there was another Person with us!"

Another Person! He is ever there to march side by side with those who trust Him!

Take His Hand and Walk with Him!

January 3

Do not be over-anxious . . . about tomorrow, for tomorrow will bring its own cares. Enough for each day are its own troubles. (Matt. 6:34 WEYMOUTH)

There are two golden days in the week, upon which, and about which, I never worry—two carefree days, kept sacredly free from fear and apprehension.

One of these days is Yesterday; Yesterday, with its cares and frets, all its pains and aches, all its faults, mistakes and blunders, has passed forever beyond my recall. I cannot undo an act that I wrought; nor unsay a word that I said. All that it holds of my life, of wrong, regret and sorrow, is in the hands of the Mighty Love that can bring honey out of the rock and sweetest waters out of the bitterest desert. Save for the beautiful memories—sweet and tender—that linger like the perfume of roses in the heart of that day that is gone, I have nothing to do with Yesterday. It *was* mine! It *is* God's!

And the other day that I do not worry about is Tomorrow; Tomorrow, with all its possible adversities, its burdens, its perils, its large promise and poor performance, its failures and mistakes, is as far beyond my mastery as its dead sister, Yesterday. It is a day of God's. Its sun will rise in roseate splendor, or behind a mask of weeping clouds—*but it will rise.*

Until then, the same Love and Patience that held Yesterday holds Tomorrow. Save for the star of hope that gleams forever on the brow of Tomorrow, shining with tender promise into the heart of Today, I have no possession in that unborn day of grace. All else is in the safe keeping of the Infinite Love that is higher than the stars, wider than the skies, deeper than the seas. Tomorrow *is* God's day! It *will be* mine!

There is left for myself, then, but one day in the week—Today. *Any man can fight the battles of Today! Any woman can carry the burdens of just one day! Any man can resist the temptations of Today!* Oh, friends, *it is when we willfully add the burdens of those two awful eternities—Yesterday and Tomorrow—such burdens as only the Mighty God can sustain—that we break down.* It isn't the experience of Today that drives men mad. It is the remorse for something that happened Yesterday; the dread of what Tomorrow may disclose.

These are God's days! Leave them with Him!

Therefore, I think and I do, and I journey *but one day* at a time! That is the easy way. That is Man's Day. Dutifully I run my course and work my appointed task on that Day of ours. God—the All-Mighty and All-Loving—takes care of Yesterday and Tomorrow. BOB BURDETTE 🦋

> *—But, Lord, tomorrow!*
> *Did I not die for thee?*
> *Do I not live for thee?*
> *Leave Me tomorrow!*
>
> CHRISTINA ROSSETTI 🦋

"Tomorrow is God's secret—but today is yours to live."

All the tomorrows of our lives have to pass Him before they can get to us.

> *I heard a voice at evening softly say,*
> *"Bear not thy yesterday into tomorrow;*
> *Nor load this week with last week's load of sorrow.*
> *Lift all thy burdens as they come, nor try*
> *To weight the present with the by and by.*
> *One step, and then another, take thy way—*
> *Live by the day."*
>
> JULIA HARRIS MAY 🦋

January 4

Whosoever drinketh of the water that I shall give him shall never thirst. (John 4:14)

My heart needs Thee, O Lord, my heart needs Thee! No part of my being needs Thee like my heart. All else within me can be filled by Thy gifts. My hunger can be satisfied by daily bread. My thirst can be allayed by earthly waters. My cold can be removed by household fires. My weariness can be relieved by outward rest. But no outward thing can make my heart pure. The calmest day will not calm my passions. The fairest scene will not beautify my soul. The richest music will not make harmony within. The breezes can cleanse the air, but no breeze can cleanse a spirit. This world has not provided for my heart. It has provided for my eye; it has provided for my ear; it has provided for my touch; it has provided for my taste; it has provided for my sense of beauty but it has not provided for my heart.

Lift up your eyes unto the hills! Make haste to Calvary, "Calvary's awful mountain-climb," and on the way there visit the slopes of Mount Olivet, where grow the trees of Gethsemane. Contemplate there the agony of the Lord, where He already tasted the tremendous cup which He drank to the dregs the next noontide on the Cross. *There* is the answer to your need.

Provide Thou for my heart, O Lord. It is the only unwinged bird in all creation. *Give it wings!* O Lord, *give it wings!* Earth has failed to give it wings; its very power of loving has often drawn it into the mire. Be Thou the strength of my heart. Be Thou its fortress in temptation, its shield in remorse, its covert in the storm, its star in the night, its voice in the solitude. Guide it in its gloom; help it in its heat; direct it in its doubt; calm it in its conflict; fan it in its faintness; prompt it in its perplexity; lead it through its labyrinth; raise it from its ruins.

I cannot rule this heart of mine; keep it under the shadow of Thine own wings. GEORGE MATHESON 🐝

> *None other Lamb! none other name!*
> *None other hope in heaven, or earth, or sea!*
> *None other hiding-place for sin and shame!*
> *None beside Thee!*
>
> *My faith burns low; my hope burns low;*
> *Only my soul's deep need comes out in me*
> *By the deep thunder of its want and woe,*
> *Calls out to Thee.*
>
> *Lord, Thou art life though I be dead!*
> *Love's Flame art Thou, however cold I be!*
> *Nor heaven have I, nor place to lay my head,*
> *Nor home, but Thee.*
>
> CHRISTINA ROSSETTI 🐝

"Come unto me . . . and I will give you rest."

January 5

And why take ye thought? (Matt. 6:28)

When a man is living on God's plan he has no need to worry himself about his trade, or about his house, or about anything that belongs to him.

Do not look at your own faith; look at God's faithfulness! Do not look around on circumstances; keep on looking at the resources of the Infinite God!

The only thing a man may be anxious about in this life is whether he is working on God's plan, doing God's work; and if that is so, all the care of everything else is back on God.

There are some things which we cannot definitely claim in prayer, because we do not know whether they are in God's mind for us. They may or may not be, but it is only by praying that we can tell. I am perfectly sure that in praying, there comes to men who dwell with God a kind of holy confidence; and when they get hold of a promise in God's Word, they look on that promise as granted.

Let us yield ourselves to God, that the living Godhead may flow through our poor, mean, frail human minds.

If the Lord careth for thee, be thyself at rest. ARCHBISHOP LEIGHTON

> *When we see the lilies*
> *Spinning in distress,*
> *Taking thought to*
> *Manufacture loveliness;*
> *When we see the birds all*
> *Building barns for store,*
> *'Twill be time for us to worry—*
> *Not before!*

If the Pilot has come on board, why should the captain also pace the deck with weary foot?

January 6

Have faith in God. (Mark 11:22)

In the catacombs, we are told, explorers take a thread with them through all the dark passages and tortuous windings, and by this thread find their way back again to the light. There is such a thread running through all the dark corridors which we tread; and if we simply, practically trust in God we shall steer past every peril and land in the world of light. This is the counsel to remember in all the perplexities of our actual life.

There is an answer to every questioning "Why?" It is this: *Have faith in God.*

Have faith that *He knows all, sympathizes with all, can rectify what is amiss in all!* Have faith in the outworking of His beneficent purpose: that the ruin will become a magnificent pile; the desert will blossom into a garden. *Have faith in God.* Keep close to Him—His side, His will—and He will teach us the true thing, the right way. Have faith that God knows, and that we shall know by and by, why things are as they are.

> *We ask and are answered not,*
> *And so we say, God has forgot,*
> *Or else, there is no God.*
>
> *The years*
> *Roll back and through a mist of tears,*
> *I see a child turn from her play,*
> *And seek with eager feet, the way*
> *That led her to her father's knee.*
>
> *"If God is wise and kind," said she,*
> *"Why did He let my roses die?"*
> *A moment's pause, a smile, a sigh,*
> *And then, "I do not know, my dear,*
> *Some questions are not answered here."*
>
> *"But is it wrong to ask?" "Not so,*
> *My child; that we should seek to know*
> *Proves right to know, beyond a doubt;*
> *And someday we shall yet find out*
> *Why roses die."*
>
> *And then I wait,*
> *Sure of my answer, soon or late;*
> *Secure that love doth hold for me*
> *The key to life's great mystery;*

And oh, so glad to leave it there,
Tho' my dead roses were so fair.

AUTHOR UNKNOWN

January 7

Take you ... twelve stones. ... That this may be a sign among you ... when your children ask ... in time to come ... What mean ye by these stones? Then ye shall answer ... the waters of Jordan were cut off: and these stones shall be for a memorial ... for ever. (Josh. 4:3, 6–7)

You will never get anywhere with God unless you take definite steps.

God was very definite in His dealings with Abraham. *He brought him to a definite place, and Abraham marked the spot.*

When the children of Israel crossed over Jordan they marked the spot on the shore with twelve stones, and also placed twelve stones in the riverbed which were later covered with water—a hidden place.

God wants us, as Christians, *to take definite steps,* and to *mark* these steps. There are places in your heart over which the Jordan's waters roll—hidden places which no one sees, or of which no one knows the meaning; but He knows. When you have committed them unto Him that He might have His say, saying, "Search me, O God, and know my heart; try me, and know my thoughts; and see if there be any wicked way in me," *He knows and answers prayer.*

Is this a crisis hour in *your* life? If it is, settle it *now.*

We must never go back on our transactions with God.

It remains to be seen what God can do with a man irrevocably given to Him. It is because we are but partially His that His work in us and for us is incomplete.

If you have given yourself to God, you have just to *reckon* that He takes what you give. A time comes when you have to *cease praying and believe.* Some Christians say, "O Lord, come and fill me." They keep on praying, and He says, "Believe I have come; reckon that I am come; if you reckon, I will come."

A friend said, "If God tells me to reckon, *He pledges Himself to make the reckoning good.*" As we go on reckoning, we will go on realizing. No man makes a mistake who does what the Lord bids him do. THOMAS COOK

17

Reckon some special time when you fully surrendered your life to the Lord. Build a pile of stones there to mark the spot, and then build another on the life side—the resurrection side! Do this today! Build a heap of stones to mark the time, and never fight the old battle again. We should not be dying and rising, and dying and rising again; we should build our memorial of stones once for all, and then *ever date from that time!*

January 8

He hath ... made me a polished shaft. (Isa. 49:2)

Corner stones, polished after the similitude of a palace. (Ps. 144:12)

∽᠗

Cut ... to Shine!

"When in Amsterdam, Holland, last summer," says a traveler, "I was much interested in a visit we made to a place then famous for polishing diamonds. We saw the men engaged in the work. When a diamond is found it is rough and dark like a common pebble. It takes a long time to polish it, and it is very hard work. It is held by means of a piece of metal close to the surface of a large wheel, which is kept going round and round. Fine diamond dust is put on this wheel, nothing else being hard enough to polish the diamond. This work is kept up for months, and sometimes for several years, before it is finished. If the diamond is intended for a king, then greater time and trouble are spent on it."

What though the precious jewel may be torn and cut until its carats are reduced tenfold! When the cutting and polishing are completed, it will shine with a thousand flashes of reflected light—every carat will be multiplied an hundredfold in value by the process of reduction and threatened destruction!

Let us *wait His time*—let us *trust His love,* that "the trial of your faith ... might be found unto praise and honor and glory at the appearing of Jesus Christ."

Rarest gems bear hardest grinding—
God's own workmanship are we.

January 9

And Jacob was left alone; and there wrestled a man with him until the breaking of the day.... And he said ... as a prince hast thou power with God ... and hast prevailed. (Gen. 32:24, 28)

If you saw one of the intimates of the King on his knees, you would marvel at the sight. Look! He is in the Audience Chamber. He has a seat set for him among the peers. He is set down among the old nobility of the Empire. The King will not put on his signet ring to seal a command, till his friend has been heard. "Command Me," the King says to him. "Ask of Me," He says, "for the things of My sons: command the things to come concerning them!" And, as if that were not enough, that man-of-all-prayer is still on his knees. He is wrestling there. There is no enemy that I can see; yet he wrestles like a mighty man. What is he doing with such a struggle? Doing? Do you not know what he is doing? He is moving Heaven and earth. He is casting this mountain, and that, into the midst of the sea. He is casting down thrones. He is smiting old empires of time to pieces. Yes, he is wrestling indeed. ALEXANDER WHYTE

> *Break through to God,*
> *He fully understands*
> *Thou art in His dear Hands,*
> *To fulfill all His commands,*
> *Break through to God!*
>
> *Break through to God,*
> *Be dauntless, faithful, strong,*
> *E'en though the fight is long,*
> *Raise to Him the victor's song,*
> *Break through to God.*
>
> *Break through to God,*
> *Though thy heart may quail,*
> *And the foe may rail,*
> *Calvary's victory shall not fail,*
> *Break through to God!*

Looking back over the Welsh Revival about 1904, the Rev. Seth Joshua wrote: "The secret of the Lord was with many even before the blessing came. I know a man, who, for five years was carried out by the Spirit, and made to weep and pray along the banks of a Welsh river. At last the travail ceased, and calm expectation followed the soul pangs of this man about whom I now write. *He lived to see the answer to his heart-cries unto the Lord.* He was present in the services in which the first historical incidents took place."

Break through to God!

January 10

Peter went up upon the housetop to pray. (Acts 10:9)

❧

He went up upon the housetop to pray, probably *for further light.* What was to be the next step in the fulfillment of his lifework? Was the cloud to move forward? Was some new development of the Divine pattern at hand which he must realize for himself? And for others?

While he prayed the heavens were opened, and God gave him a real vision of His will. Then when he was very much perplexed in himself at what the vision meant, the knocking at the gate, the voices of men that rose at noon-silence calling his name, together with the assurance of the Spirit that there was no need for fear or further hesitation—all indicated that the hour of Destiny had struck; that a new epoch was inaugurated; and that he was to lead the Church into the greatest revolution she had known since the Ascension of her Lord.

What a lesson for our perplexed and anxious hearts! We find it difficult to wait our Lord's leisure; like imprisoned birds we beat our breasts against the wires of the cage. Though we pray, we do not trust. We find it hard to obey the injunction of our Lord—to roll our care, our way, ourselves, onto God.

Give to the winds thy fears;
hope and be undismayed;
God hears thy sighs, and counts thy tears;
God shall lift up thy head.

Leave to His sovereign sway to choose
and to command;
With wonder filled, thou soon shall own
how wise, how strong His Hand!

Through waves and clouds and storms, He gently
clears thy way.

Wait thou His time, so shall thy night
soon end in joyous day.

He everywhere hath sway, and all things serve
His might.
His every act pure blessing is
His path unsullied light.

January 11

As dying, and, behold, we live. (2 Cor. 6:9)

To one who asked him the secret of service, Mr. George Müller replied: "There was a day when I died, utterly died to George Müller"—and, as he spoke, he bent lower and lower until he almost touched the floor—"to his opinions, preferences, tastes and will; died to the world, its approval or censure; died to the approval or blame of even my brethren and friends. Since then I have *studied to show myself approved only unto God.*"

We may not understand nor know
Just how the giant oak trees throw
Their spreading branches wide,
Nor how upon the mountainside
The dainty wildflowers grow.

We may not understand nor see
Into the depth and mystery
Of suffering and tears;
Yet, through the stress of patient years
The flowers of sympathy

Spring up and scatter everywhere
Their perfume on the fragrant air—
But lo! the seed must die,
If it would bloom and multiply
And ripened fruitage bear.

THOMAS KIMBER

Look at that splendid oak! Where was it born? In a grave. The acorn was put into the ground and in that grave it sprouted and sent up its shoots. And was it only one day that it stood in the grave? No, every day for a hundred years it has stood there, and in that place of death it has found its life. *"The creation of a thousand forests is in one acorn."*

How shall my leaves fly singing in the
wind unless my roots shall wither in the dark?

PERSIAN POET

January 12

Suffered the loss of all things . . . that I may win Christ.
(Phil. 3:8)

Every great life has had in it some great renunciation.

Abraham began by letting go, and going out, and all the way it was just giving up; first his home, his father and his past; next his inheritance to Lot, his selfish nephew; and finally the very child of promise on the altar of Moriah; but he became the father of the faithful, whose inheritance was as the sands of the sea and the stars of the heavens.

Hear *David* saying, "Neither will I offer burnt offerings unto the LORD my God of that which doth cost me nothing" (2 Sam. 24:24). David paid the full price. And we read, "The throne of David shall be established before the LORD for ever" (1 Kings 2:45).

Hannah gave up her boy and he became the prophet of the restoration of ancient Israel.

Paul not only suffered the loss of all things, but counted them but refuse that he might win Christ. And Paul stood before the common people, and in the palaces of kings.

So it is always: *real sacrifice, unto complete surrender of self, brings to us the revelation of God in His fullness.* As we have already seen, it was only on condition of Jacob's releasing and the brothers' bringing the best they had, Benjamin, that they could even see Joseph's face again. And when Judah went farther than this, and offered himself to be Joseph's slave forever, then it was that Joseph could keep back nothing, but found himself compelled to reveal everything to those for whom his heart yearned. It is God's own way with us. God in Jesus Christ does not, and apparently cannot, make Himself fully known in His personality and love, until we have surrendered to Him unconditionally and forever not only all we have, but all we are. *Then God can refrain no longer, but lavishes upon us, in Christ, such a revealing of Himself that it cannot be told in words.*

But the supreme sacrifice!

God had to sacrifice Himself, in Christ, in order thus to reveal Himself to us; but His sacrifice alone will not suffice. Not until we in turn have sacrificed ourself to Him is the revelation possible and complete. But what a revelation it is! *What glory does God give us in the life that is Christ as our life!* How it changes everything for us thereafter *from famine to royal abundance!* MESSAGES FOR THE MORNING WATCH 🦅

I heard a voice so softly calling:
"Take up thy cross and follow me."
A tempest o'er my heart was falling,
A living cross this was to me.

His cross I took, which, cross no longer,
A hundredfold brings life to me;
My heart is filled with joy o'erflowing,
His love and life are light to me.

SELECTED 🦅

January 13

Ye shall have a song. (Isa. 30:29)

Someone writes of sitting one winter evening by an open wood fire, and listening to the singing of the green logs as the fire flamed about them. All manner of sounds came out of the wood as it burned, and the writer, with poetic fancy, suggests that they were imprisoned songs, long sleeping in silence in the wood, brought out now by the fire.

When the tree stood in the forest the birds came and sat on its boughs and sang their songs. The wind, too, breathed through the branches making a weird, strange music. One day a child sat on the moss by the tree's root and sang its happy gladness in a snatch of sweet melody. A penitent sat under the tree's shade and with trembling tones, amid falling leaves, sang the fifty-first Psalm. And all these notes of varied song sank into the tree as it stood there, and hid away in its trunk. There they slept until the tree was cut down and part of it became a backlog in the cheerful evening fire. Then the flames brought out the music.

This is but a poet's fancy as far as the tree and the songs of the backlog are concerned. But is there not here a little parable which may be likened to many a human life? Life has its varied notes and tones—some glad, some choked in tears. Years pass and the life gives out no music of praise, sings no songs to bless others. But, at length, grief comes, and in the flames the long-imprisoned music is set free and sings its praise to God and its notes of love to cheer and bless the world. Gathered in life's long summer and stored away in the heart, it is given out in the hours of suffering and pain.

Many a rejoicing Christian never learned to sing till the flames kindled upon him. J. R. MILLER 🐟

Gather the driftwood that will light the winter fire!

January 14

For I determined not to know any thing among you, save Jesus Christ, and him crucified. (1 Cor. 2:2)

For other foundation can no man lay than that is laid, which is Jesus Christ. (1 Cor. 3:11)

In the Cross of Christ I glory,
Tow'ring o'er the wrecks of time—

Martin Luther preached the doctrine of Atoning Blood to slumbering Europe, and Europe awoke from the dead.

Amid all his defenses of Divine Sovereignty, *Calvin* never ignored or belittled the Atonement.

Cowper sang of it among the water lilies of the Ouse.

Spurgeon thundered this glorious doctrine of Christ Crucified into the ears of peer and peasant with a voice like the sound of many waters.

John Bunyan made the Cross the starting-point to the Celestial City.

Moody's bells all chimed to the keynote of Calvary.

Napoleon, after conquering almost the whole of Europe, put his finger on the red spot on the map representing the British Isles, and said, "Were it not for that red spot, I'd conquer the world!"

So says Satan about the place called Calvary, where Jesus Christ shed His Blood.

Beneath the Cross of Jesus
I fain would take my stand,
The shadow of a mighty rock
Within a weary land;
A home within the wilderness,
A rest upon the way,
From the burning of the noontide heat,
And the burden of the day.

Upon the Cross of Jesus
Mine eye at times can see
The very dying form of One
Who suffered there for me.
And from my smitten heart with tears,
These wonders I confess,
The wonder of His glorious love,
And my own worthlessness.

I take, O Cross, thy shadow
For my abiding place;
I ask no other sunshine than
The sunshine of His face;
Content to let the world go by,
To know no gain nor loss,
My sinful self my only shame,
My glory all the Cross.

Every true preacher of the Gospel strings all his pearls on the Red Cord of the Atonement. T. L. CUYLER

CALVARY COVERS IT ALL!

January 15

And he said unto me, It is done. (Rev. 21:6)

How many persons are everlastingly *doing*, but how few ever *get through* with it! How few settle a thing and know that it is accomplished and can say, "It is done"!

The moment we really believe, we are conscious that there is power. We can touch God at such times, and the fire in our souls makes us sure that something is settled forever.

Faith must be a clear-cut taking hold of God; a grasping Him with fingers of iron, with an uncompromising commitment of all to God. In learning to float you must utterly abandon yourself to the water; you must believe that the water is able to hold you up. So you must take this step of commitment, and then look up to God with confidence and say, "It is done." Our part is *to commit*; God's part is *to work*. The very moment that we commit, that very moment He undertakes. We must believe that He has undertaken what we have committed. Faith must re-echo God's promise and dare to say, *"It is done."*

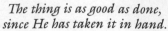

The thing is as good as done,
since He has taken it in hand.

Step out upon a bare promise right now, and "count the things that be not as though they were," and God will make your reckoning real. It will be done by actual experience. DAYS OF HEAVEN UPON EARTH 🐚

My old professor, Lord Kelvin, once said in class a very striking thing. He said that there came a point in all his great discoveries when he had to take a leap into the dark. And nobody who is afraid of such a leap from the solid ground of what is demonstrated, will know the exhilaration of believing!

To commit ourselves unreservedly to Christ is just the biggest venture in the world! The wonderful thing is that when, with a certain daring, we take Lord Kelvin's "leap into the dark" we discover it is not dark at all, but life abundant, and liberty and peace. GEORGE H. MORRISON 🐚

Believe that it is settled because God says so!

"God said, and it happened" *(Gen. 1:2–7, Finnish trans.).*

January 16

Set a watch, O LORD, before my mouth; keep the door of my lips.
(Ps. 141:3)

Let me no wrong or idle word,
Unthinking say;
Set Thou a seal upon my lips—
Just for today.

Keep still! When trouble is brewing, keep still! When slander is getting on its legs, keep still! When your feelings are hurt, keep still till you recover from your excitement at any rate! Things look different through an unagitated eye.

In a commotion once I wrote a letter and sent it, and wished I had not. In my later years I had another commotion and wrote another long letter; my life had rubbed a little sense into me, and I kept that letter in my pocket until I could look it over without agitation, and without tears, and I was glad I did—less and less it seemed necessary to send it. I was not sure it would do any harm, but in my doubtfulness I learned reticence, and eventually it was destroyed.

Time works wonders! Wait till you can speak calmly and then perhaps you will not need to speak. Silence is the most powerful thing conceivable, sometimes. It is strength in its grandeur; it is like a regiment ordered to stand still in the mad fury of battle. To plunge in were twice as easy. *Nothing is lost by learning to keep still.* HANNAH WHITALL SMITH ✒

Lord, keep me still,
Though stormy winds may blow,
And waves my little bark may overflow,
Or even if in darkness I must go,
Yet keep me still, yet keep me still.

Lord, keep me still,
The waves are in Thy hand,
The roughest winds subside at Thy command.
Steer Thou my bark in safety to the land,
And keep me still, and keep me still.

Lord, keep me still,
And may I ever hear Thy still small voice
To comfort and to cheer;
So shall I know and feel Thee ever near.
And keep me still, and keep me still.

SELECTED ✒

Silence is a great peacemaker. HENRY WADSWORTH LONGFELLOW ✒

January 17

In the year that king Uzziah died I saw . . . the Lord. (Isa. 6:1)

We have to get our eyes off others before we can have the full vision of Jesus. Moses and Elias had to pass to make possible the vision of Jesus only. *In the year that King Uzziah died,* Isaiah says, *I saw the Lord.* His eyes and hopes had been upon the mighty and victorious earthly leader, and with his death all these hopes had sunk in despair. But *the stars come out when the lights of earth fade.* It was then Isaiah's true vision and life began.

It is not enough to see Jesus along with other things and persons. What we need is to have Him fill *all* our vision, *all* our sky, *all* our heart, *all* our plans, and *all* our future. What He wants from us is *"first love,"* that is, the supreme place; and He cannot really be anything to us satisfactorily until He is everything. He is able to fill every capacity of our being and without displacing any rightful affection or occupation, yet so blend with all, so control all, so become the very essence of all thought and all delight that we can truly say, "For me to live is Christ," for "the love of Christ constraineth me," shuts me up and in from everything else as a pent-up torrent in its narrow course, to live not unto myself but "unto him that loved me, and gave himself for me."

Holy Spirit, bring us our transfiguration, take us apart to our Mount of vision, let Moses and Elias pass, and let us see no man save *Jesus only.* ECHOES OF A NEW CREATION ☙

> *Am I not enough, Mine own? Enough,*
> *Mine own, for thee?*
> *Hath the world its palace towers,*
> *Garden glades of magic flowers,*
> *Where thou wouldst be?*
> *Fair things and false are there,*
> *False things but fair,*
> *All things thou findst at last*
> *Only in Me.*
> *Am I not enough, Mine own? I, forever*
> *and alone? I, needing thee?*

SUSO ☙

January 18

I came down from heaven, not to do mine own will, but the will of him that sent me. (John 6:38)

When he was crossing the Irish Channel one dark starless night, says Dr. F. B. Meyer, he stood on the deck by the captain and asked him, "How do you know Holyhead Harbor on so dark a night as this?" He said, "You see those three lights? Those three must line up behind each other as one, and when we see them so united we know the exact position of the harbor's mouth."

When we want to know God's will there are three things which always concur: the inward impulse, the Word of God, and the trend of circumstances! God in the heart, impelling you forward; God in the Book, corroborating whatever He says in the heart; and God in circumstances, which are always indicative of His will. *Never start until these three things agree.*

Stand still at the crossroads ready to walk or run,
and you will not be kept waiting long.

When we're not quite certain if we turn to left or right—Isn't it a blessing when a *signpost* looms in sight! If there were no *signposts* we should wander miles astray—in the wrong direction if we didn't know the way.

God has set His *signposts* on Life's strange and winding road. When we're blindly stumbling with the burden of our load—He will lead our footsteps though the pathway twist and bend—In some form He guides us, through The Book, a song, a friend ... In the dark uncertain hours, we need not be afraid—When we're at the crossroads, and decisions must be made ... Though the track is unfamiliar, and the light is gray—Rest assured, there's bound to be a *signpost on the way.* PATIENCE STRONG ☙

Let us be silent unto Him, and believe that, even now, messengers are hastening along the road with the summons, or direction, or help which we need.

January 19

Can God? (Ps. 78:19)

"Can God?" the subtle Tempter breathes within,
When all seems lost, excepting sure defeat,
"Can God roll back the raging seas of sin?"
"Can God?" the fainting heart doth quick repeat.

"God can!" in trumpet tones rings faith's glad cry,
And, David-like, it fears no giant foe,
For faith dwells on the Mount, serene, and high,
While unbelief's dark clouds roll far below.

"God can!" His Saints of old did ever give
Their fullest confirmation o'er and o'er,
And He who made the long-dead bones to live,
E'en now can bring the dead to life once more.

"God can!" Then let us fear not, but arise!
Our motto be this word that He doth give,

If we have faith, before our wondering eyes
A MIGHTY ARMY SHALL ARISE AND LIVE!

J. A. R. 🍂

"Can God?" Oh, fatal question! It shut Israel out of the Land of Promise. And we are in danger of making the same mistake. Can God find me a situation, or provide food for my children? Can God keep me from yielding to that besetting sin? Can God extricate me from this terrible snare in which I am entangled? We look at the difficulties, the surges that are rolling high, and we say, "*If* Thou canst do anything, help us!" They said, "Can God?" It hurt and wounded God deeply. Say no more, "Can God?" Rather say this, "God Can!" That will clear up many a problem. That will bring you through many a difficulty in your life.

There is no strength in unbelief.

Has the life of God's people reached the utmost limit of what God can do for them? *Surely not!* God has new places, and new developments, and new resources. *He can do new things, unheard-of things, hidden things! Let us enlarge our hearts and not limit Him.* "When thou didst terrible things which we looked not for, thou camest down, the mountains flowed down at thy presence" (Isa. 64:3).

We must desire and believe. We must ask and expect that God will do *unlooked-for things!* We must set our faith on a God of whom men do not know what He hath prepared for them that wait for Him. *The Wonder-doing God ... must be the God of our confidence.* ANDREW MURRAY 🍂

The Wonder-doing God can surpass all our expectation!

January 20

And he came and dwelt in a city called Nazareth. (Matt. 2:23)

Our Lord Jesus lived for thirty years amid the happenings of the little town of Nazareth. Little villages spell out their stories in small events. *And He, the young Prince of Glory, was in the carpenter's shop!* He moved amid humdrum tasks, petty cares, village gossip, trifling trade, *and He was faithful in that which was least.*

If these smaller things in life afford such riches of opportunity for the finest loyalty, all of our lives are wonderfully wealthy in possibility and promise. Even though our house is furnished with commonplaces it can be the home of the Lord all the days of our life. J. H. JOWETT 🍂

When I am tempted to repine
That such a lowly lot is mine,
There comes to me a voice which saith,
"Mine were the streets of Nazareth."

So mean, so common and confined,
And He the Monarch of mankind!
Yet patiently He traveleth
Those narrow streets of Nazareth.

It may be I shall never rise
To place or fame beneath the skies—
But walk in straitened ways till death,
Narrow as streets of Nazareth.

But if through honor's arch I tread
And there forget to bend my head,
Ah! let me hear the voice which saith,
"Mine were the streets of Nazareth."

NETTIE ROOKER

There's sometimes a good hearty tree growin' out o' the bare rock, out o' some crack that just holds the roots, right on one o' them hills where you can't seem to see a wheelbarrowful o' good earth, but that tree'll keep a green top in the driest summer. You lay your ear down to the ground, and you'll hear a little stream runnin'. Every such tree has got its own livin' spring; there's folks made to match 'em. SARAH ORNE JEWETT

From the desire of being great, good Lord deliver us! A MORAVIAN PRAYER

January 21

Remove not the ancient landmark, which thy fathers have set. (Prov. 22:28)

Among the property owned jointly by two young brothers who were carpenters was the old tumbledown place of their birth. One of the brothers was soon to be married and the old house was to be torn down and a new one erected on its site. For years neither of the brothers had visited the cottage, as it had been leased.

As they entered now and started the work of demolishing the place, again and again floods of tender memories swept over them. By the time they reached the kitchen they were well-nigh overcome with their emotions. There was the place where the old kitchen table had stood—with the family Bible—where they had knelt every evening. They were recalling now with a pang how in later years they had felt a little superior to that time-honored custom carefully observed by their father.

Said one: "We're *better off* than he was, but we're not *better men.*"

The other agreed, saying, "I'm going back to the old church and the old ways, and in my new home I'm going to make room for worship as Dad did."

The strength of a nation lies in the homes of its people. ABRAHAM LINCOLN 🕊

Says Dr. J. G. Paton: "No hurry for market, no rush for business, no arrival of friends or guests, no trouble or sorrow, no joy or excitement, ever prevented us from kneeling around the family altar while our high priest offered himself and his children to God." And on his father's life in his home was based Dr. Paton's decision to follow the Lord wholly. "He walked with God—why not I?"

"Stand ye in the . . . old paths, where is the good way" (*Jer. 6:16*).

January 22

And when they were come into the ship, the wind ceased. (Matt. 14:32)

〜

Faith can conquer every obstacle!

Some people insist upon holding Christ at a distance, waiting before going to Him until obstacles have been removed. *When economic skies are brighter; when doubts have been cleared; when the edge of sorrow has been dulled: then they will go to Jesus.*

Peter, knowing that the Master was near, in sublime faith asked to be permitted to go to Him across the surging waters. *Fear almost conquered him, but even then Jesus lifted him by the hand.*

There are always storms of difficulty and of assailing doubts. Unanswered questions and the problems of hideous wrongs are always battling against the good purposes of Christ. Do not let the storms keep *you* from the consoling presence of Christ. Build *a bridge out of the storms, and go to Him!* SELECTED 🐦

> *"Get into the boat!" Thou didst whisper.*
> *At first how I feared to obey;*
> *I looked not at Thee, but the storm clouds,*
> *The darkness, the waves, and the spray.*
>
> *But then came the words, "Will you trust Him?*
> *Will you claim and receive at His hand*
> *All His definite fullness of blessing?*
> *Launch out at thy Master's command!"*
>
> *Thou art willing, my Lord, could I doubt Thee?*
> *Hast Thou ever proved untrue?*
> *Nay! out at Thy word I have ventured,*
> *I have trusted. Thy part is to do.*
>
> LAURA A. BARTER-SNOW 🐦

When Jesus rises, the storm stops. The calm comes from the power of His Presence. As a strong quiet man steps in majestically among a crowd of noisy brawlers, his very appearance makes them ashamed and hushes their noise; so Jesus steps in among the elements, and they are still in a moment.

January 23

I called him alone, and blessed him. (Isa. 51:2)

A celebrated Scottish nobleman and statesman once replied to a correspondent that he was *"plowing his lonely furrow."* Whenever God has required someone to do a big thing for Him, He has sent him to a *lonely furrow.* He has called him to go alone.

You may have to become the loneliest person on earth, but if you do you will be able always to see around you the chariots of God, even twenty thousand, and thousands of thousands, *and then you will forget your loneliness.*

> *The soil is hard,*
> *And the plow goes heavily.*
> *The wind is fierce*
> *And I toil on wearily—*

But His hands made the yoke!
Ah wonder—that I should bear His yoke—
It is enough, if I may but plow the furrow,
For the Sower to sow the seed.

If you have taken hold of the plow, *hold on until the field is finished.* *"Let us not cave in" (fall out and leave a gap) (Gal. 6:9, Greek).*

Says Theodore L. Cuyler, "After long and painful perplexities about accepting a certain attractive call, I opened the Book and read: *'Why gaddest thou about so much to change thy way?'"* (Jer. 2:36).

"Your present field may be limited, but you are not limited by your field. Great men have sprung from the furrows. Great men have plowed and harrowed, and leaving these things have written their names deep in history. There are heights undreamed of, ecstasies unthought of for the one who follows on. So follow on in the valley, *looking for hills.* One day you will look back with surprise, and then turning go forward with fresh courage."

You were made to MOUNT and not to crawl!

"One lonely soul on fire with the love of God may set the whole universe ablaze" *(see Acts 2:41; Rev. 5:11).*

January 24

There is nothing. (1 Kings 18:43)

Elijah was a man who hoped perfectly; hoped against hope until the abundant answer came. He continued, in the very face of darkness and perplexity, *to expect,* because the very God of hope lived *in* him and expected *through* him. And he was not ashamed, for it came to pass the seventh time his servant said, "Behold, there ariseth a little cloud out of the sea, about the size of a man's hand," and in a little while the heaven was black with clouds and there was a great rain!

Can *you* count God faithful when only *the still small voice* speaks? When there is neither wind, earthquake, nor fire? Can you start *when you see the cloud no bigger than a man's hand?* Can you say: "'There is nothing,' *but I wait on Thee.* My mind is peculiarly in the dark regarding the way I am to take, *but Thou knowest. Unto Thee do I look up!"*

"There is nothing"—though the raindrops needed sorely
and so long
Have been promised by Jehovah, by the Father true and strong.
And the sky is blue and cloudless, and the earth is parched and dry,
Yet no showers are forthcoming from the reservoir on high.

"There is nothing"—but the prophet knows and trusts his Master's word;
He is not a senseless idol, but the mighty, powerful God.
He has seen His wondrous working, he believes Him faithful still;
So he humbly waits in patience for Jehovah's perfect will.

"There is nothing"—oh, how often doth the enemy declare,
Nothing for your constant wrestlings; nothing for your cries and tears.
And the faithless heart says
"Nothing," though deceived she ne'er has been,
For the little cloud so longed for, at the seventh time is soon.

"There is nothing"—but there shall be: God is still the Great "I AM."
He is NOW Almighty, faithful, and forevermore the same;
And the tears, and cries, and wrestlings, have been recorded on high;
Not forgotten, nor neglected, to be answered by and by.

JAMES BOOBBYER

"Get thee up, eat and drink; for there is a sound of abundance of rain!"

January 25

Produce your cause, saith the LORD; bring forth your strong reasons, saith the King of Jacob. (Isa. 41:21)

Over in Canada there lived an Irish saint called "Holy Ann." She lived to be one hundred years old. When she was a young girl, she was working in a family for very small wages under a very cruel master and mistress. They made her carry water for a mile up a steep hill. At one time there had been a well dug there; it had gone dry, but it stood there year after year. One night she was very tired, and she fell on her knees and cried to God; and while on her knees she read these words: "I will open . . . fountains in the midst of the valleys: I will make . . . the dry land springs of water." "Produce your cause, saith the LORD; bring forth your strong reasons." These words struck Holy Ann, and she produced her cause before the Lord. She told Him how badly they needed the water and how hard it was for her to carry the water up the steep hill; then she lay down and fell asleep. She had pleaded her cause and brought forth her strong reasons. The next morning early she was seen to take a bucket and start for the well. Someone asked her where she was going, and she replied, "I am going to draw water from the well." "Why, it is dry," was the answer. But that did not stop Holy Ann. She knew whom she had believed, and on she went; and, lo and behold, there in the well was eighty-three feet of pure, cold water, and she told me that the well never did run dry! That is the way the Lord can fulfill His promises. "Produce your cause ... bring forth your strong reasons," and see Him work in your behalf.

How little we use this method of holy argument in prayer; and yet there are many examples of it in Scripture: Abraham, Jacob, Moses, Elijah, Daniel—all used arguments in prayer, and claimed the Divine interposition on the ground of the pleas which they presented.

January 26

I being in the way, the LORD led me. (Gen. 24:27)

"The way" means God's way, the pathway prepared for us; not our way; not any kind of way (Prov. 14:12); not man's way; but the direct way of duty and command. In such a way the Lord will be sure to lead and guide us. The Lord answered the servant's prayer *exactly* as he prayed, step by step.

"God never gives guidance for two steps at a time. I must take one step, and then I receive light for the next."

> *As thou dost travel down the corridor of Time*
> *Thou wilt find many doors of usefulness;*
> *To gain some there are many weary steps to climb,*
> *And then they will not yield! but onward press,*
> *For there before thee, in the distance just beyond*
> *Lies one which yet will open; enter there,*
> *And thou shalt find all realized thy visions fair*
> *Of fields more vast than thou hast yet conceived.*
> *Press on, faint not; though briars strew thy way,*
> *The greatest things are yet to be achieved;*
> *And he who falters not will win the day.*

No man can shut the door which God sets wide,
He bids thee enter there—thy work awaits inside.
FAIRELIE THORNTON

Keep to your post and watch His signals!

Implicitly rely on the methods of His guidance.

January 27

And a light shined in the prison: and he [the angel] smote Peter on the side . . . saying, Arise up quickly. (Acts 12:7)

If we fear the Lord, we may look for timely interpositions when our case is at its worst. Angels are not kept from us by storms, nor hindered by darkness. Seraphs think it no humiliation to visit the poorest of the heavenly family. If angels' visits are few and far between at ordinary times, they shall be frequent in our nights of tempest and tossing. Dear reader, is this an hour of distress with you? Then ask for peculiar help. Jesus is the Angel of the Covenant, and if His presence be now earnestly sought it will not be denied. What that presence brings is heart cheer. CHARLES H. SPURGEON

> *And a light shined in my cell,*
> *And there was not any wall,*
> *And there was no dark at all,*
> *Only THOU, Emmanuel.*
>
> *Light of love shined in my cell,*
> *Turned to gold the iron bars,*
> *Opened windows to the stars,*
> *Peace stood there as sentinel.*
>
> *Dearest Lord, how can it be*
> *That Thou art so kind to me?*
> *Love is shining in my cell,*
> *Jesus, my Emmanuel.*
>
> A. W. C.

January 28

Go forth, and stand upon the mount before the LORD.
(1 Kings 19:11)

A rebuke is often a blessing in disguise. Elijah needed this form of address in order to arouse him to an understanding of his causeless fear. Such a one as he has no right to be fitful and repining. If he will *go forth and stand upon the mount before the Lord,* instead of hiding away in a cave, he will find new inspiration in a new vision of His power! When we are living on earth's low levels we fail to catch the inspiring visions of God which are the true support of the prophetic life. We must come out into the sunshine and make the ascent of the mountain if we would discern those evidences of God's power which are always available for the re-creation of faith and courage.

The golden-crested wren is one of the tiniest of birds; it is said to weigh only the fifth part of an ounce; and yet, on frailest pinions, it braves hurricanes and crosses northern seas.

It often seems in nature as though Omnipotence works but through frailest organisms; certainly the Omnipotence of grace is seen to the greatest advantage in the trembling but resolute saint.

On the American prairies the butterflies start westward in their migrations and make steady progress though the wind is against them and the sea in front. The delicate butterflies rebuke me.

> *Step out on the waves*
> *That would crush you!*
> *Step out in the storm*
> *That would hush you!*
> *And you will find,*
> *As you touch the crest*
> *You feared so much,*
> *And walk on its breast,*
> *There was One walking there,*
> *The whole night through,*
> *Walking, watching,*
> *Waiting—*FOR YOU!

January 29

I will make all my mountains a way. (Isa. 49:11)

Do not try to tunnel under them, nor to squeeze through them, nor to run away from them, but to *claim them.*

Tighten your loins with the promises of God!

These mountains of difficulty are His stepping-stones; walk on them with holy joy.

Keep the strong staff of faith well in hand, and *trust God in the dark*.

We are safer with Him in the dark than without Him in the sunshine. *At the end of the gloomy passage beams the heavenly light!* When we reach heaven we may discover that the richest and most profitable experiences that we had in this world were those gained in the very roads from which we shrank back in dread.

It was because Job was on God's main line that he found so many tunnels.

The great thing to remember is that *God's darknesses are not His goals.* His tunnels must be traveled *to get somewhere else*. Therefore, be patient, my soul! The darkness is not thy bourne; the tunnel is not thy abiding home!

The traveler who would pass from the wintry slopes of Switzerland into the summer beauty of the plains of Italy, *must be prepared to tunnel the Alps.*

> *Often darkness fills the pathway of the*
> *pilgrim's onward track,*
> *And we shrink from going forward—trembling,*
> *feel like going back:*
> *But the Lord, who plans so wisely, leads us on*
> *both day and night,*
> *Till at last, in silent wonder, we rejoice in*
> *Wisdom's light.*
>
> *Though the tunnel may be tedious through the*
> *narrow, darkened way,*
> *Yet it amply serves its purpose—soon it brings*
> *the light of day:*
> *And the way so greatly dreaded, as we*
> *backward take a glance,*
> *Shows the skill of careful planning: never the*
> *result of chance!*
>
> *Is your present path a tunnel, does the darkness*
> *bring you fear?*
> *To the upright, oh, remember, He doth cause*
> *a light to cheer.*
> *Press on bravely, resting calmly, though a way*
> *you dimly see,*
> *Till, at length, so safely guided, you emerge*
> *triumphantly.*

Trust the Engineer Eternal, surely all His works
are right,
Though we cannot always trace them, faith will
turn at last to sight:
Then no more the deepening shadows of the
dark and dismal way,
There forever in clear sunlight, we'll enjoy
"the perfect day."

SELECTED

The tunnel is never on a siding—it is planned to lead somewhere!

January 30

Get thee out of thy country . . . unto a land that I will show thee.
(Gen. 12:1)

It was one of the great moments of history when this primitive caravan set out for Haran. As we dimly picture them setting forth in the pale dawn of history, we seem to see the laden camels, pacing slowly, towering above the slow-footed sheep; we hear the drovers' cries and bleating of the flocks, broken by the wail of parting women.

With those who stay behind we strain wistful eyes across the broad flood of old Euphrates, till in the wilderness beyond, the caravan is lost in a faint dust-haze—a stain and no more on the southern horizon.

Who does not feel that the grandeur of that moment centers in *the loyalty of one human soul to one word of God?*

"There's no sense in going further—it's the edge of cultivation."
So they said and I believed it—broke my land and sowed my crop—
Built my barns and strung my fences in the little
border station—
Tucked away below the foothills where the trails run out and stop.

Till a voice, as bad as conscience, rang interminable changes
On one everlasting whisper, day and night repeated so:
"Something hidden. Go and find it. Go and look behind the Ranges—
Something lost behind the Ranges, lost and waiting for you. Go!"

Anybody might have found it, but—His whisper came to me!

KIPLING

There remaineth yet very much land to be possessed!

Like the western prairies, there is no limit; it extends beyond the power of the human mind. "Eye hath not seen, nor ear heard, neither have entered into the heart of man, the things which God hath prepared for them that love him" (1 Cor. 2:9).

The Holy Ghost is looking for simple-hearted believers *who will claim for Jesus Christ the great stretches of unoccupied places of darkness.*

Who will strike the Trail?

January 31

For he shall be as a tree planted by the waters. (Jer. 17:8)

Trees that brave storms are not propagated in hothouses!

The staunchest tree is not found in the shelter of the forest, but out in the open where the winds from every quarter beat upon it, and bend and twist it until it becomes a giant in stature.

It requires storms to produce the rooting.

Out on the meadow it stands to shelter the herds and flocks. The earth about the tree hardens. The rains do little good for the water runs off.

But the terrific storm strikes. It twists, turns, wrenches, and at times all but tears it out of its place. If the tree could speak it might bitterly complain. Should nature listen and cease the storm process?

The storm almost bends the tree double. It is wrath now. What can such seeming cruelty mean? Is that love? But *wait!*

About the tree the soil is all loosened. Great cracks are opened up away down into the ground. Deep wounds they might appear to the inexperienced. The rain now comes in with its gentle ministry. The WOUNDS fill up. The moisture reaches away down deep even to the utmost root. The sun again shines. New and vigorous life bursts forth. The roots go deeper and deeper. The branches shoot forth. Now and again one hears something snap and crack like a pistol: it is getting too big for its clothes! It is growing into a giant! *It is rooting!*

This is the tree from which the mechanic wants his tools made—the tree which the wagon-maker seeks.

When you see a spiritual giant, think of the road over which he has traveled—not the sunny lane where wildflowers ever bloom, but a steep, rocky, narrow pathway where the blasts of hell will almost blow you off your feet, where the sharp rocks cut the feet, where the projecting thorns scratch the brow, and the venomous serpents hiss on every side.

The Lord provides deep roots
when there are to be wide-spreading branches.

God of the gallant trees
Give to us fortitude:
Give as Thou givest to these,
Valorous hardihood.
We are the trees of Thy planting, O God,
We are the trees of Thy wood.

Now let the life-sap run
Clean through our every vein,
Perfect what Thou hast begun,
God of the sun and rain.
Thou who dost measure the weight of wind,
Fit us for stress and strain!

A. W. C.

Blessed be storms!

February 1

Jesus knowing that the Father had given all things into his hands, and that he was come from God, and went to God; He riseth from supper, and laid aside his garments; and took a towel, and girded himself. After that he poureth water into a basin, and began to wash the disciples' feet, and to wipe them with the towel wherewith he was girded. (John 13:3–5)

Not to sit on a lifted throne, nor to rule superbly alone; not to be ranked on the left or right in the kingdom's glory, the kingdom's might; not to be great and first of all, not to hold others in humble thrall; not to lord it over the world, a scepter high and a flag unfurled; not with authority, not with pride, vain dominion, mastery wide—nothing to wish for, nothing to do—not, in short, to be ministered to! Ah, but to minister! Lowly to sup with the servant's bread and the servant's cup; down where the waters of sorrow flow; full-baptized in the stream of woe; out where the people of sorrow are, walking brotherly, walking far; known to

bitterness, known to sin, to the poor and wretched comrade
and kin; so to be helper, the last and the least serf in the kingdom,
slave at the feast; so to obey, and so to defer, and so, my Savior, to minister. Yes, for never am I alone: this is Thy glory and this is Thy throne.
Infinite Servant, well may I be bondman and vassal and toiler—with
Thee. AMOS R. WELLS ☙

I would be simply used,
Spending myself in humble task or great,
Priest at the altar, keeper of the gate,
So be my Lord requireth just that thing
Which at the needful moment I may bring.
O joy of serviceableness Divine!

Of merging will and work, dear Lord, in Thine,
Of knowing that results, however small,
Fitly into Thy stream of purpose fall.
I would be simply used!

ANONYMOUS ☙

I want to be a humble soul
Commended in the sky.

JOHN SHOBER KIMBER ☙

February 2

That it may bring forth more fruit. (John 15:2)

Two years ago I set out a rosebush in the corner of my garden. It was
to bear yellow roses. And it was to bear them profusely. Yet, during these
two years, it has not produced a blossom!

I asked the florist from whom I bought the bush why it was so barren of flowers. I had cultivated it carefully; had watered it often; had made
the soil around it as rich as possible. And it had grown well.

"That's just why," said the florist. "That kind of rose needs the poorest soil in the garden. Sandy soil would be best, and never a bit of fertilizer.
Take away the rich soil and put gravelly earth in its place. Cut the bush back
severely. Then it will bloom."

I did—and the bush blossomed forth in the most gorgeous yellow
known to nature. Then I moralized: that yellow rose is just like many lives.
Hardships develop beauty in the soul; the soul thrives on troubles; trials

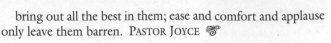

bring out all the best in them; ease and comfort and applause only leave them barren. PASTOR JOYCE 🥀

The bark by tempest vainly tossed
May founder in the calm;
And he who braved the polar frost
Faint by the isles of balm.

WHITTIER 🥀

The finest of flowers bloom in the sandiest of deserts as well as in the hothouses. God is the same Gardener.

February 3

And the chief priests accused him of many things. And Pilate again asked him, saying, Answerest thou nothing? behold how many things they accuse thee of. But Jesus no more answered anything; insomuch that Pilate marvelled. (Mark 15:3–5 ASV)

The apostle writes years afterwards of this wonderful silence of the God-man:

"Who, when he was reviled, reviled not again; when he suffered, he threatened not" *(1 Peter 2:23).*

His silence was Divine. No mere human could thus remain dumb, and innocent and guiltless allow Himself to be "led as a lamb to the slaughter," to be as a sheep dumb in the hand of the shearers. This silence before Pilate, and then the silence on the Cross in the midst of untold agony—silence, broken only seven times, with brief words of wondrous meaning—this silence of Jesus was the climax to a life of God-like silence in circumstances when men must speak; a life of silent waiting until He was thirty years of age ere He entered on public ministry, and made His lamb-like way to the Cross; a life of silence over glory unspeakable with His Father, and suffering untold at the hands of men; of tender silence over blessing to others, and over Judas' traitor path.

This is the pattern for all who would *follow His steps;* the pattern for the one who would walk as He walked, by His walking again in them. And how can it be? Only by seeing the *calling* and accepting it (1 Peter 1:15). And by taking His Cross as *our* Cross, "we having died" *in* Him and *with* Him can thus live unto God, and then the silence of Jesus can be known in truth, and we shall be:

SILENT in our lowly service among others, not seeking to be seen of men.

SILENT over the glory of the hours on the Mount, lest others think of us above that which is written.

SILENT over the depths of the Calvary pathway that led us unto God.

SILENT over the human instruments permitted of God to hand us over to the judgment hall, and the forsaking of our nearest and our dearest.

SILENT whilst we stoop to serve the very ones who have betrayed us.

SILENT over the deep things of God revealed in the secret places of the Most High, *impossible to utter* to those who have not yet been *baptized* with that baptism without which they will be *straightened* in spiritual perception *until it be accomplished.*

SILENT over questions only to be answered by God, the Holy Ghost, when *that day* dawns for the questioning heart, and silences all doubt by the glorious revelation of Him who is the answer to all our needs.

SILENT when forced by others to some position where apparent rivalry with another much-used servant of God seems imminent, only to be hushed by utter self-effacement, and our silent withdrawal without explanation, *irrespective of our rights.*

SILENT —yea, silent in the judgment hall of our co-religionists, when criticized and falsely accused of many things. TRACT

Live Thou this life in me.

February 4

We had the sentence of death in ourselves, that we should not trust in ourselves. (2 Cor. 1:9)

These are weighty words for all Christ's servants; but we must be His servants *in reality,* in order to enter into their deep significance. If we are content to live a life of indolence and ease, a life of self-seeking and self-pleasing, it is impossible for us to understand such words, or indeed to enter into any of those intense exercises of soul through which Christ's true-hearted servants and faithful witnesses, in all ages, have been called to pass.

We find, invariably, that all those who have been most used of God in public have gone through deep waters in secret. Paul could say to the Corinthians, *"Death worketh in us, but life in you."* Death working in the poor earthen vessel; but streams of life, heavenly grace, and spiritual power flowing into those to whom he ministered.

How the professing church has departed from the Divine reality of ministry! Where are the Pauls, the Gideons, and the Joshuas? Where are the deep heart-searchings and profound soul exercises which have characterized Christ's servants in other days? Flippant, worldly, shallow, empty, self-sufficient and self-indulgent are we! *Need we wonder at the small results?*

How can we expect to see life working in others, when we know so little about death working in us?

May the eternal Spirit stir us all up! May He work in us a more powerful sense of what it is to be *true-hearted, single-eyed, devoted servants of the Lord Jesus Christ!*

> *From prayer that asks that I may be*
> *Sheltered from winds that beat on Thee,*
> *From fearing when I should aspire,*
> *From faltering when I should climb higher,*
> *From silken self, O Captain, free*
> *Thy soldier who would follow Thee.*
>
> *From subtle love of softening things,*
> *From easy choices, weakenings,*
> *(Not thus are spirits fortified,*
> *Not this way went the Crucified)*
> *From all that dims Thy Calvary*
> *O Lamb of God, deliver me.*
>
> *Give me the love that leads the way,*
> *The faith that nothing can dismay,*
> *The hope no disappointments tire,*
> *The passion that will burn like fire;*
> *Let me not sink to be a clod:*
> *Make me Thy fuel, Flame of God.*

AMY WILSON CARMICHAEL

Write the death sentence upon self, that the power of resurrection life in Christ may shine forth!

February 5

Hezekiah went up unto the house of the LORD, and spread it before the LORD. (Isa. 37:14)

Does it not often happen that you are in great difficulty how to act in some particular case? Your course is not plain; your way is not open: each side seems equally balanced, and you cannot tell which to choose. Your wishes, perhaps, point one way; your fears, another. You are afraid lest you should decide wrongly; lest you should take what, in the end, may prove hurtful to you.

It is very trying to be brought into this painful conflict. And it adds to our distress if we are forced to go forward at once, and take one course or the other. Shall I tell you how you may be sure to find unspeakable relief?

Go and lay your matter before the Lord, as Hezekiah did with the king of Assyria's letter. Do not, however, deceive yourself, as many do, and seek counsel of God, *having determined to act according to your own will, and not according to His.* But, simply and honestly, ask that He would guide you. Commit your case to your Father in heaven; surrender yourself as a little child to be led as He pleases. This is the way to be guided aright, and to realize the blessing of having a heavenly Counselor. A. OXENDEN

"Confide all your works to the Lord, and He will arrange for all your plans" *(Prov. 16:3 Fenton's trans.).*

Surrendered—led alone by Thee,
And wait Thy guidance still.

February 6

If thou canst believe, all things are possible to him that believeth. (Mark 9:23)

Prayer takes the people to the Bank of Faith, and obtains the golden blessing. Mind how you pray! Pray! Make real business of it! Never let it be a dead formality! People pray a long time, but do not get what they are supposed to ask for, *because they do not plead the promise in a truthful businesslike way.* If you were to go into a bank and stand an hour talking to the clerk, and then come out again without your cash, what would be the good of it? CHARLES H. SPURGEON ❧

Have you ever given God the chance to answer the Prayer of Faith?

Do not let us lose our last chance of believing by waiting till the dawn has broken into day! LILIAS TROTTER ❧

If radio's slim finger can pluck a melody
From night, and toss it over a continent or sea;
If the petaled white notes of a violin
Are blown across a mountain or a city's din;
If songs, like crimson roses, are culled from thin
blue air—
Why should mortals wonder if God hears prayer?
ETHEL ROMIG FULLER ❧

When all things can be accomplished by prayer, why not yield to the test? Why not pray on? And through?

February 7

Before they call, I will answer; and while they are yet speaking,
I will hear. (Isa. 65:24)

In one of his great Gospel campaigns in Chicago, Moody asked his helpers to join him in prayer for $6,000 and to ask that it *might be sent at once*. They prayed long and earnestly, and before they rose from their knees a telegram was brought in. It was in some such words as these:

Your friends at Northfield had a feeling that you needed money for your work in Chicago. We have taken up a collection and there are $6,000 in the baskets.

"God had prepared the people" *(2 Chron. 29:36)*.

In connection with the work of the West London Mission, the Rev. Hugh Price Hughes and his colleagues once found themselves in pressing need of £1,000, and to get quiet they met at midnight to pray for it. After some time of pleading, one of the number burst into praise, being assured that the prayer had been heard and would be answered. Mr. Hughes did not share this absolute confidence. He believed with trembling.

When the day came for announcing the sum received, it was found that £990 had come in within a very short time and in very extraordinary ways—but there was the deficiency of £10. When Mr. Hughes went home he found a letter which he now remembered had been there in the morning, but through pressure he had left it unopened. It contained a check for £10!

I'll trust Thy grace—'tis infinite;
And knows no bound, nor end.

After Dan Crawford had passed to his eternal rest, it was written of him: "He lived (and his work was supported) by strong faith in the unlimited riches of God, and in the power of prayer. He felt, too, *that those riches and that power were available for all Africa, though he knew that not all had the same faith.*"

He had a strong sense of unity of God's work. A certain missionary in Africa, held up in some work for God, wrote to Dan Crawford asking for £100, and excused himself by saying, "You are rich." When he saw that the same weekly mail that had brought the request had brought also contributions amounting to about the sum mentioned, Dan Crawford sent the whole week's income to his correspondent with this reply: "Rich? Yes, I am rich—rich in faith for you all."

"And God is able to give you an overflowing measure of all good gifts, that all your wants of every kind may be supplied at all times, and you may give of your abundance to every good work."

He might have doled His blossoms out quite grudgingly,
God might have used His sunset gold so sparingly,
He might have put but one wee star in all the sky—
But since He gave so lavishly, why should not I?

A. C. H.

February 8

And there came thither [to Lystra] certain Jews ... who persuaded the people, and, having stoned Paul, drew him out of the city, supposing he had been dead.... The next day he departed ... to Derbe. And when they had preached the gospel to that city ... they returned again to Lystra. (Acts 14:19–21)

The cruel stones unerring fell upon him—
Until they deemed his bleeding form was dead;

His worth and work they knew not, and they cared not;
Enough, they madly hated what he said.

God touched him! and he rose, with new life given;
Nor in his bosom burned resentful pain;
And, by and by, when need and call both guided,
He to the stoning-place RETURNED AGAIN.

Perchance thou, too, hast tasted cruel stoning—
And might'st be glad if call came ne'er again
To turn to scenes where surely there awaits thee
The cruel, cutting stones which make life vain.

Yet, if "back to the stones" the Finger pointeth,
Then thou shalt know there is no better way;
And there, just there, shall matchless grace await thee,
And God Himself shall be thy strength and stay.

J. DANSON SMITH 🐦

The most sublime moments lie very close to the most painful situations.

Are *we* familiar with the road that leads back to the stones?

February 9

God led them not through the way of the ... Philistines, although that was near. (Ex. 13:17)

Why not? Because the people needed disciplining and molding as a Nation. They would have been destroyed by way of Philistia, but by the way of the wilderness they were trained slowly for the great task at their journey's end. God, who chose the route, also chose the leader. God, who disciplined the people, also disciplined the man who led them.

History and experience seem to point to the fact that God's line for us is not usually a straight line, but a winding zigzag path.

The roundabout way may be the nearest! JOSEPH PARKER 🐦

Over the Apennines there is a wonderful railroad—one passes through forty-three tunnels in less than seventy miles—magnificent outlooks, but every few minutes, a tunnel! The road has been built to carry the traveler to his destination by the shortest way; anyone getting off at the first station simply because he did not like tunnels, and striking into the mountains to find another path, would be almost sure of being lost and starving to death.

Can we not believe the same thing of God's way? His way lies through tunnels—long ones often, but it is the best and safest road. And it is not all tunnels; in the region of the high rocks there are most glorious prospects! Places so full of beauty, and commanding such outlooks of love and mercy, as ought to reconcile us to the intervals of darkness.

Be not afraid of the *winding way* if God turns you into it.

Travel the road He points out to you!

God brings men to His consummations *only by His own road.*

We climbed the height by the zigzag path
And wondered why—until
We understood it was made zigzag
To break the force of the hill.

A road straight up would prove too steep
For the traveler's feet to tread;
The thought was kind in its wise design
Of a zigzag path instead.

It is often so in our daily life;
We fail to understand
That the twisting way our feet must tread
By love alone was planned.

Then murmur not at the winding way,
It is our Father's will
To lead us Home by the zigzag path,
To break the force of the hill.

ANONYMOUS

Simply following God is the true philosophy of life.

February 10

The angel of the LORD encampeth round about them that fear him, and delivereth them. (Ps. 34:7)

A wonderful story is told by a Moravian missionary in connection with angelic protection.

An American missionary and his wife bravely went to their station, where, twenty years before, two missionaries had been killed and eaten by the natives. They said as they took up their work it seemed as if often they were surrounded not only by the hostile natives, but by the very powers of darkness. These latter were so real, that night after night they were forced to get up and strengthen their hearts by reading the Word of God. Again, they would pray.

One day a man came and said, "I would like to see your watchmen close at hand."

The missionary replied: "I have no watchmen; I have only a cook and a little herd boy. What watchmen do you mean?"

The man asked permission to look through the missionaries' home. Every corner of the house was carefully searched, and the man came out of the house greatly disappointed.

Then the missionary asked the man to tell him about the watchmen to whom he referred. Here is the man's answer.

"When you and your wife came here we determined to kill you as we did the missionaries twenty years ago. Night after night we came to carry out our intentions, but *there always stood around your house a double row of watchmen with glittering weapons, and we dared not come near.* At last we hired a professional assassin, who said he feared neither God nor devil. Last night he came close to your house—we followed at a distance— brandishing his spear. *There stood the shining watchmen,* and the killer fled in terror. So we have given up our purpose to kill you, but tell me, *who are the watchmen?*"

The missionary opened the Word of God and read: *"The angel of the* Lord *encampeth round about them that fear him, and delivereth them."*

"The beloved of the Lord shall dwell in safety by him" *(Deut. 33:12).*

"The Lord hid them" *(Jer. 36:26).*

February 11

He mounts me upon high places, that I may conquer by song. (Hab. 3:19, Trans.)

In "Marble Faun," Miriam, the brokenhearted singer, puts into a burst of song the pent-up grief of her soul. This was better, surely, than if she had let forth a wild shriek of pain.

It is nobler to sing a victorious song in time of trial than to lie crushed in grief. Songs bless the world more than wails. It is better for our own heart, too, to put our sorrows and pains into songs. *"We shall conquer by song."*

"Our minister is a skylark Christian," boasted one of his people. Fine bird! It sings morning, noon, and evening; sings as it springs from the flowery sod; sings when the ground is white with snow. What a song, too!—a shower of melody and infinite sweetness—*with no undertone of pain.*

If we could only realize the full truth and blessedness of our faith we should continually go up and down singing, until one fine day we would go up singing—up, up, beyond the sun—and come down no more, lost in the eternal light!

Help me to make of all my sorrows music for the world!

> *Turn your troubles into treasure,*
> *Turn your sorrows into song;*
> *Then all men will know the measure,*
> *In which you to Christ belong.*
> *When they see your bright behavior*
> *Under provocation great,*
> *They may ask what mighty Savior*
> *Can impart that happy state.*
>
> *Paul and Silas in the prison,*
> *With their feet fast in the stocks,*
> *Praised their glorious Lord, arisen,*
> *Till the earthquake rent the rocks.*
> *There was none to join their singing,*
> *So the earthquake roared "Amen!"*
> *And glad chains fell down a-ringing,*
> *As their voices rang again!*
>
> *Oh, then sing with us His praises*
> *When there seems least cause to praise;*
> *Faith the sweetest anthem raises*
> *When the darkness hides God's ways;*
> *He brings forth His "new creation"*
> *Only there where ends "the old."*
> *Let us praise Him for salvation,*
> *When all feels most dead and cold.*
>
> *My soul, keep up thy singing,*
> *Turn thy sorrows into song.*

ARTHUR S. BOOTH-CLIBBORN ☞

Let every sigh be changed into a *Hallelujah!* OTTO STOCKMAYER ☞

"None might enter into the king's gate clothed with sackcloth."

February 12

For thou art my lamp, O LORD: and the LORD will lighten my darkness. (2 Sam. 22:29)

There are times when a Christian needs to lie still, when our only safety is doing nothing. The voice of our Savior-God is heard beside many a Red-Sea difficulty—"*Stand still*, and *see* the salvation of the LORD." It is a hard thing to "stand still" in the presence of opposing forces. Jehovah is the *Living God*. Cloud and storm are beneath His feet and His throne remains unmoved.

"Am I in the dark?" asks Charles H. Spurgeon. "Then Thou, O Lord, 'will lighten my darkness.' Before long things will change. Affairs may grow worse and more dreary, and cloud upon cloud may be piled upon cloud; but if it grows so dark that I cannot see my own hand, still I shall see the Hand of the Lord."

When I cannot find a light within me, or among my friends, or in the whole world, the Lord who said, "Let there be light" and there was light, can say the same thing again. He will speak me into the sunshine yet. The day is already breaking. This sweet text shines like a morning star: "For thou art my lamp, O LORD: and the LORD will lighten my darkness."

Clouds pass; stars remain!

My lamp is shattered, I'm deprived of light; my lamp is shattered, and so
dark the night. My lamp is shattered,
yet to my glad sight—a star shines on.
My lamp is shattered, but a star shines bright, and by its glowing
I can wend aright. My lamp is shattered, but I still can fight—
for a star shines on.
My lamp is shattered, sad indeed my plight. My lamp is shattered,
yet I'll reach the height—for a star shines on!
WILHELMINA STITCH 🐝

February 13

And the kine took the straight way . . . and went along the high-
way, lowing as they went, and turned not aside to the right hand
or to the left. (1 Sam. 6:12)

There was another yoke upon those kine that day than the yoke of wood fashioned by the hands of Philistines: they were constrained of God. It was that that made them patient and willing to walk together; that, too, made them choose the new road. Born and stalled in Ekron, familiar with the field and the manger, they herded off to Beth-shemesh, along the road they had never been before.

Why did they do it? *It was God.*

And as surely it is God when men choose the new way and walk along the road to the heavenly kingdom. They are *apprehended of Christ,* and not only *born* of the Spirit, but *borne* of the Spirit. *Men moved of God have a new instinct.*

Nature would have sent those kine back to their calves; but something has been known to make a man forsake father and mother, renounce life or a love dearer than life, for the Kingdom of God. And

Whoso hath felt the Spirit of the Highest
Cannot confound Him, or doubt Him, or deny.

It means pain. Christ's martyrs, living or dying, though they rejoice to follow in His steps, are not insensible.

The kine went, *lowing as they went.* That was part of the proof; they had not forgotten their calves although they had forsaken them. Every low of the kine was a witness for God; and God who asks His people to sacrifice for His sake does not chide us because we feel it.

The reward of sacrifice is a call to sacrifice still more complete. The Lord never pays spiritual service in earthly currency. The impulse that carried the kine to the destined country led them to pause beside the stone that became an altar. The happy reapers of Beth-shemesh welcomed the Ark, *but the kine who under God's hand had brought it to them were not feasted and garlanded.*

"They clave the wood of the cart, and offered the kine a burnt offering unto the LORD." So the service was followed by sacrifice, and the story is in the Book to make us glad when, our active life a thing of the past, we can still render ourselves unto God in a great renunciation. GOD'S HIGHWAY 🙠

Measure all by the Cross!

February 14

He maketh me to lie down in green pastures. (Ps. 23:2)

There are times when a Christian needs to lie still, like the earth under the spring rain, letting the lesson of experience and the memories of the Word of God sink down to the very roots of his life and fill the deep reservoirs of his soul.

Those are not always lost days when his hands are not busy, any more than rainy days in summer are lost because they keep the farmer indoors. The Great Shepherd makes his servant to *lie down* there.

There are times when men say they are too busy to stop; when they think they are doing God service by going on. Now and then God makes such a one to lie down. He has been driving through the pastures so fast that he has not known their greenness, nor apprehended their sweet savor; and God does not mean that he shall lose all that, and so *He makes him lie down.*

Many a man has had to thank God for some such enforced season of rest, in which he first learned the sweetness of meditation on the Word, and of lying still in God's hands and waiting God's pleasure.

The soul cannot be hurried!

God is not in a hurry, dear!
The work He chose for you
Can wait, if He is giving you another
task to do,
Or, if He call you from your work
to quietness and rest,
Be sure that in the silence
you may do His bidding best.

You cannot be a joy to Him,
if thus with frown and fret
You turn at each new call of His,
to find new lessons set.
The old familiar tasks were dear,
and ordered by His hand;
But come and tread another way:
it is as He has planned.

And yesterday He led you there;
and now He wants you here;
And what shall be tomorrow's work,
tomorrow shall make clear.
So patiently and faithfully let each

day's course be run;
God is not in a hurry, dear,
His work will all be done.

EDITH HICKMAN DIVALL 🖋

There must be a Selah!

February 15

But the fruit of the Spirit is . . . gentleness. (Gal. 5:22)

One day at an auction a man bought a vase of cheap earthenware for a few pennies. He put into the vase a rich perfume—the attar of roses. For a long time the vase held this perfume, and when it was empty it had been so soaked through with the sweet perfume that the fragrance lingered. One day the vase fell and was broken to pieces, but every fragment still smelled of the attar of roses.

We are all common clay—plain earthenware, but if the love of Christ is kept in our hearts it will sweeten all our life, and we shall become as loving as He. That is the way the beloved disciple learned the lesson and grew into such lovingness. He leaned on Christ's breast, and Christ's gentleness filled all his life.

As John upon his dear Lord's breast,
So would I lean, so would I rest;
An empty shell in depths of sea,
So would I sink, he filled with Thee.

Like singing bird in high blue air,
So would I soar, and sing Thee there.
Nor rain, nor stormy wind can be,
When all the air is full of Thee.

And so, though daily duties crowd,
And dust of earth be like a cloud,
Through noise of words, O Lord, my Rest,
Thy John would lean upon Thy breast.

ROSE FROM BRIER 🖋

Save me from growing hard!

February 16

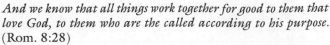

And we know that all things work together for good to them that love God, to them who are the called according to his purpose. (Rom. 8:28)

He was weaving.

"That is a strange-looking carpet you are making!" said the visitor.

"Just stoop down and look underneath," was the reply.

The man stooped. *The plan was on the other side,* and in that moment a light broke upon his mind.

The Great Weaver is busy with His plan. Do not be impatient; suffice to know that you are part of the plan and that *He never errs.* Wait for the light of the later years, and the peep at the other side. *Hope on!*

> *White and black, and hodden-gray,*
> *Weavers of webs are we;*
> *To every weaver one golden strand*
> *Is given in trust by the Master-Hand;*
> *Weavers of webs are we.*
>
> *And that we weave, we know not,*
> *Weavers of webs are we.*
> *The thread we see, but the pattern is known*
> *To the Master-Weaver alone, alone;*
> *Weavers of webs are we.*

JOHN OXENHAM

Of many of the beautiful carpets made in India it may be said that the weaving is done to music. The designs are handed down from one generation to another, and the instructions for their making are in script that looks not unlike a sheet of music. Indeed, it is more than an accidental resemblance, for each carpet has a sort of tune of its own. The thousands of threads are stretched on a great wooden frame, and behind it on a long bench sit the workers. The master in charge reads the instructions for each stitch in a strange chanting tone, each color having its own particular note.

The story makes us think of our own life web. We are all weavers and day by day we work in the threads—now dark, now bright—that are to go into the finished pattern. But blessed are they who feel sure that there is a pattern; who hear and trust the directing Voice, and so weave the changing threads to music. W. J. HART

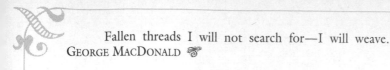

Fallen threads I will not search for—I will weave.
GEORGE MACDONALD

February 17

My presence shall go with thee, and I will give thee rest. (Ex. 33:14)

What is rest?

To step out of self-life into Christ-life; to lie still, and let Him lift you out of it; to fold your hands close, and hide your face on the hem of His garment; to let Him lay His cooling, soothing, healing hands upon your soul, and draw all the hurry and fever from its veins; to realize that you are not a mighty messenger, an important worker of His, full of care and responsibility, but only a little child, with a Father's gentle bidding to heed and fulfill; to lay your busy plans and ambitions confidently in His hands, as a child brings its broken toys at its mother's call; to serve Him by waiting; to praise Him by saying, "Holy, Holy, Holy"; to cease to hurry, so you may not lose sight of His face; to learn to follow Him, and not to run ahead of orders! to cease to live in self and for self, and to live in Him and for Him; to love His honor more than your own; to be a clear medium for His life-tide to shine and glow through. This is consecration, this is rest.

> *Thou sweet, beloved will of God,*
> *My anchor ground, my fortress hill,*
> *My spirit's silent, fair abode,*
> *In Thee I hide me and am still.*
>
> *Thy beautiful sweet will, my God,*
> *Holds fast in its sublime embrace*
> *My captive will, a gladsome bird,*
> *Prison'd in such a realm of grace.*
>
> *Upon God's will I lay me down,*
> *As child upon its mother's breast,*
> *No silken couch, nor softest bed,*
> *Could ever give me such deep rest.*

TERSTEEGEN

February 18

I will go before thee and unwind the snarls. (Isa. 45:2, Free trans.)

If any of you, beloved, seem to be in a knot of difficulty of which you cannot get the thread, look to Him who is perfect wisdom, and *let the tangle go out of your hands into His; turn the matter over to Him.* What is impossible with you is perfectly possible with Him who is Almighty!

A little child at mother's knee
Plies woolen strands and needles bright.
Small, eager hands strive earnestly
To fasten every stitch aright.

But soon perplexing knots appear
Which vex and hinder progress' flow;
Impatient fingers pull and tear,
While ever worse the tangles grow.

How surely then in wiser hands
The roughest places are made plain!
How easy now the task's demands,
How wonderful the lesson's gain!

Thus, God, we bring our snarls to Thee;
Though human sense and stubborn will
Oft clamor loud for mastery,
We hear alone Thy "Peace, be still."

EDITH SHAW BROWN

How tangled some of our problems do become as the days pass and no way appears by which the matter may be straightened out! Perhaps we have been keeping the problems too much in our own hands. No wonder, then, we cannot find the beginning or the end of the line, or how to loosen the knotted strand in just the right places. A young man writing to his father about a personal problem says: "Once again, just yesterday, I have put this whole matter in the Lord's hands, and asked Him to guide me about it all. I often think of how I'd get my fishing line all tangled up. The more I pulled the worse it got. Finally I'd hand the whole thing over to you, and you'd smooth it all out. So I generally do that with my problems now; and I'm trying to learn not to pull at the line much, before I give it to Him." Have you been pulling at the line in that problem that troubles you today? Just hand it over to your heavenly Father, and see how swiftly and lovingly He will untangle the crisscross and knotty impossibility that has troubled you so! SUNDAY SCHOOL TIMES

With thoughtless and
Impatient hands
We tangle up
The plans
The Lord hath wrought.

And when we cry
In pain, He saith,
"Be quiet, dear,
While I untie the knot."

February 19

He healeth the broken in heart, and bindeth up their wounds.
He telleth the number of the stars; he calleth them all by their
names. (Ps. 147:3–4)

A beautiful picture has just been painted by one of the greatest of the European artists: *The Consoler.* It is a picture of a bedroom in an English cottage. On the bed sits a beautiful little babe, perhaps a year in age, having in his hand a toy soldier that he is holding very lovingly to his body. He is unconscious of anything about him. Back of him on the wall is the picture of a young man in soldier's dress—the baby's father. On her knees, her head in her hands, is the young widow robed in deepest black, sobbing her heart out. One of the saddest pictures the world shall ever know—a baby to forget and never know his father; a young widow to go down through life with burdened, broken heart. But leaning over her, with the light of heaven on His beautiful face, is One who lays His hand lovingly on her shoulder. We do not wonder the great artist has called the picture *The Consoler.*

With His healing hand on a broken heart,
And the other on a star,
Our wonderful God views the miles apart,
And they seem not very far.

Oh, it makes us cry—then laugh—then sing,
Tho' 'tis all beyond our ken;
He bindeth up wounds on that poor crushed thing,
And He makes it whole again.

Was there something shone from that healed new heart
Made the Psalmist think of stars—

That bright as the sun or the lightning's dart,
Sped away past earthly bars?

In a low place sobbing by death's lone cart,
Then a flight on whirlwind's cars;
One verse is about a poor broken heart,
And the next among the stars.

There is hope and help for our sighs and tears,
For the wound that stings and smarts;
Our God is at home with the rolling spheres,
And at home with broken hearts.

MAMIE PAYNE FERGUSON

"Let God cover thy wounds," said Augustine, "do not thou. For if thou wish to cover them being ashamed, the Physician will not come. Let Him cover; for by the covering of the Physician the wound is healed; by the covering of the wounded man the wound is concealed. And from whom? From Him who knoweth all things."

The Great Lover comes close behind the storm,
And whispers softly to the broken mountaintops,
And fills their wounds with clean fresh odors.

The Great Lover knows the pain of blasted trees
And binds up tenderly their broken arms;
The Great Lover has gone through many storms.

MATTHEW BILLER

February 20

These were the potters, and those that dwelt among plants and hedges: there they dwelt with the king for his work. (1 Chron. 4:23)

Is your place a small place?
Tend it with care!—
He set you there.

Is your place a large place?
Guard it with care!
He set you there.

Whate'er your place, it is
Not yours alone, but His.
He set you there.

JOHN OXENHAM

With infinite care and forethought God has chosen the best place in which you can do your best work for the world. You may be lonely, but you have no more right to complain than the lamp has, which has been placed in a niche to illumine a dark landing or a flight of dangerous stone steps. The master of the house may have put you in a very small corner and on a very humble stand; but it is enough if it be His blessed will. Someday He will pass by, and you shall light His steps as He goes forth to seek and save that which is lost; or you shall kindle some great light that shall shine like a beacon over the storm-swept ocean. Thus the obscure Andrew was the means of igniting his brother Peter, when he brought him to Jesus.
SELECTED 🐝

When the Master of all the workmen called me into the field,
I went for Him light and happy, the tools of His service to wield;
Expectant of high position, as suited my lofty taste—
When Lo! He set me weeding and watering down in the waste.

Such puttering down in the hedges! A task so thankless and small!
Yet I stifled my vain discomfort and wrought for the Lord of all,
Till, meeker grown, as nightly I sank to my hard-won rest
I cared but to hear in my dreaming, "This one has done his best."

The years have leveled distinctions, there is no more "great" nor "small";
Only faithful service counts with the Lord of all;
And I know that, tilled with patience, the dreariest waste of clod
Shall yield the perfect ideal planned in the heart of God.
SELECTED 🐝

Are YOU willing to be a "stopper of chinks" *(Ezek. 27:9)*?

February 21

The things which happened unto me have fallen out rather unto the furtherance of the gospel. (Phil. 1:12)

∽✾∾

We cannot expect to learn much of the life of trust without passing through hard places. When they come let us not say as Jacob did, "All these things are against me" (Gen. 42:36).

Let us rather climb our Hills of Difficulty and say, *"These are faith's opportunities!"*

I would not lose the hard things from my life,
The rocks o'er which I stumbled long ago,

The griefs and fears, the failures and mistakes,
That tried and tested faith and patience so.

I need them now: they make the deep-laid wall,
The firm foundation-stones on which I raise—
To mount therein from stair to higher stair—
The lofty towers of my House of Praise.

Soft was the roadside turf to weary feet,
And cool the meadows where I fain had trod,
And sweet beneath the trees to lie at rest
And breathe the incense of the flower-starred sod;

But not on these might I securely build;
Nor sand nor sod withstand the earthquake shock;
I need the rough hard boulders of the hills,
To set my house on everlasting rock.

ANNIE JOHNSON FLINT

Crises reveal character: when we are put to the test we reveal exactly the hidden resources of our character.

February 22

Faint not. (2 Cor. 4:16)

One day a naturalist, out in his garden, observed a most unusually large and beautiful butterfly, fluttering as though in great distress; it seemed to be caught as though it could not release itself. The naturalist, thinking to release the precious thing, took hold of the wings and set it free. It flew but a few feet and fell to the ground dead.

He picked up the poor thing, took it into his laboratory and put it under a magnifying glass to discover the cause of its death. There he found the lifeblood flowing from the tiny arteries of its wings. Nature had fastened it to its chrysalis and was allowing it to flutter and flutter so that its wings might grow strong. It was the muscle-developing process that nature was giving the dear thing so that it might have an unusual range among the flowers and gardens. *If it had only fluttered long enough the butterfly would have come forth ready for the wide range; but release ended the beautiful dream.*

So with God's children: *how the Father wishes for them wide ranges in experience and truth. He permits us to be fastened to some form of struggle. We would tear ourselves free.* We cry out in our distress and sometimes think

Him cruel that He does not release us. He permits us to flutter and flutter on. Struggle seems to be His program sometimes.

Prayer alone will hold us steady while in the struggles; so we keep sweet and learn, oh, such wonderful lessons.

> *God laid upon my back a grievous load,*
> *A heavy cross to bear along the road.*
>
> *I staggered on, and lo! one weary day,*
> *An angry lion sprang across my way.*
>
> *I prayed to God, and swift at His command*
> *The cross became a weapon in my hand.*
>
> *It slew my raging enemy, and then*
> *Became a cross upon my back again.*
>
> *I reached a desert. O'er the burning track*
> *I persevered, the cross upon my back.*
>
> *No shade was there, and in the cruel sun*
> *I sank at last, and thought my days were done.*
>
> *But lo! the Lord works many a blest surprise—*
> *The cross became a tree before my eyes!*
>
> *I slept; I woke, to feel the strength of ten.*
> *I found the cross upon my back again.*
>
> *And thus through all my days from then to this,*
> *The cross, my burden, has become my bliss.*
>
> *Nor ever shall I lay the burden down,*
> *For God someday will make the cross a crown!*
>
> AMOS R. WELLS

You are bound to a cross. I entreat you not to struggle. The more lovingly the cross is carried by the soul, the lighter it becomes!

February 23

Hope thou in God: for I shall yet praise him. (Ps. 42:5)

During a truce in the Civil War in America, when the hostile armies sat sullenly facing each other with a field between them, a little brown bird rose suddenly from the long grass and darted skyward. There, a mere speck in the blue, it poured forth its liquid music of which the lark alone has the secret. And steely eyes melted to tears, and hard hearts grew pitiful and tender. There was a God who cared. There was hope for men.

Hope is like the lark on the battlefield. It will not sing in a gilded cage. It cannot soar in an atmosphere of religious luxury. But brave souls, exposing themselves fearlessly for God and their fellow-men on the battlefield of life, hear its song and are made strong and glad. E. HERMAN ✺

Persons who held on in hope, with seemingly little for which to hope, were known to say:

Then was our mouth filled with laughter . . .
We were like them that dream.

The tide may turn, the wind may change. New eras have been heard of before now!

In "hope against hope," I wait, Lord,
Faced by some fast-barred gate, Lord,
Hope never says "Too late," Lord,
Therefore in Thee I hope!

Hope though the night be long, Lord,
Hope of a glowing dawn, Lord,
Morning must break in song, Lord,
For we are "saved by hope."
HYMNS OF CONSECRATION AND FAITH ✺

"Hope thou in God!"

February 24

After he had seen the vision, immediately we endeavored to go into Macedonia, assuredly gathering that the Lord had called us for to preach the gospel unto them. (Acts 16:10)

⟨∽∾⟩

There is a simplicity about God in working out His plans, yet a resourcefulness equal to any difficulty, an unswerving faithfulness to His trusting child, and an unforgetting steadiness in holding to His purpose. Through a fellow-prisoner, then a dream, He lifts Joseph from a prison to a premiership. And the length of stay in the prison prevents dizziness in the premier.

It's safe to trust God's methods, and to go by His clock. THE BENT KNEE TIME, BY S. D. GORDON ✺

The path was veiled! The Master's will was hidden,
And further progress for the time was stayed;
But in good time he would again be bidden
And, waiting meantime, he was unafraid.

Then came that night when, maybe, softly sleeping,
The vision came—the clarion call to move;
And once again, with all in God's good keeping,
He could step forth, God's faithfulness to prove.

No human voice conveyed the word of leading;
No human hand was sent, his way to guide;
No human heart full knew his depth of needing,
Or could assist him to his steps decide.

And so, without to other minds appealing,
"Assuredly" he "gathered" now God's will,
Yet—to his inner soul there came revealing—
He started forth, God's purpose to fulfill.

Perhaps, O soul, thou waitest for His leading,
Thy longing heart His further will would'st know;
Rest thou in God: His ear hath heard thy pleading,
The "further steps" He yet to thee will show.

Keep looking Himwards—He alone can lead thee;
Nor count from choicest friends thy way to glean;
He knoweth best where He Himself doth need thee,
And He can lead thee on by means unseen.

"Assuredly" thy longing heart shall "gather"
The guidance thou dost long for; therefore wait;
Fret not thyself! Ah, no! But learn this rather—
God's guidance never comes to us too late.

J. DANSON SMITH

February 25

Jesus taketh Peter, James, and John his brother, and bringeth
them up into an high mountain apart, And was transfigured
before them.... Then ... Peter ... said unto Jesus, Lord, it is good
for us to be here. (Matt. 17:1–2, 4)

It is good to be the possessor of some mountaintop experience. *Not to know life on the heights is to suffer an impoverishing incompleteness.*

Those times when the Lord's presence is marvelously manifest to you—the moments of self-revelation—*do not despise them.* But beware of *not acting upon what you see in your moments on the mount with God!*

Horizons broaden when we stand on the heights. There is always, we find, the danger that we will make of life too much of a dead-level existence; a monotonous tread of beaten paths; a matter of absorbing, spiritless, deadening routine.

Do not drop your life into the passing current, to be steadily going you scarcely know *where,* or *why.*

Christian life, writes one, *is not all a valley of humiliation. It has its heights of vision.*

Abraham saw in the glorious depths of the starry firmament visions that no telescope could ever have revealed! Jacob's stony pillow led up to the ladder of vision!

Joseph's early dreams kept him in the hours of discouragement and despair that followed!

Moses, who spent one-third of his life in the desert, we find crying out: "I beseech thee, show me thy glory!"

Job's vision showed him God and lifted him out of himself!

The mariner does not expect to see the sun and stars every day, but when he does, he takes his observations and sails by their light for many days to come.

God gives days of special illumination that we may be able to call to memory in the days of shadow, and say: "Therefore will I remember thee from the land of Jordan, and of the Hermonites, from the hill Mizar."

In the life of Paul, we find a few of these blessed interludes—when the Lord gave to him words of promise to remember in his days of trial that followed.

If these special experiences came too often they would lose their flavor!

> *He walks in glory on the hills,*
> *And longs for men to join Him there.*

February 26

There came a woman having an alabaster box of ointment of spikenard very precious; and she brake the box, and poured it on his head. (Mark 14:3)

And the house was filled with the odour of the ointment.
(John 12:3)

Mary wanted it to be known that this act of hers was done *for Him exclusively.* Just for HIM, without thought of self, or anything else. Martha was serving, but it was *not exclusively for Him.* It might be in His honor, but it was done for others also. Simon might entertain, but others were included in the entertainment also. What Mary did was for HIM ALONE. "When *Jesus understood it,* he said unto them, Why trouble ye the woman?"

JESUS UNDERSTOOD!

Jesus said to Peter: "Lovest thou Me?" Peter replied: "Thou knowest that I love Thee." Jesus said to him: "Feed my sheep FOR ME.... Feed my lambs FOR ME" (John 21:15–17, Syriac version).

"Take this child away, and nurse it FOR ME, and I will give thee thy wages" (Ex. 2:9).

> *Under an Eastern sky*
> *Amid a rabble cry*
> *A Man went forth to die*
> *For me—for me.*
>
> *Thorn-crowned His blessed Head,*
> *Bloodstained His every tread,*
> *To Calvary He was led*
> *For me—for me.*
>
> *Pierced were His Hands, His Feet,*
> *Three hours o'er Him did beat*
> *Fierce rays of noonday heat,*
> *For me—for me.*
>
> *Since Thou wast made all mine,*
> *Lord, make me wholly Thine.*
> *Grant strength and grace Divine*
> *For me—for me.*
>
> *Thy will to do, Oh, lead*
> *In thought and word and deed*
> *My heart, e'en though it bleed,*
> *To Thee—to Thee.*

SELECTED

FOR ME!

"For Him! For Him!" the man cries as he planes his boards, sells his goods, adds his figures, or writes his letters. "For Him! For Him!" sings the woman as she plies her needle, makes her bed, cooks her food, or dusts her house.

All day long the hand is outstretched to touch the invisible Christ, and at night the work done is brought to Him for His benediction.

February 27

A vessel unto honour, sanctified, and meet for the master's use, and prepared unto every good work. (2 Tim. 2:21)

Here, O my Father, is Thy making stuff!

Set Thy wheel going; let it whir and play.
The chips in me, the stones, the straws, the sand,
Cast them out with fine separating hand,
And make a vessel of Thy yielding clay.

Martin Wells Knapp was once undergoing a severe trial, and in his secret devotions he asked God to remove his trial. As he waited before the Lord the vision of a rough piece of marble rose before him with a sculptor grinding and chiseling. Watching the dust and chips fill the air, he noticed a beautiful image begin to appear in the marble. The Lord spoke to him and said, "Son, you are that block of marble. I have an image in My mind, and I desire to produce it in your character, and will do so if you will stand the grinding; but I will stop now if you so desire." Mr. Knapp broke down and said, *"Lord, continue the chiseling and grinding."*

When God wants to drill a man,
And thrill a man,
And skill a man,
When God wants to mold a man
To play the noblest part;
When He yearns with all His heart
To create so great and bold a man
That all the world shall be amazed,
Watch His methods, watch His ways!
How He ruthlessly perfects
Whom He royally elects!
How He hammers him and hurts him,

And with mighty blows converts him
Into trial shapes of clay which
Only God understands;
While his tortured heart is crying
And he lifts beseeching hands!
How He bends but never breaks
When his good He undertakes;
How He uses whom He chooses,
And with every purpose fuses him;
But every act induces him
To try His splendor out—
God knows what He's about.

S<small>ELECTED</small> 🐚

Life is a quarry, out of which we are to mold and chisel and complete a character. G<small>OETHE</small> 🐚

February 28

Up . . . is not the L<small>ORD</small> gone out before thee? (Judg. 4:14)

God has guided the heroes and saints of all ages to do things which the common sense of the community has regarded as ridiculous and mad. Have *you* ever taken any risks for Christ? C<small>HARLES</small> E. C<small>OWMAN</small> 🐚

"Have not I sent thee?" *(Judg. 6:14)*.

God knows, and you know, what He has sent you to do. God sent Moses to Egypt to bring three millions of bondmen out of the house of bondage into the Promised Land. Did he fail? It looked at first as if he were going to. But *did* he? God sent Elijah to stand before Ahab, and it was a bold thing for him to say that there should be neither dew nor rain: but did he not lock up the heavens for three years and six months? Did he fail?

And you cannot find any place in Scripture where a man was ever sent by God to do a work in which he ever failed. D. L. M<small>OODY</small> 🐚

Had Moses failed to go, had God
Granted his prayer, there would have been
For him no leadership to win;
No pillared fire; no magic rod;
No wonders in the land of Zin;
No smiting of the sea; no tears

Ecstatic, shed on Sinai's steep;
No Nebo with a God to keep
His burial; only forty years
Of desert, watching with his sheep.

J. R. MILLER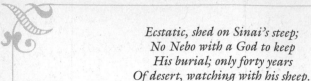

Our might is His Almightiness.

March 1

Pass through the host . . . armed. (Josh. 1:11, 14)

Pass through, pass through, nor sit among
The hosts encamped around.
The glorious Victor paved the way,
Put all His armor on you may.
With shield of faith held well in view,
Thy song ere long—"He brought me through!"

E. N. P.

After a step of faith most persons are looking for sunny skies and unruffled seas, and when they meet a storm or tempest they are filled with astonishment and perplexity. *But this is just what we must expect if we have received anything of the Lord.* The best token of His presence is the adversary's defiance, and the more real our blessing the more certainly it will be challenged. It is a good thing to go out looking for the worst, then if it comes we are not surprised; while if our path be smooth and the way unopposed it is all the more delightful because it comes as a glad surprise.

But let us quite understand what we mean by *temptation.* You, especially, who have stepped out with the assurance that you have died to self and sin, may be greatly amazed to find yourself assailed with a tempest of thoughts and feelings that seem to come wholly from within, and you will be impelled to say, "Why, I thought I was dead, but I seem to be alive!" This, beloved, is the time to remember that in temptation the instigation is not your sin but only the voice of the evil one. A. B. SIMPSON

Why does the battle thicken so—
The darts rain fast upon my breast,
While missiles hurled with cruel force
Ring loud against my burnished crest?
Above the din I seem to hear

My Captain's voice in accents clear,
"Because your shield is down!"

Why does the enemy advance
And hem us 'round on every hand
While we, the army of the Lord,
Can scarce his arrogance withstand?
Above the shouts I seem to hear
My Captain's voice in accents clear,
"Because your shields are down!"

Ah! Now it's brighter—now I see
The enemy is taking flight,
And lo, the banner of the Cross
Streams red against the morning light;
But as they flee I seem to hear
My Captain call in accents clear,
"Let not your shields go down!"

THOMAS KIMBER

Failure in our faith is fatal. Faith is our spiritual shield
protecting us from the darts of the devil. Lay this shield aside
even for a moment, and disaster follows. Any departure
from the living God is the result of unbelief.

March 2

And apart to his disciples he explained all. (Mark 4:34, Englishman's Greek N.T.)

God may not explain to you a thousand things which puzzle your reason in His dealings with you, but if you always see yourself to be His love-slave, He will awaken in you a jealous love, and bestow upon you many blessings which come only to those who are in the inner circle.

I can still believe that a day comes for all of us, however far off it may be, when we shall understand; when these tragedies that now blacken and darken the very air of heaven for us will sink into their places in a scheme so august, so magnificent, so joyful, that we shall laugh for wonder and delight. ARTHUR CHRISTOPHER BENSON

Will not the end explain
The crossed endeavor, earnest purpose foiled,

The strange bewilderment of good work spoiled,
The clinging weariness, the inward strain?
Will not the end explain?

Meanwhile He comforteth
Them that are losing patience. 'Tis His way:
But none can write the words they heard Him say,
For men to read; only they know He saith
Sweet words and comforteth.

Not that He doth explain
The mystery that baffleth; but a sense
Husheth the quiet heart, that far, far hence
Lieth a field set thick with golden grain
Wetted in seedling days by many a rain.
The end—it will explain.

GOLD CORD ❦

March 3

Where there is no vision, the people perish. (Prov. 29:18)

We must see something before we make our ventures! Faith must first have visions: faith sees a light, if you will, an imaginary light, and leaps! Faith is always born of vision and hope! We must have the gleam of the thing hoped for shining across the waste before we can have an energetic and energizing faith.

Are we not safe in saying that the majority of people have no fine hopes, are devoid of *the vision splendid,* and therefore, have no spiritual audacity in spiritual adventure and enterprise? Our hopes are petty and peddling, and they don't give birth to crusades. There are no shining towers and minarets on our horizon, no new Jerusalem, and therefore we do not set out in chivalrous explorations.

We need a transformation in "the things hoped for." We need to be *renewed in mind,* and renewed in mind *daily.* We need to have the far-off towering summits of vast and noble possibilities enthroned in our imaginations. Our gray and uninviting horizons must glow with the unfading colors of immortal hopes. SELECTED ❦

So few men venture out beyond the blazed trail,
'Tis he who has the courage to go past this sign

That cannot in his mission fail.
He will have left at least some mark behind
To guide some other brave exploring mind.

No man is of any use until he has dared everything. ROBERT LOUIS
STEVENSON

March 4

God shall hear. (Ps. 55:19)

I was standing at a bank counter in Liverpool waiting for a clerk to
come. I picked up a pen and began to print on a blotter in large letters two
words which had gripped me like a vise: *"PRAY THROUGH."* I kept talking
to a friend and printing until I had the desk blotter filled from top to bottom with a column. I transacted my business and went away. The next day
my friend came to see me, and said he had a striking story to tell.

A businessman came into the bank soon after we had gone. He had
grown discouraged with business troubles. He started to transact some
business with the same clerk, over that blotter, when his eye caught the
long column of *"PRAY THROUGH."* He asked who wrote those words and
when he was told exclaimed, "That is the very message I needed. *I will pray
through.* I have tried in my own strength to worry through, and have
merely mentioned my troubles to God; now I am going to pray the situation through until I get light." CHARLES M. ALEXANDER

> *Don't stop praying, but have more trust;*
> *Don't stop praying! for pray we must;*
> *Faith will banish a mount of care;*
> *Don't stop praying! God answers prayer.*
>
> C. M. A.

All I *have seen* teaches me to trust the Creator for *what I have not seen!*

March 5

*So the children of Joseph, Manasseh and Ephraim, took their
inheritance.* (Josh. 16:4)

A dying judge said to his pastor, "Do you know enough about law to understand what is meant by *joint tenancy?*"

"No," was the reply; "I know nothing about law; I know a little about grace, and that satisfies me."

"Well," he said, "if you and I were joint tenants on a farm, I could not say to you, 'That is your field of corn, and this is mine; that is your blade of grass, and this is mine,' but we would share alike in everything on the place. I have just been lying here and thinking with unspeakable joy that Christ Jesus has nothing apart from me; that everything He has is mine, *and that we will share alike through all eternity.*"

God wants you to have *all* that He has—His Son, His life, His love, His Spirit, His glory. "All things are yours; and ye are Christ's; and Christ is God's." "Son, thou art ever with me, and *all that I have is thine*" (Luke 15:31). What a privilege! What a life for a child of God! *Only unbelief can blind us to the Father's love.* Only with a false humility the children of the King set limitations about their lives that He never appointed. The full table is set for us, and we eat so sparingly, forgetful of the voice that cries, "Eat, O friends: drink, yea, drink abundantly, O beloved!"

"The resources of the Christian life," says Dr. Robert F. Horton, *"are just Jesus Christ."* He IS *our regal provision for the way.* He *is the way.* Let us draw upon these Divine resources. *Whom* should He bless, even on earth, *if not His own?*

Supply yourself from Him!

God is to be adored, but He is also to be *used.* Merely to worship Him in the awe of His greatness and holiness is not to please Him fully. He wants us to draw upon Him as an asset of our practical life, and as a priceless possession. We live in Him; but He also lives in us to bring to our soul the power of His own infinite life. *To possess HIM is to possess all things and to have power to attain our noblest purposes.*

He is always at our service. Use Him, then; for He is there and waits for you to use Him. *All the unclaimed wealth of the forty thousand checks in the bankbook of the Bible is ours!* And "He satisfieth [satiates] the longing soul" (Ps. 107:9). *God is our God to be used for things we need Him for.*

> *My need and Thy great fullness meet,*
> *And I have all in Thee.*

God has a separate inheritance for each one. Do not fail to enter upon *yours.*

"The right of inheritance is thine" *(Jer. 32:8).*

March 6

For me and thee. (Matt. 17:27)

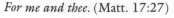

Peter had been a fisherman. Jesus had said, "Follow me," and Peter had given up his fishing business to follow. We read that *straightway* he forsook his nets, and followed. That must have been a tremendous experience for Peter—giving up his means of livelihood, upkeep of his home, not to mention the money for those taxes. Peter, the Fisherman, left *all* to follow Christ. The Lord knew that he had given up his means of livelihood to answer His call, and from the very thing that Peter had given up for His sake—*fish*—the Lord met His servant's need when the time for paying the taxes came around. *No servant of Christ will ever be the loser.*

So our dear Lord is always thinking in advance of *our* needs, and He loves to save us from embarrassment and anticipate our anxieties and cares by laying up His loving acts and providing before the emergency comes. "For me and thee," He had said, bracketing those words together in a wondrous, sacred intimacy. He puts Himself first in the embarrassing need, and bears the heavy end of the burden for His distressed and suffering child. He makes our cares, *His* cares; our sorrows, *His* sorrows; our shame, *His* shame.

> *The tax was due—the Master's and disciple's,*
> *And to the sea the Master strangely sent:*
> *A fish would yield the needful piece of silver!*
> *Strange bank, indeed, from which to pay that rent.*
>
> *"One piece of silver!" Not two equal portions!*
> *One piece of silver—one, and shining bright;*
> *"That use for Me and thee," thus spoke the Master,*
> *"That claims on Me and thee we thus unite."*
>
> *Blest, happy bond! May I thus sweetly know Him!*
> *Am I His servant? Hath He use of me?*
> *Then, O my soul, why shouldst thou own law's limit,*
> *If thy dear Lord doth find delight in thee?*
>
> *If thou art His—joint-heir in all His riches,*
> *Then, O my soul, a simpler spirit grow;*
> *"How shall He not, with Him, why, give us all things,"*
> *All that we need, to do His work below!*

J. DANSON SMITH

March 7

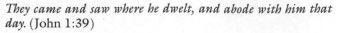

They came and saw where he dwelt, and abode with him that day. (John 1:39)

I wonder what it was that lured your feet to follow Him upon His homeward way. Was it mere eagerness to see the street, and house in which He sojourned, and to stay at closer quarters with Him for one day?

... Or, did you feel a strange attractive Power, which lured you from your boat beside the bay; when, heeding not the passing of the hour, and caring not what other folk might say, you made your home with Him for that brief day?

... Perhaps you felt a holy discontent, after the hours spent in that presence fair? Certain it is you thenceforth were intent on fishing men; for, from His side you went, and straightway brought your brother to Him there!

... Oh, Andrew! you could never be the same, after the contact of that wondrous day. You ne'er again could play with passion's flame, or harbor pride or hate, or grasp for fame, or give to avarice a place to stay.

... Rather, I think, you might be heard to say, "Something about Him burned my pride away, and cooled my hate and changed it for Love's way ... *After the healing contact of that stay, I must bring Simon to have one such day!*"

... And, ever after, as men passed your way, they would be conscious of some strange, new spell; some unexplained, mysterious miracle. Then, in an awe-filled whisper they would say, *"Andrew is greatly altered since that day!"*

... Oh! Wondrous Sojourner on life's dark way. Savior! Who understands what sinners say, *Grant me to come beneath Thy magic sway, lest, rough-edged, loveless, sin-stained, I should stay, lacking the impress of just such a day!* ELEANOR VELLACOTT WOOD ☙

Stradivari of Cremona is said to have marked every one of the priceless violins which he made, with the name of Jesus, and so well-known did this become that his work is still called *"Stradivarius del Gesu."*

If our lives might become equally well known because of that sacred mark by which He said that *all men shall know,* there would be more people who, like the blind beggar, would come to Him that they might receive their sight, and who, too, would *worship Him.*

March 8

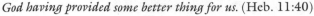

God having provided some better thing for us. (Heb. 11:40)

Our heavenly Father never takes any earthly thing from His children, unless He means to give them *something better instead.*   GEORGE MÜLLER

An easy thing, O Power Divine,
To thank Thee for these gifts of Thine!
For summer's sunshine, winter's snow,
For hearts that kindle, thoughts that glow;
But when shall I attain to this:
To thank Thee for the things I miss?

For all young fancy's early gleams,
The dreamed-of joys that still are dreams,
Hope unfulfilled, and pleasures known
Through others' fortunes, not my own,
And blessings seen that are not given,
And ne'er will be—this side of heaven.

Had I, too, shared the joys I see,
Would there have been a heaven for me?
Could I have felt Thy presence near
Had I possessed what I held dear?
My deepest fortune, highest bliss,
Have grown, perchance, from things I miss.

Sometimes there comes an hour of calm;
Grief turns to blessing, pain to balm;
A Power that works above my will
Still leads me onward, upward still;
And then my heart attains to this:
To thank Thee for the things I miss.
THOMAS WENTWORTH HIGGINSON

Instead of the dry land, springs of water!
Instead of heaviness, the garment of praise!
Instead of the thorn, the fir tree!
Instead of the brier, the myrtle tree!
Instead of ashes, beauty!
ISAIAH 41:18; 55:13; 61:3

Now Jacob's well was there. Jesus therefore, being wearied with his journey, sat thus on the well: and it was about the sixth hour. (John 4:6)

I have known thy continued enduring, and thy being patient, and thy unwearied painstaking for My Name's sake. (Rev. 2:2–3, Tamil)

Our Lord took His apostles aside when they were fatigued, and said, "Let us rest awhile." He never drove His overtired faculties. When tired, "He sat by the well." He used to go and rest in the home of Martha and Mary after the fatigue of working in Jerusalem. The Scripture shows it was His custom. He tells us all—you, and me, and all—to let tomorrow take care of itself, and merely to meet the evil of the present day.

As Elijah slept under a juniper tree, an angel touched him and said, "Arise and eat." God had sent His wearied servant to sleep. In his over-wrought condition sleep was his greatest need, and it is precisely under such conditions that sleep is often wooed in vain. Are we ever astonished at the miracle of sleep? Remember you have to do with the same God who ministered to Elijah, and

> *Though thy way be long and dreary,*
> *Eagle strength He'll still renew.*

Real foresight consists in reserving our own forces. If we labor with anxiety about the future, we destroy that strength which will enable us to meet the future. If we take more in hand now than we can well do, we break up and the work is broken up with us.

Bakers of bread for others to eat must be very careful to husband their strength. They are not much seen, but much felt; unknown multitudes would feel their loss and their failing means others famishing.

We need to take lessons of Sir William Cecil, once Lord Mayor of London. Upon throwing off his gown at night he would say to it, "Lay there, Lord Treasurer!" and forget all the cares of State until he resumed his official garb in the morning. THE GOLDEN MILESTONE ❧

"Be still, and know!"

The Hebrew word signifies more than quietness and meditation before God; it means to let the tension go out of our life, just as the great cable holds in place the great steamer until the vessel reaches its channel and can go with its own steam. JOHN TIMOTHY STONE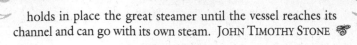

March 10

Faultless . . . with exceeding joy! (Jude 24)

When a young girl, an intense passion for music was awakened within my soul. Father brought great joy into my life by presenting me with a beautiful organ. It would thrill me to the very fiber of my being, as the days slipped by, to be able to draw forth such wonderful harmony from my beloved instrument.

I used to sit at the organ in the early morning hours, just as the birds began to awaken, and through the open windows listen to their sweet little bird notes as they mingled with the melody of the organ, like a paean of praise to our Creator!

Then, one morning, quite suddenly, and at a time when I was preparing with girlish enthusiasm for my first concert appearance, one of the notes became faulty. How the discordant sound grated upon my sensitive ear. Father, sensing my grief, said: "Never mind, daughter, I will have the tuner come." Long hours the tuner worked on that faulty note before it again rang out all sweet and true with the others. And the concert was a success, *because the tuner was successful!*

> *Good Tuner, why*
> *This ruthless, slow examination?*
> *Why, on that one poor note,*
> *Expend such careful concentration?*
> *Just pass it by.*
> *How I will let my soul respond to thee!*
> *And see*
>
> *But, no! Again, and yet again,*
> *With skilled determination,*
> *Rang out that meaningless reiteration.*
> *While, ever and anon, through the great aisle's dim space,*
> *Echoed the reverent chord; the loud harmonious phrase,*
>
> *Till day began to wane.*
> *And still, more patiently, the Tuner wrought*
> *With that one faulty note; until, with zest,*
> *All sweet and true, it answered like the rest.*

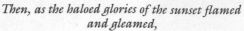

Then, as the haloed glories of the sunset flamed
and gleamed,
Swift through the storied windows long shafts of crimson streamed:
And we poor whispering wayfarers heard, round about and o'er us,
The throbbing, thundering triumphs of the Hallelujah Chorus!

THE TOWER IN THE CATHEDRAL,
BY FAY INCHFAWN 🙠

March 11

*And thou shalt be like a watered garden, and like a spring of
water, whose waters fail not.* (Isa. 58:11)

Holiness appeared to me to be of a sweet, pleasant ... calm nature. It seemed to me ... that it made the soul like a field or garden of God, with all manner of pleasant flowers—all pleasant, delightful and undisturbed; enjoying a sweet calm, and the gently vivifying beams of the sun.

The soul of a true Christian appeared like such a little white flower as we see in the spring of the year—low and humble on the ground—opening its bosom to receive the pleasant beams of the sun's glory—rejoicing, as it were, in a calm rapture—diffusing around a sweet fragrancy.

Once I rode out into the woods for my health. Having alighted from my horse in a retired place as my manner commonly had been, to walk for Divine contemplation and prayer, I had a view—that was for me extraordinary—of the glory of the Son of God. As near as I can judge, this continued about an hour; and kept me the greater part of the time in a flood of tears and weeping aloud. I felt an ardency of soul to be—what I know not otherwise how to express—*emptied and annihilated; to love Him with a holy and pure love; to serve and follow Him; to be perfectly sanctified, and made pure with a Divine and heavenly purity.* JONATHAN EDWARDS 🙠

*I never thought it could be thus, month after month to know
The river of Thy peace without one ripple in its flow;
Without one quiver in the trust, one flicker in the glow.*

March 12

If we suffer, we shall also reign with him. (2 Tim. 2:12)

There is only one place where we can receive *no answer but peace* to our question "Why?" All torturing questions find answer beneath those old gray olive trees. An hour at the foot of the Cross steadies the soul as nothing else can. Love that loves like that can be trusted with this question.
"O Christ Beloved, Thy Calvary stills all questions."

> *For Calvary interprets human life;*
> *No path of pain but there we meet our Lord;*
> *And all the strain, the terror and the strife*
> *Die down like waves before His peaceful word,*
> *And nowhere but beside the awful Cross,*
> *And where the olives grow along the hill,*
> *Can we accept the unexplained, the loss,*
> *The crushing agony, and hold us still.*

ROSE FROM BRIER

Every Gethsemane has beside it the serene, sweet heights of the Mount of Olives, and from its summit the resurrection into the heaven of heavens.

We have missed human history if we have not seen that out of the shadows of suffering have sprung the great literatures, the great paintings, the great philosophies, the great civilizations. All of them have blossomed into the light out of the shadows of suffering.

"Where a great thought is born," said one who knew by bitter experience, "there is always Gethsemane."

> *The mark of rank in nature is capacity for pain,*
> *And the anguish of the singer makes the sweetness of the strain.*

In Scotland there is a battlefield on which the Scots and their Saxon foes met in deadly conflict. A monument marks the spot; and here and there, tradition tells us, a little blue flower grows. It is called the *Flower of Culloden*. The baptism of blood, tradition avers, brought the flower into fertilization.

The choicest flowers are always "Culloden flowers." They spring only from the soil on which lifeblood of a brave heart has been spilt. CHARLES KINGSLEY

March 13

That your love may abound yet more and more. (Phil. 1:9)

Tradition says that when they carried Saint John for the last time into the church, he lifted up his feeble hands to the listening congregation, and said,
"Little children, love one another."
The words are echoing yet throughout the world.

More precious and important even than faith is heavenly love. Without it faith must ultimately wither. Many of God's most powerful workers after a time lose their power *because they lose the spirit of love.* This is the crowning grace of Christian character. *It has a thousand shades, and it is in the finer touches that its glory consists.* Every new experience of life is but a school to learn some lesson of love. Let us not try to expel our teachers. *Let us welcome them* and so learn the lesson, that they may soon pass on and leave us to make new advances.

If mountains can be removed by faith is there less power in love?

The immense arms from either side of the *Forth Bridge* had been completed; slowly and steadily they had been built out; all that was now needed at the center of the mighty arch was the final riveting.

The day fixed was cold and chilly, and cold contracts metals. In spite of fires set under the iron to expand it the inch or two required, the union could not be completed and the day's program was a failure.

But the next day the sun rose bright; under its genial warmth the iron expanded, the holes came opposite each other, and the riveters had nothing to do but drive the binding bolts home.

"Love unbinds others by its bonds."

Love through me, Love of God,
There is no love in me,
O Fire of love, light thou the love,
That burns perpetually.

Flow through me, Peace of God,
Calm river, flow until
No wind can blow, no current stir
A ripple of self-will.

Shine through me, Joy of God,
Make me like Thy clear air

Which Thou dost pour Thy colors thro'
As though it were not there.

O blessed Love of God,
That all may taste and see
How good Thou art, once more I pray:
Love through me, even me.

A. W. C. 🖃

"Love never faileth!"

March 14

Behold, he cometh! (Rev. 1:7)

The exclamation is a striking one. The Greek word "behold" means "See; look!" It is used to quickly call attention to some striking spectacle which suddenly breaks upon the gaze—as though one should say of some great sight appearing in the heavens before all eyes, "Behold the meteor!" Suddenly in mid-heaven, without a second's warning, is staged by God the most stupendous sight upon which human eyes have ever gazed—the out-flashing, dazzling, awful splendor of the personal coming of the Lord Jesus Christ in His glory.

The earth beholds and thrills with the first ecstatic moment of her deliverance from the bondage of corruption into the glorious liberty of the sons of God.

The angels behold and cry, "The kingdoms of this world are become the kingdoms of our Lord, and of his Christ" (Rev. 11:15).

The kings and princes of the world behold and cry to the rocks and hills to fall upon them and hide them from His presence.

The Antichrist beholds and falls palsied and helpless before the breath of His mouth and the glory of His coming.

The nations of the earth behold and wail because of Him.

B E H O L D !

Let *us* study the picture as the Scripture word-paints it. For not since the skies were stretched by the omnipotent hand of God in the ages that are past, has their blue canopy been the setting for such a scene as now floods them with its glory. JAMES H. McCONKEY 🖃

"Midnight is past," sings the sailor on the Southern Ocean; "midnight is past; the Cross begins to bend."

"It is high time to awake out of sleep." "Our Lord will come."

The Morning Cometh!

A shout!
A trumpet note!
A Glorious Presence in the azure sky!
A gasp,
A thrill of joy,
And we are with Him in the twinkling of an eye!

A glance,
An upward look,
Caught up to be with Christ forevermore!
The dead alive!
The living glorified!
Fulfilled are all His promises that came before!

His face!
His joy supreme
Our souls find rapture only at His feet!
Blameless!
Without a spot!
We enter into heaven's joy complete!

Strike harps,
Oh, sound His praise . . .
We know Him as we never knew before!
God's love!
God's matchless grace!
'Twill take eternity to tell while we adore!
ANNE CATHERINE WHITE

"His going forth is certain as the dawn" *(Hos. 6:3, Arabic).*

March 15

Married to another, even to him. (Rom. 7:4)

The most joyous moment in the life of the bride ought to be the moment when she loses her own name and self-dependence at the marriage altar, taking her husband's name instead of her own, and merging her life in his. And the most blissful moment of our life ought to be that in which we, by renouncing our right to self-ownership, become the bride of Another, the Lord Jesus Christ.

In marriage the wealth of the husband is, of course, placed at the disposal of the wife. Many will recall the story of the Earl of Burleigh, which Tennyson has immortalized. Under the guise of a landscape painter, the Earl won the heart of a simple village maiden. Imagining they were going to the cottage of which he had spoken, in which they were to spend their happy wedded life, they passed one beautiful dwelling after another, until . . .

> . . . a gateway she discerns
> With armorial bearings stately,
> And beneath the gate she turns,
> Sees a mansion more majestic
> Than all those she saw before:
> Many a gallant gay domestic
> Bows before him at the door.
> And they speak in gentle murmur,
> When they answer to his call,
> While he treads with footstep firmer,
> Leading on from hall to hall.
> And while now she wonders blindly,
> Nor the meaning can divine,
> Proudly turns he round and kindly,
> "All of this is mine and thine."

So by the union of hearts and lives the simple village maiden became the Lady of Burleigh, and *all* her husband's wealth was *hers*.

Who shall tell of the wealth which they inherit who are truly united to Jesus?

> "The exceeding riches of his grace" *(Eph. 2:7).*
> "The unsearchable riches of Christ" *(Eph. 3:8).*

> *Oh, sacred union with the Perfect Mind,*
> *Transcendent bliss, which Thou alone canst give;*
> *How blest are they this Pearl of Price who find,*
> *And, dead to earth, have learnt in Thee to live.*

> *Thus in Thine arms of love, O God, I lie,*
> *Lost, and forever lost to all but Thee.*
> *My happy soul, since it hath learnt to die,*
> *Hath found new life in Thine Infinity.*

Go then, and learn this lesson of the Cross,
And tread the way the saints and prophets trod:
Who, counting life and self and all things loss,
Have found in inward death the life of God.

Give up your identity!

March 16

And, lo, it was the latter growth after the king's mowings.
(Amos 7:1)

Our Lord is so intent on the life harvest of the saints, that He Himself often mows our fields for us, and takes away the things that seem to us *good*, in order to give us *the best*.

Our great King Himself is far more concerned for the worker than for the work.

When your heart fails you God sends His sunshine and the rain, and your hopes that were laid low sprout again, new growths appear—fertilized, perhaps, by your tears; perhaps by your heart's blood. Not only is the latter growth given after the king's mowing, but *because* of it. Like a grass lawn, the saints' lives become better the more they are beaten and rolled and mown. Do not think, then, that some strange thing has befallen you when you are tempted or tried. *It is by these things men live.*

There are, it may be, lives where the first growth is the worthiest, but I have seen few, and these—though beautiful—have not been strong.

The second crop of roses is the best, and *the greatest saints are those who have felt the scythe.* But *if the King is He who mows, then welcome the mowing that brings Him into the life.*

Better a bare field *with Christ* than the best harvest *without Him!*

Where He comes, Heaven's verdure springs; where He treads, earth's virtues grow. GOD'S HIGHWAY 🌿

They took them all away—my toys—
Not one was left;
They set me here, shorn, stripped of humblest joys,
Anguished, bereft.

I wondered why. The years have flown;
Unto my hand

Cling weaker, sadder ones who walk alone—
I understand.

ANONYMOUS

March 17

Doth the plowman plow all day to sow? (Isa. 28:24)

Is not the plowing merely a preparation for the seed-sowing to follow, and after that for the wheat which is to feed many? *When the plowshare goes through human hearts, surely it is for something!* Someday we shall see when the ripe ears of corn appear, that the plowshare had to come for a season. We thought it would kill us! And no plowshare goes through the earth but some life *is* destroyed, *but only that something better than that life may come.*

Be still, poor heart! God is effectual in working. "Let him do what seemeth him good."

> *God will not let my field lie fallow.*
> *The plowshare is sharp, the feet of the oxen are heavy.*
> *They hurt.*
> *But I cannot stay God from His plowing.*
> *He will not let my field lie fallow.*

KARLE WILSON BAKER

I have seen a farmer drive his plowshare through the velvet greensward, and it looked like a harsh and cruel process; but the farmer's eye foresaw the springing blades of wheat, and knew that within a few months that torn soil would laugh with a golden harvest.

Deep soul-plowing brings rich fruits of the Spirit. There are bitter mercies as well as sweet mercies; *but they are all mercies,* whether given in honey or given in wormwood. T. L. CUYLER

The iron plowshare goes over the field of the heart until the night-time . . . down the deep furrows the angels come and sow.

March 18

I have chosen you. (John 15:16)

Myron Niesley, California tenor, is called the highest-paid radio singer because he receives £5 for singing *one note*—the final and top one of a theme song, which others in the chorus cannot hit so perfectly.

God has *just one person to come at the right moment;* a place which no one can fill *but that person* and *at that time!*

Toil-worn I stood and said,
"O Lord, my feet have bled,
My hands are sore,
I weep, my efforts vainly poor.
With fainting heart I pray of Thee,
Give some brave other, work designed for me."

But my Lord answer made,
"O child of Mine,
I have looked through space and searched through time,
There is none can do the work called thine."

Soul-sick I knelt and cried,
"Let me forever hide
My little soul
From sight of Him who made me whole,
My one small spirit in the vast,
Vast throngs of like mean myriads, present, past!"

But my Lord answer made,
"O child of Mine,
I have looked through space and searched through time,
But I find no soul is like to thine!"

FRANCES BENT DILLINGHAM

Ask God if you are in His place for you.

Our life is but a little holding lent
To do a mighty labor. We are one
With heaven and the stars when it is spent
To do God's will.

It is possible for us to cross God's plan for our lives.

March 19

From henceforth let no man trouble me: for I bear in my body the marks of the Lord Jesus. (Gal. 6:17)

Do *we* carry any wound marks? Have we sought the protected areas while others met clash on clash the onset of the evil one? Has compromise robbed us of our war trophies? *Shall we not have done with such?* Someday we shall see Him face to face; shall see the nailprints in His hands. Shall we stand ashamed in His presence because we wear no scars of battle? DAILY COMMUNION

> *Hast thou no scar?*
> *No hidden scar on foot, or side, or hand?*
> *I hear thee sung as mighty in the land,*
> *I hear them hail thy bright ascendant star,*
> *Hast thou no scar?*
>
> *Hast thou no wound?*
> *Yet I was wounded by the archers, spent,*
> *Leaned me against a tree to die; and rent*
> *By ravening wolves that compassed me, I swooned;*
> *Hast thou no wound?*
>
> *No wound? No scar?*
> *Yet, as the Master shall the servant be,*
> *And pierced are the feet that follow Me;*
> *But thine are whole; can he have followed far*
> *Who hath no wound nor scar?*
>
> A. W. C.

Our path does not lie all the way through Beulah.

Garibaldi, the great Italian reformer of a past generation, in a fiery speech urged some thousands of Italy's young men to fight for the freedom of their homeland. One timid young fellow approached him, asking, "If I fight, Sir, what will be my reward?" Swift as a lightning flash came the uncompromising answer: "Wounds, scars, bruises, and perhaps death. But remember that through your bruises Italy will be free."

Are you not willing to endure scars in order to liberate souls?

The roughest road goes straight to the hilltop!

March 20

Bread corn is bruised. (Isa. 28:28)

Be content; ye are the wheat growing in our Lord's field; and, *if* wheat, ye must go under our Lord's threshing instrument on His barn floor, and through His sieve; and through His will be bruised, as was the Prince of your salvation (Isa. 53:10); that ye may be found good bread in your Lord's house. SAMUEL RUTHERFORD

When the wheat is carried home
And the threshing time has come,
Close the door.
When the flail is lifted high,
Like the chaff I would not fly;
At His feet, oh, let me lie,
On the floor!

All the cares that o'er me steal,
All the sorrows that I feel
Like a dart,
When my enemies prevail,
When my strength begins to fail—
'Tis the beating of the flail,
On my heart!

It becomes me to be still,
Though I cannot all His will
Understand.
I would be the purest wheat
Lying humbly at His feet,
Kissing oft the rod that beats,
In His hand!

By and by I shall be stored
In the garner of my Lord
Like a prize;
Thanking Him for every blow
That in sorrow laid me low,
But in beating made me grow
For the skies!

VOICE OF TRIUMPH

"Look at God's method of producing corn, and see something of His method of producing saints."

March 21

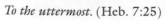

To the uttermost. (Heb. 7:25)

John B. Gough, the world's greatest temperance lecturer, was given a text by his godly mother, which indeed became like buried treasure, for it lay hidden within his heart for seven long years of dissipation. It was

> *He is able to save them to the uttermost*
> *that come unto God by him.*

His sins rose mountain-high before him; they seemed indelible; the past could not be undone! But he met Jesus Christ and found that His Blood availed for even him. "I have suffered," he cried, "and come out of the fire scorched and scathed with the marks upon my person, and with the memory of it burnt right into my soul." He likened his life to a snowdrift that had been badly stained; no power on earth could restore its former whiteness and purity. "The scars remain! The scars remain!" he used to say with bitter self-reproaches.

Giant Yesterday pointed to the black, black past derisively; held it a threat over the poor penitent's bowed and contrite head; told in tones that sounded like thunderclaps that there was no escape.

> *Wounds of the soul, though healed, will ache;*
> *The reddening scars remain*
> *And make confession.*
> *Lost innocence returns no more,*
> *We are not what we were*
> *Before transgression!*

Jesus is able to save to the uttermost. Says a writer, "God paints in many colors, but He never paints so gorgeously as when He paints in white." The crimson of the sunset; the azure of the ocean; the green of the valleys; the scarlet of the poppies; the silver of the dewdrops; the gold of the gorse: these are exquisite—so perfectly beautiful, indeed, that we cannot imagine an attractive heaven without them. But in the soul of John B. Gough we feel that the Divine art is at its very best.

Forty-four years have passed away since he had that grim struggle with sin. Gough is again in America, addressing a vast audience of young men in Philadelphia.

"Young men," he cries, perhaps with a bitter memory of those seven indelible years. "Young men, keep your record clean!" He pauses—a longer pause than usual, and the audience wonders. But he regains his voice.

"Young men," he repeats, more feebly this time, "keep your record clean!" Another pause—longer than the previous one. But again he finds the power of speech.

"Young men," he cries the third time, but in a thin, wavering voice. "Young men, keep your record clean!"

He falls heavily on the platform. Devout men carry him to his burial, and make lamentation over him. His race is finished; his voyage completed; his battle won. The promise has been literally and triumphantly fulfilled. The grace that saved him has kept him *to the very last inch, of the very last yard, of the very last mile; to the very last minute, of the very last hour, of the very last day! For* "He is able to save them *to the uttermost* that come unto God by him"! SELECTED

March 22

And told him, saying, Joseph is yet alive, and he is governor over all the land of Egypt. . . . It is enough; Joseph my son is yet alive: I will go and see him before I die. (Gen. 45:26, 28)

There are *heartbreaks of joy in God's plan for His children.* We can no more imagine the good things He has waiting ahead for us, both in this life and in the life to come, than Jacob could have imagined his lost boy alive and ruling Egypt. *That is the sort of miracle-surprise awaiting me daily in the tingling, vibrant, throbbing life of Jesus Christ who is my life, when I let Him fulfill His will and lavish Himself and His gifts and surprises upon me; when I let Him become all that there is of me. What a here and hereafter He gives me,* when I can say, "To me to live is Christ, and to die is gain"! MESSAGES FOR THE MORNING WATCH

I have a heritage of joy
That yet I must not see;
The Hand that bled to make it mine
Is keeping it for me.
My heart is resting on His truth
Who hath made all things mine,

Who draws my captive will to Him
And makes it one with Thine!

A. L. WARING

"Thou surprisest him" *(Ps. 21:3, Kay's trans.)*.

March 23

God is our refuge and strength, a very present help in trouble.
(Ps. 46:1)

Constrained at the darkest hour to confess humbly that without God's help I was helpless, I vowed a vow in the forest solitude that I would confess His aid before men. A silence as of death was around me; it was midnight and I was weakened by illness, prostrated with fatigue and worn with anxiety for my white and black companions, whose fate was a mystery. In this physical and mental distress I besought God to give me back my people. Nine hours later we were exulting with rapturous joy. In full view of all was the crimson flag with the crescent and beneath its waving folds was the long-lost rear column. HENRY M. STANLEY

My horse was very lame, and my head did ache exceedingly. Now what occurred I here avow as truth—though let each man account for it as he will.

Suddenly I thought, "Cannot God heal man or beast as He will?"

Immediately my weariness and headache ceased, and my horse was no longer lame! JOHN WESLEY

March 24

Peace I leave with you, my peace I give unto you. . . . Let not your heart be troubled, neither let it be afraid. (John 14:27)

The late Bishop Moule has told how once, during the war, at the close of an entertainment given for men going out to the front, a young officer arose at his Colonel's request to express the thanks of the men. He did so in genial words of charm and humor. Then suddenly, as if in afterthought, and in a different tone, he added: "We are soon crossing to France and to the trenches, and very possibly of course to death. Will any of our friends here tell us how to die?" There was a long, strained silence. Then the answer came. One of the singers made her way quietly forward to the front of the stage and began to sing the great *Aria from Elijah*, "O Rest in the Lord." There were few dry eyes when the song was concluded.

Here, above all else, is what each one of us needs in the battle of life: *a heart that has come to rest in God; a will fully surrendered.* That is the great secret. *That, alone, will bring us through with honor.* JAMES STEWART

When the soldiers of Napoleon were weak and discouraged on the Alpine ascent, we are told that their leader ordered: "Sound the French *Gloria*"; and the music gave the men new heart, and triumphantly they pressed forward. Beloved, whatever your cross, look up to your loving Master and sound the *Gloria!*

> *And when the fight is fierce, the warfare long,*
> *Steals on the air the distant triumph song,*
> *And hearts are brave again, and hands are strong,*
> *Alleluia!*

> *The music of the Gospel leads us Home!*

March 25

Fill up that which is behind of the afflictions of Christ.
(Col. 1:24)

The suggestion is this: *all ministry for the Master must be possessed of the sacrificial spirit of the Master.* If Paul is to help in the redemption of Rome, he must himself incarnate the death of Calvary. If he is to be a minister of Life, he must "die daily." The spirit of Calvary is to be reincarnate in Ephesus, in Athens, in Rome ... the sacrificial succession is to be maintained through the ages, and *we* are to *"fill up that which is behind of the sufferings of Christ."*

Here, then, is a principle: *the gospel of a broken heart demands the ministry of bleeding hearts. As soon as we cease to bleed we cease to bless. When our sympathy loses its pangs we can no longer be the servants of the Passion.* I do not know how any Christian service is to be fruitful if the servant is not primarily baptized in the spirit of a suffering compassion. *We can never heal the needs we do not feel. Tearless hearts can never be the heralds of the Passion. We must bleed if we would be the ministers of the saving blood.* We must, by our own suffering sympathies, "fill up that which is behind of the sufferings of Christ."

Are we in the succession? J. H. JOWETT

Ignatius said, when facing the lions in the arena, *"I am a grain of God. Let me be ground between the teeth of lions if I may thus become bread to feed God's people."* Were such martyred lives wasted? Thrown away? Is any life wasted that becomes seed-corn to produce bread for the world?

The way to make *nothing* of our lives is to be very careful of them. The way to make our lives an *eternal success* is to do with them just what Christ did with His.

Watch the opportunities to *"fill up that which remains behind of the afflictions of Christ."* How many of us can show Him wounds that worship *Him?* SEED THOUGHT CALENDAR

March 26

Get thee hence . . . and hide thyself. (1 Kings 17:3)

This is not a very gratifying endorsement of Elijah. Doubtless the man's heart swelled with eagerness to start a great reformation; his mind expanded with dreams of world-empire. To flee now, when the audacious approach to the king has been made, is to contradict all accepted methods of operation. Nothing now but solitude? But God knows His plans and Elijah, his servant. There is wholesome truth here. To trust where we cannot trace is to give our God the full sovereignty that He longs for. The most formidable barrier in His dealings with His children is their self-will. *"Let him do what seemeth him good"* (1 Sam. 3:18) *is not resignation, but triumphant faith, if we trust.*

And so by the brook Cherith the lonely man abides. It is lost time in the judgment of the flesh-depending critics; here is a thread in the fabric of society capable of great accomplishment, doing nothing. But they who argue so fail to see what God is to do. If we weigh things in the scales of human reasoning we shall always deal with economics and expediency; but no time is lost if God can have His way. *The real truth is, that He is to come into the life of His servant to better qualify him for a more vital revelation of Himself;* for with God *"the worker is more than the work."*

There may be many dear saints of God who doubt their saintship because their activities have been taken from them. Circumstances have closed in upon them; doors have been shut in their faces; funds for the prosecution of their work have ceased. It may be that, physically exhausted, they lie on their beds wondering why He can consent to so unreasonable a situation. Be assured of one thing: *Elijah is not to remain in obscurity and inactivity for all time*. Our error lies in mentally fixing our future according to present conditions. Let us arouse ourselves from this deadly coma. There is always the *afterward* of His gracious promising. KENNETH MACKENZIE

"He knows, and loves, and cares!"

"Immediately I conferred not with flesh and blood," says Paul, and he went away into a desert place.

A desert place ... and rest!

March 27

Bringing into captivity every thought. (2 Cor. 10:5)

"They compassed me about like bees," the Psalmist says.

Every second we get a sting from some fiery shaft, some imagination, some memory, some foreboding, some fear, some care, and God lets us get them in order that they may be destroyed and we so armed against them that they can never hurt us anymore. The only way to be armed against them is to refuse them and the source from which they come.

There is a world of truth here that most Christians have entirely overlooked. They give their spirit and heart to the Lord and they keep their head to themselves. Our intellect must be sanctified by being slain and replaced by *the mind of Christ*.

The only remedy for bad thoughts is to stop thinking all our own thoughts, to be spiritually decapitated, and to be delivered from the natural mind as well as the natural heart. God will, therefore, put us to school in the difficult task of stopping thinking. We will not only try to think right, but *we will stop our thoughts* and *wait for Him to give us His mind*.

This may seem to you like annihilation; but you will come to it if you are going to enter into the deepest, sweetest, strongest life, until *you shall be afraid to think at all until God first thinks in you*.

Have you given your thoughts to God? Have you learned the meaning of that cry of David, "I hate thoughts, but thy law do I love"? A. B. SIMPSON

Each sin has its door of entrance.
Keep—that—door—closed!
Bolt it tight!
Just outside, the wild beast crouches
In the night.
Pin the bolt with a prayer,
God will fix it there.
BEES IN AMBER, BY JOHN OXENHAM

"Carelessness with thoughts is as dangerous as toying with explosives!"

Bolt that door!

March 28

He made it again another vessel, as seemed good to the potter to make it. (Jer. 18:4)

God wants to make the very best He can of each of His children. He puts us on His wheel, and subjects us to the discipline which He deems most likely to secure our greatest blessedness and usefulness. But alas! How often He finds a marred vessel left on His hands when He desired and sought perfect beauty and strength! This is through no failure on His part; but because some bubble of vanity or grit of self-will has hindered Him.

When this has been the case, He does not cast us utterly away; but puts us afresh on the wheel and "makes us again." If He cannot do what He desired at first, He will still make the best of us; and the weakness of God is stronger than men. *Yield yourselves afresh to God.* Confess that you have marred His work. Humbly ask that He should make you again, as He made Jacob again, and Peter, and John, and Mark.

There is simply no limit to the progress and development of the soul which is able to meet God with a never-faltering "Yes." *Be very prompt to obey all that He may impress upon you as being His holy will. Let the lifelike clay in the potter's hands, be plastic to the Maker's touch!* DAILY DEVOTIONAL COMMENTARY

The potter worked at his task
With patience, love and skill.
A vessel, marred and broken,
He altered again to his will.
It was blackened, bent and old

But with traces of beauty left,
So he worked, this mender of pottery,
To restore the charm bereft,
Till at last it stood transformed
And he viewed it with tender eyes,
The work of his hands and love,
This potter, patient and wise.

I know a Mender of broken hearts,
And of lives that are all undone;
He takes them all, as they come to Him
And He loves them, every one.
With patience, love and skill
That surpasses the knowledge of men,
This Master Potter gathers the lost
And restores to His image again.
O Lover of folk with broken lives,
O wonderful Potter Divine,
I bring my soul for Thy healing touch;
In me, let Thy beauty shine.

There is no type of failure that He has not taken hold of and remade.

March 29

He is faithful that promised. (Heb. 10:23)

Oftentimes it is difficult to see how certain promises of God are to be realized. *We have nothing to do with that whatever!* God keeps our hands off His promises quite as surely as He keeps them off His stars. If He will not let us intermeddle with His planets, He will not ask us to have anything to do with the outworking and realization of His promises. He asks that their fulfillment be left to Him; and afterwards He will challenge our own life as the witness and answer, and confirmation of all that is gracious and all that is sure in the outworking of His words of promise. JOSEPH PARKER

The One who rolls the stars along
Speaks all the promises.

Trust the untraceable ways of God and remember that "these are parts of his ways."

In Thy strong arms I lay me down,
So shall the work be done;
For who can work so wondrously,
As the Almighty One!

March 30

And she went up, and laid him on the bed of the man of God,
and shut the door upon him, and went out. (2 Kings 4:21)

The Shunammite woman had lost her only son who had been given to her as the special gift of God. She held him dead in her arms. What could she do? She had a consecrated room where she entertained the prophet of God, and this room meant to her the very presence of God. She took up her precious burden *and she went up* there. How blessed it is to be able *to go up to the secret place of the Most High,* and *to bring our troubles under the shadow of the Almighty!* This is the place of refuge where the weary, helpless and heartbroken find relief.

"And she ... laid him on the bed of the man of God." This is a beautiful picture of committal—laying our trouble, our business, our whole way over on God.

"Commit ... trust ... and He worketh" (Ps. 37:5).

This poor bereaved mother was laying her burden on the Lord and leaving it there. That is one of the most difficult things to do: to *leave* our burdens with the Lord after we have placed them there.

"And shut the door ... and went out." The temptation is *not* to shut the door. We still see our trouble; we still handle it; we go over it again and again; we think our presence is needed, while His presence is more than sufficient. It takes faith to *"shut the door"* and go out. It takes real confidence for us to let the matter that is troubling us pass entirely *out of our* hands *into God's* hands. *In no other way can God fully work.*

The corn of wheat *must be hidden from the eyes of man if it is to bring forth fruit!* This Shunammite woman committed her dead son entirely to God and went out, shutting the door. No wonder that she could then say when questioned regarding her son, *"It is well."* There is no safer place in all the universe in which to leave our loved ones than in the hands of God. *No wonder that she received her dead son back to life!*

We certainly believe that there is many a son and daughter given as a special gift of God and now dead in trespasses and sins, *who, if fully committed to God in definite faith, would certainly be restored and saved.*

We certainly believe, also, that in every burden, trial, or care, *which we thus fully leave with God, and for which we fully trust Him, He will work above all we ask or think.* C. H. P. ☞

> When thou hast shut thy door,
> Shut out from thee its anxious care
> With all its sharp temptations sore,
> For He is there.
>
> When thou hast shut thy door,
> Shut out from thee its pain and grief,
> Bereavements—pressures to the core;
> He gives relief.
>
> When thou hast shut thy door,
> And left all there behind that wall
> Of God's own care, forevermore—
> He takes it all.
>
> When thou hast shut thy door,
> Shut out thyself—He only in,
> Nothing for thee but to adore—
> He works within.

L. S. P. ☞

March 31

The Spirit itself maketh intercession for us. (Rom. 8:26)

The highest ideal of prayer is to have the Holy Spirit pray through us. He is in us *to inspire our desires and longings, to quicken our minds and hearts,* and *giving us prayers, to pray them through us.* A great deal has been said about "praying through"; and when it means to pray until we believe God it is a most helpful and scriptural suggestion. However, if we approach this subject of prayer from the Divine standpoint, it may be truly said that all effectual prayer is only that which the Holy Spirit *prays through us.*

In His *praying through us* He quickens and uses our individual powers of will, intellect, and affection. His action is just as natural as if it had all originated with and was carried on by ourselves, but He is the *pray-er* for we have yielded ourselves to Him by an act of the will in definite faith for His working.

Although His praying is as natural as our own would be, yet when He is the *pray-er,* there is often the consciousness of a depth and power unutterable. These are God's infinitely loving desires striving to find expression through finite and human channels. Beside, there will be the leading out in prayer for objects and persons that otherwise would have been neglected, and *such spirit of prayer will come upon us just as there is need, and may sometimes even seem to be at the most unlikely time and place.*

How limitless are the possibilities of prayer when we have such a mighty, loving Helper! *How certain we may be of the answer when He breathes the prayer through us!* What wonderful fellowship this kind of prayer gives!

We can only realize His ideal for our prayer-life by abiding in Him and trusting Him moment by moment *to pray through us with His own mighty intercessions.* C. H. P.

Can it be that some souls are still in sins "retained" because you and I have shrunk from the travail of intercession?

April 1

His heart is fixed, trusting. (Ps. 112:7)

Before my window is a beautiful branch of a tree now in full spring dress. Only a few weeks ago that same branch was loaded with ice—it seemed as if it must break! I remember one hour: it seemed it could not keep up. I expected to see it give way; but it did not break. Today it is beautiful!

There are many in this sad world who are as my bare branch was—loaded with ice. Their sorrows seem like hailstorms, and how to keep up, how to hold on, seems to be the one vital question. If one such should read about my branch, let me say to that one, "Don't break; cling for your life to the one truth, *that God has not forgotten you!* He holds the winds in His fists; and the waves that now seem as though they would swallow you up, in the hollow of His hands." You may look up and say,

> *Thou hast a charge no waves can wash away;*
> *And let the storm that does Thy work*
> *Deal with me as it may.*

And so, by simple faith in God's goodness and love you hold on, and when in the future—like the branch near my window—it shall be all spring with you, you will remember your sorrows as waters that have passed away. "Hold on! It is not always winter; spring is coming. The birds are yet to sing on the very branch loaded with ice. *Only, don't break!*"

My branch did not have a will of its own, but we have wills, and God can energize them. We must use our wills and say, "Though He slay me, yet will I trust in Him," and *He never slays but to make alive.*

Thus trusting, though you may bend to the blast, *you will not break; you will hold on; you will see your Spring!*

And I know not any trouble, for I have the tempest's King
To change my winter's fury to the gladness of His spring.

Blessed is the man who, when the tempest has spent its fury, recognizes his Father's Voice in the undertone.

April 2

Be still, and know that I am God. (Ps. 46:10)

There is immense power in stillness. A great saint once said, "All things come to him who knows how to trust and be silent." The words are pregnant with meaning. A knowledge of this fact would immensely change our ways of working. Instead of restless struggles, we would "sit down" inwardly before the Lord, and would let the Divine forces of His Spirit work out in silence the ends to which we aspire. You may not see or feel the operations of this silent force, but be assured it is always working mightily, and will work for you, if you only get your spirit still enough to be carried along by the currents of its power. HANNAH WHITALL SMITH

There is a stillness in the Christian's life:
An inner stillness only known to him
Who has so gladly laid at Jesus' feet
His all, and now He reigns alone within,
Master of every motion, wish, and plan.
In stillness crowned, He rules supreme as King,
And in that inner chamber of the heart
Has made a little sanctuary within.

There is a stillness in the Christian's life:
The corn of wheat must fall into the ground

And die, then if it die, out of that death
Life, fullest life, will blessedly abound.
It is a mystery no words can tell,
But known to those who in this stillness rest;
Something Divinely incomprehensible:
That for my nothingness, I get God's best!

Leave it all quietly with Him: failures, fears, foes, future!

April 3

Say unto the peoples: the Lord reigneth from the tree.
(Ps. 96:10, Latin)

Home of our hearts, lest we forget
What our redemption meant to Thee,
Let our most reverent thought be set
Upon Thy Calvary.

A. W. C.

When Christ hung on the Cross of Calvary He was, apparently, the biggest failure the world had ever seen; for no other man had even dared to make such astounding claims as He, yet there He hung; nailed to the cross of shame, exposed to the view of a coarse, mocking crowd; cut off in early manhood; betrayed by one of His own personal friends; deserted by all of the other apostles—one of whom, after loud professions of devotion had denied Him with oaths and curses. It seemed as if that most wonderful and touching of all intercessory prayers (recorded in John 17) had never reached the Father's ear; and as if the words "Father, the hour is come; glorify thy Son" were impossible of fulfillment.

Not one soul, even of those who loved the Savior best, understood Him and His lifework; therefore not one friend could really sympathize with the God-man, who, on His human side, so hungered for sympathy.

If you and I are truly following in the Master's footsteps, we too must be willing to risk apparent failure in the eyes of the world; and, harder still, must often be content to be misunderstood by our fellow-Christians. It is only when we have learned the faith and obedience which leave all consequences with God, that we can know the power and deep joy contained in these words, that once sounded so terrible—"I am crucified with Christ." E. A. G.

Jesus, thou living bread,
Ground in the mills of death,
Let me by Thee be fed;
Thy servant hungereth.

Jesus, thou choicest vine,
Nailed to the Cross of woe,
Now let Thy life Divine
Into my being flow.

Strength for the coming day
Thy Body doth impart,
Thy Blood doth cleanse away
The sins that stain my heart.

Let not my heart be cold,
Nor doubt when faith doth prove
That in my hand I hold
Thy Sacrament of love.

Jesus, be not a guest
That tarrieth but a day;
Come to my longing breast,
Come, and forever stay.

R. F. Pechey

He reigneth! He reigneth, but let us never forget that it is from the throne on Golgotha!

April 4

Repair the breaches. (2 Kings 12:5)

A God-fearing Armenian Christian was sending some merchandise to a distant city. There were no railroads in that part of the country, and as it was a valuable lot of goods the merchant himself accompanied the caravan.

Such caravans usually camp at night, and this is an opportune time for the highwaymen, who make their living by attacking caravans, to steal unnoticed upon the campers. At the chosen time, under cover of the night, the Kurds drew near. All was strangely silent. There seemed to be no guards. But as they pressed closer, imagine their astonishment to find *high walls where walls had never stood before.* The next night they found the same impassable walls. On the third night they found the same walls, but there were breaches in them through which the robbers entered.

The captain of the marauding band was so terrified by the mystery that he woke up the Armenian, asking what it meant. He told how his band had followed intent on robbing them; how they had found the high walls around the caravan on the first and second nights; but on this night they had been able to enter through breaches. "If you will tell us the secret of all this, we will not molest you," said the captain.

The merchant himself was puzzled. "My friends," he said, "I have done nothing to have walls raised about us. All I do is pray every evening, committing myself and those with me to God. I fully trust in Him to keep me from all evil; but tonight, being very tired and sleepy, I made a rather halfhearted prayer. That must be why you were allowed to break through."

The Kurds were overcome by this testimony. Then and there they accepted the Lord Jesus Christ as their Savior. *But the Armenian never forgot the breach in the wall of prayer.*

Have you broken your tryst with God?

April 5

And he bearing his cross went forth into ... Golgotha.
(John 19:17)

When the two single beams were lifted from the Lord's bleeding shoulders and laid on those of the sturdy Cyrenian, Simon became what none ever had been, or ever would be, in all the history of the Lord's Passion—he became for a brief space *the substitute of Jesus!* Simon came into Jerusalem that morning, from the village home where he had been a guest, unconscious of the tragedy enacted there during the night, and was soon caught in the throng accompanying Jesus to Calvary. Through the dense excited mass of life this heavily-built countryman forced his insistent body till he came to the edge of the procession. From this vantage point he could peer in and get sight of Jesus—could catch the weariness of His face. Was it the merest accident that Simon was taken into the heart of the tragedy? The guard looked round and saw Simon—his prominence and bulk—perhaps an unconscious sympathy growing on his face—and before Simon knew what had happened he had been dragged out from among the people and the cross was on his shoulders, and *he was walking beside Jesus to Calvary.*

O good fortune of the Cyrenian to have a stout body—to be born a countryman—to carry a kindly heart! It had won him an honor *denied to kings and conquerors.*

And none so favored as this Cyrenian, for *they journeyed together* within an iron wall—no man could interrupt or annoy—neither priest nor people; they were so close together *that the cross seemed to be on them both.* That Jesus spoke to Simon as He did to few in all His ministry, there can be little doubt, since no one could render Jesus the slightest service without being instantly repaid, and this man had succored Him in His dire extremity. What Jesus said to *His substitute* Simon never told. But one thing is certain: in the heart of the tragedy on the way to Calvary, *Simon met Jesus.* And with what kindness Jesus must have spoken to *His cross-bearer* as they went forward together under one cross—one common disgrace! *Alone with the Redeemer* one gathers precious treasure!

For a short while *this man carried the load of wood.* In return, *Jesus carried his sin, and that of his children after him;* for by the time this Gospel was given unto the world Simon was known as the head of a distinguished Christian house—a man honored in his sons, Alexander and Rufus.

Nothing save . . . a few drops of blood on the ground remained of the great tragedy as Simon journeyed homeward that evening; but, in the meantime, *Jesus had accomplished the deliverance of the world*—and *Simon, the Cyrenian, had carried the Lord's cross!* What a privilege!

Taken from the throng to carry another's cross—Via Dolorosa with Jesus! JOHN WATSON 🐦

April 6

In all these things we are more than conquerors. (Rom. 8:37)

This is one of the greatest chapters in the Bible. If doubt overtakes you, read it. If your sorrows have been too consuming, this chapter has a message for you. If you are weak, it will give you strength. If you are discouraged, hope will be restored by its inescapable logic. Read it often; become familiar with its truths, its reasoning process, its conclusion. Believe it. Live it. *Here is not only promised victory, but more than victory!*

How can we be "more than conquerors"? The American Indians believed that every foe tomahawked sent fresh strength into the warrior's arm. Temptation victoriously met increases our spiritual strength and equipment. It is possible not only to defeat the enemy but to capture him and make him fight in our ranks. God wants all His children *to turn the storm clouds into chariots.*

The ministry of thorns has often been a greater ministry to man than the ministry of thrones. Appropriate this truth.

Face the forces of darkness today Fearlessly!

> *I dare not be defeated*
> *Since Christ, my conquering King,*
> *Has called me to the battle*
> *Which He did surely win.*
> *Come, Lord, and give me courage,*
> *Thy conquering Spirit give,*
> *Make me an overcomer,*
> *In power within me live.*
>
> *I dare not be defeated,*
> *Just at the set of sun,*
> *When Jesus waits to whisper,*
> *"Well done, beloved, well done!"*
> *Come, Lord, bend from the Glory,*
> *On me Thy Spirit cast,*
> *Make me an overcomer,*
> *A victor to the last.*

THE VERSES OF A PILGRIM

April 7

The LORD is my shepherd. (Ps. 23:1)

Who is it that is your Shepherd? The Lord! Oh, my friends, what a wonderful announcement! The Lord God of heaven and earth, and Almighty Creator of all things; He who holds the universe in His Hand as though it were a very little thing. He is your Shepherd, and has charged Himself with the care and keeping of you, as a shepherd is charged with the care and keeping of his sheep. If your hearts could really take in this thought you would never have a fear or a care again; for with such a Shepherd how could it be possible for you ever to want any good thing? HANNAH WHITALL SMITH

Come, my sheep, shadows deep fall over land and sea,
Fast the day fades away;
Come and rest with me. Come, and in my fold abide—
Dangers lurk on every side—till at last night is past;
In my fold abide.

Come, my sheep, I will keep watch the long night through.
Safe from harm and alarm,
I will shelter you. Through the night my lambs shall rest
Safe upon the Shepherd's breast, folded there free from care
Through the night shall rest.

Come, my sheep, calmly sleep sheltered in the fold,
Weary one homeward come—
Winds are blowing cold. Rest until the dawn shall break,
Then with joy my flocks shall wake; pastures new wait for you
When the dawn shall break.

DOROTHY B. POLSUE

The Shepherd is responsible for the sheep; not the sheep for the Shepherd. The worst of it is, that we sometimes think we are both the Shepherd and the sheep, and that we have both to guide and follow. Happy are we when we realize that He is responsible; that He goes before, and goodness and mercy follow.

April 8

He was oppressed, and he was afflicted. (Isa. 53:7)

Christ was *chosen out of the people,* that He might know our wants, and sympathize with us. I believe some of the rich have no notion whatever of what the distress of the poor is. They have no idea of what it is to labor for their daily bread. They have a very faint conception of what a rise in the price of bread means; they do not *know* anything about it. And when we put men in power who never were of the people, they do not understand the art of governing us. But our great and glorious Jesus Christ is one *chosen out of the people;* and therefore He knows our wants.

Jesus suffered *temptation and pain* before us; our *sicknesses* He bore; *weariness*—He has endured it, for weary He sat by the well; *poverty*—He knows it, for sometimes He had no bread to eat save that bread of which the world knows nothing; *to be houseless*—He knew that, too, for the foxes

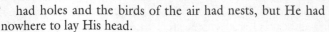

had holes and the birds of the air had nests, but He had nowhere to lay His head.

My fellow-Christian, there is no place where thou canst go, where Christ has not been before thee—sinful places alone excepted. *He hath been before thee;* He hath smoothed the way; He hath entered the grave, that He might make the tomb the royal bedchamber of the ransomed race, the closet where they lay aside the garments of labor to put on the vestments of eternal rest.

In all places whithersoever we go, the Angel of the covenant has been our forerunner. Each burden we have to carry has once been laid on the shoulders of Immanuel.

> *His way was much rougher and darker than mine;*
> *Did Christ my Lord suffer and shall I repine?*

Dear fellow-traveler, take courage! Christ has consecrated the road.
CHARLES H. SPURGEON

> *And is Thy spotless life on earth to end*
> *Ere Thy young manhood has but scarce begun?*
> *Will not Thy Father heaven's guardians send?*
> *Thou art His Son.*
>
> *Is there no other way to save mankind*
> *Without Thine agony and utter loss?*
> *Is there no road which Heavenly Love may find*
> *Beside the Cross?*
>
> *There is no path His weary feet may know*
> *But that which leads Him to the shameful tree;*
> *That Great Forgiving Love will even go*
> *To Calvary.*

NO OTHER ROAD,
BY E. LILLIAN LOWTHER

April 9

By reason of breakings they purify themselves. (Job 41:25)

Do you know the lovely fact about the opal: that, in the first place, it is made of desert dust, sand and silica, and owes its beauty and preciousness to a defect? It is a stone with a broken heart. It is full of minute fissures, which admit air, and the air refracts the light. Hence, its lovely hues and that sweet "lamp of fire" that ever burns at its heart; for *the breath of the Lord is in it.*

You are only conscious of the cracks and desert sand, but so He makes *His precious opals.*

We must be broken in ourselves before we can give back the lovely hues of His light, and the lamp of the Temple can burn in us and never go out. ELLICE HOPKINS

Then hush! oh, hush! for the Father knows what thou knowest not,
The need and the thorn and the shadow linked with the fairest lot;
Knows the wisest exemption from many an unseen snare,
Knows what will keep thee nearest, knows what thou could'st not bear.

Hush! oh, hush! for the Father portioneth as He will,
To all His beloved children, and shall they not be still?
Is not His will the wisest, is not His choice the best?
And in perfect acquiescence is there not perfect rest?

Hush! oh, hush! for the Father, whose ways are true and just,
Knoweth and careth and loveth, and waits for thy perfect trust;
The cup He is slowly filling shall soon be full to the brim,
And infinite compensations forever be found in Him.

FRANCES RIDLEY HAVERGAL

April 10

Be filled with the Spirit. (Eph. 5:18)

General Gordon regretted that no one had told him when he was a young man that there was a Holy Spirit which he could possess and which could possess him. The knowledge would have saved him weakness, and sorrow, and loss. But when the later loneliness came, Gordon knew the inner strengthening of the Spirit. A power not his own came to his help. He was "strengthened with all might."

This is the apostle's sense of the magnitude of the Spirit. There is nothing we can need at any time of pressure, whether of duty or of danger, of temptation or of anxiety, but the Divine Ally will make Himself the resource of the soul to meet and endure the strain.

The apostle urges *that the utmost room should be made for the Spirit; that a man possess the Divine gift in its utmost measure.* He seems to suggest that there are degrees of possession; there are measurements we make, limitations we impose, and in his eager way he urges *that we make the utmost room for the Spirit's fullness.* Do not go in for small measures; do not restrict your allowance. The gift of the Spirit is not on a rationing basis. Do not confine yourself to mean and petty degrees of the Spirit. "Be filled with the Spirit." There is no surfeit here, nor need there be any restriction. THE LIFE OF A CHRISTIAN, BY JOHN MACBETH 🐝

> *There are deep things of God. Push out from shore,*
> *Hast thou found much? Give thanks and look for more.*
> *Dost fear the generous Giver to offend?*
> *Then know His store of bounty hath no end.*
> *He doth not need to be implored or teased;*
> *The more we take the better He is pleased.*

Beside the common inheritance of the land, there are some special possessions. A. B. SIMPSON 🐝

"Have ye received the Holy Ghost since ye believed?"

April 11

Instead of the thorn shall come up the fir tree, and instead of the brier shall come up the myrtle tree: and it shall be to the LORD for a name, for an everlasting sign that shall not be cut off. (Isa. 55:13)

At the Jerusalem Conference on Good Friday we were out on the Mount of Olives, and our hearts were deeply and strangely moved as we thought about *His* going out of the city yonder, up the hillside, to die. I said to myself, "I would like to follow in His train, and catch the same passion and the same vision." As the meeting was closing I thought, "I will take something by which to remember this hour." I leaned over to pluck a flower, one of the flowers that bloom in lovely profusion across the hillsides of Palestine. As I was about to pick my wildflower, an inner voice said, "No, not the wildflower; here is the thornbush yonder; take a piece of that." It was the thornbush from which the crown of thorns was taken, and crushed upon the brow of Jesus. I protested, "The thornbush is not beautiful, it is ugly; I would rather have the flower," and I again leaned over to pick my flower. The voice was more imperious this time, and said, "No, not the flower, but the thornbush; there is something in the thornbush you do not see now; take it!"

Rather reluctantly I turned away from the wildflower and plucked a piece from the thornbush and put it in the folds of my Bible. No, deeper; I put it within the folds of my heart and wore it there.

Weeks went by—months. One day I chanced to look at my thornbush I had worn within my heart, and to my amazement I found it was all abloom! The Rose of Sharon was there in lovely profusion. There was something else in the thornbush I had not seen.

"From thy brier, dear heart, shall blow a rose for others."

To some people there comes this cross, the *absence* of the Cross. There is always the shadow of the Cross. Suppose God took it away, what then?

> *And shall there be no cross for me*
> *In all this life of mine?*
> *Shall mine be all a flowery path*
> *And all the thorns be Thine?*

April 12

If thou hadst been here. (John 11:21)

"*If* only my circumstances and my environment were altered ...

"*If* only So-and-So were not trying to live with ...

"*If* only I had the opportunities, the advantages, that other people have ...

"*If* only that insurmountable difficulty, that sorrow, that trouble, could be moved out of my life; then how different things would be! and how different I should be."

Ah, dear friend, you are not the only one who has had such thoughts. No less a person than Paul the Apostle besought the Lord three times that the thorn in the flesh might depart from him; *and yet, it was allowed to remain.*

A certain gentleman had a garden which might have been very beautiful had it not been disfigured by an immense boulder which reached far under the soil. He tried to blast it out with dynamite, but in the attempt only shattered the windows of the house. Being very self-willed he used without success one harsh method after another to get rid of the disfigurement until finally he died of worry and blighted hopes.

The heir, a man who *not only had common sense but used it,* soon perceived the hopelessness of striving to budge the boulder and therefore set to work to convert it into a rockery, which he covered with frescoes, flowers, ferns, and vines. It soon came about that the visitors to the garden commented on its unsurpassed beauty, and the owner could never quite decide which gave him the greater happiness—the harmonious aspect of his garden, or the success in adapting himself to the thing that was too deep to move.

So the unsightly boulder which could not be removed, proved to be the most valuable asset in that garden *when dealt with by one who knew how to turn its very defects to account.* SELECTED

God often plants His flowers among rough rocks!

April 13

He is risen. (Mark 16:6)

Arise! for He is risen today;
And shine, for He is glorified!
Put on thy beautiful array,
And keep perpetual Eastertide.

A little lad was gazing intently at the picture in the art store window: the store was displaying a notable picture of the crucifixion. A gentleman approached, stopped, and looked. The boy, seeing his interest, said: "That's Jesus." The man made no reply, and the lad continued: "Them's Roman soldiers." And, after a moment: "They killed Him."

"Where did you learn that?" asked the man.

"In the Mission Sunday school," was the reply.

The man turned and walked thoughtfully away. He had not gone far when he heard a youthful voice calling: "Say, Mister," and quickly the little street lad caught up with him. "Say, Mister," he repeated, "I wanted to tell you that He rose again."

That message, which was nearly forgotten by the boy, is the message which has been coming down through the ages. It is the Easter message— the story of the eternal triumph of life over death; the promise and pledge of man's immortality.

The grave to Him was not a terminus!
This is the day of glad tidings! Go quickly, and tell the message!
"He is risen!" Hallelujah! Christ is risen! Hades could not hold Him! Corruption could not devour Him! "I am He that liveth and was dead; and, behold, I am alive forevermore, Amen; and have the keys of death and Hades." Blessed be God! Jesus lives to die no more! Go quickly, and tell everywhere the glad news!

And I think the Shining Ones marvel much
As they gaze from the world above,
To see how slowly we spread the news
Of that Sacrifice of love.

There is, to my mind, a natural sequence in one of the accounts of that first Easter morning, as beautiful as it is suggestive. It is the story of the women who hastened to the sepulcher, and it says: *"They came unto the sepulcher at the rising of the sun."*

The glory of Easter morn is the sacrificial red
on the morning sky!

April 14

Be strong in the grace that is in Christ Jesus. . . . Endure hardness, as a good soldier of Jesus Christ. (2 Tim. 2:1, 3)

The post of honor in war is so called because it is attended by difficulties and dangers to which but few are equal; yet generals usually allot these hard services to their favorites and friends, who on their part eagerly take them as tokens of favor and marks of confidence.

Should we not, therefore, account it an honor and a privilege when the Captain of our salvation assigns us a difficult post, since He can and does inspire His soldiers, which no earthly commander can, with wisdom, courage, and strength suitable to their situation?

Listen to Ignatius shouting as the lion's teeth tear his flesh, "Now I begin to be a Christian!"

The Christian's badge of honor here, has ever been the Cross.

No church or movement can survive unless it is ready to be crucified.
BISHOP OF WINCHESTER

If I did not see that the Lord kept watch over the ship, I should long since have abandoned the helm. But I see Him! through the storm, strengthening the tackling, handling the yards, spreading the sails—aye more, commanding the very winds! Should *I* not be a coward if I abandoned *my* post? Let Him govern, let Him carry us forward, let Him hasten or delay, *we will fear nothing!* MARTIN LUTHER

For us, swords drawn, up to the gate of heaven:
Oh, may no coward spirit seek to leaven
The warrior code, the calling that is ours!
Forbid that we should sheathe our sword in flowers!

Captain beloved, battle wounds were Thine,
Let me not wonder if some hurt be mine.
Rather, O Lord, let my deep wonder be
That I may share a battle wound with Thee.

GOLD CORD

April 15

Although the fig tree shall not blossom, neither shall fruit be in the vines; the labor of the olive shall fail, and the fields shall yield no meat; the flock shall be cut off from the fold, and there shall be no herd in the stalls: Yet I will rejoice in the LORD, I will joy in the God of my salvation. (Hab. 3:17–18)

How irrational it seems! We, with whom God hath dealt bountifully, can understand praising Him, but we should have the greatest respect for a man, who under these circumstances would not repine. To bring it closer home than the time of Habakkuk, translate all this into current experience. Instead of flocks and herds, use profits; instead of figs and olives, read credit balances; for husbandry and its terms, use business and its terms; for flocks and stalls, substitute bank balances and securities; for Chaldean invasion, the economic blizzard which is sweeping through the world—and then see where you stand!

Although there shall be no balances and securities, and all dividends shall be passed, and though I be reduced to utter penury, yet will I rejoice in the Lord!

You say that is impossible! Of course, apart from some supernatural aid he could not have done it, nor can we. Habakkuk learned that life cannot be a solo affair: it is a duet. If life were a solo, it would mean a tragic breakdown when the high notes must be reached, or the low ones melodiously sounded. A duet means harmony—*human life linked on to Divine purpose and power.* Habakkuk's experience shows that *you have lost nothing if you have not lost God.*   J. STUART HOLDEN ✺

Pilgrim, look up!

The road is dusty; the journey is long. Look up! *Look up in the early morning* when the sun comes peeping over the horizon, out of the shadows of the night. Look up *in the noontide* when the resting-spot is still afar in the distance. Look up *when you see the evening star.*

Look up! There shines the City!

April 16

Speak unto the children of Israel, that they go forward.
(Ex. 14:15)

Let us move on and step out boldly, though it be into the night where one can scarcely see the way. The path will open as we press on, like the trail through the forest, or the Alpine pass which discloses but a few rods of its length. There are things God gives us to do without any light or illumination at all except His own command, but *those who know the way to God can find it in the dark.*   ALEXANDER MACLAREN ✺

The God of Israel, the Savior, is sometimes a God that hideth Himself, but never a God that absenteth Himself; sometimes in the dark, but never at a distance.   MATTHEW HENRY ✺

There was a rift tonight;
I saw a gray cloud break and let the light
Shine through—a ray of hope to all the earth;
Long had I waited here; I found it hard to say,
"The clouds will drift apart, the darkness melt away
Before the radiance of the night's new birth."

That promised glow to guide a wayward one;
At last, after long hours of doubt and fear,
Came light again and life, and sweet security,
As though a hidden ray from God's eternity
Peeped out, that I might look and see it there.

So, if I can but wait,
I know that God will send it, soon or late—
This break within my life's gray cloud; His gift
To me, one star of perfect love to shine and show
That they who walk by faith are told the way to go,
And after storm will come the blessed rift.

RUTH M. GIBBS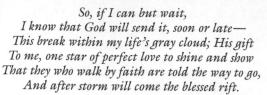

April 17

Blessed is that servant, whom his lord when he cometh shall find so doing. (Matt. 24:46)

A story is related, which has to do with the Second Coming of our blessed Lord; and the general dissemination of this precious truth. At last it reached the black people in the South as they worked in the cotton fields. Said one of the old black brethren, *"What's de use of us pickin' cotton if de Lawd is comin' back?"* And scores of others agreed. The cotton pickers stopped their work and the cotton wasted in the fields. Everybody was busy attending conferences and camp meetings, singing the praises of God, and looking for His return.

The following winter was one of great need and privation, because their crops had been so woefully neglected.

Then one of their number, an evangelist, began preaching on this text: *"Blessed is that servant, whom his lord when he cometh shall find so doing."*

Before long the black people were once again tilling their ground, and picking cotton in the rows. It remained for Bertrand Shadwell to give us the following poem which suggests their change in attitude:

There's a King and Captain high,
Who'll be coming by and by;
And He'll find me hoeing cotton when He comes.
You can hear His legions charging in the thunder of the sky;
And He'll find me hoeing cotton when He comes.
When He comes!
When He comes!
All the dead shall rise, in answer to His drums.
Oh, the fires of His encampment star the firmament on high;
And the heavens shall roll asunder, when He comes.

There's a Man they thrust aside,
Who was tortured till He died;
And He'll find me hoeing cotton when He comes.
He was spat upon and mocked at;
He was scourged and crucified;
And He'll find me hoeing cotton when He comes.
When He comes!
When He comes!
He'll be loved by saints and angels when He comes;
They'll be calling out "Hosanna!" to the Man that men denied;
And I'll kneel among the cotton—
When He comes!

"Occupy till I come."

April 18

And he brought him forth abroad, and said, Look now toward heaven, and tell the stars, if thou be able to number them: and he said unto him, So shall thy seed be. (Gen. 15:5)

We are profoundly impressed with the unlimited resources of the God of the Bible. He never does anything small. When He makes an ocean He makes it so deep that no man can fathom it. When He makes a mountain He makes it so large that no one can measure or weigh it. When He makes flowers, He scatters multiplied millions of them where there is no one to admire them but Himself. When He makes grace, He makes it without sides or bottom and leaves the top off. Instead of giving salvation with a medicine dropper, He pours it forth like a river.

When God sets out to do a thing for us, *He does it with a prodigality of love-prompted abundance that fairly staggers one who reckons things by the coldly calculating standards of earth.*

Whatever blessing is in our cup it is sure to *run over.* With Him the calf is always the *fatted calf;* the robe is always the *best robe;* the joy is *unspeakable;* the peace *passeth understanding;* the grace is *so abundant that the recipient has all-sufficiency for all things, and abounds to every good work.*

There is no grudging in God's benevolence; He does not measure out His goodness as the apothecary counts his drops and measures his drams, slowly and exactly, drop by drop. God's way is always characterized by multitudinous and overflowing bounty, like that in nature which is so profuse in beauty and life that every drop of the ocean, every square inch of the forest glade, every molecule of water, teems with marvels and defies the research and investigation of man. Well may we cry with the apostle,

"I have all, and abound."

April 19

When thou prayest, enter into thy closet. (Matt. 6:6)

The apostolic men, the saintly men, the heroic servants of God, the strong soldiers of Jesus Christ, have everywhere and always *prayed without ceasing.*

If Francis of Assisi knew how to do battle among men, it was because he loved to "fly away as a bird to its nest in the mountains." John Welsh spent eight hours out of the twenty-four in communion with God; therefore he was equipped and armed and dared to suffer! David Brainerd rode through the endless American woods praying, and so fulfilled his ministry in a short time. John Wesley came out from his seclusion to change the face of England. Andrew Bonar did not once miss his mercy seat, and his fellowship with heaven made him the winsome Christian that he was. John Fletcher sometimes prayed all night. Adoniram Judson won Burma for Christ through unwearied prayer. Such was *the habit of those who wrought nobly for God.*

If we would attempt great things for God, and achieve something before we die, we must pray at every moment and in every place. *God commits Himself into the hands of those who truly pray.*

> *Alone, dear Lord, in solitude serene,*
> *Thy servant Moses was constrained to go,*
> *Into the silent desert with the sheep;*
> *The silvery stars his lovely vigil know.*

> *And Paul, the fiery warrior, zealous, bold,*
> *In desert places, 'neath Arabian skies,*
> *Learned God's own lessons, harkened to His voice,*
> *Grew calm, resourceful, humble, meek and wise.*

> *Alone, dear Lord, I fear to be alone;*
> *My heart demands the blest companionship*

Of those that love Thee; friendship's nectar sweet,
With those beloved, I evermore would sip.

But in the desert, Moses, David, Paul,
Were not alone, afar from love or care:
They companied with heav'nly visitors,
They knew no loneliness, for Thou wert there.

ALICE E. SHERWOOD

The first-century Christians were said to be *power conscious*. We are *problem* conscious. What did *they* believe about prayer? What do *we*?

April 20

But he himself went a day's journey into the wilderness, and came and sat down under a juniper tree: and he requested for himself that he might die; and said, It is enough.... And, behold, the LORD passed by, and a great ... wind ...; but the LORD was not in the wind: ... an earthquake; but the LORD was not in the earthquake: ... a fire; but the LORD was not in the fire: and after the fire a still small voice.... And the LORD said unto him, Go, return on thy way ... and ... anoint Hazael to be king over Syria. (1 Kings 19:4, 11–12, 15)

When a man loses heart he loses everything. To keep one's heart in the midst of life's stream, and to maintain an undiscourageable front in the face of its difficulties is not an achievement that springs from anything that a laboratory can demonstrate, or that logic can affirm. *It is an achievement of faith.*
If you lose your sky, you will soon lose your earth.

From under the juniper tree Elijah is called into an audience with the King of Kings. While listening to his own defeated wail, the accents of the still small Voice fall upon his weary ear. God refused him his unworthy request; rested him from his service; reminded him that he was still needed; and returned him to his work. He thought his work was done and that life had left him in the shadows. God says: "No, I am commissioning you to go forth and anoint kings and prophets, and climax the service of other days."

Not till His hour strikes is our day done; as long as we live we serve the King!

The tempter is always ready to take advantage of a time of weariness and reaction. *He loves to fish in troubled waters.*

Juniper trees make poor sanctuaries.

It is good to have things settled by faith, before they are unsettled by feeling.

April 21

God hath chosen the weak things of the world to confound the things which are mighty. (1 Cor. 1:27)

We must not be fainthearted because we are consciously poor instruments. The main question is *the mastery of Him who uses the instruments.*

Once Paganini, standing before a vast audience, broke string after string of his violin. Men had come to hear his greatest sonata, "Napoleon." They hissed as he seemed to destroy all hope for continuing his performance. Then the artist held up his violin: "One string—and Paganini," and on that one string he made the first complete manifestation of his greatness!

It would be a poor violin, indeed, out of which Paganini could not bring music; a poor pencil with which Raphael could not create a masterpiece; and *the power of the Spirit behind the least gifted one can work to glorious issues.*

It is said that Gainsborough, the artist, longed also to be a musician. He bought musical instruments of many kinds and tried to play them. He once heard a great violinist bringing ravishing music from his instrument. Gainsborough was charmed and thrown into transports of admiration. He bought the violin on which the master played so marvelously. He thought that if he had the wonderful instrument that he could play, too. But he soon learned that the music was not in the violin, but was in the master who played it.

Are you discouraged because there is so little strength, no ability you can call your own? Are you dejected because you have no resources? Think, then, what this may mean: *one hour, one talent—and God!* Let me put myself wholly at God's service, whatever I may be; *greatness is not required,* but *meetness for the Master's use.*

Only let Him have a free hand!

They called him a genius,
The Fiddler;
But he said, "I am only

The strings
Of God's instrument, He
Playing on it.
It is not I, but the fiddle
That sings."

GOD'S FIDDLER 🕊

April 22

By faith Moses . . . choosing rather to suffer. (Heb. 11:24–25)

"By faith Moses . . . refused." Faith rests on promise; to faith the promise is *equivalent to fulfillment;* and if only we have the one, we may dare to count on the other as already ours. It matters comparatively little that the thing promised is not given; it is sure and certain because God has pledged His word for it, and in anticipation we may enter on its enjoyment. Had Moses simply acted on what he saw, he would never have left Pharaoh's palace. But his faith told him of things hidden from his contemporaries; and these led him to act in a way which to them was perfectly incomprehensible.

One blow struck when the time is fulfilled is worth a thousand struck in premature eagerness. It is not for thee, O my soul, to know the times and seasons which the Father hath put in His own power; wait thou only upon God; let thy expectation be from Him.

It was a rude surprise when he essayed to adjust a difference between two Hebrews to find himself repulsed from them by the challenge, "Who made thee a prince and a judge over us?" *"For he supposed his brethren would have understood how that God by his hand would deliver them"* (Acts 7:25). Evidently, then, God's time had not arrived; nor could it come until the heat of his spirit had slowly evaporated in the desert air, and he had learned the hardest of all lessons, that *"by strength shall no man prevail."*

Faith is only possible when we are on God's plan and stand on God's promise. It is useless to pray for increased faith until we have fulfilled the conditions of faith. It is useless to waste time in regrets and tears over the failures which are due to our unbelief. *"Wherefore liest thou thus upon thy face?"* Faith is as natural to right conditions of soul, as a flower is to a plant.

Ascertain your place in God's plan, and get on to it. Feed on God's promises. When each of these conditions is realized, faith comes of itself; and there is absolutely nothing which is impossible. The believing soul will then be as the metal track along which God travels to men in love, grace, and truth.

Oh, for grace to wait and watch with God! F. B. MEYER ☞

Faith is not a magic drug, a spiritual anesthetic: it is the victory that overcometh the world by doing battle with it. E. HERMAN ☞

April 23

Faith which worketh by love. (Gal. 5:6)

Faith without works is dead. (James 2:26)

❧

God never gave us faith to play with. It is a sword, but it was not made for presentation on a gala day, nor to be worn on state occasions only, nor to be exhibited upon a parade ground. It is a sword that was meant to cut and wound and slay; and he who has it girt about him may expect that between here and heaven, he shall know what battle means. *Faith is a sound seagoing vessel, and not meant to lie in dock and perish of dry rot.* To whom God has given faith, it is as though one gave a lantern to his friend because he expected it to be dark on his way home. *The very gift of faith is a hint to you that you will want it; that at certain points and places you will especially require it; and that, at all points and in every place you will really need it. Faith must begin to use its resources!*

Use the faith God has already given you. You have faith, or you could not be a Christian. Use your little faith and it will increase by use. Plant a few grains of it, and you will find it will grow and multiply. George Müller said that when he began his ministry it was as hard to believe for a pound as it was forty years later to believe for one thousand pounds. He was like the Thessalonians to whom Paul wrote, "Your faith groweth exceedingly."

Do not be satisfied with prayer and desire, but DO!

April 24

Lord, teach us to pray. (Luke 11:1)

Pray ye. (Matt. 9:38)

❧

Dr. John Timothy Stone tells of a visit which he paid to the old church of Robert Murray McCheyne. The aged sexton showed him around. Taking Dr. Stone into the study he pointed to a chair and said, "Sit there; that is where the master used to sit." Then he said, "Now put your elbows on the table." This was done. "Now bow your head upon your hands." Dr. Stone did so. "Now let the tears flow; that is the way the master used to do."

The visitor was then taken up into the pulpit, and the old sexton said, "Stand there behind the pulpit." Dr. Stone obeyed. "Now," said the sexton, "lean your elbows on the pulpit and put your face in your hands." This having been done, he said, "Now let the tears flow; that is the way the master used to do."

Then the old man added a testimony which gripped the heart of his hearer. With tearful eyes and trembling voice he said, *"He called down the power of God upon Scotland, and it is with us still."* SUNDAY SCHOOL TIMES

Oh, that *we* had a passion to save others! It was a compact between that holy Indian missionary known as "Praying Hyde," and God—that each day He should have at least four souls.

And Brainerd tells us that one Sunday night he offered himself to be used by God and for Him. "It was raining and the roads were muddy; but this desire grew so strong, that I kneeled down by the side of the road, and told God all about it. While I was praying, I told Him that my hands should work for Him, my tongue speak for Him, if He would only use me as His instrument—when suddenly the darkness of the night lit up, and I knew that God had heard and answered my prayer; and I felt that I was accepted into the inner circle of God's loved ones."

April 25

Go unto him at midnight. (Luke 11:5)

Summoned to the couch of a dying little girl, the mighty Master had time to tarry by the way until a poor helpless woman was healed by a touch of His garment. Meanwhile that little life had ebbed away, and human unbelief hastened to turn back the visit which was now too late. "Trouble not the Master; she is dead." It was then that His strong and mighty love rose to its glorious height of power and victory. *"Be not afraid,"* is His calm reply; *"Only believe and she shall be made whole."*

"Too late," says Martha. "Four days buried." But He only answers, *"Said I not unto thee, that, if thou wouldest believe, thou shouldest see the glory of God?"*

"Go unto Him at midnight!" Let us go when all other doors are barred and even the heavens seem brass, for the gates of prayer are open evermore; and it is only when the sun is gone down and our pillow is but a stone of the wilderness, that we behold the ladder that reaches unto heaven with our Infinite God above it, and the angels of His providence ascending and descending for our help and deliverance. He is a friend in extremity. He is able for the hardest occasions. He is seated on His throne for the very purpose of giving help in time of need.

No matter if the case is wholly hopeless, and your situation one where you have nothing, and the hour is dark as midnight, *"Go unto Him."* Go unto Him at midnight. *He* loves the hour of extremity. It is His chosen time of Almighty interposition.

"There's a budding morrow in midnight," so fold your griefs away, and wait for the bud to open, a fragrant and fair new day. Wait for the bud to open, cease to worry and grope, "there's a budding morrow in midnight," its name is *The Dawn of Hope.* A NEW TRAIL

"God will help us when the sun comes up" *(Ps. 46:5, Spanish).*

April 26

I plead with you therefore, brethren, by the compassions of God, to present all your faculties to him as a living and holy sacrifice acceptable to him. This with you will be an act of reasonable worship. (Rom. 12:1 WEYMOUTH)

Someone has said very pertinently, "There was no rudder to Noah's ark." It was hardly necessary. He had obeyed God and now was shut in, with God only to steer his ark; for he was on God's errand. The man who could endure what he endured for more than a century, while preaching the Word amidst a hostile people, did not have any fears as to where he was going. The fulfillment of the prophecy regarding the deluge must have confirmed a faith already strong.

It is a delightful experience when we really believe that God is steering our little bark over life's tempestuous sea. *Only supreme and absolute abandonment to the will of God will give perfect rest of soul.* It is this that enlarges the soul. Fenelon says: "If there be anything that is capable of setting the soul in a large place it is *absolute abandonment to God*. It diffuses in the soul a peace that flows like a river and the righteousness which is as the waves of the sea" (Isa. 48:18). If there be anything that can render the soul calm, dissipate its scruples and dispel its fears, sweeten its sufferings by the anointing of love, impart strength to all its actions, and spread abroad the joy of the Holy Ghost in its countenance and words, it is this simple and childlike repose in the arms of God.

God could give to Abraham, because he had made such a wide opening into his life. God can give only into an open hand. This hand was opened wide. This door swung clear back. God had a free swing and He used it. He *could,* and He did. He always does. Let this be our rule: "Give all He asks; then take all He gives." And the cup will be spilling joyously over the brim. S. D. GORDON

"Beware of every hesitation to abandon to God!"

April 27

Is any thing too hard for the LORD? (Gen. 18:14)

GOD *wants us to ask Him for the impossible!* God can do things that man cannot do. He would not be God if this were not so. That is why He has graciously made prayer a law of life. *"If ye shall ask ... I will do."* This inviting promise from the Lord means that He will do for us what we cannot do for ourselves; He will do for others what we cannot do for them—*if we but ask Him.* How little do we avail ourselves of this immense privilege!

Someone spoke this searching word at Edinburgh in 1910: *"We have lost the eternal youthfulness of Christianity, and have aged into calculating manhood. We seldom pray in earnest for the extraordinary, the limitless, the glorious. We seldom pray with any confidence, for any good to the realization of which we cannot imagine a way. And yet, we suppose ourselves to believe in an Infinite Father."*

The natural man calculates results. Calculations have no place in our relation with God.

That matter which has been so burdening us just now, and with which we can see no way of dealing, *how are we praying about it? In anxiety, or with thanksgiving?*

Worrying prayer defeats its own answer; rejoicing prayer gets through. "In nothing be anxious; but in everything by prayer and supplication with thanksgiving let your requests be made known unto God." Then will come the answer *"exceeding abundantly above all that we ask or think."*

The more we are cut off from human help, the greater claim we can make on Divine help. The more impossible a thing is to human or mortal power, the more at peace can we be when we look to Him for deliverance.

"Only those who see the invisible can do the impossible!"

> *God will answer when to thee,*
> *Not a possibility*
> *Of deliverance seems near;*
> *It is then He will appear.*
>
> *God will answer when you pray;*
> *Yea, though mountains block thy way,*
> *At His word, a way will be*
> *E'en through mountains, made for thee.*
>
> *God who still divides the sea,*
> *Willingly will work for thee;*
> *God, before whom mountains fall,*
> *Promises to hear thy call.*

M. E. B.

April 28

Here have we no continuing city, but we seek one to come. (Heb. 13:14)

Mr. Rothschild was the wealthiest man in the world, but he lived and died in an unfinished mansion. He had power to frighten a nation by calling for gold. Yet, one of the cornices of his house was purposely unfinished, to bear testimony that he was a pilgrim in the land. He was an orthodox Jew, and the house of every Jew, according to the Talmud, must be left unfinished. The unfinished cornice says: "Beautiful as this is, it is not my home; I am looking for a city."

Beloved, does the unfinished cornice appear in your life? Do you know that you are a stranger as were our fathers?

One place have I in heaven above—
The glory of His throne;
On this dark earth, whence He is gone,
I have one place alone;
And if His rest in heaven I know,
I joy to find His path below.

One lowly path across the waste,
The lowly path of shame;
I would adore Thy wondrous grace
That I should tread the same.
The Stranger and the Alien, Thou—
And I the stranger, alien, now.

G. T. S. 🖎

We bless Thee, that life is a pilgrimage; that the earth is not our rest; that every day brings us nearer our home in the city of God, and that Thou art willing to be our Companion in every step of the desert march!

Am I a pilgrim or a tramp?

"Build thee more stately mansions, O my soul!"

April 29

God is ever true to His promises. (1 Cor. 1:9 WEYMOUTH)

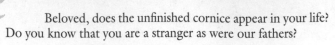

God puts Himself within our reach in His promises; and when we can say to Him, "Thou saidst," He cannot say nay—He must do as He has said. In prayer, be sure to *get your feet on a promise;* it will give you purchase enough to force open the gates of heaven and to take it by force! When once you can lay hold of a promise, you have a leverage with God which enables you to count upon the fulfillment of your petition. God cannot go back from His plighted word. F. B. MEYER 🖎

"God could no more disappoint faith than He could deny Himself."

A friend gives me a check which reads: "Pay to the order of C. H. Spurgeon the sum of ten pounds." His name is good and his bank is good, but I get nothing from his kindness until I put my own name on the back of the check. It is a very simple act but the signature cannot be dispensed with. There are many nobler names than mine, but none of these can be used instead of my own. If I wrote the Queen's name it would not avail me . . . I must affix my own name.

Even so, each one must personally accept, adopt, and endorse the promise of God by his own individual faith, or he will derive no benefit from it. If you were to write Miltonic lines in honor of the bank, or exceed Tennyson in verses in praise of the generous benefactor, it would avail nothing. The simple, self-written name is demanded, and nothing will be accepted instead of it. We must *believe the promise*, each one for himself, and declare that we know it to be true, or it will bring us no blessing. CHARLES H. SPURGEON

"God is always greater than His promises; He does not only fulfill His promises, He over-fulfills them" *(see Eph. 3:20).*

Upon Thy Word I rest
Each pilgrim day;
This golden staff is best
For all the way.
What Jesus Christ hath spoken
Cannot be broken!

Upon Thy Word I rest
So strong, so sure!
So full of comfort blest,
So sweet, so pure!
The charter of salvation,
Faith's broad foundation.

Upon Thy Word I stand,
That cannot die;
Christ seals it in my hand,
He cannot lie!
Thy Word that faileth never,
Abideth ever.

FRANCES RIDLEY HAVERGAL

April 30

John . . . was in the isle that is called Patmos, for the word of God.
(Rev. 1:9)

Can we not imagine how eagerly John would lay himself out for a life in incessant service for His Divine Master and Lord? No task would seem too great, no toil too arduous, if only His Lord might be glorified; and we can well imagine how all his plans, ambitions, desires would center round the extension of the kingdom of Jesus Christ. Then, suddenly—Patmos! What now became of all his hopes and longings, his plans and projects? Surely he buried them all as he set foot on Patmos. They died when he first heard his sentence; they were interred with no prospect of a resurrection. Patmos was, for the beloved disciple

The Island of Buried Hopes!

But John soon discovered that Patmos had its compensations. True, he could no longer entertain the hope of carrying out all his plans, yet he learned in Patmos that truer and nobler service would yet be his than any he had ever contemplated. To him came the assurance that not only has the Lord *loved us, and washed us from our sins in His own blood,* but *He hath set us apart as both kings and priests, and nothing can ever terminate that royal priesthood.* John had caught sight of a far greater honor and holier service awaiting him in the land that lies beyond.

It might have been thought that John in his dreary exile was terribly isolated. Someone has said *not isolated, but insulated,* and there is a world of difference between the two. True, the island was small and his confines narrow, but that was only the outer circumstance of his life, his daily environment.

Nothing to see! Alone! Ah, but John found it not so! The overwhelming glory of the sight of his risen Lord robbed him of his strength until he felt the gracious gentle pressure of the pierced Hand resting upon him. Again and again he tells us that he heard a Voice speaking to him. Whilst these things were so he could never feel that there was nothing to see! He could never feel alone! And the Spirit so insulated John *that God's messages might pass through him to the entire world!*

Most of us are well acquainted with this experience. We may not have had to suffer at the hands of any earthly potentate, but there must be comparatively few who have not, at some time, had to bury their fondest hopes, their most eager desires. Oh, weary troubled heart, if God has led *you to the Island of Buried Hopes,* it is that He may show you yet more wonderful things. He has not failed you, nor forgotten you, but has led you into the darkened room because, in His own time and way, *He would reveal to you the unsuspected glory of His grace and power.*

Is our life lonely? Monotonous? We need opened eyes. Standing near us all the time is the same wonderful Lord who stood by John in Patmos. *Oh, the joy, even of Patmos, when it is filled with the presence of Jesus!*

Patmos HAS its compensations!

But if we would share in them, and Patmos is to be a blessing to us, we must fulfill certain conditions. Here is the secret that transforms all disappointments, suffering, monotony, loneliness—*love to Christ,* that impels us to learn of Him day by day, to lean upon Him in constant communion, to look upon Him as the all-sufficient Savior.

To those who fulfill these conditions there is no Patmos that is not irradiated by a glory that is not of earth. SELECTED ☞

Our Father makes no mistakes!

May 1

Minding himself to go afoot (Acts 20:13)

Why did Paul prefer to go *afoot?* And how may we account for his desire to go *alone?*

There are times in every man's life when he wants no comrade on the road with him. A precious part of our Creed is "I believe in the communion of saints," but, after all, it is not in such communion that we have the closest fellowship with God in Christ. It is *in secret* that we learn the secret of the Lord.

It was in the eerie solitude of Beth-el, and in the gray dawn by the ford Jabbok that Jacob was granted visions of God.

It was when he was alone in the silent desert that Moses was shown the burning bush, and received the Divine commission.

It was when Joshua walked unattended under the stars by the wall of Jericho that the Captain of the Lord's hosts stood before him.

It was when Isaiah was alone in the Temple that a live coal touched his lips.

It was when Mary was alone that the angel brought to her the message of the Lord.

It was when Elisha was plowing his lonely furrow that the prophet's mantle fell upon his shoulders.

Noah built and voyaged alone. His neighbors laughed at his strangeness and perished.

Abraham wandered and worshiped alone; Sodomites smiled at the simple shepherd, followed the fashion, and fed the flames.

Daniel dined and prayed alone.

Jesus lived and died alone.

Ah, it is good to be "minded . . . to go afoot" sometimes; when even our nearest and dearest go by another road. *For when we are alone we have a better chance of One joining us, and making our hearts burn while He talks with us by the way.*

I love the lonely creative hours with God. MADAME GUYON

> *When storms of life are round me beating,*
> *When rough the path that I have trod,*
> *Within my closet doors retreating,*
> *I love to be alone with God.*
>
> *What tho' the clouds have gathered o'er me*
> *What tho' I've passed beneath the rod?*
> *God's perfect will there lies before me,*
> *When I am thus alone with God.*
>
> *Alone with God the world forbidden,*
> *Alone with Him, O blest retreat!*
> *Alone with God and in Him hidden,*
> *To hold with Him communion sweet.*

HYMNAL

May 2

They looked unto him and were radiant. (Ps. 34:5, American Rev.)

> *How lovely are the faces of*
> *The men who talk with God—*
> *Lit with an inner sureness of*
> *The path their feet have trod;*
> *How gentle is the manner of*
> *A man who walks with Him!*
> *No strength can overcome him, and*
> *No cloud his courage dim.*
> *Keen are the hands and feet—ah yes—*
> *Of those who wait His will,*
> *And clear as crystal mirrors, are*
> *The hearts His love can fill.*
>
> *Some lives are drear from doubt and fear*
> *While others merely plod;*

But lovely faces mark the men
Who walk and talk with God.

MARKED FOR HIS OWN,
BY PAULINE PROSSER-THOMPSON

I presume everybody has known saints whose lives were just radiant. Joy beamed out of their eyes; joy bubbled over their lips; joy seemed to fairly run from their fingertips. You could not come in contact with them without having a new light come into your own life. They were like electric batteries charged with joy.

If you look into the eyes of such radiantly happy persons—not those people who are sometimes on the mountaintop, and sometimes in the valley, but people who are always radiantly happy—you will find that every one is a man or a woman who spends a great deal of time in prayer with God alone. *God is the source of all joy, and if we come into contact with Him, His infinite joy comes into our lives.*

Would *you* like to be a radiant Christian? You may be. Spend time in prayer. You cannot be a radiant Christian in any other way. Why is it that prayer in the Name of Christ makes one radiantly happy? It is because prayer makes God real. *The gladdest thing upon earth is to have a real God!* I would rather give up anything I have in the world, or anything I ever may have, than give up my faith in God. You cannot have vital faith in God if you give all your time to the world and to secular affairs, to reading the newspapers and to reading literature, no matter how good it is. *Unless you take time for fellowship with God, you cannot have a real God. If you do take time for prayer you will have a real, living God, and if you have a living God you will have a radiant life.* R. A. TORREY

Of all the lights you carry in your face,
Joy will reach the farthest out to sea.

H. W. BEECHER

It was said by Chesterfield, the heartless dandy, upon his return from visiting Fenelon, the Archbishop of Cambrai: "If I had stayed another day in his presence, *I am afraid I would have had to become a Christian; his spirit was so pure, so attractive and beautiful.*"

May 3

No man, having put his hand to the plow, and looking back, is fit for the kingdom of God. (Luke 9:62)

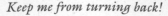

Keep me from turning back!

Deep indeed is the world's debt to people who would not quit!

Suppose Columbus had not sailed! Suppose Anne Sullivan, discouraged, had lost hope for Helen Keller! Suppose Louis Pasteur, searching for a cure for rabies, had not said to his weary helpers: "Keep on! The important thing is not to leave the subject!"

Many a race is lost at the last lap! Many a ship is washed on the reefs outside the final port! Many a battle is lost on the last charge!

What hope have *we* of completing the course upon which we have embarked? What hope? Ah! *He is able to keep.* "He is able to save them *to the uttermost* that come unto God by him."

God cannot help us until we stop running away. We must be willing to stand somewhere and trust Him. He has reinforcements to send, but there must be somebody there to meet them when they come, and *fear takes flight as well as fright.* "Fear not" is the first step.

> *Keep me from turning back*
> *My hand is on the plow, my faltering hand:*
> *But all in front of me is untilled land,*
> *The wilderness and solitary place,*
> *The lonely desert with its interspace.*
> *What harvest have I but this paltry grain,*
> *These dwindling husks, a handful of dry corn,*
> *These poor lean stalks? My courage is outworn.*
> *Keep me from turning back.*
> *The handles of my plow with tears are wet,*
> *The shares with rust are spoiled, and yet, and yet,*
> *My God! My God! Keep me from turning back.*

AUTHOR UNKNOWN

May 4

But the God of all grace, who hath called us unto his eternal glory by Christ Jesus, AFTER THAT YE HAVE SUFFERED A WHILE, makes you perfect. (1 Peter 5:10, emphasis added)

What a singular wish! The singular thing about it is the blot in the middle—*after ye have suffered a while.* What would you think of receiving this wish from a friend?

Yet this is what Peter desired for those to whom he wrote: all the gifts and the graces of the Christ-life in perfection, but not until after they had "suffered a while." Peter wrote out of the bitter experience of his own past: *he* had come into his kingdom too soon; he had obtained his crown before he could support its cares. His faith had been drenched in the brine; his love had been cooled in the judgment hall as he sat by the fire and cried, "I know not the man."

In essence he is saying, "I do not want you to find the keys too soon." He does not want them to be innocent only; pure because there is no temptation; loyal because there is no danger.

There is a peace, which is not the peace of the Son of God. Be not *that* our peace, O God!

We cannot know Thy stillness until it is broken. There is no music in the silence until we have heard the roar of battle! We cannot see Thy beauty until it is shaded. LEAVES FOR QUIET HOURS 🌿

"After the shadows, the sunlight will come."

May 5

When he saw the wagons . . . the spirit of Jacob . . . revived. (Gen. 45:27)

A very simple sight: just some farm wagons laden with corn—food for the starving household. It was these wagons turning into the courtyard that raised the fast-falling hopes of Jacob to expectancy. They remind me of other wagons laden and sent by another One greater than Joseph, even our Lord Jesus Christ. These wagons of His are a great stimulus to our faith. They come unseen to us in our hours of darkness—when our hopes are dashed to the ground. Yes, *when we are in the awful grips of spiritual starvation, how blessed are these wagons as they are seen approaching!*

Lift up your eyes! Look out for them! When they come they will not be empty! You will be fed and nourished with the choicest of His stores.

"Blessed be the Lord, who daily loadeth us with benefits."

> *"All these things are against me!" Yet those things,*
> *Those very things, were God's machinery*
> *For working out your heart's imaginings,*
> *For turning hope to blessed certainty.*
> *Oh, man who walked by sight,*

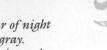

You should have known the darkest hour of night
Is just before the earliest streak of gray.
Your wagons, all the time, were on their way!

Faith? Yes, but with a flaw.
Here was a man who trusted when he saw!
And yet,
The Holy One has set
His name beside two men of saintly will,
And calls Himself the "God of Jacob" still!
That you and I,
Lacking in faith, maybe, or gentleness
May yet stretch out weak hands of hopelessness,
And find the GOD OF JACOB very nigh.

Oh, sorrowful soul! Trust just a little longer.
Who knows, but o'er your bare, brown hill
The wagons may be coming nearer still?
Give faith a chance. For soon, how soon it may
Give place to sight; and then
Never again
Will you have opportunity to show
That you can trust, albeit you cannot know.

FAY INCHFAWN

May 6

He answered . . . never a word. (Matt. 27:14)

Not railing for railing; not a word. How much is lost by a word! Be still! Keep quiet! If they smite you on one cheek turn the other also. Never retort! Hush—not a word! *Never mind your reputation or your character; they are in His hands; you mar them by trying to retain them.*

Do not strive. Open not your mouth. Silence! A word will grieve, disturb the gentle dove. Hush—not a word!

Are you misunderstood? Never mind! Will it hurt your influence and weaken your power for good? *Leave it to Him*—His to take care and take charge.

Are you wronged and your good name tarnished? All right! Be it yours to be meek and lowly; simple and gentle—not a word! *Let Him keep you in perfect peace; stay your mind on Him; trust in Him.*

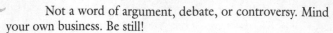

Not a word of argument, debate, or controversy. Mind your own business. Be still!

Never judge, condemn, arraign, censure. Not a word! Never a disparaging remark of another. *As you would others should do to you, so do you.*

Pause! Be still! Selah! Not a word, emphatically; not even a look that will mar the sweet serenity of the soul. Get still! Know God! *Keep silence before Him!* Stillness is better than noise.

Not a word of murmuring or complaining in supplication; not a word of nagging or persuading. Let language be simple, gentle, quiet; you utter not a word, but give Him opportunity to speak. *Hearken to hear His voice.*

This is the way to honor and to know Him. Not a word—not the least word! Listen to obey. Words make trouble. *Be still! This is the voice of the Spirit.*

Restlessness, fret, worry, makes the place of His abiding unpleasant. *He is to keep in perfect peace;* take it not out of His hands.

I rode with a dear brother in the cars, and poured my weighty burdens in his ears. I took his earnest advice to my heart. His counsel was not the mind of the Spirit, and when I returned to my seat in the car the Spirit gently said to me: "So you went to him! Could you not trust me?" I confessed, was forgiven, restored. And I determined *never again to take my case out of His hands.*

"Ye are my witnesses." Witness in love. Not a word! And, like the dew of the morning, or the sweet breeze of eventide, you will be quietly blessed, and you will be so glad that you uttered—*never a word!* STEPHEN MERRITT

> *Let me no wrong or idle word*
> *Unthinking say;*
> *Set Thou a seal upon my lips,*
> *Just for today.*

May 7

And he went down with them ... and was subject unto them.
(Luke 2:51)

An extraordinary exhibition of submissiveness! And "the disciple is not above his master."

Think of it! Thirty years at home with His brothers and sisters who did not believe in Him! We fix on the three years which were extraordinary, and forget altogether the thirty years of absolute submissiveness.

If God is putting you through a spell of submission, and you seem to be losing your individuality and everything else, *it is because Jesus is making you one with Him.*

Let Dr. A. J. Gossip, the great gifted Scottish preacher, tell us how once on a day in France, the bonniest of experiences befell him.

He had been for weeks amid the appalling desolation and sickening sights of the war front. Then they had gone back to rest where there were budding hedgerows, a shimmer of green on living trees, grass and flowers—glorious flowers in the first splendor of spring. It seemed Heaven! Then came the order to return to Passchendaele and the battlefront.

"It reached us," says Dr. Gossip, "on a perfect afternoon of sunshine; and with a heart grown hot and hard I turned down a little land with a brown burn wimpling beside it and a lush meadow—all brave sheets of purple and golden flowers—on either side. The earth was very beautiful, and life seemed very sweet, and it was hard to go back into the old purgatory and face death again. And, with that, through the gap in the hedge there came a shepherd laddie tending his flock of some two dozen sheep. He was not driving them in our rough way, with two barking dogs: he went first, and they were following him; if one loitered he called it by name and it came running to him. So they moved on down the lane, up a little hill, up to the brow and over it, and so out of my life. I stood staring after them, hearing as if the words were spoken aloud, to me first, and to me only:

"And when he putteth forth his own sheep, he goeth before them."

> *Peter, outworn,*
> *And menaced by the sword,*
> *Shook off the dust of Rome;*
> *And, as he fled,*
> *Met one, with eager face,*
> *Hastening cityward,*
> *And, to his vast amaze,*
> *It was the Lord.*
>
> *"Lord, whither goest Thou?"*
> *He cried, importunate;*
> *And Christ replied,*
> *"Peter, I suffer loss,*

I go to take thy place,
To bear thy cross."

Then Peter bowed his head,
Discomforted;
Then, at the Master's feet,
Found grace complete,
And courage, and new faith,
And turned, with Him
To death.

JOHN OXENHAM

May 8

Under utterly hopeless circumstances he hopefully believed. (Rom.
4:18 WEYMOUTH)

When God is going to do something *wonderful,* He begins with a difficulty. If it is going to be something *very wonderful,* He begins with an impossibility. CHARLES INWOOD

O God of the impossible!
Since all things are to Thee
But soil in which Omnipotence
Can work almightily,

Each trial may to us become
The means that will display
How o'er what seems impossible
Our God hath perfect sway!

The very storms that beat upon
Our little bark so frail,
But manifest Thy power to quell
All forces that assail.

The things that are to us too hard,
The foes that are too strong,
Are just the very ones that may
Awake a triumph song.

O God of the impossible,
When we no hope can see,

Grant us the faith that still believes
ALL possible to Thee!

J. H. S.

May 9

Come unto me, all ye that labor and are heavy laden, and I will
give you rest. (Matt. 11:28)

I wonder why the easiest thing in the Christian life is the most difficult? I wonder why I work by a guttering candle when there is an electric light switch within easy reach of my hand? The answer, of course, is that I don't. I am not so foolish—except in one direction, and that is Godward. In our spiritual life many of us seem to be content struggling along with all the poor primitive resources of a weak, human nature, while all the infinite power of the Godhead is at our disposal. There is no condition of human nature, no circumstance of human life, that is not completely provided for in the all-embracing love of our Father God; yet the vast majority of His children struggle along life's road, bearing burdens that He is eager to carry, and has urged them to entrust to Him. I wonder why?

> *It should be an easy thing, an alluring thing,*
> a thrilling thing to talk to God,

to hold converse with Christ. Yet, strange to relate, prayer is the most neglected of all the Christian ministries. The most perfunctory, abbreviated and ofttimes omitted exercise of many a Christian's life is the prayer-time. I wonder why?

Perhaps the difficulty lies in its very ease, its utter simplicity. Just to kneel at your bedside, and with the old abandon of childhood and the same unquestioning faith, leave all burdens and cares and needs with the Father! How childlike, but how difficult! How hard to relax; to spare an hour or even half that time out of our busy, rushing, worried lives, and go quietly to our room, shut the door and be still in His presence! How hard to divest ourselves of our sophistication, of our self-consciousness and self-centeredness, and ever-present feeling that I have to face and meet and shoulder all these cares and responsibilities! How hard just to be a child again, and with a great, happy sigh, settle down carefree at His feet, perfectly assured that He careth; that the government is upon His shoulder.
A. STUART M'NAIRN

May 10

Yield . . . ye your members as instruments . . . unto God. (Rom. 6:13)

God can do nothing with us if *we do not yield.* We recall a day of sight-seeing in the palace of Genoa. We entered a room seemingly empty; bare walls, floors, and tables greeted us. Presently the guide led us across the room to the wall at the farther side. There we espied a niche in the wall. It was covered with a glass case. Behind the case was a magnificent violin, in perfect preservation—Paganini's favorite violin; the rich old Cremona upon which he loved most of all to display his marvelous skill. We gazed intently upon the superb instrument, with its warm rich tints, sinuous curves, and perfect model. And then we tried to imagine the wondrous strains the touch of the great master would bring forth if he were there in that quiet palace chamber . . . Nay, but this could not be! He could not possibly do so! For *it was locked up against him!* It gave the master no chance.

It is not how much do you have, but how *much of yours does God have. Present your members as instruments to God.* To present means "to place near the hand of one." *Yielded, reachable, usable*—this gives God a chance.

Make it a real transaction!

God-yielded wills find the God-planned life.   JAMES H. McCONKEY

> I owned a little boat a while ago
> And sailed a Morning Sea without a fear,
> And whither any breeze might fairly blow
> I'd steer the little craft afar or near.
>
> Mine was the boat, and mine the air,
> And mine the sea; not mine, a care.
>
> My boat became my place of nightly toil.
> I sailed at sunset to the fishing ground.
> At morn the boat was freighted with the spoil
> That my all-conquering work and skill had found.
>
> Mine was the boat, and mine the net,
> And mine the skill, and power to get.
>
> One day there passed along the silent shore,
> While I my net was casting in the sea,

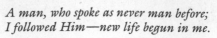

A man, who spoke as never man before;
I followed Him—new life begun in me.

Mine was the boat, but His the voice,
And His the call; yet mine, the choice.

Ah, 'twas a fearful night out on the lake,
And all my skill availed not at the helm,
Till Him asleep I waken, crying "Take,
Take Thou command, lest waters overwhelm!"

His was the boat, and His the Sea,
And His the Peace o'er all and me.

Once from His boat He taught the curious throng,
Then bade me let down nets out in the Sea;
I murmured, but obeyed, nor was it long
Before the catch amazed and humbled me.

His was the boat, and His the skill,
And His the catch—and His, my will.

JOSEPH ADDISON RICHARDS 🐦

Give God a chance!

May 11

God's tilled land. (1 Cor. 3:9 RSV margin)

God's farm. (Trans.)

The plowing and harrowing are painful processes. And surely the Divine Plowman is at work in the world as never before. He plows *by His Spirit, by His Word, and by His providences.* Though painful be the processes of cultivation, they are essential.

Could the earth speak, it would say, "I felt the hard plow today; I knew what was coming; when the plow-point first struck me I was full of pain and distress and I could have cried out for very agony for the point was sharp and driven through me with great energy; but now, I think, *this means the blade, the ear, the full corn in the ear, the golden harvest and harvest-home.*"

When the plow of God's providence first cuts up a man's life, what wonder if the man should exclaim a little; yea, if he should give way to one hour's grief! But the man may come to himself, ere eventide, and say, "Plow on,

Lord! I want my life to be *plowed all over,* that it may be sown all over, and *that in every corner there may be the golden grain or the beautiful flowers.* Pity me that I exclaimed when I first felt the plowshare. Thou knowest my frame; Thou rememberest that I am dust. But now I recollect; I put things together; I see Thy meaning; *so drive on, Thou Plowman of Eternity!"*

He does not use the plow and harrow without intention. Where God plows, He intends to sow. *His plowing is a proof He is* FOR *and not against you.*

> "For, behold, I am for you, and I will turn unto you, and ye shall be tilled and sown" *(Ezek. 36:9).*

Let us never forget that the Husbandman is never so near the land as when He is plowing it, the very time when we are tempted to think He hath forsaken us.

His plowing is a proof that He thinks you *of value,* and *worth chastening;* for *He does not waste His plowing on the barren sand.* He will not plow continually, but only for a time, and for a definite purpose. Soon He will close that process. "Doth the plowman plow continually to sow? Doth he continually open and break the clods of His ground?" (Isa. 28:24 RSV). Verily, No! Soon, aye soon, we shall, through these painful processes and by His gentle showers of grace become *His fruitful land.*

"The desolate land shall be tilled. . . . And they shall say, This land that was desolate is become like the garden of Eden" (Ezek. 36:34–35), and thus we shall be a praise unto Him.

> *Come ill, come well, the cross, the crown,*
> *The rainbow or the thunder—*
> *I fling my soul and body down*
> *For God to plow them under.*
> A PRINCE OF THE CAPTIVITY, BY JOHN BUCHAN

May 12

As an eagle stirreth up her nest. (Deut. 32:11)

God, like the eagle, stirs our nest. Yesterday it was the place for us; today there is a new plan. He wrecks the nest, although He knows it is dear to us; perhaps, because it *is* dear to us. He loves us too well not to spoil our meager contentment. Let not our minds, therefore, dwell on second causes. It is His doing! Do not let us blame the thorn that pierces us.

Though the destruction of the nest may seem wanton, and almost certainly come at an hour when I do not expect it; though the things happen that I least anticipate—let me guard my heart and be not forgetful of God's care, lest I miss the meaning of the wreckage of my hopes. He has *something better for me*.

God will not spoil our nest, and leave us without a nest, *if a nest is best for us*. His seeming cruelty is love; therefore, *let us always sit light with the things of time*.

The eaglet says, *"Teach me to fly!"* The saints often sit idly *wishing that they were like to their Lord*. Neither is likely to recognize that the prayer is heard *when the nest is toppled over!*

The breaking up of a nest an act of God's benevolence? What a startling thought!

Yet, here is an old writer who makes it a subject of praise; blesses God for it; declares it to be the first step of my education! I can understand praising Him for His gifts to body and soul; but I lose my breath in surprise when I am asked to make the first stanza of my hymn the adoration of His mercy in loosing the ties of home!

Nay, my soul, it is to *strengthen these ties* that my Father breaks up the nest; not to get rid of home, but to teach thee to fly! Travel with thy Teacher and thou shalt learn that

The Home is wider than any nest!

He would have thee learn of the many mansions of which thy nest is only one. He would tell thee of a brotherhood in Christ, which includes, yet transcends, thy household fires. He would tell thee of the family altar, which makes thee brother to the outcast, sister to the friendless—in kinship to all.

Thy Father hath given thee wings in the breaking of thy ties!

The storm that shook thy nest taught thee to fly! LEAVES FOR QUIET HOURS 🦋

God spreads broad wings;
And by His lifting, holy grace,
We find a wider, fairer place,
The freedom of untrammeled space;
Where clearer vision shows us things
The nest-view never brings.

The wing-life is characterized by comprehensiveness. High soaring gives wide seeing! J. H. JOWETT 🦋

May 13

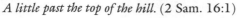

A little past the top of the hill. (2 Sam. 16:1)

It was a hard climb up that hill for a man with a burdened heart; he was tired and done. Then came God's provision for him through Ziba.

Are you a little past the top of the hill? Feeling tired and almost done? Take heart! God has something ready at the precise moment! God's help will meet you!

Just a little farther on—and all who honor Me, with joy shall prove My promise true; they too shall honored be. Full well I know thy heart's desire, the heights to which thou dost aspire, thy love which burns with holy fire—and all to honor Me.

Just a little farther on—the "Victor's song will then be sung by all who honor Me." Thou hast done well, yet still press on—and greater works I'll trust to thee, and grander glories thou shalt see; thus thou shalt fully honored be—a little farther on! *see John 12:26; Ps. 91:15*

> *Just over the hill, by the climbing way,*
> *Is a place where all good travelers stay—*
> *Just over the hill and up along.*
>
> *At the side of the road is a garden-gate,*
> *Which is always open, early and late—*
> *Just over the hill and up along.*
>
> *And inside the gate is a House of Rest,*
> *Where the Host will give you His very best—*
> *Just over the hill and up along.*
>
> JOHN OXENHAM

God never permits any of His children to come up a steep hill along life's pathway without having provided at the foot of the hill a cooling spring from which the traveler may drink in refreshment and strength ere he begins to climb.

He climbs beside you; lean upon Him!

God has no road without its springs!

May 14

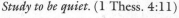

Study to be quiet. (1 Thess. 4:11)

Beloved! this is our spirit's deepest need. It is thus that we can learn to know God. It is thus that we receive spiritual refreshment and nutriment. It is thus that we are nourished and fed. It is thus that we receive the Living Bread. It is thus that our very bodies are healed, and our spirits drink in the life of our risen Lord, and we go forth to life's conflicts and duties like the flower that has drunk in, through the shades of the night, the cool and crystal drops of dew. But the dew never falls on a stormy night, so the dews of His Grace never come to the restless soul.

We cannot go through life strong and fresh on constant express trains with ten minutes for lunch: we must have quiet hours, secret places of the Most High, times of waiting upon the Lord, when we renew our strength and learn to mount up on wings as eagles, and then come back to run and not be weary, and to walk and not faint.

The best thing about this stillness is, that it gives God a chance to work. "He that is entered into His rest hath ceased from his own works, even as God did from His"; and when we cease from our thoughts, God's thoughts come into us; when we get still from our restless activity, "God worketh in us, both to will and to do of His good pleasure," and we have but to work it out.

Beloved! let us take His stillness!

A. B. SIMPSON

Jesus, Deliverer, come Thou to me;
Soothe Thou my voyaging,
Over life's sea!

May 15

This he said to prove him: for he himself knew what he would do.
(John 6:6)

At this very hour you may have to come face to face with a most tremendous need, and Christ stands beside you looking at it and questioning you about it. He says, in effect, "How are you going to meet it?"

He is scrutinizing you ... watching you with a gentle tender sympathy. How many of us have failed in the test! We have taken out our pencil and our paper and commenced to figure out the two hundred pennyworth of bread; or we have run off hither and thither to strong and wealthy friends to extricate us; or we have sat down in utter despondency; or we have murmured against Him for bringing us into such a position. Should we not have turned a sunny face to Christ saying: *Thou hast a plan! Thine is the responsibility, and Thou must tell me what to do. I have come so far in the path of obedience to Thy Guiding Spirit: and now, what art Thou going to do?*

They understood not how that God by his hand would deliver them (Acts 7:25). *It is so today.*

> Leave the HOW with Jesus,
> Secret things He knows;
> Infinite in wisdom,
> Time will all disclose.
>
> Leave the HOW with Jesus,
> He will comfort bring;
> Thro' the storm He'll hide thee
> Underneath His wing.

"God does not explain to us His technique."

"My times are in thy hand." If you quote this verse to the native of Congo, he will translate it in the gorgeous words: *"All my life's whys and whens and wheres and wherefores are in God's Hand!"* DAN CRAWFORD

We want to know more than the silent God deems it good to tell; to understand the "why" which He bids us wait to ask; to *see* the path which He has spread on purpose in the dark. The Infinite Father does not stand by us to be catechized and to explain Himself to our vain minds; He is here for our trust.

May 16

At even my wife died; and I did in the morning as I was commanded. (Ezek. 24:18)

"At even my wife died." The light of the home went out. Darkness brooded over the face of every familiar thing. The trusted companion who

had shared all the changes of the ever-changing way was taken from my side. The light of our fellowship was suddenly extinguished as by some mysterious hand stretched forth from the unseen. I lost "the desire of mine eyes." I was alone. "At even my wife died; and . . . in the morning . . ." Aye, what about the next morning, when the light broke almost obtrusively upon a world which had changed into a cemetery containing only one grave? *"In the morning I did as I was commanded."*

The command had been laid upon him in the days before his bereavement. Life in his home had been a source of inspiring fellowship. In the evening-time, after the discharge of the burdensome tasks of the day, he had turned to his home as weary dust-choked pilgrims turn to a bath; and immersed in the sweet sanctities of wedded life he had found such restoration of soul as fitted him for the renewed labor of the morrow. But "at even my wife died." The home was no longer a refreshing bath, but part of the dusty road; no longer an oasis, but a repetition of the wilderness.

How now shall it be concerning the prophet's command? "At even my wife died; and in the morning" the commandment? How does the old duty appear in the gloom of the prophet's bereavement? Duty still, clamant and clamorous now in the shadows as it was loud and importunate in the light. What shall the prophet do? Take up the old burden, and faithfully trudge the old road. Go out in his loneliness, and go on with the old tasks. But why? You will find the secret of it all in the last clause of the chapter:

"Thou shalt be a sign unto them;
and they shall know that I am the LORD."

A brokenhearted prophet patiently and persistently pursuing an old duty, and by his manner of doing it compelling people to believe in the Lord! That is the secret motive of the heavy discipline.

The great God wants our conspicuous crises to be occasions of conspicuous testimony; our seasons of darkness to be opportunities for the unveiling of the Divine. *He wants duty to shine more resplendently because of the environing shadows.* He wants tribulation only to furbish and burnish our signs. He wants us to manifest the sweet grace of continuance amid all the sudden and saddening upheavals of our intensely varied life. This was the prophet's triumph. He made his calamity a witness to the eternal. He made his very loneliness minister to his God. He made his very bereavement intensify his calling. He took up the old task, and in taking it up he glorified it. "At even my wife died; and in the morning I did as I was commanded."

The evening sorrow will come to all of us: what shall we be found doing in the morning? We shall have to dig graves; have burials: how shall it be with us when the funeral is over? J. H. JOWETT ☙

May 17

To sojourn in the land are we come; for thy servants have no pasture for their flocks; for the famine is sore in the land of Canaan.... The land of Egypt is before thee; in the best of the land make thy father and brethren to dwell. (Gen. 47:4, 6)

Did you ever come to a time of the most awful famine—spiritual famine—in your life, when there was no pasture upon which to feed? At such a time Christ Himself takes the matter for us to the throne of God. He tells God we are His own brothers. And what is the answer? "The kingdom of heaven is before thee; *in the best of the kingdom make thy brethren to dwell.*" Do you realize what it means *to have Jesus Christ intercede for you*—the Christ whom you repudiated by your own sin? Pharaoh knew not these men; but he knew Joseph, and nothing was too good for Joseph and every relative of Joseph.

We are "joint-heirs with Christ." Because of Christ, God flings wide open the whole kingdom, and simply asks *that we take its best.* Out of famine—into the best that the kingdom affords! Not only that, but rulers of the King's own property! Oh, Lord Jesus, forgive my unfaith! Open my sin-bound, self-centered eyes to the wonders of Thy love. Teach me how to receive more. *The best of the kingdom:* that means *Thee.* I take Thee, Lord, as my feast of Eternal Life. MESSAGES FOR THE MORNING WATCH

> I am not the brood of the dust and sod,
> Nor a shuttled thread in the loom of fate;
> But the child Divine of the living God,
> With eternity for my life's estate.
> I am not a sport of a cosmic night,
> Nor a thing of chance that has grown to man;
> But a deathless soul on my upward flight,
> And my Father's heir in His wondrous plan.
>
> ALVA ROMANES

We are His only heirs.

May 18

They need not depart. (Matt. 14:16)

What a task lay before the Lord on that day! There were five thousand men, besides women and children. To feed such a crowd at a moment's notice might well-nigh seem impossible. Well might the disciples say, "Send the multitude away, that they may go into the villages, and buy themselves victuals." Well might they look startled when the reply came back. "They need not depart; give ye them to eat." Their hearts must have sunk within them as their eyes again and again scanned that surging crowd.

The prospect of feeding that multitude did not alarm the Lord. He asked Philip, indeed, "Whence shall *we* buy bread, that these may eat?" but we learn immediately that He said this "to prove him." The Lord Jesus is perfectly confident that He can meet our needs and He would have us confident, too; for He is the One who for thousands of years has met the needs of those who put their trust in Him. As the God of providence He keeps the barrel of meal from wasting, and the cruse of oil from failing. He draws from one the testimony: "I have been young, and now am old; yet have I not seen the righteous forsaken, nor his seed begging bread." And from another, "There hath not failed one word of all his good promise." SELECTED

Say not, my soul, "From whence
Can God relieve my care?"
Remember that Omnipotence
Hath servants everywhere.

His help is always sure,
His methods seldom guessed;
Delay will make our pleasure pure:
Surprise will give it zest.

His wisdom is sublime,
His heart profoundly kind;
God never is before His time,
And never is behind.

Hast thou assumed a load
Which none will bear with thee?
And art thou bearing it for God,
And shall He fail to see?

Be comforted at heart,
Thou art not left alone;

Now thou the Lord's companion art—
Soon thou shalt share His throne.

J. J. LYNCH 🍂

Jesus fed the multitude in a desert place.

May 19

God, even our own God, shall bless us. (Ps. 67:6)

When ye pray, say . . . Father. (Luke 11:2)

It is strange how little use we have of the spiritual blessings which God gives us, but it is stranger still *how little use we make of God Himself.* Though He is "our own God," we apply ourselves but little to Him. How seldom do we ask counsel at the hands of the Lord! How often do we go about our business without seeking His guidance! In our troubles how constantly do we strive to bear our burdens ourselves, instead of casting them upon the Lord that He may sustain us! This is not because we *may* not, for the Lord seems to say, "I am thine, soul; come and make use of Me as thou wilt; thou mayst come freely to My store, and the oftener the more welcome." It is our own fault if we do not make free with the riches of our own God.

Then, since thou hast such a Friend, and He invites thee, draw from Him daily. *Never want whilst thou hast a God to go to; never fear or faint whilst thou hast God to help thee; go to thy treasure and take whatever thou needest—there is all that thou canst want.*

Learn the Divine skill of making God all things to thee. He can supply thee with all; or, better still, He can be to thee instead of all. Let me urge thee, then, to make use of thy God. Make use of Him in prayer; go to Him often, because *He is thy God.* Oh, wilt thou fail to use so great a privilege? Fly to Him; tell Him all thy wants. Use Him constantly by faith at all times. If some dark providence has beclouded thee, use thy God as a "sun"; if some strong enemy has beset thee, find in Jehovah a "shield"; *for He is a sun and a shield to His people.* If thou hast lost thy way in the mazes of life, use Him as a "guide"; *for He will direct thee.* Whatever thou art, and wherever thou art, remember God is just *what thou wantest,* and just *where thou wantest* and that He *can do all thou wantest!* CHARLES H. SPURGEON 🍂

The life of faith is the life that uses the Lord. H. C. G. MOULE 🍂

O little heart of mine! Shall pain
Or sorrow make thee moan,
When all this God is all for thee—
A Father all thine own?

May 20

And being in an agony he prayed ... Father, if thou be willing,
remove this cup from me: nevertheless, not my will, but thine, be
done. And there appeared an angel unto him from heaven,
strengthening him. (Luke 22:42–44)

There is a story of a woman who had had many sorrows: parents, husband, children, wealth, all were gone. In her great grief she prayed for death, but death did not come. She would not take up any of her wonted work for Christ. One night she had a dream: she thought she had gone to heaven. She saw her husband and ran to him with eager joy, expecting a glad welcome. But, strange to say, no answering joy shone on his face—only surprise and displeasure. "How did you come here?" he asked. "They did not say that you were to be sent for today; I did not expect you for a long time yet." With a bitter cry she turned from him to seek her parents. But instead of the tender love for which her heart was longing she met from them only the same amazement and the same surprised questions. "I'll go to my Savior," she cried. "He will welcome me if no one else does." When she saw Christ, there was infinite love in His look, but His words throbbed with sorrow as He said: "Child, child, who is doing your work down there?" At last she understood; she had no right yet to be in heaven; her work was not finished; she had fled away from her duty.

This is one of the dangers of sorrow: *that in our grief for those who are gone we lose our interest in those who are living, and slacken our zeal in the work which is allotted to us.* However great our bereavements we may not drop our tasks until the Master calls us away. J. R. MILLER 🖎

Finish thy work, the time is short;
The sun is in the west,
The night is coming down; till then
Think not of rest.

Rest? Finish thy work, then rest;
Till then, rest never.

The rest prepared for thee by God
Is rest forever.

Finish thy work, then sit thee down
On some celestial hill,
And of heaven's everlasting bliss
Take thou thy fill.

Finish thy work, then go in peace,
Life's battle fought and won;
Hear from the throne the Master's voice,
"Well done! Well done!"

Finish Thy work, then take the harp,
Give praise to God above;
Sing a new song of mighty joy
And endless love!

Take not your rest too soon, else you will never enter into *your real rest*. It is not here on this plank amid the billows, but yonder on that shore. GEORGE BOWEN

Nothing ever happens but once in this world. What I do now I do once and forever. It is over, it is gone with a still eternity of solemn meaning.

May 21

Make this valley full of ditches. (2 Kings 3:16)

Do we say, "Lord, I want my life to be a channel through which Thy power may flow"? Then let the spade of His Word go down into the depths of your heart, that the hidden things may be revealed. Blessing must be prepared for. You can hinder it, and shirk it; you can shut your ears to His voice; or you can get alone with the Lord Jesus and let Him have His way. *God has a glorious work to do in every yielded life;* He has a glorious fullness to bestow. But there is also a work for *us* to do; there must be a digging down into the depths of our heart; we must resolve to get rid of all the rubbish, and to prepare for the living water. H. EARNSHAW SMITH

Lord, spare nothing in me that would hinder the flowing of the rivers of water of life. Carry Thy cross to every root and corner of my most secret being.

Do you recall the bit of teaching brought out in connection with the river of the Sanctuary? *Waters to the ankles—waters
to the knees—waters to the loins.* Afterward the prophet measured it again,
and it was a *river! Waters to swim in!*

*"Beware of paddling in the ocean of God's truth, when you should
be out swimming!"*

Go deeper into me, Lord Jesus;
Yes, deeper every day,
Till Thou hast conquered me, Lord Jesus;
Go deeper all the way.

Go deeper into me, Lord Jesus;
Search all the secret springs
Of thought and action, words and feelings,
Of great and little things.

Go deeper into me, Lord Jesus,
Cleanse all the hidden part,
Where pride, or touchiness, or temper,
May lurk within my heart.

Go deeper into me, Lord Jesus,
Till Thou canst really rise,
Out of the depths of this my being,
Through Thy great Sacrifice.

As Thou dost rise in me, Lord Jesus,
The life shall be Thine own,
Till o'er my humbled broken spirit
Thou reignest on Thy throne.

E. E. B. Rogers

"We get no deeper into Christ than we allow Him to get into us."

May 22

He giveth quietness. (Job 34:29)

The calm sea says more to the thoughtful soul than the same sea in a
storm and tumult. But we need the understanding of eternal things, and
the sentiment of the Infinite to be able to feel this.

Napoleon, with his arms crossed over his breast, is more expressive
than the furious Hercules beating the air with his athletic fists.

People of passionate temperament never understand this. AMIEL'S JOURNEY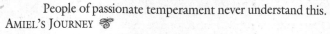

The lovely things are quiet things
Soft falling snow,
And feathers dropped from flying wings
Make no sound as they go.

A petal loosened from a rose,
Quietly seeks the ground,
And love, if lovely, when it goes,
Goes without sound.

The silent seasons of life are imperative. The winter is the mother of spring; the night is the fountain of the physical forces of the day; the silent soil is the womb where vegetable life is born. The greatest things in our spiritual life come out of our waiting hours, when all activity is suspended and the soul learns to be "silent unto God" while He shapes and molds us for future activities and fruitful years.

The greatest forces in nature are quiet ones. The law of gravitation is silent, yet invincible. So, back of all our activities and actions the law of faith is the mightiest force of the spiritual world, and mightiest when quietest and least demonstrative. When the soul is anchored to the will of God and His exceeding great and precious promises, with the calm unwavering confidence that His power and love are behind us and can never fail us until all His will for us is accomplished, *our life must be victorious.*

In the center of the whirlpool, while the waters rush around,
There's a space of perfect stillness, though with turmoil it is bound;
All is calm, and all is quiet, scarcely e'en a sense of sound.
So with us—despite the conflict—when in Christ His Peace is found.

There is no other real peace; how comparatively few know the secret.

God's noiseless workers own His calm control. NORA C. USHER

We need not be noisy if we are sure. MARY E. SHANNON

May 23

Though it tarry, wait for it; because it will surely come, it will not tarry. (Hab. 2:3)

Some things have their cycle in an hour and some in a century; but His plans shall complete their cycle whether long or short. The tender annual which blossoms for a season and dies, and the Columbian aloe which develops in a century, each is true to its normal principle. Many of us desire to pluck our fruit in June rather than wait until October, and so, of course, it is sour and immature; but God's purposes ripen slowly and fully, and faith waits while He tarries, knowing He will surely come and will not tarry too long.

It is perfect rest to fully learn and wholly trust this glorious promise. We may know without a question that His purposes shall be accomplished when we have fully committed our ways to Him, and are walking in watchful obedience to His every prompting. This faith will give a calm and tranquil poise to the spirit and save us from the restless fret of trying to do too much ourselves.

> *Wait, and every wrong will righten;*
> *Wait, and every cloud will brighten,*
> *If you will only wait.*

A. B. SIMPSON

How much depends upon knowing when the time is exactly ripe! Not to interfere before the crisis arrives; not to let the opportunity pass when the crisis has arrived. This power of discernment, of patience, of promptitude, is a gift of superlative value.

Who knows the psychological moment like the Keeper of Israel? He does not interfere too soon; He allows the enemy rope enough to hang himself; He waits until His people know their weakness and peril, and are shut up to Him. He does not interpose too late; at the critical juncture He smites the pride of His people.

We see in nature how precisely God works by the clock; certainly He is not less exact in the times and seasons of human life. We often speak of "the hour and the man"; let us remember "the hour and the God."

May 24

And they departed into a desert place by ship privately. (Mark 6:32)

If you have a desert place in your heart to which you must sometimes go, you should depart to it in a ship *privately. No man should make a thor-*

oughfare of his desert. Keep your grief for the private ship.
Never go into company with an abstracted mind; that is to display your desert.

You have sometimes refrained from God's table of communion because your thoughts were away. You did well. Man's table of communion has the same need. If you are bidden to a feast when you are troubled in your mind, try first whether you can carry your burden privately away. If you can, then leave the desert behind you; *"anoint thine head, and wash thy face; that thou appear not unto men to fast."* But if you cannot, if there is no ship that can take away your burden in secret, then *come not yet* to the feast. Journey not while the cloud is resting over the tabernacle. Tarry under the cloud. Watch one hour in the garden. Bury thy sorrow in the silence. Let thy heart be reconciled to the Father, and then come to the world and offer thy gift.

Hide your thorn in the rose. Bury your sigh in the song. Keep your cross, if you will, but keep it hidden under a wreath of flowers. Keep a singing heart!

O Thou that hast hid Thy thorn beneath a rose, steer the ship in which I conceal my burden! Thou hast gone down to the feast of Cana from the fast in the wilderness; where hast Thou hid the print of the nails? In love. Steer me to that burying ground! Let the ship on its way to my desert touch for an hour at the desert of my brother! Let me feel the fellowship of grief, the community of sorrow, the kindredness of pain! Let me hear the voices from other wildernesses, the sighs from other souls, the groans from other graves! And, when I come to my own landing-place and put down my hand to lift up my burden, I shall meet a wondrous surprise. *It will be there, but it will be there half-sized.* Its heaviness will be gone, its impossibility will have vanished. I shall lift it easily; I shall carry it lightly; I shall bury it swiftly. I shall be ready for Cana in an hour, ready for Calvary in a few minutes. I shall go back to enter into the struggle of the multitude; and the multitude will say, *"There is no desert with him!"*

> *Give others the sunshine,*
> *Tell Jesus the rest.*

Leaves for Quiet Hours 🐝

> *Lie down and sleep,*
> *Leave it with God to keep*
> *This sorrow which is part*
> *Now of thy heart.*

When thou dost wake
If still 'tis thine to take,
Utter no wild complaint,
Work waits thy hand.
If thou shouldst faint
God understands.

May 25

Take root downward, and bear fruit upward. (Isa. 37:31)

Why is it that the mountain hemlocks can attain such stateliness in spite of fierce winter gales and crushing snows? If you look at one of them closely you will see that it has foliage almost as delicate as a fir, its dark needles being as dainty as fairy feathers. Yet if you try to break a twig or a bough you will learn that therein lies the strength and the tenacious power of the hemlock. It will bend and yield but it will not break. Winds may whip and toss it this way and that, but they cannot break it—nor can elements, however fierce, pull its roots out of the ground. For months it may have its graceful form held down by a mighty weight of snow, but when the warm breath of summer winds and the melting influence of summer's sun relieve it of its burden it straightens up as proud and as noble as it was before.

Beautiful, wonderful hemlock of the mountains—what a lesson you bring to us! Though we may be storm-tossed and bent by the winds of sorrow, we need not be crushed and broken *if our souls are anchored to the Rock of Ages.*

Lord, make me strong! Let my soul rooted be
Afar from vales of rest,
Flung close to heaven upon a great Rock's breast,
Unsheltered and alone, but strong in Thee.

What though the lashing tempests leave their scars?
Has not the Rock been bruised?
Mine, with the strength of ages deep infused,
To face the storms, and triumph with the stars!

Lord, plant my spirit high upon the crest
Of Thine eternal strength!
Then, though life's breaking struggles come at length,
Their storms shall only bend me to Thy breast.

DOROTHY CLARK WILSON

May 26

I am the resurrection, and the life. (John 11:25)

Bishop Foster was one of the leading bishops of the Methodist Church in his day, and was a very godly man. After an earnest search for thirty years he found what is here related in the hope that it may be a help to some other hearts who sought light as he did.

"I have perused all of the books written on the immortality of the soul, bought them at great prices, studied them with great earnestness. I have spent thirty years at it, hoping someday I might be able to present the argument with more force and make its impression stronger upon the mind and heart of the world.

"But when death came to my home and struck down my darlings, when I went and looked into their graves, I saw nothing but utter darkness. With an anguish I cannot express I went out into the deep woods, and looked up into the great vault above, and beat upon my breast and cried to my Father until my heart was crushed and broken. In speechless silence I lay with my face upon the earth to see if I could not hear Him; but I found that it was dark and silent; not a ray, not a voice.

"I went and sat down by the philosophers, but now I found they gave me nothing but husks. I read their arguments which once had cheered me, but now they broke my heart. There was nothing in them, not even enough for me to found a conjecture upon. I was desolate with an utter desolation. I wrung my hands in an agony I cannot describe.

"Nor did I find relief until I heard a Voice coming through the gloom. Out of the darkness and silence, with heavenly music and sweetness in it, it said:

> *I am Jesus, the resurrection and the*
> *life; and thy dead shall live again.*

"And with that single idea that I could rest my hope and my faith upon, He has revealed that great doctrine; He has established the truth which ever eluded mankind till He came down out of heaven telling the story of the Fatherhood of God and the immortality of His own spiritual children."

> *I know not how that Bethlehem's Babe*
> *Could in the Godhead be:*
> *I only know the Manger Child*
> *Has brought God's life to me.*

I know not how that Calvary's Cross
A world from sin could free:
I only know its matchless love
Has brought God's love to me.

I know not how that Joseph's tomb
Could solve death's mystery:
I only know a living Christ,
Our immortality.

MAJOR HARRY W. FARRINGTON 🐝

May 27

I rejoice at thy word, as one that findeth great spoil. (Ps.
119:162)

It has pleased the Lord to teach me a truth, the benefit of which I have
not lost for more than fourteen years. The point is this: I saw more clearly
than ever that the first great and primary business to which I ought to
attend every day was *to have my soul happy in the Lord.*

The first thing to be concerned about was not how much I might serve
the Lord; but how I might get my soul in a happy state, and how my inner
man might be nourished. For I might seek to set the truth before the uncon-
verted, I might seek to benefit believers, I might seek to relieve the distressed,
I might in other ways seek to behave myself as it becomes a child of God in
this world; and yet, not being happy in the Lord and not being strengthened
in my inner man day by day, all this might not be attended to in the right
spirit. Before this time my practice had been, at least for ten years previously,
as an habitual thing to give myself to prayer after having dressed myself in the
morning. Now I saw that the most important thing I had to do was *to give
myself to the reading of the Word of God, and to meditate on it,* that thus my
heart might be comforted, encouraged, warmed, reproved, instructed; and
that thus, by means of the Word of God, whilst meditating on it, my heart
might be brought into experimental communion with the Lord.

I began therefore to meditate on the New Testament from the beginning, early in the morning. The first thing I did, after having asked in a few
words the Lord's blessing upon His precious Word, was to begin to meditate on the Word of God, searching as it were every verse to get a blessing out of it, not for the sake of the public ministry of the Word, not for
the sake of preaching upon what I had meditated upon, but *for obtaining
food for my own soul.*

The result I have found to be almost invariably this, that after a few minutes my soul has been led to confession, or to thanksgiving, or to intercession, or to supplication; so that, though I did not as it were give myself to prayer, but to meditation, yet it turned almost immediately more or less into prayer. When thus I have been for a while making confession or intercession or supplication, or have given thanks, I go on to the next words or verse, turning all as I go on into prayer for myself or others as the Word may lead to it, but still continually keeping before me that *food for my own soul is the object of my meditation.*

Formerly I often spent a quarter of an hour, or half an hour, or even an hour on my knees, before being conscious of having derived comfort, encouragement, humbling of soul, etcetera and often, after having suffered much from wandering of mind for the first ten minutes, or a quarter of an hour, or even half an hour, I only then began to really pray. I scarcely ever suffer now in this way; for my heart being nourished by the truth, being brought into experimental fellowship with God, I speak to my Father and to my Friend (vile though I am and unworthy) about the things that He has brought before me in His precious Word. It often now astonishes me that I did not sooner see this point.

> *Take the golden key, He calleth thee.*
> *Enter into the holy place.*

George Müller's Secret

Do you know this secret?

May 28

In a great trial of affliction, the abundance of their joy and their deep poverty abounded unto the riches of their liberality. (2 Cor. 8:2)

Joy is not gush; Joy is not jolliness. Joy is simply perfect acquiescence in God's will, because the soul delights itself in God Himself. "I delight to do thy will," said Jesus, though the cup was the Cross, in such agony as no man knew. *It cost Him blood.* Oh, take the Fatherhood of God in the blessed Son the Savior, and by the Holy Ghost; rejoice in the will of God, and nothing else. Bow down your heads and your hearts before God, and let the will, the blessed will of God, be done. PREBENDARY WEBB-PEPLOE

"Joy and deep poverty!" Truly strange blending.
Fullness and emptiness! Contrasting themes.
Spiritual richness and temporal leanness!
None but the Spirit could wed such extremes.

"Joy and deep poverty!" Servant of Jesus,
Doth it perplex that thy portion is this?
Doth it offend that reward for thy faithfulness
Seemeth to lie much in things thou must miss?

"Joy and deep poverty!" Pause thee, and ponder!
Joy for thy spirit—the world cannot give;
If therewith leanness—extreme limitation—
Mayhap 'tis by e'en such need thou shalt LIVE!

J. DANSON SMITH

One of the happiest men who ever lived—
Saint Francis de Assisi—was one of the poorest.

May 29

And there stood no man with him, while Joseph made himself known. (Gen. 45:1)

In the secret places of the stairs, let me see thy countenance, let me hear thy voice; for sweet is thy voice. (Song 2:14)

There are feelings and experiences too tender and too sacred for the public gaze. Joseph could not reveal himself to his brethren in the face of the Egyptian Court. The stranger could not be allowed to intermeddle with the demonstration of his love.

It is so with Christ's revelation of Himself to the human soul. Not in the busy marketplace, not in the social circle, not even in the crowded sanctuary do we come into the closest touch with the heart of our Elder Brother and our Friend. In the hour of silent communion, when the door is shut; when the world is excluded; in the hush of breathless and holy silence there comes to us the fullest apocalypse of the Divine affection. It is then that we see with clearest vision the glory of the face of Christ, and hear most distinctly the melody of the Divine voice as it tells to us the story of His love.

No public feast with Him can compensate for the loss of the private interview.

Make time to be alone with God. He has visions to reveal to us that are not for the eye of the worldling. *Alone with God*—to know the depth and sweetness of our relationship to Him!

> *Precious, gentle, holy Jesus!*
> *Blessed Bridegroom of my heart,*
> *In Thy secret inner chamber*
> *Thou wilt whisper what Thou art.*

A calm hour with God is worth a whole lifetime with man. ROBERT MURRAY MCCHEYNE

May 30

I have finished my course. (2 Tim. 4·7)

There is a course prepared for each believer from the moment of his new birth, providing for the fullest maturity of the new life within him, and the highest which God can make of his life in the use of every faculty for His service. To discover that *course* and fulfill it is the one duty of every soul. Others cannot judge what that course is; God alone knows it. And God can just as certainly make known and guide the believer into that course today, as He did with Jeremiah and other prophets, Paul and Timothy and other apostles. J. P. L.

> *Why do I drift on a storm-tossed sea,*
> *With neither compass, nor star, nor chart,*
> *When, as I drift, God's own plan for me*
> *Waits at the door of my slow-trusting heart?*
>
> *Down from the heavens it drops like a scroll,*
> *Each day a bit will the Master unroll,*
> *Each day a mite of the veil will He lift.*
> *Why do I falter? Why wander, and drift?*
>
> *Drifting, while God's at the helm to steer;*
> *Groping, when God lays the course so clear;*
> *Swerving, though straight into port I might sail;*
> *Wrecking, when heaven lies just within hail.*
>
> *Help me, O God, in the plan to believe;*
> *Help me my fragment each day to receive.*

Oh, that my will may with Thine have no strife!
God-yielded wills find the God-planned life.

JAMES H. MCCONKEY ✼

Allow God to carry out His plans for you without anxiety or inter-ference.

May 31

There came a woman having an alabaster box of ointment of spikenard very precious; and she brake the box, and poured it on his head. (Mark 14:3)

The very nature of God is extravagance. How many sunrises and sun-sets does God make?

> *Gloriously wasteful, O my Lord, art Thou!*
> *Sunset faints after sunset into the night . . .*

How many flowers and birds, how many ineffable beauties all over the world, lavish desert blossoms that only His eyes see?

Mary's act was one of spontaneous extravagance. Mary of Bethany revealed in her act of extravagant devotion, that the unconscious sympathy of her life was with Jesus Christ. "She hath done what she could"—to the absolute limit of what a human can do. It was impossible to do more. The only thing that Jesus Christ ever commended was this act of Mary's, and He said: "Wheresoever this gospel shall be preached throughout the whole world, that also which this woman hath done shall be spoken of for a memorial of her," because in the anointing our Lord saw an exact illustra-tion of what He, Himself, was about to do. He put Mary's act alongside His own Cross. God shattered the life of His own Son to save the world. *Are we prepared to pour out our lives for Him?* Our Lord is carried beyond Himself with joy when He sees any of us doing what Mary of Bethany did. *Have I ever produced in the heart of the Lord Jesus what Mary of Bethany pro-duced?* "She hath done what she could"—to the absolute limit. *I have not done what I could until I have done the same.* OSWALD CHAMBERS ✼

Is the precious ointment poured on the feet of the Master ever wasted? Eternity will answer the question. GOLD CORD ✼

The only way to keep a thing is to throw it away!

> *Seeds which mildew in the garner*
> *Scattered, fill with gold the plain.*

To keep your treasure is to die—to lose it is to live—
The angels keep the records in God's countinghouse—so give!
PATIENCE STRONG

June 1

Pray without ceasing. (1 Thess. 5:17)

Is it hypocritical to pray when we don't feel like it?

Perhaps there is no more subtle hindrance to prayer than that of our *moods*. Nearly everybody has to meet that difficulty at times. Even God's prophets were not wholly free from it. Habakkuk felt as if he were facing a blank wall for a long time. What shall we do when moods like this come to *us*? Wait until we *do feel like* praying? It is easy to persuade ourselves that it is hypocrisy to pray when we do not feel like it; but we don't argue that way about other things in life. If you were in a room that had been tightly closed for some time you would, sooner or later, begin to feel very miserable—so miserable, perhaps, that you would not want to make the effort to open the windows, especially if they were difficult to open. But your weakness and listlessness would be proof that you were beginning to need fresh air very desperately—that you would soon be ill without it.

If the soul *perseveres* in a life of prayer, there will come a time when *these seasons of dryness will pass away and the soul will be led out,* as Daniel says, *"into a large place"* (margin "into a *moist* place"). Let nothing discourage you. If the soil is dry, *keep cultivating it.* It is said, that in a dry time this harrowing of the corn is equal to a shower of rain.

When we are listless about prayer *it is the very time when we need most to pray.* The only way we can overcome listlessness in anything is to put more of ourselves, not less, into the task. To pray when you do not feel like praying *is not hypocrisy*—it is faithfulness to the greatest duty of life. Just *tell the Father* that you don't feel like it—ask Him to show you what is making you listless. *He will help us to overcome our moods,* and give us courage to persevere in spite of them.

"When you cannot pray as you would, pray as you can."

If I feel myself disinclined to pray, then is the time when I need to pray more than ever. Possibly when the soul leaps and exults in communion with God it might more safely refrain from prayer than at those seasons when it drags heavily in devotion. CHARLES H. SPURGEON

167

June 2

Unload on Him all your cares. (1 Peter 5:7, French)

Hurling all your care upon him. (Greek)

Who among us has not occasionally experienced anxiety? And yet the Bible clearly prohibits it, and as clearly provides an unfailing remedy: *"Blessed is the man who trusteth in Jehovah, and whose confidence Jehovah is; for he shall be like a tree ... which stretcheth forth its roots by the water course, so that it shall not fear when heat cometh, but its leaf shall be verdant; which is not uneasy in the year of drought."* SPURRELL

Not uneasy! Not uneasy in the year of drought—in a time of spiritual darkness. Not uneasy about spiritual supplies; not uneasy concerning temporal supplies—food or raiment; not uneasy concerning our lip witness—how, or what to say. Then what is there left about which we may be anxious? Nothing. For the Lord went on to say, *"Why take ye thought for the rest?"* And Paul further says, *"Be careful for nothing,"* or, *"In nothing be anxious."* And again, Peter says, *"Do not begin to be anxious."*

Anxiety is therefore prohibited in the Bible. But how is it to be prevented? By hurling all your care or worry upon Him, *because with Him there is care about you.*

Blessed is the man who is not *uneasy!* APHRA WHITE

June 3

Though the root thereof wax old in the earth, and the stock thereof die in the ground; yet through the scent of water it will bud, and bring forth boughs like a plant. (Job 14:8–9)

My root was spread out by the waters, and the dew lay all night upon my branch. My glory was fresh in me, and my bow was renewed in my hand. (Job 29:19–20)

Once there was an oak tree that clung to a crag on a mountainside. The wind swept its crest, and the snows and rains tore at its soil. Its roots ran along a pathway and were trampled by the feet of men. But the rain and the snows ran down the mountain, and the oak tree was dying of drought. Patiently and persistently its underground tendrils had gone forth in every direction for relief. All its power was put into the quest by which it would save its life. And, by and by, the roots reached the mountain spring. The faithful stream that touched the lips of man and beast ran up the trunk and laved the branches and gave new life to the utmost twig. The tree stood in the same place; it met the same storms; it was trodden by the same hurrying feet. *But it was planted by the rivers of water and its leaf could not wither.* Out into the same old life *you* must go today as ever, but *down underneath you can be nourished by the everlasting streams of God.*

Travelers returning from Palestine report that beneath the streets of Shechem there are rivers flowing. During the daytime it is impossible to hear the murmuring of the waters because of the noise. But when night comes and the clamor dies away, then can be heard the music of the hidden rivers.

Are there not "hidden rivers" flowing under the crowded streets of our twentieth-century life? If we can be assured that there is still the music of deep-flowing waters beneath all the noise and tumult of the working hours, we can walk the way of the conqueror.

Keep your roots deep in the living waters.

June 4

The hand of the LORD was there upon him. (Ezek. 1:3)

Bones cannot be quickened into life by manipulation. Only the touch of God can give them life.

Some of us must be taught this by bitter experiences of failure. So writes Dr. A. C. Dixon.

"While I was pastor of the Baptist Church in Chapel Hill, the university town of North Carolina, I was made to realize that, as a preacher, I was a dismal failure. Parents all over the state wrote me and requested that I look after the spiritual welfare of their sons in the university. I prepared sermons with the students in mind, and was glad to see that they showed their appreciation by attending our Sunday services in large numbers. We appointed a week of prayer and preaching with the single purpose of winning them to Christ, and they attended the evening meetings.

"About the middle of the week their interest seemed to turn into opposition; the spirit of mischief possessed them—one night they tried to put out the lights. As I walked through the grove around the university buildings, I sometimes heard my voice coming from behind a tree: a bright student had caught a part of my sermon the night before, and he was giving it in thought and tone for the benefit of his fellow students, who showed their appreciation by applause and laughter. As I walked before an open window I heard my voice in prayer floating out. I felt I was defeated and was seriously considering resigning the pastorate. Not one had been saved.

"After a restless night I took my Bible and went into the grove and remained there until three o'clock in the afternoon. As I read I asked God to show me what was the matter, and the Word of God searched me through and through giving me a deep sense of sin and helplessness, such as I had never had before.

"That evening the students listened reverently, and at the close two pews were filled with those who had responded to the invitation. The revival continued day after day until more than seventy of the students had confessed Christ.

"Now the practical question is *what did it*? Certainly not I; I fear it was the *I* that kept God from doing it for a long time. There came to me out of the day's experience a clear-cut distinction between influence and power. Influence is made up of many things: intellect, education, money, social position, personality, organization—all of which ought to be used for Christ. Power is God Himself at work *unhindered by our unbelief and other sins.*

"The word *influence* occurs but once in the Bible, and that in Job where Jehovah speaks to the old patriarch of *the sweet influences of the Pleiades*—a good text for a young minister to preach on in the springtime, but not sufficient in dealing with a group of mocking university students.

"The New Testament word *power* holds the secret, and *the power from on high* was no other than God the Holy Spirit *touching the soul through the living word, and giving it a birth from above.*

"I had been trusting and testing many other good things, only to fail; *the touch of God* did in a minute what my best efforts could not do."

June 5

And God heard their groaning, and God remembered his covenant with Abraham, with Isaac, and with Jacob. (Ex. 2:24)

God always hears, and He never forgets. His silence does not mean that He is not listening and is not planning. Probably it means that the best time of deliverance has not come yet, and that He is patiently waiting for the moment to arrive when He may prove His love and His power.

Cromwell said to his soldiers just before a great battle: "Know ye soldiers all, that *God always comes to man's help in the nick of time.*"

Yes, God is always *on time; never behind* and *never ahead.* Happy the man who learns *to wait as he prays,* and never loses patience with God. MEN WHO PRAYED

There is a set time for putting into the furnace, and a set time for taking out of the furnace.

There is a time for pruning the branches of the vine, and there is a time when the husbandman lays aside the pruning hook.

Let us wait His time; "He that believeth shall not make haste." God's time is the best time. But shall we come out the same as we went in? Ah, no! We "shall come forth as gold." We shall become purer vessels to hold the sweet-smelling incense of praise and prayer. We shall become holy golden vessels for the Master's use in time and in Eternity.

"When a great issue is in the balance and the path is obscure, wait; but with that waiting shirk not the work that lieth before thee, for *in that task may be the solution of thy problem.*"

God will justify you before the universe in His own time. OTTO STOCKMAYER

June 6

He delivers magnificently, and showeth loving-kindness. (Ps. 18:50, French trans.)

Someone who knew what it was to trust God once said: "During the last two years, though I have said little about them, I have had many a crevasse open up before me. The ice has seemed to split asunder, and I have looked down into the blue depths.

"It is a glorious thing to have a big trouble, a great Atlantic billow, that takes you off your feet and sweeps you right out to sea, and lets you sink down into the depths, into old ocean's lowest caverns, till you get to the foundation of the mountains, and there see God, and then come up

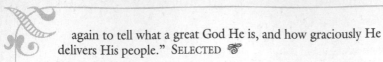

again to tell what a great God He is, and how graciously He delivers His people." SELECTED ☞

"He calmeth the storm to a whisper" *(Ps. 107:29, Rotherham).*

Life is to be just hard enough to bring out the heroic! I shall go across battlefields and into twisting storms that I may have an experience of the Father's care, protection and glorious deliverance. *I am to share in the tremendous experiences of the great!*

Only when Christ opened thine ear to the *storm*, did He open thine ear to the *stillness.* GEORGE MATHESON ☞

Prize your storms!

June 7

God was in Christ, reconciling the world unto himself. (2 Cor. 5:19)

There is on record a story of how a tribe of North American Indians who roamed in the neighborhood of Niagara offered, year by year, a young virgin as a sacrifice to the Spirit of the Mighty River.

She was called *the Bride of the Falls.*

The lot fell one year on a beautiful girl who was the only daughter of an old chieftain. The news was carried to him while he was sitting in his tent; but on hearing it the old man went on smoking his pipe, and said nothing of what he felt.

On the day fixed for the sacrifice a white canoe, full of ripe fruits and decked with beautiful flowers, was ready, waiting to receive "the Bride."

At the appointed hour she took her place in the frail bark, which was pushed out into midstream where it would be carried swiftly toward the mighty cataract.

Then, to the amazement of the crowd which had assembled to watch the sacrifice, a second canoe was seen to dart out from the river's bank a little lower down the stream. In it was seated the old chieftain. With swift strokes he paddled toward the canoe in which sat his beloved child. Upon reaching it he gripped it firmly and held it fast. The eyes of both met in one last long look of love; and then, close together, father and daughter were carried by the racing current until they plunged over the thundering cataract and perished side by side.

In their death they were not divided. The father was *in it* with his child!

"*God was in Christ, reconciling the world unto himself.*" He did not have to do this. Nobody forced Him. *The only force behind that sacrifice was the force of His seeking love for His lost world.* SELECTED

June 8

We glory in tribulations ... knowing that tribulation worketh patience; And patience, experience; and experience, hope: And hope maketh not ashamed. (Rom. 5:3–5)

A story is told of the great artist Turner, that one day he invited Charles Kingsley to his studio to see a picture of a storm at sea. Kingsley was rapt in admiration. "How did you do it, Turner?" he exclaimed. Turner answered: "I wished to paint a storm at sea; so I went to the coast of Holland, and engaged a fisherman to take me out in his boat in the next storm. The storm was brewing, and I went down to the boat and bade him bind me to its mast. Then he drove the boat out into the teeth of the storm. The storm was so furious that I longed to be down in the bottom of the boat and allow it to blow over me. But I could not: I was bound to the mast. *Not only did I see that storm, and feel it, but it blew itself into me until I became part of the storm. And then I came back and painted the picture.*"

His experience is a parable of life: sometimes cloud and sometimes sunshine; sometimes pleasure, sometimes pain. *Life is a great mixture of happiness and tragic storm. He who comes out of it rich in living, is he who dares to accept it all, face it all, and let it blow its power, mystery and tragedy into the inmost recesses of the soul. A victory so won in this life will then be an eternal possession.* CHARLES LEWIS SLATTERY

June 9

They shall mount up with wings as eagles. (Isa. 40:31)

Those who wait upon the Lord shall obtain a marvelous addition to their resources: *they shall obtain wings!* They become endowed with power to rise above things. Men who do not soar always have small views of things. Wings are required for breadth of view. The wing-life is characterized by a

sense of proportion. To see things aright we must get away from them. An affliction looked at from the lowlands may be stupendous; looked at from the heights, it may appear little or nothing. This "light affliction, which is but for a moment, worketh for us a far more exceeding and eternal weight of glory." What a breadth of view!

And here is another great quotation: "The sufferings of this present time are not worthy to be compared with the glory which shall be revealed in us." This is a bird's-eye view. It sees life as a whole. How mighty the bird from which the picture is taken! "As eagles!" What strength of wing! *Such is to be ours if we wait upon the Lord.* We shall be able to soar above disappointment—no matter how great—and to wing our way into the very presence of God. *Let us live the wing-life!*

> *The little bird sat on a slender limb,*
> *Upward swinging,*
> *And though wind and rain were rough with him,*
> *Still kept singing.*
> *"O little bird, quick, seek out your nest!"*
> *I could not keep from calling;*
> *"The bleak winds tear your tender breast,*
> *Your tiny feet are falling."*
> *"More need for song*
> *When things go wrong,*
> *I was not meant for crying;*
> *No fear for me,"*
> *He piped with glee,*
> *"My wings are made for flying!"*
>
> *My heart had been dark as the stormy sky*
> *In my sorrow,*
> *With the weight of troubles long passed by,*
> *And the morrow.*
> *"O little bird, sing!" I cried once more,*
> *"The sun will soon be shining.*
> *See, there's a rainbow arching o'er*
> *The storm cloud's silver lining."*
> *I, too, will sing*
> *Through everything;*
> *It will teach blessing double;*
> *Nor yet forget.*
> *When rude winds fret,*
> *To fly above my trouble.*

SELECTED

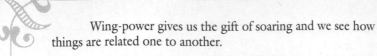

Wing-power gives us the gift of soaring and we see how things are related one to another.

Wide soaring gives wide seeing!

June 10

The LORD thy God shall bless thee in all that thou doest. (Deut. 15:18)

Art thou suddenly called to occupy a difficult position full of responsibilities? Go forward, counting on *Me!* I am giving thee the position full of difficulties for the reason that Jehovah thy God will bless thee in all thy works, and in all the business of thy hands.

This day I place in thy hands a pot of holy oil. Draw from it freely, My child, that all the circumstances arising along thy pathway, each word that gives thee pain, each manifestation of thy feebleness, each interruption trying to thy patience, may be anointed with this oil.

Interruptions are Divine instructions.

The sting will go in the measure in which thou seest *Me* in all things.

"Set your hearts unto all the words which I testify among you this day . . . because it is your life" (Deut. 32:46–47).

"I will now turn aside, and see this great sight."

Our Father is always trying to get us to the place of spiritual discoveries. God is not interested in getting mere information into our souls; He wants us to have a revelation of Himself. God has challenging futures for us, and will go to miracle lengths to get us to pay attention. If God calls me from ease and idleness, it will be that His undergirdings are sufficient for a great service. *"I will turn aside,"* for it is God who calls me.

As *"my expectation is from him,"* I will listen today.

June 11

I will awake the dawn. (Ps. 57:8, Smith's trans.)

Take time. Give God time to reveal Himself to you. Give yourself time to be silent and quiet before Him, waiting to receive through the Spirit the assurance of His presence with you, His power working in you. Take time to read His Word as in His presence; that from it you may know what He asks of you and what He promises you. Let the Word create around you, create within you, a holy heavenly light in which your soul will be refreshed and strengthened for the work of daily life. ANDREW MURRAY ❧

We repeatedly come upon entries in the diary of Dr. Chalmers which express what he called the "morning grace of appropriation."

"Began my first waking moments with confident hold upon Christ as my Savior."

"A day of quietness."

"My faith took hold of the precious promises this morning."

"The morning makes the entire day. To think of morning is to think of a bloom and fragrance which if missed, cannot be overtaken later on in the day. The Lord stands upon the shore in the morning and reveals Himself to the weary, disillusioned men who had toiled all night and taken nothing. *He* ever stands upon life's most dreary and time-worn shores, and as we *gaze* upon Him the shadows flee and *it is morning*."

> *I met God in the morning*
> *When the day was at its best,*
> *And His presence came like glory*
> *Of the sunrise in my breast.*
>
> *All day long the Presence lingered,*
> *All day long He stayed with me,*
> *And we sailed in perfect calmness*
> *O'er a very troubled sea.*
>
> *Other ships were blown and battered,*
> *Other ships were sore distressed.*
> *But the winds that seemed to drive them,*
> *Brought to us a peace and rest.*
>
> *Then I thought of other mornings,*
> *With a keen remorse of mind.*
> *When I too, had loosed the moorings*
> *With the Presence left behind.*
>
> *And I think I know the secret,*
> *Learned from many a troubled way;*
> *You must seek God in the morning*
> *If you want Him through the day.*
>
> RALPH CUSHMAN ❧

"The early morning hour has always been a time of visions. What discoveries the saints have made while others slept!"

June 12

Is thy God . . . able to deliver thee from the lions? (Dan. 6:20)

> *Thou servant of the living God,*
> *Whilst lions round thee roar,*
> *Look up and trust and praise His Name,*
> *And all His ways adore;*
> *For even now, in peril dire,*
> *He works to set thee free,*
> *And in a way known but to Him,*
> *Shall thy deliverance be.*
>
> *Dost wait while lions round thee stand?*
> *Dost wait in gloom, alone,*
> *And looking up above thy head*
> *See but a sealed stone?*
> *Praise in the dark! Yea, praise His Name,*
> *Who trusted thee to see*
> *His mighty power displayed again*
> *For thee, His saints, for thee.*
>
> *Thou servant of the living God,*
> *Thine but to wait and praise;*
> *The living God, Himself, will work,*
> *To Him thine anthem raise;*
> *Though undelivered thou dost wait,*
> *The God who works for thee,*
> *When His hour strikes, will with a word*
> *Set thee forever free.*

M. E. B. 🐝

"*Believe ye that I am able to do this?*"
"*Yea, Lord.*"
Strengthen yourself in the Omnipotence of God. Do not say, "Is God able?" Say, rather, "God is able." Andrew Murray 🐝

"*The supernatural always slumbers when faith lies sleeping, or dead.*"

June 13

Who for the joy that was set before him endured the cross, despising the shame. (Heb. 12:2)

The joy of the spirit is no cheap joy. It has scars on it—radiant scars! It is joy won out of the heart of pain. Those who know it have found one of life's deepest and most transforming secrets; the transmuting of pain into a paean. Sorrow becomes not something to escape; we can make it sing. We can set our tears to music, and no music is so exquisite, so compelling. The Christians learned immediately and at once the truth which the philosopher Royce puts in these words: "Such ills we remove only as we assimilate them, take them up into the plan of our lives, give them meaning, set them in their place in the whole." When their heartstrings were stretched upon some cross of pain and the winds of persecution blew through them, then from this human aeolian harp men heard the very music of God. They did not *bear pain,* they *used* it. SELECTED

Where the rain does not fall we have deserts. When the soil is not torn up by the plow and the harrow we get no crops.

Joy is a rare plant; it needs much rain for its growth and blossoming.

> I heard an old farmer talk one day,
> Telling his listeners how
> In the wide, new country far away
> The rainfall follows the plow.
> "As fast as they break it up, you see,
> And turn the heart to the sun,
> As they open the furrow deep and free
> And the tillage is begun,
> The earth grows mellow, and more and more
> It holds and sends to the sky
> A moisture it never had before,
> When its face was hard and dry.
> And so wherever the plowshares run
> The clouds run overhead,
> And the soil that works and lets in the sun
> With water is always fed."
> I wonder if that old farmer knew

The half of his simple word,
Or guessed the message that, heavenly true,
Within it was hidden and heard.
It fell on my ear by chance that day,
But the gladness lingers now,
To think it is always God's dear way
That the rainfall follows the plow.

Endure with faith and courage through the frost, and you will see a glorious spring.

June 14

I have commanded the ravens ... a widow woman there.
(1 Kings 17:4, 9)

We must be where God desires. Elijah spoke of himself as always standing before the Lord God of Israel. He could as distinctly stand before God when hiding beside Cherith, or sheltering in the widow's house at Zarephath, as when he stood erect on Carmel, or listened to the voice of God at Horeb.

If we are where God wants us to be, He will see the supply of our need. It is as easy for Him to feed us by the ravens as by the widow woman. As long as God says *stay here,* or *there,* be sure that He is pledged to provide for you. Though you resemble a lonely sentinel in some distant post of missionary service God will see to you. The ravens are not less amenable to His command than of old: and out of the stores of widow women He is able to supply your need as He did Elijah's at Zarephath.

When God said to Elijah, "Hide thyself by the brook Cherith," a carbon copy of the order was given to the ravens. They brought food morning and evening to *the place of Divine appointment.*

When Jesus said, "Go ye into all the world, and preach the gospel," He placed all the resources of heaven at the disposal of the going group.

When I was ordered toward the front in France, I got permission to remain behind ten days for letters. None came. When I reached my objective, where men were dying without a Chaplain's comfort, I found the last thirty days' post. The commanding officer said:

"In the army, the letters go where the orders read."

In the kingdom of God the blessings and equipment are found only where the orders read. Let us all go and tell the story. JOSIAH HOPKINS

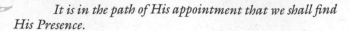

It is in the path of His appointment that we shall find His Presence.

June 15

I sought the LORD, and he heard me. (Ps. 34:4)

Andrew Murray says: It is one of the terrible marks of the diseased state of the Christian life in these days, *that there are so many that rest content without the distinct experience of answered prayer.* They *pray daily,* but know little of direct, definite *answer to prayer as the rule of their daily life.*

And it is this the Father wills. He seeks daily intercourse with His children in *listening to and granting* their petitions. He wills that I should come to Him day by day with distinct requests. He wills day by day to do for me what I ask.

There may be cases in which the answer is a refusal, but our Father lets His child know when He cannot give him what he requests, and like the Son in Gethsemane, he will withdraw his petition.

Whether the request be according to His will or not, God will by His Word and His Spirit *teach those who are teachable* and who will give Him time. Let us withdraw our requests if they are not according to God's mind, or persevere until the answer comes.

Prayer is appointed to obtain the answer!

It is in prayer and its answer that *the interchange of love between the Father and His child takes place.*

Are your prayers answered?

June 16

O that thou hadst hearkened to my commandments! then had thy peace been as a river. (Isa. 48:18)

Do we not see how God's purposes are thwarted and deferred by human perversity? At the very time when God had determined upon the election and consecration of Aaron to the priesthood, Aaron was spending his time in molding and chiseling the golden calf.

We might have been crowned fifty years ago, but just as the coronation was about to take place we were discovered in the manufacture of an idol. *The Lord was just ready to make kings of us when we made fools of ourselves.* JOSEPH PARKER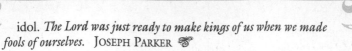

> *One small life in God's great plan—*
> *How futile it seems as the ages roll,*
> *Do what it may or strive how it can*
> *To alter the sweep of the infinite whole!*
> *A single stitch in the endless web,*
> *A drop in the ocean's flow or ebb;*
> *But the pattern is rent where the stitch is lost,*
> *Or marred where the tangled threads have crossed:*
> *And each life that fails of true intent*
> *Mars the perfect plan that its Master meant.*

Remember the awful truth *that I can limit Christ's power in the present,* although I can never alter God Almighty's order for a moment. SEED THOUGHTS CALENDAR

> *There is a niche in God's own Temple, it is thine;*
> *And the hand that shapes thee for it, is Divine.*

June 17

The crooked shall be made straight, and the rough places plain: And the glory of the LORD *shall be revealed, and all flesh shall see it together.* (Isa. 40:4–5)

And what is God's glory? It is the ministration of love. We are not to wait for a union of *opinions;* we are to begin with a union of hearts. *We are to be united, while yet we do not "see together."* You and I may look at the same stars and call them by different names. You are an astronomer, and I am a peasant; to you they are masses of worlds; to me they are candles in the sky set up to light me home.

What matter? Shall we not enjoy the glory though we do not agree about it? *Let us join hands over the message ere we settle the dispute about the messenger.*

Ye who stand upon the shore and wrangle about the number of the waves, there is meantime a work for you to do, *and to do together.* There are shipwrecked voyagers out yonder, crying and calling. They have folded their hands in prayer, and have heard no answer save the echo of their cry. Shall they call in vain? Shall they wait till you have counted the billows that consume them? Shall they stand shivering in the storm while you are disputing the name of the lifeboat? *What matter how we name the lifeboat if only we each believe in it?*

Come out to the wreck, my brothers. Come to the souls who have lost their compass, to lives that have broken their helm, to hearts that have rent their sails. They will not ask *the name of your lifeboat;* even Jacob's angel had no name. You may not see together, *but you shall reveal together*—reveal the glory of the Lord. You shall be the church of united sympathizers. *You shall see together the face of the Master,* but *you shall touch together the print of the nails. Tomorrow, you shall see Him as He is.* GEORGE MATHESON

> *When crew and captain understand each other to the core,*
> *It takes a gale and more than a gale to put their ship ashore;*
> *For the one will do what the other commands,*
> *although they are chilled to the bone;*
> *And both together can live through weather*
> *that neither could face alone.*
>
> KIPLING

A battleship cannot go into action with a mutiny raging on board.

June 18

Who maketh the clouds his chariot. (Ps. 104:3)

We cannot ride in our own chariots and God's at the same time. God must burn up with the fire of His love *every earthly chariot* that stands in the way of our mounting into His.

Would you mount into God's chariots? Then take each thing that is wrong in your life as one of God's chariots for you. Ask Him daily to *open your eyes,* and you will see His unseen chariots of deliverance.

Whenever we mount into God's chariots we have a translation—not into the heavens above us as Elijah did, but into the heaven *within us;* away from the low, groveling plane of life, up into the heavenly places in Christ Jesus, where we shall ride in triumph over all below. But the chariot that carries the soul over this road is generally some chastening, *that for the present doth not seem joyous but grievous.*

NEVERTHELESS AFTERWARD!

No matter what the source of these chastenings, look upon them as God's chariots sent to carry your soul into the high planes of spiritual achievement and uplifting. You will find, to your glad surprise, that it is God's love that sends the chariots—His chariots in which you may *ride prosperously* over all darkness.

Let us be thankful for every trial that will help to destroy our earthly chariots, and will compel us to take refuge in the chariots of God, which always stand ready and waiting beside us in every trial.

"My soul, wait thou *only* upon God; for my expectation is from him. *He only* is my rock and my salvation: he is my defense; I shall not be moved."

We have to be brought to the place where all other refuges fail, before we can say HE ONLY. We say, He *and* my experience; He *and* my church relationships; He *and* my Christian work. All that comes after the *and* must be taken away from us, or must be proved useless, before we can come to the *He only*. Only then we mount into God's chariots.

If we want to ride with God *upon the heavens,* all earth riding must be brought to an end.

He who rides with God rides above all earthborn clouds!

> *Oh, may no earthborn cloud arise*
> *To hide Thee from Thy servant's eyes.*

No obstacle can hinder the triumphant course of God's chariots! HANNAH WHITALL SMITH ☙

June 19

I will be as the dew. (Hos. 14:5)

Hosea leads us to the source of *the dew-drenched life.* It is from *Him* that this priceless gift comes. Those who spend much time with the Master come forth with the dew of blessing upon their lives.

The dew falls in the still night when all nature is hushed to rest. What is true in nature holds true in spiritual things: in this we have the key reason why so many of God's people are living dewless lives. They are restless, anxious, impatient, fussy, busy, with not time at all to be still before the Lord.

The finer things are being sacrificed for the coarser, the things of value for the worthless.

In Job 38:28 the question is asked, "Who hath begotten the drops of dew?" It is one of God's secrets. It comes quietly, and yet works so mightily. We cannot produce it, but we may receive it and live, moment by

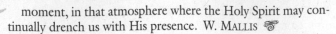

moment, in that atmosphere where the Holy Spirit may continually drench us with His presence. W. MALLIS

> *But the sensitive dew and the stillness are friends,*
> *In the storm, it is true that it never descends.*
> *Let me fuss not, nor pine, but on God cast my care,*
> *And the dew shall be mine in the quiet of prayer.*
>
> *Let Him hush the sad riot of temper and will,*
> *Till rested and quiet the cleansed heart is still.*
> *When the atmosphere's so, 'tis attractive to dew,*
> *And the first thing you know 'twill be falling on you.*
>   MAMIE PAYNE FERGUSON

"Thy dew is as the dew of herbs."

God feeds the wildflowers on the lonely mountainside without the help of any man, and they are as fresh and lovely as those that are daily watched over in our gardens. So God can feed His own planted ones without the help of man, by the sweet falling dew on his spirit. ROBERT MURRAY MCCHEYNE

"Wait before the Master until your whole heart is drenched by Him, and then go forth in the power of a fresh, strong, and fragrant life."

Lord, let Thy Spirit bedew my dry fleece!

June 20

And the song sang, and the trumpeters sounded: this continued until the burnt offering was finished. (2 Chron. 29:28, margin)

There is a joy that is *attained* and another joy that is *given*. The first joy needs things to make it joy—congenial circumstances, attentive friends; the second joy joys because it is filled with a bubbling spring of internal and eternal gladness—a gladness because it is *always in God, and God is always in it*. It glows and grows under all circumstances—it sings *because it is a song*.

It sings after prayer. "Ask, and ye shall receive, that your joy may be full." This implies that there must have been a need, a place to fill. As we believe and receive, *the song sings!*

It sings after faith. "Though now ye see him not, yet believing, ye rejoice with joy unspeakable and full of glory." Nothing seen and nothing sensed, at least not by natural sense—yet *the song sang*, and with a fullness of glory not before known.

It sings after yielding. "The meek also shall increase their joy in the LORD." Making room for the Lord is a secret of receiving more of Himself.

It sings after sorrow. "Weeping may endure for a night, but singing [margin] cometh in the morning." He, who is *Light,* who gives the morning signal to every feathered songster to tune his song, will also give you a *song that sings.*

It sings after sacrifice. "Neither count I my life dear unto myself, so that I might finish my course with joy."

Did you ever find *the song that sang of itself* in the quiet of your closet, when you heard His "Yes" to your prayer for His glory to come on earth? When nothing was seen of His working for you and your loved ones, did you hear the sweet strains of *the song that sang?*

The world awaits you—the singer with the new song!

June 21

This God is our God. (Ps. 48:14)

God is *great* in great things, but *very great* in little things," says Henry Dyer.

A party stood on the Matterhorn admiring the sublimity of the scene, when a gentleman produced a pocket microscope, and having caught a fly placed it under the glass. He reminded us that the legs of the household fly in England are naked, then called attention to the legs of this little fly which were thickly covered with hair; thus showing that the same God who made the lofty Swiss mountain attended to the comfort of His tiniest creatures, even providing socks and mittens for the little fly whose home these mountains were. *This God is OUR God!*

A doubting soul beheld a robin's nest in a gigantic elm and heard a still small voice saying, "If God spent a hundred years in creating a tree like that for a bird, He will surely take care of you." God is so interested, that He takes us one by one and arranges for every detail of our life. To Him, *there are no little things.*

"The God of the *infinite* is the God of the *infinitesimal.*"

I saw a human life ablaze with God,
I felt a power Divine
As through an empty vessel of frail clay
I saw God's glory shine.

Then woke I from a dream, and cried aloud:
"My Father, give to me
The blessing of a life consumed by God
That I may live for Thee."

June 22

Not I, but Christ. (Gal. 2:20)

Full of the Holy Ghost. (Acts 11:24)

We would in Thee abide,
In Thee be glorified,
And shine as candles "lighted by the Lord."

For long the wick of my lamp had served my purpose, silently ministering as I read beside it. I felt ashamed that I had not before noticed its unobtrusive ministry. I said to the wick:

"For the service of many months I thank thee."

"What have I done for thee?"

"Hast thou not given light upon my page?"

"Indeed, no; I have no light to give, in proof whereof take me from my bath of oil, and see how quickly I expire. Thou wilt soon turn from me as a piece of smoking tow. It is not I that burns, but *the oil with which my texture is saturated.* It is this that lights thee. I simply mediate between the oil in the cistern and the fire on my edge. This blackened edge slowly decays, but the light continually burns."

"Dost thou not fear becoming exhausted? See how many inches of coil remain! Wilt thou be able to give light till every inch of this is slowly charred and cut away?"

"I have no fear so long as the supply of oil does not fail, if only some kindly hand will remove from time to time the charred margin ... exposing a fresh edge to the flame. This is my twofold need: *oil and trimming.* Give me these and I shall burn to the end!"

God has called His children to shine as "lights in the world." Let us, then, beware of hiding our light—whether household candle, street lamp, or lighthouse gleam—lest men stumble to their death.

It is at variance with the teaching of the wick to try and accumulate a stock of grace in a sacrament, a convention, or a night of prayer. The wick has no such stores, but is always supplied!

You may seem altogether helpless and inadequate; but a living fountain of oil is prepared to furnish you with inexhaustible supplies: *Not by your might or power, but by His Spirit.* Hour after hour the oil climbs up the wick to the flame!

YOU CANNOT EXHAUST GOD!

Let us not *flinch* when the snuffers are used; they only cut away the black charred debris. He thinks so much of His work that He uses *golden* snuffers! And the Hand that holds the snuffers bears *the nailprint of Calvary!* F. B. MEYER 🖋

June 23

Men ought always to pray, and not to faint. (Luke 18:1)

That little "ought" is emphatic. It implies obligation as high as heaven. *Jesus* said, "Men ought *always* to pray," and added, "and *not to faint.*"

I confess I do not always *feel* like praying—when, judging by my feelings, there is no one listening to my prayer. And then these words have stirred me to pray:

> I ought *to pray—*
> I *ought* always *to pray—*
> I should not grow faint *in praying.*

Praying is a form of work. The farmer plows his field often when he does not *feel* like it, but he confidently expects a crop for his labors. Now, if prayer is a form of work, and *our labor is not in vain in the Lord,* should we not pray regardless of feelings? Once when I knelt for morning prayers I felt a sort of deadness in my soul, and just then the "accuser of the brethren" became busy reminding me of things that had long since been under the Blood. I cried to God for help, and the blessed Comforter reminded me that my Great High Priest was pleading my case; that I must come boldly to the throne of grace. I did, and the enemy was routed! What a blessed time of communion I had with my Lord! Had I fainted instead of *fighting* I could not have received wages because I had not labored fervently in prayer; I could not have *reaped* because I had not *sown.* COMMISSIONER BRENGLE 🖋

June 24

Yet amid all these things we are more than conquerors through him who has loved us. (Rom. 8:37 WEYMOUTH)

The best steel is subjected to the alternatives of extreme heat and extreme cold. In a cutlery you will notice that knife blades are heated and beaten, and then heated again and plunged into the coldest water in order to give them the right shape and temper. You will also observe a large heap of rejected blades, rejected because they would not bear the tempering process; when put upon the grindstone little flaws appeared in some that up to that point had seemed perfect; others would not bear the tempering process.

Souls are heated in the furnace of affliction, plunged into the cold waters of tribulation, and ground between the upper and nether stones of adversity and disaster. Some come out ready for the highest services; others are unfit for any but the lowest uses. Would you be of account among the forces which are working out the salvation of the world? *Be still in the Hands of God until He tempers you.*

"Stop now!" says the Knife-blade to the Cutler. "I have been in the fire often enough! Would you burn the life out of me?"

But again it goes into the glowing furnace and is heated to white heat.

"Stop hammering! I have been pounded enough already."

But down comes the sledge.

"Keep me out of this cold water! One moment in the fiery furnace, and the next in ice water. It is enough to kill one!"

But in it goes.

"Keep me off the grindstone! You'll chafe the life out of me!"

But it is made to kiss the stone until the Cutler is satisfied.

Now see! You may bend it double; yet it springs back straight as an arrow. It is as bright as polished silver, hard as a diamond, and will cut like a Damascus blade. *It has been shaped, tempered, and polished; it is worth something.*

Be still, and *let God temper and polish you, and you will be worth something, too. Allow yourself to be prepared for usefulness. He will give you a post of holy renown if you will let Him fit you for it.*

Be still in the furnace fire *while the Holy Ghost molds and polishes your soul.* R. V. LAWRENCE

June 25

I told them of the hand of my God which was good upon me.
(Neh. 2:18)

Is the work God's work? Has He called you to do it, and equipped you for it? *Be sure on these points.* Take time to consider and pray and find what the will of the Lord is. Then, when the difficulties have been considered and the needs fairly measured, and the clear conviction remains that God calls you to rise and build, then, *put your hand to the plow and never look back.*

Power to endure to the end—patience to outlast all discouragements—zeal that will not die out, and that will enkindle the zeal of others—*all these are given and secured to him who knows that the work and call are from God.*

For every worker and every work in the kingdom of God the principles are the same. The only way to avoid being repelled and discouraged in the work, so as to give it up in irritation, disgust or despair, is to get the work put upon the *right lines* from the very start. These must *begin* in the secret place of the Most High—the Holy of Holies—*alone with God.* They must *proceed* to the Holy Place, for the light and strength contained therein—the guidance and equipment needed. Then, and not till then can they safely *come out,* their success secure and their permanence established, because they are thus truly *"wrought in God."* HUBERT BROOKE

While the yoke of the Lord Jesus is easy and His burden light, nevertheless the furrow that He calls us to undertake is not always by any means easy plowing. There is no yoke that fits so smoothly and handily as His, but there is no work that requires more steady trudging and persistent faithfulness than His. Three stages of that work are strikingly set forth by Hudson Taylor when he says: "Commonly there are three stages in work for God: *Impossible, Difficult, Done!"*

Said General William Booth, *"God loves with a special love the man who has a passion for the impossible."* Are you confronting today the *impossible* in work for God? Praise Him for that, because you are in a way to discover the blessing of finding that *work difficult,* and then to experience the deep joy of finding it *done,* by the same Lord who started you on the furrow.

Am I Thy friend?
And canst Thou count on me,
Lord, to be true to Thee?
Canst Thou depend

On sympathy and help of mine,
In purpose, aim,
Or work of Thine,
And trust me with the honor of Thy name?

June 26

Lo, I am with you alway, even to the close of the age. (Matt. 28:20, Trans.)

Many with lacerated feet have come back to tell the story and to testify that when the very foundations of earth seemed giving way, He remained whom no accident could take away, no chance ever change. This is the power of the Great Companionship.

Stretched on a rack, where they were torturing him piteously, one of the martyrs saw with cleansed and opened eyes, a Young Man by his side—*not yet fifty years old*—who kept wiping the beads of sweat from his brow.

When the fire is hottest, He is there. *"And the form of the fourth is like the Son of God" (Dan. 3:25). "He that is near Me is near the fire."* That is why the heart of the Divine furnace is the place of the soul's deepest peace. There is always ONE beside us when we go through the fire.

When John G. Paton stood beside that lonely grave in the South Sea Islands; when he with his own hands made his wife's coffin, and with his own hands dug her grave, the savages were looking on. They had never seen it in this fashion. That man must fill in the sepulcher, and soon leave it. He says, "If it had not been for Jesus and the Presence that He vouchsafed me there, I would have gone mad and died beside that lonely grave." But John G. Paton found his Master with him through the dire darkness.

Sir Ernest Shackleton and two of his companions spent thirty-six hours among the snow mountains of New Georgia, seeking for a station that meant life or death to them and their waiting crew on Elephant Island. Writing of that journey, he says, *"It seemed to me, often, that we were four, not three."* He refers to the "guiding Presence" that went with them. Then in closing he writes, "A record of our journey would be incomplete without a reference to a subject so near to our hearts."

Paul was not peculiarly privileged when he saw the Living One while en route to Damascus.

Kahlil Gibran, the Syrian, explaining his remarkable modern painting of Jesus, said: "Last night I saw His face again, clearer than I have ever seen it."

Handel, composer of the "Hallelujah Chorus," declared: "I did see God on His throne."

During the terrible stress of war many affirmed positively that they saw "The White Comrade."

Phillips Brooks testified, "He is here. I know Him. He knows me. It is not a figure of speech. It is the realest thing in the world."

No distant Lord have I,
Loving afar to be;
Made flesh for me, He cannot rest
Until He rests in me.

Brother in joy or pain,
Bone of my bone was He;
Now—intimacy closer still—
He dwells Himself in me.

I need not journey far,
This dearest Friend to see;
Companionship is always mine,
He makes His home with me.

MALTBIE D. BABCOCK

June 27

Stormy wind fulfilling his word. (Ps. 148:8)

Did you ever go into the woods late in the afternoon on a day of howling wind and driving rain; and did you ever see a drearier spectacle, or hear drearier sounds? The sough of the winds through the almost bare branches, the drip, drip of the rain upon the masses of withered leaves, the air filled with flying leaves fluttering down in the gloom of the forest as into a grave, the delicate colors of trunk and moss all changed and stained and blended by the soaking of the rain: how hard to believe that such dreariness is related in any way to the beauty of the summer forest!

And yet we know that it is that very wind which is rocking the trees and howling so dismally—just that streaming rain and those rotting leaves which will help to clothe the forest trees next year with verdure, and to make the woods sing with joy and pulsate with life. All winds and weathers are favorable to the development of the sturdy, well-rooted tree; even the hurricane which strips it of its leaves and branches, quickens all its vital powers, challenging it to put forth greater strength.

If the tree is cut down in part, the result is a sturdier trunk and a more compact and symmetrical growth. Even if it is toppled over by a storm, its acorns are scattered and become the seeds of the forest. In its ruin it goes back to the soil from which spring other trees.

So you are better and purer and stronger today because of the tears and the sighing and the desolation. You know, and the world knows, that your life is richer, better poised, more trustful, less selfish, more detached from the things of sense—that the whole atmosphere is somehow purer and more vitalizing.

"Stormy wind fulfilling his word," and the soul that hears in their tumult the rustling of Almighty Wings praises God for the storm—the storm that swings free from enervating ease; the flood that casts upon the Eternal Rock.

Storms make a strong tree—
Sufferings make a strong saint!

June 28

With God nothing shall be impossible. (Luke 1:37)

Those who have had the joy of climbing the Swiss mountains in springtime will have learned to love the Soldanella, with its delicate little mauve bells. Many years ago there appeared a booklet by Lilias Trotter, "The Glory of the Impossible," with a sketch of this little plant just above the snow. We have never forgotten her exquisite application of the lesson, as she traced the power of this fragile plant to melt its way through the icy covering into the sunshine overhead.

We love to see the impossible done and so does God!

"Canst thou prevail
To pierce the snow?
Thou art so frail,
And icy winds do blow!"
"I will lift up my head
And trusting, onward go."

"Now hard as rock
Frozen and dry,
Thy strength to mock,
What profits it to try?
The snow will bar thy way."
"On God I will rely."

"Thou art so weak,
Tender and fair,
Why not go, seek
A balmier softer air?"
"God chose my lot for me,
And will sustain me there."

"Wilt thou keep on?
Alas! the fight
Is stern from dawn
Till eve." "Tis not by might
The victory is won;
God puts my foes to flight."

And now above
In blaze of day,
Wonder of love,
We see the flower and say,
"Naught is impossible
To him who trusts alway."

JUST TRUSTING, BY J. B. L. 🍃

The incense buds of the kiku (chrysanthemum) will open even in the frost. JAPANESE PROVERB 🍃

June 29

Thy people shall be a freewill offering in the day of thy power . . . thou shalt have the dew of thy youth. (Ps. 110:3, Trans.)

This is what the term *consecration* properly means. It is the voluntary surrender or self-offering of the heart, by the constraint of love *to be the Lord's*. Its glad expression is "I am my Beloved's."

It must spring, of course, from faith. There must be the full confidence that we are safe in this abandonment; that we are not falling over a precipice, or surrendering ourselves to the hands of a judge, but that we are sinking into the Father's arms and stepping into an infinite inheritance. Oh, *it is an infinite inheritance!* Oh, it is an infinite privilege to be permitted thus to give ourselves up to One who pledges Himself to make us all that we would love to be; nay, all that His infinite wisdom, power, and love will delight to accomplish in us!

It is the clay yielding itself to the potter's hands, that it may be shaped into a vessel of honor, meet for the Master's use.

It is the poor street waif consenting to become the child of a prince, that he may be educated and provided for; that he may be prepared to inherit all the wealth of his guardian. DAYS OF HEAVEN UPON EARTH

> *He ventured all: the loss of place,*
> *and power, and love of kin—*
> *O bitter loss! O loneliness and pain!*
> *He gained the Christ! Who would not dare*
> *the loss*
> *Such priceless bliss to win?*
> *Christ for today, and each tomorrow—*
> *Christ!*
> PAUL, BY J. MANNINGTON DEXTER

Make a supreme consecration!

June 30

And there was a voice from the firmament ... when they stood, and had let down their wings. (Ezek. 1:25)

> *If in God's starry universe there throbbed*
> *No heart but His and mine, I would not plod*
> *With eyes earthbound, hungry of soul, and robbed*
> *Of a sweet sense of nearness to my God.*
> *For mystic notes that issue from His soul*
> *Would wing their shining way in singing showers*
> *Into my waiting heart, when spared the toll*
> *Of intercourse with men that wastes my powers.*
>
> *Alone with God! My soul, invite the art,*
> *As One who climbed the heights alone to pray,*
> *And in the gentle stillness, heart to heart,*
> *Let Heaven's dew transform this house of clay.*
> *Oh, God is everywhere. Yes, God is here!*
> *Only my faith is dim ... the world too near.*
> EDITH ALICE BANG

In the silences I make in the midst of the turmoil of life I have appointments with God. From these silences I come forth with spirit refreshed, and

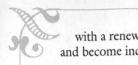

with a renewed sense of power. I hear a Voice in the silences, and become increasingly aware that it is the Voice of God.

Oh, how comfortable is a little glimpse of God! DAVID BRAINERD ✒

July 1

Having spoiled principalities and powers, he made a show of them openly, triumphing over them in it. (Col. 2:15)

Here Satan is represented as a conquered foe, and even as a degraded and disarmed antagonist. He has been "spoiled." One is reminded of the figure of a scarecrow on a farmer's field where the dead birds are hung up as warnings against other depredators. He cannot harm us although he may alarm us. He is beaten before the battle begins. We enter the fray with the prestige of victors. Let us hold this high place as we meet our adversary. Let us treat him as a defeated enemy. Let us not honor him by our doubts and fears. It is not our valor or our victory. It is *our confidence in Christ, the Victor, that wins.*

"This is the victory that overcometh the world, even our faith." Our triumph has already been won by our Leader, *but we must identify ourselves with His victory. Let us never dare to doubt!*

"And the hostile princes and rulers He shook off from Himself, and *boldly displayed them as His conquests* when by the Cross He triumphed over them" (Col. 2:15 WEYMOUTH).

Says Dr. Weymouth: "Stand your ground in the day of battle, and having fought to the end, remain victors on the field!" "Victors on the field"— I am thrilled by the inspiring word. After every temptation—the temptation which comes to me in sunshine or the temptation that comes to me in the gloom—after every fight, victors on the field, the Lord's banner flying, and the evil one and all his hosts in utter rout, and in full and dire retreat! J. H. JOWETT ✒

Describing the force of the waves which beat on the Eddystone Lighthouse a writer says: "But without a quiver the lighthouse supports those terrible attacks. Yet it bends toward them as if to render homage to the power of its adversaries."

Let us meet the storms of life with the fixedness and plasticity with which the lighthouse overcomes the wild tempest.

July 2

When I was hemmed in, Thou hast freed me often. (Ps. 4:1, Trans.)

It is a little thing to trust God as far as we can see Him, as far as the way lies open before us; but to trust Him when we are hedged in on every side and can see no way to escape, this is good and acceptable with God. This is the faith of Abraham, our father.

"Under hopeless circumstances, he hopefully believed."

Abraham Lincoln, during the Civil War, once said: "I have been driven many times to my knees by the overwhelming conviction that I had nowhere else to go. My own wisdom and that of all about me seemed insufficient for the day."

The greatest men, without God, are nothing but dismal failures.

> *The devil may wall you 'round*
> *But he cannot roof you in;*
> *He may fetter your feet and tie your hands*
> *And strive to hamper your soul with bands*
> *As his way has ever been;*
> *But he cannot hide the face of God*
> *And the Lord shall be your light,*
> *And your eyes and your thoughts can rise to the sky,*
> *Where His clouds and His winds and His birds go by,*
> *And His stars shine out at night.*
>
> *The devil may wall you 'round;*
> *He may rob you of all things dear,*
> *He may bring his hardest and roughest stone*
> *And thinks to cage you and keep you alone,*
> *But he may not press too near;*
> *For the Lord has planted a hedge inside,*
> *And has made it strong and tall,*
> *A hedge of living and growing green;*
> *And ever it mounts and keeps between*
> *The trusting soul and the devil's wall.*

The devil may wall you 'round,
But the Lord's hand covers you,
And His hedge is a thick and thorny hedge,
And the devil can find no entering wedge
Nor get his finger through;
He may circle about you all day long,
But he cannot work as he would,
For the will of the Lord restrains his hand,
And he cannot pass the Lord's command
And his evil turns to good.

The devil may wall you 'round,
With his gray stones, row on row,
But the green of the hedge is fresh and fair,
And within its circle is space to spare,
And room for your soul to grow;
The wall that shuts you in
May be hard and high and stout,
But the Lord is sun and the Lord is dew,
And His hedge is coolness and shade for you,
And no wall can shut Him out.

ANNIE JOHNSON FLINT

July 3

Your reasonable service. (Rom. 12:1)

Why are we saved? We are saved in order *to be sacrificed*. There is a striking lesson in God's saving certain of the clean beasts and clean fowl at the time of the flood. At God's direction, Noah brought these, as well as other beasts and fowl that were not clean, into the ark of salvation. These clean creatures were favored above those that were lost in the flood. It must have been a wonderful experience to step out from the ark onto dry land again. But what happened then?

"And Noah builded an altar unto the LORD; and took of every clean beast, and of every clean fowl, and offered burnt offerings on the altar" (Gen. 8:20).

Thus it appears *that certain of these creatures were saved in order to be sacrificed after their salvation was complete.* If this surprises us,

197

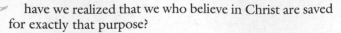

have we realized that we who believe in Christ are saved for exactly that purpose?

"I beseech you therefore, brethren, by the mercies of God, that ye present your bodies a living sacrifice" *(Rom. 12:1).*

This is *acceptable unto God,* and it is *our reasonable service.*

Noah's sacrifice of the clean animals brought great blessing to the earth, as the record goes on to show us; and the "living sacrifice" of God's children brings great blessing to mankind.

Let us thank God, indeed, that we are saved to be sacrificed. SUNDAY SCHOOL TIMES

> *Laid on Thine altar, O my Lord, Divine,*
> *Accept this day my gift for Jesus' sake.*
> *I have no jewels to adorn Thy shrine,*
> *Nor any world-famed sacrifice to make;*
> *But here I bring within my trembling hand*
> *This will of mine: a thing that seemeth small;*
> *And only Thou dear Lord, canst understand*
> *That when I yield Thee this, I yield Thee all.*
> *It hath been wet with tears and dimmed with sighs,*
> *Clenched in my clasp, till beauty it hath none.*
>
> *Now from Thy footstool, where it vanquished lies,*
> *The prayer ascendeth: "Let Thy will be done."*
> *Take it, O Father, ere my courage fail,*
> *And blend it so with Thine own will, that e'en*
> *If in some desperate hour my cry prevail,*
> *And Thou giv'st back my gift, it may have been*
> *So changed, so purified, so fair have grown,*
> *So one with Thee, so filled with peace Divine,*
> *I may not know nor feel it as my own,*
> *But gaining back my will may find it Thine.*
>
> *All I have I am bringing to Thee!*

July 4

He shall dwell in the heights: his place of defense shall be the munitions of rock. . . . Thine eyes . . . shall behold the land of far distances. (Isa. 33:16–17, margin)

Up yonder on the rocky cliff in a rough nest of sticks lies an egg. The eagle's breast-feathers warm it; the sky bends down and invites it; the abysses of the air beckon it, saying:

All our heights and depths are
for you; come and occupy them.

And all the peaks and the roomy places up under the rafters of the sky, where the twinkling stars sit sheltered like twittering sparrows, call down to the pent-up little life, "Come up hither!" and the live germ inside hears through the thin walls of its prison, and is coaxed out of its shell, and out of the nest, and off the cliff, and then up and away into the wide ranges of sunlit air, and down into the deep gulfs that gash mountains apart. A PILGRIM OF THE INFINITE

I stand upon the mount of God
With sunlight in my soul;
I hear the storms in vales beneath,
I hear the thunders roll.

But I am calm with Thee, my God,
Beneath these glorious skies;
And to the height on which I stand,
No storms, nor clouds, can rise.

Oh, THIS is life! Oh, this is joy!
My God, to find Thee so;
Thy face to see, Thy voice to hear,
And all Thy love to know.

HORATIUS BONAR

July 5

I will not be afraid of ten thousands of people, that have set themselves against me round about. (Ps. 3:6)

Evening. Felt much turmoil of spirit, in prospect of having all my plans for the welfare of this great region and this teeming population, knocked on the head by savages tomorrow. But I read that Jesus said: "All power is given unto me in heaven and in earth. Go ye therefore, and teach all nations

... and, lo, I am with you always, even unto the end of the world"! *It is the word of a Gentleman, of the strictest and most sacred honor.* So there's an end of it! I will not cross furtively tonight as I intended. Should such a man as I flee? Nay, verily, I shall take observations for latitude and longitude tonight, though they may be the last. I feel quite calm now, thank God! FROM THE DIARY OF DAVID LIVINGSTONE 🖎

During the terrible days of the Boxer uprising in China, as one report followed another of mission stations destroyed and missionaries massacred, Hudson Taylor sat quietly at his desk singing softly the hymn he loved so dearly:

> *Jesus, I am resting, resting,*
> *In the joy of what Thou art.*

When our confidence is in God we may be superior to circumstances. "If God be for us, who can be against us?" However impossible it may seem to the reasoning of the earthly-minded, it is nevertheless a blessed reality to the trustful child of God, that *"Faith can sing through days of sorrow: 'All, ALL is well!'"*

"Though I was afraid of many things," said John Buchan, *"the thing I feared most mortally was being afraid."*

> *Fierce was the wild billow,*
> *Dark was the night;*
> *Oars labored heavily;*
> *Foam glimmered white.*
> *Trembled the mariners,*
> *Peril was nigh;*
> *Then said the God of Gods,*
> *"Peace! It is I."*
>
> *Ridge of the mountain wave,*
> *Lower thy crest.*
> *Wail of the stormy wind,*
> *Be thou at rest.*
> *Peril there none can be;*
> *Sorrow must fly,*
> *Where saith the Light of Life,*
> *"Peace! It is I."*

SELECTED 🖎

Come into port greatly, or sail with God the seas! RALPH WALDO EMERSON 🖎

July 6

For I reckon that the sufferings of this present time are not worthy to be compared with the glory which shall be revealed in us.
(Rom. 8:18)

For developing character an imperfect man needs the stimulus and discipline of a *developing* environment, not yet perfected—a world of struggle and resistance: obstacles to be overcome, battles to be won, baffling problems to be solved. He needs not a soft world of ease to lull him to sleep, but a changing environment of action and reaction: cold and heat, summer and winter, sunshine and shadow, light and darkness, pleasure and pain, prosperity and adversity.

As Dr. Hillis said: "He who would ask release from suffering *would take the winter out of the seasons, the glory of the night out of the round of day, the cloud and rainstorms out of the summer; would expel the furrows from the face of Lincoln; would rob Socrates of his dignity and majesty; would make Saint Paul a mere esthetic feeling; would steal the sweetness from maternity; would rob the Divine Sufferer of His sanctity."*

When the little girl told her music teacher that it hurt her fingers to practice the piano, the teacher answered: *"I know it hurts, but it strengthens them, too."* Then the child packed the philosophy of the ages in her reply: "Teacher, *it seems that everything that strengthens, hurts."*

God never wastes His children's pain!

God loves much those whom He trusts with sorrow, and designs some precious soul enrichment which comes only through the channel of suffering.

There are things which even God cannot do for us unless He allows us to suffer. *He cannot have the result of the process without the process.*

If you are among "them that love God," *all things are yours!* The stars in their courses fight for you. Every wind that blows can only fill your sails.

God does not test worthless souls!

July 7

He performeth the thing that is appointed for me. (Job 23:14)

Let us have confidence in the *purposes of God.* The thought occurs in the writings of Goulburn, Adolph Monod, and others, that the Lord owed that wonderful calmness which marked His life—a calmness which never forsook Him, whether teaching, or traveling, however engaged, however tried—very much to the fact that His Father had a plan for Him; not a plan for a lifetime merely, but a plan for each day; and that He had but to discover what the plan was, and then carry it out; and so, however puzzling and perplexing the maze of duties through which He had to thread His way, nothing ever perplexed or puzzled Him, because, putting His hand in His Father's, *He just walked in the paths prepared for Him.*

Well, now, what if God should have a plan for everyone? What if God should have a plan for *you*? In such a case—surely it is the true case—everything we have to do, everything we have to bear, comes to us as part of a prearranged plan. Things that disturb our work, things that upset our purposes, things that thwart our wishes, interruptions, annoyances—these may all be a part of the plan—God's plan—and should be met accordingly. LIVING WATERS ✄

> *I doubt not through the ages*
> *One Eternal purpose runs.*

There's a throne above the world. There's a Man on the throne. He has a plan for things down here during this time of turmoil and strife. His Spirit is down here to get that plan done. He needs each one of us. He puts His Hand on each Christian life and says, "Separate yourself from all else for the bit I need you to do." His Hand is on *you*. Are you doing it? *Anything else classes as failure.* THE BENT KNEE TIME, BY S. D. GORDON ✄

July 8

I was crushed. (2 Cor. 1:8, Trans.)

"You smell delightfully fragrant," said the Gravel Walk to the bed of Camomile flowers under the window.

"We have been trodden on," replied the Camomiles.

"Does that cause it?" asked the Gravel Walk. "Treading on me produces no sweetness."

"Our natures are different," answered the Camomiles. "Gravel walks become only the harder by being trodden upon; but the effect on our own selves is that, if pressed and bruised when the dew is upon us we give forth the sweet smell you now delight in."

"Very delightful," replied the Gravel Walk.

Trials come alike to the Christian and to the man of the world. The one grows bitter and hardened under the experience, while the other becomes mellow and Christlike. It is because their natures are different.

Oh, beautiful rose, please tell me,
For I would like to know,
Why I must crush your petals
That sweet perfume may flow.

Oh, life that is clothed in beauty,
Perhaps like that beautiful rose,
You will need to be crushed by suffering
Ere you give out your best; who knows?

A life that is crushed by sorrow
Can feel for another's grief,
And send out that sweet perfume of love
That will bring some heart relief.

Oh, do not repine at your testing,
When called to pass under the rod,
It is that life might the sweeter be,
And comes from the Hand of God.

He knows how much we are needing,
Of sorrow, or suffering, or test,
And only gives to His children
The things that He knoweth are best.

Then let us rejoice when He sendeth
Some sorrow or hardship that tries,
And be glad to be crushed as the rose leaf,
That a sweeter perfume may arise.

FLORA L. OSGOOD

July 9

My soul thirsteth for thee, my flesh longeth for thee in a dry and thirsty land. (Ps. 63:1)

An interesting story is told concerning the northern reindeer. It seems that on those far-off plains, a hundred miles from the sea, at a certain season, in the midst of the Laplander's village a young reindeer will raise his broad muzzle to the north wind, and stare at the limitless distance for the space of a minute or more. He grows restless from that moment, but he is yet alone. The next day a dozen of the herd look up from cropping the moss, snuffing the breeze. Then the Laps nod to one another, and the camp grows daily more unquiet.

At times the whole herd of young deer stand and gaze, as it were, breathing hard through wide nostrils, then jostling each other and stamping the soft ground. They grow unruly and it is hard to harness them into the light sleds. As the days pass the Laps watch them more and more closely, well knowing what will happen sooner or later.

And then, at last, in the northern twilight, the great herd begins to move! The impulse is simultaneous, irresistible; their heads are all turned in one direction. They move slowly at first, still biting here and there at the bunches of rich moss. Presently the slow step becomes a trot, they crowd more closely together, while the Laps hasten to gather up their last unpacked possessions, their cooking utensils and their wooden gods.

The great herd together breaks from a trot to a gallop, from a gallop to a breakneck pace; the distant thunder of their united tread reaches the camp for a few minutes, and then they are gone out of sight and hearing, to drink of the Polar Sea.

The Laps follow after them, dragging painfully their laden sledges in the broad track left by the thousands of galloping beasts; a day's journey, and they are yet far from the sea, and the track is yet broad.

On the second day the path grows narrower, and there are stains of blood to be seen; far on the distant plain before them their sharp eyes distinguish in the direct line a dark, motionless object, another, and yet another. The race has grown more desperate and more wild as the stampede nears the sea. The weaker reindeer have been trampled by their stronger fellows. A thousand sharp hoofs have crushed and cut through hide and flesh and bone. Ever swifter and more terrible in their motion, the ruthless herd has raced onward, careless of the slain, careless of the food, careless of any drink but the sharp, salt water ahead of them. And when the Laplanders reach the shore, their deer are once more quietly grazing, once more tame and docile, once more ready to drag the sled.

Once in its life the reindeer must taste of the sea in one long satisfying draft, and if he is hindered, he perishes! Neither man nor beast dare stand between him and the ocean, in the hundred miles of his arrowlike path!

I hear the voice of Jesus say,
"Behold, I freely give

The living water; thirsty one,
Stoop down, and drink, and live!"
I came to Jesus, and I drank
Of that life-giving stream;
My thirst was quenched, my soul revived,
And now I live in Him.

"Come, O come YE to the Waters!"

July 10

And the LORD *took me as I followed the flock.* (Amos 7:15)

"Whom have You left behind to carry out the work?" asked the angels.

"A little band of men and women who love Me," replied the Lord Jesus.

"But what if they should fail when the trial comes? Will all You have done be defeated?"

"Yes, if they should fail all I have done will be defeated; but *they will not fail!*"

And the angels wondered as they saw the sublime confidence of love which this betokened!

"Wilt thou follow Me?"
The Savior asked.
The road looked bright and fair,
And filled with youthful hope and zeal
I answered, "Anywhere."

"Wilt thou follow Me?"
Again He asked.
The road looked dim ahead;
But I gave one glance at His glowing face
"To the end, dear Lord," I said.

"Wilt thou follow Me?"
I almost blanched,
For the road was rough and new,
But I felt the grip of His steady Hand,
And it thrilled me through and through.

"Still followest thou?"
'Twas a tender tone,

And it thrilled my inmost heart.
I answered not, but He drew me close,
And I knew we would never part.

SELECTED

The way lies through Gethsemane, through the city gate, outside the camp. The way lies alone, and the way lies until there is no trace of a footstep, only the Voice, "Follow Me!" But in the end it leads to "the joy that was set before him" and to the Mount of God. Selected 🌿

The hour is desperately dark; your flame is needed.

July 11

He leadeth me beside the waters of quietness. (Ps. 23:2, margin)

Is it worthwhile, this ceaseless chase by which so many are affected? Does it pay? And, after all, why this exciting pace which has all too truly become a part of our national program?

Must the sons of men be forever driven like so many beasts of prey? Is there no escape from the feverish haste which persists in manifesting itself in all the walks of life?

It is possible for a Christian to make his active life restful. He may carry the atmosphere of the closet into the street. The Shepherd promises to lead him beside still waters; and those are the deepest waters.

This feverish hurried life which too many of us lead *is not in God's economy, depend upon it.* If we live in this way it is because we push on before the Shepherd instead of letting Him lead us beside still waters.

If we were more docile, we should be more restful.

Only when the soul is brimful of the life of faith does it work in rest. Not until we shall have let our life drop back behind God, *to follow at the rate which He prescribes,* shall we learn what the words mean,

> *"Thou wilt keep him in perfect peace,*
> *whose mind is stayed on thee."*

Our little restless earth, and our little breathless lives will take on dignity and deeper worth if we catch step with the rhythmic movement of the quiet stars.

Most strong men know times of silence. Abraham, alone with God, made the father of a Nation; Moses, in the quietness and stillness of the desert, received God's message at the burning bush. The most of their training was in the school of silence.

It takes time to be spiritual; it doesn't happen!

In the deep jungles of Africa, a traveler was making a long trek. Men had been engaged from a tribe to carry the loads. The first day they marched rapidly and went far. The traveler had high hopes of a speedy journey. But the second morning these jungle tribesmen refused to move. For some strange reason they just sat and rested. On inquiry as to the reason for this strange behavior, the traveler was informed that they had gone too fast the first day, and that *they were now waiting for their souls to catch up with their bodies.*

This whirling rushing life which so many of us live does for us what that first march did for those poor jungle tribesmen. The difference: *they knew* what they needed to restore life's balance; too often *we do not.*

> *Jesus calls us o'er the tumult*
> *Of our life's wild restless sea.*

July 12

I am pressing on ... forgetting everything which is past. (Phil. 3:12–13 WEYMOUTH)

In the very depths of yourself, dig a grave. Let it be like some forgotten spot to which no path leads; and there, in the eternal silence, bury the wrongs that you have suffered. Your heart will feel as if a weight had fallen from it, and a Divine peace come to abide with you. CHARLES WAGNER

To be misunderstood even by those whom one loves is the cross and bitterness of life. It is the secret of that sad melancholy smile on the lips of great men which so few understand. It is what must have oftenest wrung the heart of the Son of Man. AMIEL

> *Blasted rock and broken stone,*
> *Ordinary earth,*
> *Rolled and rammed and trampled on,*
> *Forgotten, nothing worth,*
> *And blamed, but used day after day;*
> *An open road—the king's highway.*
>
> *Often left outside the door,*
> *Sometimes in the rain,*

Always lying on the floor,
And made for mud and stain:
Men wipe their feet, and tread it flat,
And beat it clean—the master's mat.

Thou wast broken, left alone,
Thou wast blamed, and worse,
Thou wast scourged and spat upon,
Thou didst become my curse—
Lord Jesus, as I think of that
I pray, make me Thy road, Thy mat.

GOLD CORD

"The power to help others depends upon the acceptance of a trampled life."

July 13

The place whereon thou standest is holy ground. (Ex. 3:5)

We cannot depend upon great events, striking circumstances, exalted moments and great occasions to measure our zeal, courage, faith, and love. These are measured by the commonplace, workaday tasks, the homely hidden paths of common life.

Thank God for the new vision, the beautiful idea, the glowing experience of the mountain; but unless we bring it down to the level of life, and teach it to walk with feet, work with hands, and stand the strain of daily life, we have worse than lost it—we have been hurt by it. *The uncommon life is the product of the day lived in the uncommon way.* Conspicuous efficiency in a lowly sphere is the best preparation for a higher one.

The incidents of which Jesus' work was made up are, humanly speaking, very humble and unpretentious. Human details fill the compass of His vast experience and work. He might have stilled a tempest every night. He could have walked upon the sea or flown over it, had the need existed. He could have transfigured Himself before Pilate and the astonished multitude in the Temple. He could have made visible ascensions at noon every day, had He been minded so to do.

The most faithful cannot compare with Jesus in lowliness of manner: He taught only one woman at Jacob's well; He noticed a finger-touch on the hem of His garment; He stooped to take little children up in his arms and bless them; even so small a thing as a cup of cold water, He said, would yield its recompense of a heavenly reward. SELECTED ☙

It may be on a kitchen floor,
Or in a busy shopping store,
Or teaching, nursing, day by day,
Till limb and brain almost give way;
Yet if, just there, by Jesus thou art found,
The place thou standest on is Holy Ground.

M. COLLEY ☙

"I will make the place of my feet glorious," said the Lord. Be it never so rough, be it never so steep, be it never so miry—*the place of His feet is glorious!*

Take God on thy route and thou shalt banish wrinkles from thy brow. Gethsemane itself shall not age thee if thou tread by the side of Jesus; for it is not the place of thy travel that makes thee weary—it is the heaviness of thy step. GEORGE MATHESON ☙

July 14

The chariots of God are twenty thousand. (Ps. 68:17)

Chariots of victory, or deliverance. (Hab. 3:8, Variorum)

But Lord, they do not *look* like chariots. They look instead like enemies, sufferings, trials, defeats, misunderstandings, disappointments, unkindnesses; juggernaut cars of misery and wretchedness that are only waiting to roll over us and crush us into the earth.

But they *are* chariots; chariots of triumph in which we may rise to those very heights of victory for which our souls have been longing and praying.

Earthly chariots are subject to the laws of matter and may be hindered or overturned; *God's* chariots are controlled by spiritual forces, *and triumph over all hindering things!*

"Very many" says the text; and although our spiritual eyes may not as yet have been opened to see them, all around us on every side *they must be waiting for us.*

Elisha prayed, and said, LORD, I pray thee, open his eyes, that he may see. And the LORD opened the eyes of the young man; and he saw: and, behold, the mountain *was full of horses and chariots. 2 Kings 6:17,* emphasis added

Chariots the King of Syria was unable to see; nor could the servant of the prophet see them. But the prophet himself sat calmly in his house without fear—his eyes had been opened to see the invisible. Now, what he asked for his servant was, "LORD . . . *open his eyes, that he may see.*"

Open our eyes that we may see!

I have not a shadow of a doubt that if all our eyes were opened today we would see our home, our places of business, the streets we traverse, filled with the "chariots of God." There is no need for any one of us to walk for lack of a chariot in which to ride: that cross inmate of your household, who has hitherto made life a burden to you, and who had been the juggernaut car to crush your soul into the very dust, may henceforth be a glorious chariot to carry you to the heights of heavenly patience and long-suffering; that misunderstanding, that mortification, that unkindness, that disappointment, that loss, that defeat—these are the chariots waiting to carry you to those places of victory you have so often longed to reach.

Somewhere in the trial His will must be hidden, and you must accept His will whether known or unknown, and so hide yourself in His invisible arms of love. Say, "Thy will be done! Thy will be done!" again and again. Shut out every other thought but the one thought of submission to His will and of trust in His love. Thus will you find yourself *riding with God* in a way you never dreamed could be.

No words can express the glorious places to which that soul shall arrive who travels in the chariots of God! *Would YOU ride on the high places of the earth?*

Then get into the chariots that will take you there! HANNAH WHITALL SMITH

July 15

He shall receive the crown of life . . . promised. (James 1:12)

The greatest helpers of humanity have been its cross-bearers. The leaders of men have suffered in loneliness; the prophets have learned their lessons in the school of pain. The corals in the sheltered lagoon grow rank and useless; those that are broken and crushed by the surf form the living rock and the foundations of continents. Ease has not produced greatness.

Men who have had to struggle with an unfavorable environ-
ment, to fight cold, to buffet the storm, to blast the rock or wring a
livelihood from a niggardly soil, have won character by their pains.

The bird rises against a strong head wind, not only in spite of the wind, but *because of it.*

The *opposing force* becomes a *lifting force* if faced at the right angle.

The storm may buffet ships and rend the rigging, but it makes strong hands and brave hearts. Oh, fellow-voyager amid the storms and calms of life's wide sea,

"Spread thy sails to catch the favoring breezes of adversity."

If the greatest character of all time, even He who was the very touchstone of destiny, could be made perfect only through suffering, is it not probable that you and I must be also?

The best things all lie beyond some battle plain: you must fight your way across the field to get them!

> High natures must be thunder-scarred
> With many a scarring wrong!
> Naught unmarred with struggle hard
> Can make the soul's sinews strong.

LOWELL ✤

Take the hardest thing in your life—the place of difficulty, outward or inward, and expect God to triumph gloriously in that very spot. Just there He can bring your soul into blossom. LILIAS TROTTER ✤

July 16

In the LORD put I my trust. (Ps. 11:1)

That is a jubilant bird note, but the bird is singing, not on some fair dewy spring morning, but in a cloudy heaven, and in the very midst of a destructive tempest. A little while ago I listened to a concert of mingled thunder and birdsong. Between the crashing peals of thunder, I heard the clear thrilling note of the lark. The melody seemed to come out of the very heart of the tempest. The environment of this Psalm is stormy. The sun is down. The stars are hid. The waters are out. The roads are broken up. And in the very midst of the darkness and desolation one hears the triumphant cry of the Psalmist, "In the LORD put I my trust." The singer is a soul in difficulty. He is the victim of relentless antagonists. He is pursued by implacable foes. The fight would appear to be going against him. The enemies are overwhelming, and, just at this point of seeming defeat and imminent disaster, there emerges this note of joyful confidence in God. "In the LORD put I my trust." It is a song in the night. J. H. JOWETT

There is a bird of the thrush family found in the South of Ireland, called "The Storm Thrush," from its peculiar love of storms. In the wildest storms of rain and wind it betakes itself to the very topmost twig of the highest tree and there pours out its beautiful song—its frail perch swaying in the wind.

A beautiful story is told of some little birds whose nest had been ruined. As the poet walked among the trees in his garden after the storm, he found a torn nest laying on the ground. He began to brood sadly over it, pitying the birds whose home had thus been wrecked. But as he stood there and mused he heard a twittering and chattering over his head; looking up he saw the birds *busy building again their ruined nest!*

I heard a bird at break of day
Sing from the autumn trees
A song so musical and calm,
So full of certainties,
No man, I think, could listen long
Except upon his knees.
Yet this was but a simple bird
Alone among dead trees.

Robert Louis Stevenson closes one of his prayers with these words: "Help us with the grace of courage that we be none of us cast down while we sit lamenting over the ruins of our happiness. *Touch us with the fire of Thine altar, that we may be up and doing, to rebuild our city.*"

Begin to build anew!

July 17

And God made a wind to pass over the earth, and the waters assuaged. The fountains also of the deep and the windows of heaven were stopped, and the rain from heaven was restrained; And the waters returned from off the earth continually. (Gen. 8:1–3)

All this because God remembered Noah! The forces of heaven and earth were enlisted, reversed, ordered about, solely because God remembered Noah and had plans for him.

God has not forgotten *you*. He will as readily order about the forces of the universe on your account as He did on Noah's. His plans for Noah were also plans for the whole world through Noah. So they are for you. He will use you for the good of the whole world if you will let Him.
SELECTED ☞

We may forget; God does not!

God's time is never wrong,
Never too fast nor too slow;
The planets move to its steady pace
As the centuries come and go.

Stars rise and set by that time,
The punctual comets come back
With never a second's variance,
From the round of their viewless track.

Men space their years by the sun,
And reckon their months by the moon,
Which never arrive too late
And never depart too soon.

Let us set our clocks by God's,
And order our lives by His ways,
And nothing can come and nothing can go
Too soon or too late in our day.
ANNIE JOHNSON FLINT ☞

"There are no dates in His fine leisure."

July 18

Whereby shall I know that I shall inherit it? ... Take me an heifer.... And when the fowls came down ... Abram drove them away. (Gen. 15:8–9, 11)

When God promises us a great blessing, and we ask how we may know that we shall have it, the answer is always the same: *By your own sacrifice to Me.* God cannot fulfill His richest promises to any of us until we have offered up to Him, *in utter completeness of surrender, ourselves. Then He can do glorious things for and with our lives.*

And then, also, "the birds of prey" attack a life as never before. The devil does not like to see any life sacrificed to God, *for he knows how mightily God will use that life to defeat the works of darkness.* So the birds of prey come down. We must expect to be attacked and tempted more fiercely and continuously after our life has been *wholly surrendered to God* than we ever were before. MESSAGES FOR THE MORNING WATCH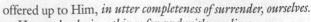

There is a Chinese legend of a potter who sought for many years to put a certain tint on the vases he made, but all his efforts failed. At last discouraged and in despair he threw himself into his furnace and his body was consumed in the fire; then, when the vases were taken out they bore the exquisite color which he had striven so long to produce.

The legend illustrates that truth that we can do our noblest and best work only at cost of self. The alabaster box must be broken before its odors can flow out.

Christ lifted up and saved the world not by an easy, pleasant, successful life in it; but by suffering and dying for it. And *we* can never bless the world merely by having a good time in it; but only by giving our lives for it.

It takes heart's blood to heal hearts. *Saving of life proves, in the end, the losing of it.*

> *My wild will was captured, yet under the yoke*
> *There was pain and not peace at the press of the load;*
> *Till the glorious burden the last fiber broke,*
> *And I melted like wax in the furnace of God.*
>
> *And now I have flung myself recklessly out,*
> *Like a chip on the stream of His infinite will;*
> *I pass the rough rocks with a smile and a shout,*
> *And just let my God His dear purpose fulfill.*

July 19

For all the promises of God in him are yea, and in him Amen. (2 Cor. 1:20)

Sometimes Christians go for a good while in trouble, not realizing that riches are laid up for them in a familiar promise.

When Christian and Hopeful strayed out of the path upon forbidden ground, and found themselves locked up in Doubting Castle by Giant Despair for their carelessness, there they lay for days, until one night they began to pray. "Now a little before it was day, Good Christian, as one half-amazed, broke out in passionate speech: 'What a fool!' quoth he, 'am I, thus to lie in this horrible dungeon, when I may as well walk at liberty. I have a key in my bosom called PROMISE, that will, I am persuaded, open any lock in Doubting Castle.' Then said Hopeful, 'That's good news good brother; pluck it out of thy bosom and try.' Then Christian pulled it out of his bosom, and began to try the dungeon door, whose bolts gave back, and the door flew open with ease, and Christian and Hopeful came out." PILGRIM'S PROGRESS, BY JOHN BUNYAN ☙

Often you cannot get at a difficulty so as to deal with it aright and find your way to a happy result. You pray, but have not the liberty in prayer which you desire. A definite promise is what you want. You try one and another of the inspired words, but they do not fit. You try again, and in due season a promise presents itself which seems to have been made for the occasion; it fits exactly as a well-made key fits the lock for which it was prepared. Having found the identical word of the living God you hasten to plead it at the throne of grace, saying, "O Lord, Thou hast promised this good thing unto Thy servant; be pleased to grant it!" The matter is ended: sorrow is turned to joy; prayer is heard. CHARLES H. SPURGEON ☙

> *Faith, mighty faith, the promise sees*
> *And looks to God alone,*
> *Laughs at impossibilities,*
> *And cries, "It shall be done."*

Try all your keys! Never despair! God leaves no treasure-house locked against us!

July 20

Hitherto have ye asked nothing in my name: ask, and ye shall receive, that your joy may be full. (John 16:24)

Alexander the Great had a famous, but indigent, philosopher in his court. This man adept in science was once particularly straightened in his circumstances. To whom should he apply but to his patron, the conqueror of the world? His request was no sooner made than granted. Alexander gave him a commission to receive of his treasury whatever he wanted. He immediately demanded in his sovereign's name ten thousand pounds. The treasurer, surprised at so large a demand, refused to comply, but waited upon the king and represented to him the affair, adding withal how unreasonable he thought the petition and how exorbitant the sum. Alexander listened with patience, but as soon as he heard the remonstrance replied, "Let the money be instantly paid. I am delighted with this philosopher's way of thinking; he has done me a singular honor: by the largeness of his request he shows the high idea he has conceived both of my superior wealth and my royal munificence."

Saints have never yet reached the limit to the possibilities of prayer. Whatever has been attained or achieved *has touched but the fringe of the garment of a prayer-hearing God.* We honor the riches both of His power and love *only* by large demands. A. T. PIERSON

You cannot think of prayer so large that God, in answering it, will not wish that you had made it larger. *Pray not for crutches, but for wings!* PHILLIPS BROOKS

> *Make thy petition deep.*
> *It is thy God who speaks with love o'erflowing,*
> *Thy God who claims the rapture of bestowing,*
> *Thy God who whispers, all thy weakness knowing,*
> *"Wouldst thou in full reap?*
> *Make thy petition deep."*

> *Make thy petition deep.*
> *Now to the fountainhead thy vessel bringing,*
> *Claim all the fullness of its glad upspringing;*
> *At Calvary was proclaimed its boundless measure;*
> *Who spared not then, withholds from thee no treasure;*
> *This word—His token, keep:*
> *Make thy petition deep.*

If Alexander gave like a King, shall not Jehovah give like a God?

July 21

What things soever ye desire . . . ye shall have them. (Mark 11:24)

Oh, the victories of prayer! They are the mountaintops of the Bible.

They take us back to the plains of Mamre, to the fords of Peniel, to the prison of Joseph, to the triumphs of Moses, to the victories of Joshua, to the deliverances of David, to the miracles of Elijah and Elisha, to the holy story of the Master's life, to the secret of Pentecost, to the keynote of Paul's unparalleled ministry, to the lives of saints and the deaths of martyrs, to all that is most sacred and sweet in the history of the church and the experience of the children of God.

And when for us the last conflict shall have passed, and the *footstool of prayer shall have given place to the harp of praise,* the scenes of time that shall be gilded with eternal radiance shall be those linked with deepest sorrow and darkest night, over which we have written

Jehovah Shammah (The Lord was there).

> *Beyond thy utmost wants,*
> *His power can love and bless;*
> *To trusting souls He loves to grant*
> *More than they can express.*

July 22

Unto you that fear my name shall the Sun of righteousness arise with healing in his wings. (Mal. 4:2)

A South American traveler tells of a curious conflict which he once witnessed between a little quadruped and a poisonous reptile of great size. The little creature seemed no match for its antagonist that threatened to destroy it by a blow, as well as its helpless young, but it fearlessly faced its mighty enemy and rushing at him, struck him with a succession of fierce and telling blows, but received at the onset a deep and apparently fatal wound from the poisonous fangs, which flashed for a moment with an angry fire, and then fastened themselves deep into the flesh of the daring little assailant.

For a moment it seemed as if all were over, but the wise little creature immediately retired into the forest, and hastening to the plantain tree eagerly devoured some of its leaves, and then hurried back, seemingly fresh and restored, to renew the fray with vigor and determination. Again and again this strange spectacle was repeated: the serpent, although greatly exhausted, ferociously attacked, and again and again wounded its antagonist to death, as it seemed; but the little creature each time repaired to its simple prescription, and returned to renewed victory. In the course of an hour or two the battle was over—the mammoth reptile lay still and dead and the little victor was unharmed, in the midst of the nest and the helpless little ones.

How often we are wounded by the dragon's sting—wounded, it would seem to death! and if we had to go through some long ceremony to reach the source of life, we must faint and die. But blessed be His Name as near at hand as that which the forest holds in its shade, *there is ever for us a Plant of healing to which we may continually repair* and come back refreshed, invigorated, transfigured—like Him who shone with the brightness of celestial light as He prayed in the mount; who, as He prayed in the garden arose triumphant over the fear of death, strengthened from on high to accomplish the mighty battle of our redemption. A. B. SIMPSON

It is His wings that heal our pains,
And soothe the serpent's poisoned stings;
Close to His bosom we must press
To feel His healing wings.

July 23

Whatsoever . . . that the Father may be glorified in the Son. (John 14:13)

Do we pray for HIS glory?

This is the privilege and possibility for every man who can speak to God *"in His Name."*

In the Lone Star Mission at Ongole, India, a faithful few had held on believingly and courageously year after year. Now the mission was about to be abandoned. The work had apparently failed; money had failed. The only hope now was God.

Dr. Jowett and his wife took with them that famous old Hindu woman, Julia, nearly one hundred years of age, and ascended the hills above Ongole to ask God to save the Lone Star Mission and the lost souls of India. The old Hindu saint mingled her tears with her description of the most important and most thrilling moment of her life—that memorable sunrise meeting on "Prayer Meeting Hill," as she rehearsed the story one night in Nellore, India, to Dr. Cortland Myers.

"They all prayed, and they all believed! They talked and then they prayed again! They wrestled before heaven's throne in the face of a heathen

world, like Elijah on Carmel. At last the day dawned. Just as the sun rose above the horizon Dr. Jowett arose out of darkness and seemed to see a great light. He lifted his hand heavenward and turned his tear-stained face toward the great Heart of Love. He declared that his vision saw the cactus field below transformed into a church and mission buildings!

"*His faith grasped and gripped the great fact!* He claimed the promise and challenged God to answer *a prayer that was entirely for His own glory and the salvation of men!*

"The money came *immediately,* and *clearly from God's hand!*

"The man—God's choice, came *immediately!* Clearly it was of God that Dr. Clough was called to put new life and hope into the almost abandoned mission.

"Today on that very cactus field stands the Christian church with the largest membership of any church on earth—20,000 members! If it had not been divided by necessity there would now be 50,000 members—the greatest miracle of the modern missionary world.

"On that well nigh abandoned field, Dr. Clough baptized 10,000 persons in one year; 2,222 in one day!

"Prayer Meeting Hill *moved the throne of God,* and made the world to tremble! The battlements of heaven must have been crowded to watch these many workings of a prayer for *His* glory!"

July 24

Blessed are they that have not seen, and yet have believed. (John 20:29)

There are those to whom no visions come, no moments upon the mount suffused with a glory that never was on land or sea. Let not such envy the men of vision. It may be that the vision is given to strengthen a faith that else were weak. It is to the people who can live along the line of what others call the commonplace, and yet trust, that the Master says, "Blessed."

Beware of a life of fitful impulse. Live and act on sustained principle. It is a poor thing—the flash of summer lightning, compared with the steady luster of moon and star.

"The darkest night has stars in it!"

When the low mood comes, open your New Testament.

Read it imaginatively: stand on the shore at Capernaum; visit the home at Bethany; sit by Jacob's well and in the Upper Room; look into the eyes of Jesus; listen to His voice; take a walk around by Calvary; remember the crown of thorns; then tell yourself (for it is true), *"All this was for me! The Son of God loved me, and gave Himself for me."* And see if a passion of praise does not send the low mood flying.

"Praise and service are great healers." When life grows sore and wounding, and it is difficult to be brave, *praise God!* Sing something, and you will rally your own heart with the song!

You must learn to swim and hold your head above the water even when the sense of His Presence is not with you to hold up your chin. GARDEN OF SPICES

Do not depend on *frames* or *feelings.* You cannot always live in the tropics.

July 25

To whomsoever I shall send thee thou shalt go. (Jer. 1:7)

Have you ever read George Eliot's poem called "Stradivarius"? Stradivari was the famous old violin maker whose violins, nearly two centuries old, are almost worth their weight in gold today. Says Stradivari in the poem:

> *If my hand slacked,*
> *I should rob God—since He is fullest good,*
> *Leaving a blank instead of violins.*
> *He could not make Antonio Stradivari's violins*
> *Without Antonio.*

You are God's opportunity in your day. He has waited for ages for a person just like you. If you refuse Him, then God loses His opportunity which He sought through you, and He will never have another for there will never be another person on the earth just like you.

> *Bring to God your gift, my brother,*
> *He'll not need to call another,*
> *You will do;*
> *He will add His blessing to it,*
> *And the two of you will do it,*
> *God and you.*

R. E. NEIGHBOUR

Get taken clear out into the purpose of God and let Him lade you with merchandise for others.

We find scores of people in middle life who are in the unhappy position of doing everyday work which they hate and which does not express the personality, when each one might have done brilliantly in another sphere if he had given a day's prayerful thought to a decision which affected half a century.

July 26

He breathed on them, and saith unto them, Receive ye the Holy Ghost. (John 20:22)

I had an opportunity to preach in a little schoolhouse two miles from my first pastorate—an afternoon meeting. After the morning church service the rain was pouring in torrents. It seemed useless to go two miles through such a storm, for who would venture out in such weather? But a young woman had come for me in her buggy, and I went with her rather reluctantly.

There were seven men present; the young woman went home to get out of the rain. My first impression was that it was hardly worthwhile to preach a sermon to so small an audience, but I repented of that and gave them the best I had. The dew of heaven was upon us: we were conscious of God's presence, and two of the seven men, who were not Christians, expressed a desire to be saved.

An old farmer arose and said: "My young brother, God is working in our midst. Will you not preach tonight? The clouds are clearing away and we will go out and tell the people about the meeting." I consented, though it rather upset my plans for the following day. That night about twenty-five persons came, and there were six or seven inquirers and two or three decisions for Christ.

The meetings went on from day to day for two weeks. There were over seventy conversions, and on Sunday morning I baptized forty new members of my church. I could not explain it; no one seemed to be expecting a revival, or praying for it. It seemed like a case of God's sovereignty in giving His *breath-touch* without demanding that anyone should pray for it.

The last day of the meetings solved the mystery. At the close of the service a plainly dressed, gray-haired, motherly woman grasped my hand

and said: "This is my home, though I spend most of my time teaching school sixty miles from here. When my niece wrote that you were preaching at three in the afternoon and at seven-thirty in the evening, I dismissed my school a half hour earlier than usual, that I might spend in prayer every minute that you preached. And, sir, *I have come to see what God has been doing. Those you baptized this morning were all my neighbors and friends, and among them my brother, nephew, and niece.*"

Neither my preaching or praying brought that revival. It was the good woman sixty miles away, whose prayers brought the *breath-touch* of God upon dead souls of that community.

Let no day pass without a prayer to God for His *breath-touch* upon the spiritual dry bones of your community.

> *Breathe on me, Breath of God*
> *Till I am wholly Thine,*
> *Till all this earthly part of me*
> *Glows with Thy fire Divine.*

In Wales during the great revival there was no accounting for the way the Spirit worked. It was all *"a-bend to God."*

July 27

Thy name shall be called no more Jacob, but Israel: for as a prince hast thou power with God and with men, and hast prevailed. (Gen. 32:28)

Napoleon was once reviewing his troops near Paris. The horse on which he sat was restless, and the Emperor having thoughtlessly dropped the reins from his hand in the eagerness of giving a command, the spirited animal bounded away and the rider was in danger of being hurled to the ground. A young private standing in the lines leaped forward and, seizing the bridle, saved his beloved Commander from a fall. The Emperor glancing at him said in his quick abrupt way, "Thank you, Captain." The private looked up with a smile and asked, "Of what regiment, sir?" "Of my guards," answered Napoleon, and instantly galloped to another part of the field.

The young soldier laid down his musket with the remark, "Whoever will may carry that gun; I am done with it," and proceeded at once to join a group of officers who stood conversing at a little distance. One of them, a General, observing his self-possessed approach, angrily said, "What is this insolent fellow doing here?"

"This insolent fellow," answered the young soldier looking the other steadily in the eye, "is a Captain of the Guards." "Why, man," responded the officer, "you are insane; why do you speak thus?" *"He said it,"* replied the soldier, pointing to the Emperor, who was far down the lines. "I beg your pardon, Captain," politely returned the General, "I was not aware of your promotion."

To those looking on he was still a private, dressed in the coarse rough garb of a common soldier; but in the bold assertion of his dignity, he could meet all the jeers of his comrades and all the scoffs of his superiors with the ready reply, "He said it."

He said it! He said it!!

July 28

Why . . . this waste? (Mark 14:4)

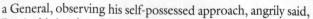

There is nothing that seems more prodigal than the waste of nature. The showers fall and sink into the ground, and seem to be lost. The rain cometh down from heaven and returneth not thither; the rivers run into the sea, and become absorbed in the ocean's brine. All this seems like a waste of precious material; and yet, science has taught us that no force is ever wasted, but simply converted into another form in which it goes on its way with an altered ministry, but an undiminished force.

Someone has represented in a sort of poetic parable a little raindrop trembling in the air, and questioning with the Genius of the sky whether it should fall upon the earth or still linger in the beautiful cloud.

"Why should I be lost and buried in the dirty soil? Why should I disappear in the dark mud, when I may glisten like a diamond or shine like an emerald or ruby in the rainbow's arch?"

"Yes," the Genius agrees; "but, if you fall in the earth you will come forth with a better resurrection in the petal of the flower, in the fragrance of the rose, in the hanging cluster of the vine."

And so, at last, the timid crystal drops one tear of regret, disappears beneath the soil, and is speedily drunk by the parched ground; it has gone out of sight—apparently out of existence. But lo! the root of yonder lily drinks in the moisture; the sap vessels of that damask rose absorb its refreshing draft; the far-reaching rootlet of yonder vine has found that fountain of life—and in a little while that raindrop comes forth in the snowy blossom of the lily, in the rich perfume of the rose, in the purple cluster of the vine, and as it meets once more the Genius of the air it answers back its glad acknowledgment: "Yes, I died, but I have risen, and now I live in a higher ministry, in a larger life, in a better resurrection." A. B. SIMPSON

Pour out thy love like the rush of a river,
Wasting its waters forever and ever,
Through the burnt sands that reward not the giver:
Silent or songful, thou nearest the sea.
Scatter thy life as the summer's shower pouring;
What if no bird through the pearl rain is soaring?
What if no blossom looks upward adoring?
Look to the life that was lavished for thee!

So the wild wind strews its perfumed caresses:
Evil and thankless the desert it blesses;
Bitter the wave that its soft pinion presses;
Never it ceases to whisper and sing.
What if the hard heart give thorns for thy roses?
What if on rocks thy tired bosom reposes?
Sweeter is music with minor-keyed closes,
Fairest the vines that on ruin will cling.

July 29

What! know ye not that your body is the temple of the Holy Ghost which is in you, which ye have of God, and ye are not your own? For ye are bought with a price: therefore glorify God in your body, and in your spirit, which are God's. (1 Cor. 6:19–20)

The Christian who truly enters into these two verses has solved some of the deepest problems in life. Those who recognize God's absolute proprietorship of their bodies are not long in doubt as to where they should go, or what they should do. *Consecration is simply a matter of letting God have what He has paid for, or returning stolen property.*

"Ye are bought with a price." It was an infinite price that God paid. It was something more than silver and gold—the precious Blood of His only begotten Son (see 1 Peter 1:18–19). God emphasizes the tremendous cost of redemption as an appeal to the heart of the redeemed. The price He has paid measures His estimate of us. He does not give *a life so dear to Him for a soul that is worth nothing to Him.* He has laid down the gold of His heart—even Jesus Christ. If we would go and stand on Calvary's hill, and consider what it has cost heaven to purchase our salvation, we could not long withhold from Him what He rightfully owns—*the full service of spirit, soul, and body.* Yet how many are satisfied to say, "Jesus is mine," who never go on to say, "I am His." *One who takes this higher ground is bound to be careful what he does with property which belongs to another.*

When the thought of His proprietorship becomes uppermost, then we will simultaneously recognize the fact that being His, we are temples of the Holy Spirit. Conscious of God's ownership, and thoughtful of our Divine Guest—the Holy Spirit—it is only natural that *we should glorify God in our bodies and in our spirits, which are His.* To glorify Him thus, is simply to exhibit the power and character of God in that which is His.

The Christian's greatest joy is found in letting God possess His own property.

July 30

The Lord will be the place of repair of His people. (Joel 3:16, Trans.)

Soldiers may be wounded in battle and sent to the hospital. A hospital isn't a shelf; it is a place of repair.

A soldier on service in the spiritual army is never off his battlefield. He is only removed to another part of the field when a wound interrupts what he meant to do, and sets him doing something else.

Is it not joy, pure joy, that there is no question of *the shelf?* No soldier on service is ever "laid aside"; he is only given another commission to fight among the unseen forces of the field. Never is he shelved as of no further use to his beloved Captain! The soldier must let his Captain say when and for what He needs him most, and he must not cloud his mind with questions. A wise master never wastes his servant's time, nor a commander his soldiers'. So let us settle it once for all and find heart's ease in doing so. *There is no discharge in warfare*—no, not for a single day. We may be called to serve on the visible field, going continually into the invisible both to renew our strength and to fight the kind of battle that can only be fought there. Or, we may be called off the visible altogether for a while and drawn deep into the invisible. That dreary word "laid aside" is never for *us. We* are soldiers of the King! ROSE FROM BRIER

Place of repair: O blessed place of refuge!
How gladly will I come to meet Him there,
To cease awhile from all the joy of service
To find a deeper joy with Him to share.

Place of repair: for tired brain and body!
How much I need that place just out of sight
Where only He can talk, and be beside me,
Until again made strong by His great might.

Place of repair: when trials press upon me
And God permits the unexpected test,
'Tis there I learn some lesson sweet and precious
As simply on His faithfulness I rest.

Place of repair: the place to take my sorrow,
The thing that hurts and would be hard to bear,
But somehow in the secret place I'm finding
That all the hurt is healed since He is there.

Place of repair: to wait for fresh enduement
I silently with Him alone would stay
Until He speaks again, and says, "Go forward
To help some other sheep to find the way."

Place of repair: O trysting-place most hallowed,
The Lord Himself is just that place to me,
His grace, His strength, His glory and His triumph,
Himself alone my all-sufficiency.

July 31

Unto him shall the gathering of the people be. (Gen. 49:10)

What a scene of unimaginable grandeur that will be, when at last *all nations are gathered to His Feet!* That will include representatives from all the European States, from Iceland in the far North to Greece in the South, and from Portugal in the West to hidden saints of God in Soviet Russia in the East. There will be many from Algeria, Morocco, and the Atlas mountains; from Egypt and the Nile Valley; from the sandy deserts and the mountains of the Sahara; from the great lakes in Central Africa, from the banks of the Niger, the Calabar, the Congo, and the Zambesi rivers; and from the uplands of South Africa. There will be *gathered to Christ* many from Palestine, Transjordan, and Arabia; India will contribute her millions; and even from closed lands like Nepal, Sikkim, and Tibet, *Christ will gather His own.*

From the Islands in the Dutch East Indies they will come—Java, Sumatra, Bali, Celebes, Lombok, Soembawa, Borneo, and the rest, and *will be gathered to the feet of the Redeemer.* From the teeming millions of Central Asia, from China, Japan, Korea, Manchukuo and Mongolia, there will be an immense home-going to the Savior. From the myriad Islands of the Pacific the peoples of Polynesia and Melanesia will *be gathered to the Lord who redeemed them.*

From Australia and New Zealand there will be multitudes who will *join in the glad song of praise.* From every republic of Central, South, and North America, and from the West Indies Islands—Cuba, Haiti, Jamaica, Puerto Rico, and the Lesser Antilles, *they will come.* From the far-off forests and lakes of Canada *there will be a similar home-going.*

Whether the tongues be those of the white race, or of the red, or of the black, *the gathering to Christ* will be overwhelmingly splendid.

From earth's wide bounds, from ocean's farthest coast,
Through gates of pearl streams in the countless host,
Singing to Father, Son, and Holy Ghost, "Hallelujah!"
BIBLE SOCIETY RECORD 🐝

I hear ten thousand voices singing
Their praises to the Lord on high;
Far distant shores and hills are ringing
With anthems of their nation's joy:

Praise ye the Lord! for He hath given
To lands in darkness hid, His light,
As morning rays light up the heaven,
His word has chased away our night.

Hark! Hark! a louder sound is booming
O'er heaven and earth, o'er land and sea;
The angel's trump proclaims His coming—
Our day of endless Jubilee.

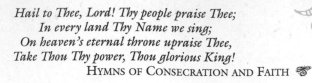

Hail to Thee, Lord! Thy people praise Thee;
In every land Thy Name we sing;
On heaven's eternal throne upraise Thee,
Take Thou Thy power, Thou glorious King!
HYMNS OF CONSECRATION AND FAITH ☙

August 1

Tell me, O thou whom my soul loveth ... where thou makest thy
flock to rest at noon? (Song 1:7)

We have lost the art of *"resting at noon."* Many are slowly succumbing to the strain of life *because they have forgotten how to rest.* The steady stream, the continuous uniformity of life, is what kills.

Rest is not a sedative for the sick, but a tonic for the strong. It spells emancipation, illumination, transformation. It saves us from becoming slaves even of good works.

One of our Cambridge naturalists told me once of an experiment he had made with a pigeon. The bird had been born in a cage and had never been free; one day his owner took the bird out on the porch of the house and flung it into the air. To the naturalist's surprise the bird's capacity for flight was perfect. Round and round it flew as if born in the air; but soon its flight grew excited, panting, and the circles grew smaller, until at last the bird dashed full against its master's breast and fell to the ground. What did it mean? It meant that, though the bird had inherited the instinct of flight it had not inherited the capacity to stop, and if it had not risked the shock of a sudden halt the little life would have been panted out in the air.

Isn't that a parable of many a modern life: completely endowed with the instinct of action, but without the capacity to stop? Round and round life goes in its weary circle until it is almost dying at full speed. Any shock, even some severe experience, is a mercy if it checks the whirl. Sometimes God stops such a soul abruptly by some sharp blow of trouble, and the soul falls in despair at His Feet, and then He bends over it and says: "*Be still,* my child; be still, and know that I am God!" until by degrees the despair of trouble is changed into submission and obedience, and the poor, weary, fluttering life is made strong to fly again.

When, spurred by tasks unceasing or undone,
You would seek rest afar,

And cannot, though repose be rightly won—
Rest where you are.

Neglect the needless; sanctify the rest;
Move without stress or jar;
With quiet of a spirit self-possessed
Rest where you are.

Not in event, restriction, or release,
Not in scenes near or far,
But in ourselves are restlessness or peace:
Rest where you are.

Where lives the soul lives God; His day, His world,
No phantom mists need mar;
His starry nights are tents of peace unfurled:
Rest where you are.

Is it so long since we trod the road to our "resting-place," that the path has become a jungle?

August 2

They waited for me as for the rain; and they opened their mouth wide as for the latter rain. (Job 29:23)

The LORD shall ... satisfy thy soul in drought ... and thou shalt be like a watered garden, and like a spring of water, whose waters fail not. (Isa. 58:11)

Travelers are enthusiastic over a species of palm tree which grows in South America. They call it *the rain tree*. This tree has the remarkable power of attracting, in a wondrous degree, atmospheric moisture, which it condenses and drops on the earth in refreshing dew. It grows straight up in the parched and arid desert and daily distributes its refreshing showers, with the result that around it an oasis of luxuriant vegetation soon springs up. The floodgates of heaven refuse to open, the fountains cease to flow, the rivers evaporate—all true, but the rain tree getting its moisture from above, renews the garden which it has created about its base, and gives the weary traveler shade and fruit, a new life and a delightful rest!

God would have *us* to be like the rain tree growing alongside the desert highways of the world—sources of new spiritual life. God HIMSELF is our atmosphere, and we carry our atmosphere with us wherever we go.

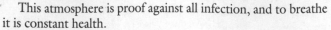

This atmosphere is proof against all infection, and to breathe it is constant health.

Christ's power was in His separateness. He did not withdraw Himself from the world, but lived in the very midst of it. No man ever came into such close external contact with the devil. Jesus was not a recluse. He was social—mingling with men; yet He kept intact His separateness from the world. He was *Jesus!* Men felt this! This was His power!

In the secret of Christ's power we see the secret of *our* power. If we are to have any power in the world we must become partakers of His holiness; we must be *separated* with Him; and be *kept separated* and set apart to the same great life.

> *The angel, grateful for each borrowed sense,*
> *Gazed at the sight:*
> *A girl so white,*
> *With slender fingers tense*
> *Upon the table edge (around his head*
> *The smell of new-baked bread)*
> *The while unhurried tones fell low, and clear,*
> *And near.*
> *Alone, yet not alone, yet not alone,*
> *She fell not prone;*
> *But leaning a little against the wall,*
> *The while the sun grew late,*
> *She knew . . . she knew . . . she knew—why all*
> *Her life she had been separate.*
> THE ANNUNCIATION, BY FLORENCE G. MAGEE

"To reveal his Son in me" *(Gal. 1:16).*

August 3

Christ in you, the hope of glory. (Col. 1:27)

The greatest thing that any of us can do is not to live for Christ but to live Christ. What is holy living? It is Christ-life. It is not to be Christians, but Christ-ones. It is not to try to do or be some great thing but simply to have Him and let Him live His own life in us; abiding in Him and He in us, and letting Him reflect His own graces, His own faith, His own consecration, His own love, His own patience, His own gentleness, His own words in us, while we "show forth the virtues of Him who hath called us out of darkness into His marvelous light." *This is at once the sublimest and the simplest life that it is possible to live.* It is a higher standard than human perfection, and yet it is possible for a poor, sinful, imperfect man to realize it through the perfect Christ who comes to live within us.

God help us so to live, and thus to make real to those around us the simplicity, the beauty, the glory, and the power of the Christ life.

"I cannot tell," said the humble shepherd's wife, "what sermon it was that led me into a life of victory. I cannot even explain the creed or the catechism, but I know that something has changed me entirely. Last summer John and I washed the sheep in yonder stream. I cannot tell you where the water went, but I can show you the clean white fleece of the sheep. And so I may forget the doctrine, but I have its blessed fruit in my heart and life."

Two of us were chatting with Sadhu Sundar Singh in my office one morning. The Sadhu had just arrived in London. We knew little concerning him, and my friend was anxious to find out if he knew the doctrine of that "perfect love" of which Saint John speaks.

"Does he understand?" asked my friend, turning to me.

The Sadhu smiled and quietly said: "When I throw a stone at the fruit tree, the fruit tree throws no stone back, but gives me *fruit*. Is it that?" Then he went on to ask: "Should not we, who love the Lord Jesus, be like sandalwood, which imparts its fragrance to the ax which cuts it?" SELECTED

August 4

The LORD is good unto them that wait for him, to the soul that seeketh him. It is good that a man should both hope and quietly wait for the salvation of the LORD. (Lam. 3:25–26)

It is easier to work than to wait. It is often more important to wait than to work. *We can trust God to do the needed working while we are waiting; but if we are not willing to wait, and insist upon working while He would have us be still, we may interfere with the effective and triumphant working that He would do in our behalf. Our waiting may be the most difficult thing we can do; it may be the severest test that God can give us.*

Oswald Chambers has said truly: "One of the greatest strains in life is the strain of *waiting for God*. God takes the saint like a bow which He stretches; we get to a certain point and say *I cannot stand any more;* but

God goes on stretching. He is not aiming at our mark, but at His own, and the patience of the saints is that we hold on until He lets the arrow fly straight to His goal. If we are willing to remember God's call and assurance there need be no strain at all while we are waiting. The "stretched bow" time may be a time of unbroken rest for us as we "rest in the LORD, and wait patiently for him" (Ps. 37:7).

Unless a violin string is stretched until it cries out when the bow is drawn over it, there is no music. A loose violin string with no strain upon it is of no use—it is dead, has no voice. But when stretched till it strains it is brought to the proper tone, and then only is it useful to the music-maker. A. B. SIMPSON

> *In God's eternal plan, a month, a year,*
> *Is but an hour of some slow April day,*
> *Holding the germs of what we hope or fear,*
> *To blossom far away.*

> *The Almighty is tedious,* but He's sure!

August 5

My God with his loving kindness shall come to meet me at every corner. (Ps. 59:10, Lit.)

It matters not how great the scheme if God draws it out; it matters not how insurmountable the difficulties appear if God undertakes the responsibility. *If we, His children, when we get into tangled corners even by our own folly and sometimes wrongdoing, would only turn to God as a King and as a Father and cast ourselves upon Him, He would work for us and lead us out of our troubles safely and in a manner worthy of a King.*

> *This morning, Lord, I pray*
> *Safeguard us through the day,*
> *Especially at corners of the way.*

> *For when the way is straight,*
> *We fear no sudden fate,*
> *But see ahead the evening's open gate.*

> *But few and far between*
> *Are days when all is seen*
> *Of what will come, or yet of what has been.*

For unexpected things
Swoop down on sudden wings
And overthrow us with their buffetings.

And so, dear Lord, we pray,
Control and guard this day
Thy children at the corners of their way.

CORNERS, BY M. G. L.

Dr. S. D. Gordon says in his writings: *"It is a good thing for us to be put in a tight corner.* To be pushed and hemmed in on every side until you are forced to stand with your back to the wall, facing a foe at every angle, with barely standing room—*that is good.* For one thing, you find out that *no matter how close the fit of that corner may be, it still can hold another in addition to yourself.* Its very tightness brings you and your Lord into the very closest quarters. And *only at closest touch will you find out what a wondrous Friend He is.*

"*Tight corners are famous places for chamber concerts.* The acoustics are wonderful. David's exile Psalms have rung out a strangely sweet melody down all the ages, and out through all the world, and into thousands of hearts."

August 6

No plan [which comes] from thee can be hindered. (Job 42:2, Lit.)

We believe in the providence of God, but we do not believe half enough in it. Remember that Omnipotence has servants everywhere, set in their places at every point of the road. In the old days of the post horses, there were always swift horses ready to carry onward the king's mails.

It is wonderful how God has His relays of providential agents; how when He has done with one there is always another ready to take his place. Sometimes you have found one friend fail you—he is just dead and buried. "Ah!" you say, "what shall I do?" Well, well, *God knows how to carry on the purposes of His providence;* He will raise up another. How strikingly punctual providence is! You and I make appointments and miss them by half an hour; but *God never missed an appointment yet!* God never is before His time though *we* often wish He were; but He is never behind—no, *not by one tick of the clock.*

When the children of Israel were to go down out of Egypt, all the Pharaohs in the pyramids, if they had risen to life again, could not have kept them in bondage another half minute. "Thus saith the LORD . . . Let my people go!" It was time, and go they must! All the kings of the earth, and all the princes thereof, are in subjection to the kingdom of God's providence, and He can move them just as He pleases. And now, trembler, wherefore are you afraid? "Fear thou not; for I am with thee." *All the mysterious arrangements of providence work for our good.* CHARLES H. SPURGEON 🖅

August 7

I AM THAT I AM. (Ex. 3:14)

God is His own equivalent, and God needs nothing but Himself to achieve the great purposes on which He has set His heart.

God gave Moses a blank, and as life went forward for the next forty years, Moses kept filling in the blank with his special need. He *filled in fearlessness* before Pharaoh. He *filled in guidance* across the Red Sea. He *filled in manna* for the whole population. He *filled in water* from the rock. He *filled in guidance* through the wilderness. He *filled in victory* over Amalek. He *filled in clear revelation* at Sinai. And so Moses, for the rest of his life, had little else to do than to go quietly alone, and taking God's blank checkbook, signed by God's name, I AM THAT I AM, write in *I AM guidance; I AM bread*. He presented the check and God honored it.

And whenever you come to live upon God's plan as Moses from that moment did, *you may absolutely trust God*. And when you come down to the hoar-head you will say, *"Not one thing hath failed of all the good things which the LORD your God spake concerning you"* (Josh. 23:14). A. B. SIMPSON 🖅

Joshua had tried God forty years in the brick kilns, forty years in the desert, and thirty years in the Promised Land, and this was his dying testimony. D. L. MOODY 🖅

Whatever life may bring to you,
"God" will ring true to you:
Star in your sky—
Food in your store—

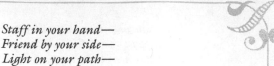

Staff in your hand—
Friend by your side—
Light on your path—
Joy in your heart—
In your ears music—
In your mouth songs.
Yes, rapid as your race may run,
And scorching as may shine your sun,
And bitter as may blow your blast,
And lonely as your lot be cast—
Whatever life may bring to you,
"God" will aye ring true to you.

CHARLES HERBERT

August 8

He shall come down like rain upon the mown grass. (Ps. 72:6)

How grateful the soft rain must feel to the mown grass, all cut as it is, and, as we imagine it, so sore! But the rain is healing: and so God says He will come to His people, "Like rain upon the mown grass."

There is so much in life that is like the cutting-machine, and the heart becomes sore and needs the healing influences that come from God. No matter what we may call that which is healing to us it is God coming "like rain upon the mown grass." And may it not be with us as with the beautiful lawns we admire: the more cutting and the more rain, the more beautiful we shall be; but *it must not be one, but both.* SELECTED

The absence of joy does not mean the absence of God.

The pruned vine does not suggest an absent vine-dresser, and even if the vine be bleeding it does not mean that he has gone away.

The mower's scythe had passed o'er summer fields,
The grass lay bleeding 'neath the summer sun;
Strong hands swift stored the harvest's wealthy yields,
And left the fields deserted, one by one.

Their glory gone, their beauty swept away,
Still smarting from the swift, keen cut of death,
Their woe the sharp, short work of one brief day
That dawned with sunshine in its balmy breath.

235

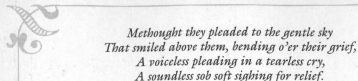

Methought they pleaded to the gentle sky
That smiled above them, bending o'er their grief,
A voiceless pleading in a tearless cry,
A soundless sob soft sighing for relief.

And heaven heard the fervor of their call,
And sent them healing balm at eventide,
Sweet raindrops breathing blessing in their fall,
And weeping gently o'er their wounded pride.

Thus shall He come as rain on new-mown grass,
And withered hopes spring up to grace His path,
New life be born where'er His footsteps pass,
And tender grass spring forth—"God's Aftermath."

FRANCES BROOK 🍂

August 9

His praise shall continually be in my mouth. (Ps. 34:1)

I heard a joyous strain—
A lark on a leafless bough
Sat singing in the rain.

I heard him singing early in the morning. It was hardly light! I could not understand that song; it was fairly a lilt of joy. It had been a portentous night for me, full of dreams that did disturb me. Old things that I had hoped to forget, and new things that I had prayed could never come, trooped through my dreams like grinning little bare-faced imps. Certainly I was in no humor to sing. What could possess that fellow out yonder to be telling the whole township how joyous he was? He was perched on the rail fence by the spring run. *He was drenched.* It had rained in the night and evidently he had been poorly housed. I pitied him. What comfort could he have had through that night bathed in the storm? He never thought of comfort. His song was not bought by any such duplicity. It was in his heart. Then I shook myself: *The shame that a lark has finer poise than a man!* G. A. LEICHLITER 🍂

"Nothing can break you as long as you sing."

August 10

But what things were gain to me, those I counted loss for Christ.
(Phil. 3:7)

If God has called you to be really like Christ, He may draw you into a life of crucifixion and humility, and put on you such demands of obedience that He will not allow you to follow other Christians, and in many ways He will seem to let other good people do things which He will not let you do.

Other Christians, who seem very religious and useful, may push themselves, pull wires, and work schemes to carry out their plans, but *you cannot do it;* and if you attempt it you will meet with such failure and rebuke from the Lord as to make you sorely penitent.

Others may boast of themselves, of their work, of their success, of their writing, but *the Holy Spirit will not allow you to do any such thing,* and if you begin it He will lead you into some deep mortification, that will make you despise yourself and all your good works.

Others will be allowed to succeed in making money ... but it is likely *God will keep you poor,* because He wants you to have something far better than gold, and that is a helpless dependence on Him, that He may have the privilege of supplying your needs day by day out of an unseen treasury.

The Lord will let others be honored and put forward, *and keep you hid away in obscurity* because He wants to produce some choice fragrant fruit for His coming glory.

He will let others be great, *but keep you small.* He will let others do a work for Him, and get the credit for it, *but He will make you work and toil without knowing how much you are doing.*

The Holy Spirit will put a strict watch over you ... rebuking you for little words and feelings, or for wasting time.

God is an Infinite Sovereign: *He has a right to do as He pleases with His own.*

Settle it forever, then, that *you are to deal directly with the Lord Jesus—that He is to have the privilege of tying your tongue, chaining your hand, or closing your eyes* in ways that He does not deal with others.

Then, *you will have found the vestibule of heaven.*

"Others may. You cannot!"

August 11

Now therefore be not grieved, nor angry with yourselves, that ye sold me hither: for God did send me before you to preserve life. (Gen. 45:5)

When you are disappointed or vexed or hedged in or thwarted; when you are seemingly abandoned, *remember, son of God, heir of Heaven, that you are being prepared for the higher life.* You need courage, patience, perseverance, and it is in the hard places that they are developed. You need faith, and you will never have it unless you are brought to circumstances in which you are compelled to act by the invisible rather than the visible. You need those Christian graces of which the Bible speaks, and of which the pulpit preaches; and practical life, with its various vicissitudes, is God's school in which you are to acquire these things. Do not be discouraged or cast down.

When you are bestead, remember that God is dealing with you as a good schoolmaster. You will thank Him for His severity by and by.

When God is dealing with you, do not accuse Him. Do not cry out, "Why hast thou forsaken me?" Remember, that to those who are exercised thereby God shows His love and His Fatherhood. Bow yourselves meekly to the chastisements of God, and study not how you can get away from the trouble, but how you can rise above it by being made better by it.

> *I knew I had been sold,*
> *For circumstance*
> *Dark as a desert pit*
> *And dismal as the slaver's caravan*
> *Surrounded me,*
> *And seemed to crush me down;*
> *I had been sold.*
>
> *I also had been sent.*
> *The circumstance*
> *Shone with the light Divine,*
> *And through the wrath of men*
> *God put me in His own appointed place.*
> *He set on high*
> *And none could bow me down.*
> *I HAD BEEN SENT.*
> JOSEPH, BY M. MANNINGTON DEXTER

Had *we* no tests, no great hedged-in experiences, *we would never know what a wonderful Deliverer and triumphant Guide we have!*

He never limits us, except to liberate us!

August 12

See how dear he held him. (John 11:36 WEYMOUTH)

He loved, yet lingered. We are so quick to think that delayed answer to prayer means that the prayer is not going to be answered. Dr. Stuart Holden has said truly: "Many a time we pray and are prone to interpret God's silence as a denial of our petitions; whereas, in truth, He only defers their fulfillment until such time as we ourselves are ready to cooperate to the full in His purposes." Prayer registered in heaven is prayer dealt with, although the vision still tarries.

Faith is trained to its supreme mission under the discipline of patience. The man who can wait God's time, knowing that *He* edits his prayer in wisdom and affection, will always discover that He never comes to man's aid one minute too soon or too late.

God's delay in answering the prayer of our longing heart is the most loving thing God can do. He may be waiting for us to come closer to Him, prostrate ourselves at His feet and abide there in trustful submission, *that His granting of the longed-for answer may mean infinitely greater blessing than if we received it anywhere else than in the dust at His feet.*

> *O wait, impatient heart!*
> *As winter waits, her songbirds fed.*
> *And every nestling blossom dead;*
> *Beyond the purple seas they sing!*
> *Beneath soft snows they sleep!*
> *They only sleep. Sweet patience keep*
> *And wait, as winter waits the spring.*

Nothing can hold our ship down when the tide comes in!

The aloe blooms but once in a hundred years; but every hour of all that century is needed to produce the delicate texture and resplendent beauty of the flower.

Faith heard the sound of "the tread of rain," and yet God made Elijah wait!

God never hastens, and He never tarries!

August 13

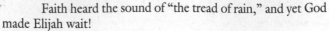

He is able to save to the uttermost. (Heb. 7:25)

What a magnificent prospect! Does it not take your breath away?

It may well do so; but nevertheless it is true, gloriously and eternally true, for it is written in the Word of God. *Grip that fact; grip it with your whole heart; take risks on it; stake your all on it; whisper it to yourself with clenched teeth when you are in the heat of the fight; shout it to the heavens when you see the enemy about to flee; triumph in it; exult in it!*

Faith in this one thing can transfigure your whole life, and lift you to the heights of victory and glory that once seemed to you as far off and remote as the distant snows of some shining mountain summit seem to the traveler when, through a haze of sunshine, he lifts up his eyes to gaze as at some holy thing up in the blue air.

Remember, that *the life of sanctification and spiritual power can never be had cheaply. To bestow it upon us the Lord Jesus paid the price of Calvary.* To receive it we must be at least willing to pay the price of obedience to His simple conditions. Remember, too, *it is the only life worth living.* READER HARRIS ❧

It costs to have a vision, but it costs too much to remember only the price.

August 14

If it die . . . much fruit. (John 12:24)

Infinite wisdom takes us in hand, and leads us through deep interior crucifixion to our fine parts, lofty reason, brightest hopes, cherished affections, our pious zeal, our spiritual impetuosity, our narrow culture, our creed and churchism, our success, our spiritual experience, our spiritual comforts.

The crucifixion goes on until we are dead and *detached from all creatures, all saints, all thoughts, all hopes, all plans, all tender heart-yearnings, all preferences; dead to all trouble, all sorrow, all disappointments, all praise or blame, success or failure, comforts and annoyances, climates or nationalities;* dead to all desires but Himself.

There is no field without a seed,
Life raised through death is life indeed.
The smallest, lowliest little flower
A secret is, of mighty power.
To die—it lives—buried to rise—
Abundant life through sacrifice.
Wouldst thou know sacrifice?
It is through loss;
Thou can'st not save but by the Cross.
A corn of wheat except it die,
Can never, never multiply.
The glorious fields of waving gold,
Through death are life a hundredfold.
Thou who for souls dost weep and pray,
Let not hell's legions thee dismay.
This is the way of ways for thee,
The way of certain victory.

THE SOUL WINNER'S SECRET

Let go of the old grain of wheat if you want a harvest.

August 15

Thinketh no evil. (1 Cor. 13:5)

"Let it rest!"

Ah! how many hearts on the brink of anxiety and disquietude, by this simple sentence have been made calm and happy!

Some proceeding has wounded us by its want of tact; *let it rest;* no one will think of it again.

A harsh or unjust sentence irritates us; *let it rest;* whoever may have given vent to it will be pleased to see it forgotten.

A painful scandal is about to estrange us from an old friend; *let it rest,* and thus preserve our charity and peace of mind.

A suspicious look is on the point of cooling our affection; *let it rest;* our look of trust will restore confidence.

Fancy! we, who are so careful to remove the briars from our pathway for fear they should wound, yet take pleasure in collecting and piercing our hearts with thorns that meet us in our daily intercourse with one another! How childish and unreasonable we are! GOLD DUST 🐝

The rents made by Time will soon mend if you will let God have His way.

August 16

Be silent unto God and let him mold thee. (Ps. 46:10, Trans.)

> *Let thy soul walk softly in thee*
> *Like a saint in heaven unshod,*
> *For to be alone with silence*
> *Is to be at home with God.*

Quiet hearts are as rare as radium. We need every day to be led by the Divine Shepherd into the green pastures and beside the still waters. We are losing the art of meditation. Inner preparation is necessary to outer service.

"Rest pauses" contribute to the finer music of life. "*He* went out into a mountain to pray." "And as *he* prayed, the fashion of his countenance was altered." Therein we have the example of our Lord.

We have yet to learn the power of silence. Not in the college or academy, but in the silence of the soul, do we learn the greater lessons of life and become rooted in spiritual inwardness.

The geologist says that certain crystals can only come to their perfect form in stillness. *In the undistracted moment men are in touch with God and everlasting things.*

The strenuousness of life and the increasing distractions of the world demand a zone of silence and the Quiet Hour.

And Jesus said to them: "Come away to some lonely spot and get a little rest (for there were many coming and going, and they could get no time even to eat). So they went privately in the boat to a lonely spot" (Mark 6:31–32). Let *us* find that spot every day, and the fellowship of silence. On such moments infinite issues hinge!

> *In every life*
> *There's a pause that is better than onward rush,*

Better than hewing or mightiest doing;
'Tis the standing still at Sovereign will.

There's a hush that is better than ardent speech,
Better than sighing or wilderness crying;
'Tis the being still at Sovereign will.

The pause and the hush sing a double song
In unison low and for all time long.
O human soul, God's working plan
Goes on, nor needs the aid of man!
Stand still, and see!
Be still, and know!

August 17

I am not eloquent. (Ex. 4:10)

Nothing is more dishonoring to God, or more dangerous for us, than a mock humility. When we refuse to occupy a position which the grace of God assigns us, because of our not possessing certain virtues and qualifications, this is not humility, for if we could but satisfy our own consciences in reference to such virtues and qualifications, we should then deem ourselves entitled to assume the position. If, for instance, Moses had possessed such a measure of eloquence as he deemed needful, we may suppose he would have been ready to go. Now the question is, how much eloquence would he have needed to furnish him for his mission? The answer is, without God no amount of human eloquence would have availed; but with God the merest stammerer would have proved an efficient minister. This is a great practical truth.

Unbelief is not humility, but thorough pride. It refuses to believe God because it does not find in self a reason for believing. This is the very height of presumption. C. H. M. ☞

Move to the fore;
Say not another is fitter than thou.
Shame to thy shrinking! Up! Face thy task now.
Own thyself equal to all a soul may,
Cease thy evading—God needs thee today.
Move to the fore!

God Himself waits, and must wait till thou come;
Men are God's prophets though ages lie dumb.
Halts the Christ Kingdom with conquest so near?
Thou art the cause, thou soul in the rear.
Move to the fore!

Find your purpose and fling your life out into it; and the loftier your purpose is, the more sure you will be to make the world richer with every enrichment of yourself. PHILLIPS BROOKS 🐝

August 18

And the angel of the LORD went further, and stood in a nar-row place, where was no way to turn either to the right hand or to the left. (Num. 22:26)

"A narrow place!" *You know that place; you have been there—you will very likely be there again before long—some of you may be there at this very moment;* for it is not merely a defile away somewhere among the mountains to the east of Moab. It is a life passage in individual experience—a time when there we are brought face to face with some inevitable question. . . . Temptation is such a "narrow place." In the serious crisis of the soul's history, it is alone. *It is a path on which there is room only for itself, and before it there is God. Between these two always the matter has to be settled. Yes, or no, is the hinge on which everything turns. Shall I yield and dishonor God, or shall I resist and triumph in His might? There is no possible compromise; for compromise with sin is itself the most insidious form of sin.* No man can pass through these crises, and be after them what he was before. *He has met God face to face, and he must either be the better or the worse for that experience.* Either, like Jacob at Peniel he can say, "My life is preserved," or like Saul after he had thrown off his allegiance to his God, "Jehovah has departed from me, and is become my enemy." WILLIAM M. TAYLOR 🐝

The harder the place the more He loves to show His power. If you wish to find Him real, come to Him in some great trouble. He has no chance to work until you get in a hard place. He led Israel out of the usual way till He got them to the Red Sea. Then there was room for His power to be manifested. God loves the hard places and the narrow places.

Rejoice if you are in such a place! Even if it is in the very heart of the foe, God is able to deliver you. Let not your faith in Him waver for a moment, and you will find *His omnipotence is all upon your side for every difficulty in which you can be placed.*

"When you get into a tight place," said Harriet Beecher Stowe, "and everything goes against you, till it seems as if you could not hold on a minute longer, never give up then, *for that is just the place and the time that the tide will turn.*"

August 19

Whatsoever thy soul desireth, I will even do it for thee. (1 Sam. 20:4)

It is sometimes difficult to realize that the promises of God *are to be taken at their face value.* Too often they are regarded as a part of the general spiritual instruction of the Word, but not to be appropriated for our own need.

We fail to realize because we do not appropriate!

No matter what may be our requirements—guidance, spiritual refreshing, physical or temporal needs, God has given us *some specific word on which to base our faith.*

Then, since the promises are definite, should not our prayers be definite? Prayerfully *search the Word to find the promise that will fit the case. Prove Him!* Back of the word of the Lord is the person and character of God Himself; *God, who cannot lie.*

God honors the person who trusts Him implicitly.

It is not *our* worth, but *Christ's,* which has secured for us *immediate access to the Throne,* "For all the promises of God *in him* are yea, and *in him* Amen" (2 Cor. 1:20).

With such a basis and assurance, *why hesitate to claim the things the Lord has provided?* Can you not trust the *One* who made the promise?

Whatever desire the Father permits to live in the heart of one of His saints, *He will grant the fulfillment thereof.* S. CHADWICK

Prove the immutable promises of God!

August 20

Whosoever will save his life shall lose it. (Mark 8:35)

The laying down of life is not only the foundation of a new life for ourselves, but also the foundation of a new life for others, just as the laying down of our Lord's life has brought forth its abundant harvest all through the years.

It is the laying down of life for the sake of the harvest; it is the grain of wheat falling into the ground to die in order that it may not abide alone.

John Coleridge Patterson's life was equipped with every gift to make it rich and happy in his own land; yet he laid it down to go to his hard and toilsome life in the South Seas. Had he been asked, *"Are you regretful for what you have turned your back upon?"* he would have answered, *"The promise has been fulfilled to me."*

An American Consul General in China once said to Matthew Culbertson, *"You might have been a Major-General if you had stayed at home."* He had been the best man in his class at West Point, but his mother's prayers had borne their fruitage and he became a missionary. He was the man of military genius in Shanghai's time of need. *"No,"* he said, *"I do not regret it. The privilege of preaching the Gospel to four hundred millions of one's fellow creatures is the greatest privilege any man can have on earth."* He had *found* his life!

To be sure, Livingstone lost his life, but he had *found* another—a life which spread through Africa, which abides in Africa, which molded the world's thought of Africa.

Henry Martyn put his hand to the plow with these words, "Now, let me burn out for God!" No "looking back." No relinquishing the handles even for a holiday!

Think of James Gilmore in Mongolia in his uncompanioned life! Mongolia stretches from the Sea of Japan on the east to Turkestan on the west—a distance of three thousand miles; from the southern boundary of Asiatic Russia to the Great Wall of China—nine hundred miles. What a field! But what a plowman! He died in the furrow!

Nineteen hundred years ago our Lord lost His life and His fame. Or *did He?*

Speak, history! Who are life's victors? Unveil thy long annals and say,
Are they those whom the world calls the victors, who won
the success of a day?
Thy martyrs, or Nero? The Spartans, who fell at Thermopylae's tryst,
Or the Persians and Xerxes? His judges, or Socrates? Pilate or Christ?
WILLIAM WETMORE STORY

August 21

Turn to ashes. (Ps. 20:3, margin)

Oh, not for Thee my fading fires,
The ashes of my heart.

May I tell you a tale of the African veld? It concerns the *fire lily.*

A grass fire in a hill country is one of the most wonderful sights in a wonderful land, surpassing in subtle attraction the grandeur of a veld fire on the plain with its roaring flames leaping skyward as they lick up the tall dry grass. Among the mountains where the grass is much shorter you watch with tireless fascination the long running lines of light on the distant heights—something like the illumination of a town seen from far away. With morning the scene is changed. You lift your eyes to greet the mountains you love, and they answer you with blackened faces. A little longer and these same hills are clothed in springing green, and, from the ashes, one of the first of the flowers, rises the *fire lily* like a little scarlet flame.

Beauty for ashes! Here are the very words of God incarnate in His works. The matchless message of Isaiah 61:3 comes with a deeper meaning as we consider the *fire lily.* Its story unfolds the Old Testament promise in the radiance of New Testament light; for it shows *by what means* God would make actual in our own experience *the glorious possibility of resurrection life.*

When we surrender our old nature to God that He may carry out the death sentence pronounced upon it, He accepts it in the only way He ever accepted a sacrifice, by turning it to ashes (Ps. 20:3, margin). And where the fire has been there springs from the ashes of the old life the fire lily of the beauty of Christ. As more ground is daily yielded, on the fire-swept hills of our inner life will be wrought the miracle of life out of death, and the bare slopes will burst with blossom. One unburnt hill will mean a jungle growth of grass and weeds; one valley spared will mean less Christfulness. This is the law of God—both natural and spiritual—*no fire, no fire lily; no ashes, no beauty.* This is the secret of the fire lily. *This is the meaning of surrender.* P. E. SHARP

But there were only ashes when He came
Saying, "My daughter, thou hast tried to serve

In thine own way? but now, stretch forth thy hands
That I may lead thee out of self's dark cell
And work My will through thee—
When thou hast ceased to be.

I said, "My youth is gone; my strength is gone;
My life—it lies before Thee bare and sere.
For very shame I cannot offer Thee
These ashes that are left me, gray and drear.
Yet, work Thy will in me
And teach me not to be."

Then through the ashes of that fading fire
He breathed His breath; and when the ash had fled,
Laid on some smoldering embers a live coal
That was His life, His love, all flaming red.
"Thy will be done to me,
So shall I live in Thee."

AUTHOR UNKNOWN

"Before God gives a blessing He writes a sentence of death on the means leading up to it!"

August 22

So are ye in mine hand. (Jer. 18:6)

Ole Bull, the world's most noted violinist, was ever wandering about. One day he became lost in the interminable forests. In the dark of the night he stumbled against a log hut, the home of a hermit. The old man took him in, fed and warmed him; after the supper they sat in front of a blazing fireplace, and the old hermit picked some crude tunes on his screechy, battered violin. Ole Bull said to the hermit, "Do you think I could play on that?" "I don't think so; it took me years to learn," the old hermit replied. Ole Bull said, "Let me try it."

He took the old marred violin and drew the bow across the strings, and suddenly the hermit's hut was filled with music Divine; and, according to the story, the hermit sobbed like a child.

We are battered instruments; life's strings have been snapped; life's bow has been bent. *Yet, if we will only let Him take us and touch us,* from this old battered, broken, shattered, marred instrument, He will bring forth music fit for the angels.

I never knew the old, brown violin,
That was so long in some dark corner thrust,
Its strings broken or loose, its pegs run down,
Could ever be of use again. The dust
Of years lay on its shabby case, until
One day a Master took the instrument,
And with caressing fingers touched the wood,
Adjusted pegs and strings; his mind intent
On making music as he drew his bow.
Then from the violin, long silent, sprang
Once more arpeggios, runs, trills. The wood
Quivered, leapt into life, and joyous sang.

I now believe that any broken life,
Jangling with discords, unadjusted, tossed
In some far corner, wasted, thrown aside,
Can yet be of some use; need not be lost
From Heaven's orchestra. A Master's Hand
Scarred with old wounds, can mend the broken thing
If yielded to Him wholly; and can make
The dumb life speak again, and joyous sing
In praise of One who gave His life that none
Need perish. And this message, glad, most blest,
I now believe; for placing in His Hand
My life, I find my world is now at rest.

DOROTHY M. BARTER-SNOW

August 23

I . . . brought you unto myself. (Ex. 19:4)

How we have wondered at those events which stirred us up and set us loose from ties of home and friends; and how we have marveled at the ruthlessness of those providences which sent us headlong from our assured places into the uncertainties of what seemed empty space around and beneath us. *But now we understand that every experience was in God's love and for the fulfillment of His high purposes toward us. No matter what happened, we soon saw His form and heard His heartening cry; and never did we grow weary but we immediately found that strong wings were beneath us. And oh, the wonder of it! when God brought us home to our resting-place beside Himself!* HENRY W. FROST

Unto Myself, my dear child, I would bring thee!
Who like Myself thy sure solace can be?
Who can reach down, down so deeply within thee?
Give to thy heart such a full sympathy?

Mournest thou sore that thy loved ones have failed thee?
Failed, sadly failed thy true comfort to be?
"Why did they fail" dost thou ask? Let Me whisper—
"That thou should'st find thy heart's comfort in Me."

Unto Myself! Ah, no not unto others,
Dearest, or sweetest, or fairest, or best;
Only in Me lieth unchanging solace;
Only in Me is thy promise of rest!

Child of My love, to Myself I would bring thee!
Not to some PLACE of most heavenly bliss:
Places, like people, may all disappoint thee,
Till thou hast learned to drink higher than this.

Unto Myself, my dear child, I would bring thee!
None like Myself thy full portion can be!
While, in my heart, there is hunger and longing
That I might find choicest treasure in thee.

Unto Myself! To Myself—not My service!
Then to most sweetly and certainly prove
That I can make thee My channel of blessing,
Use thee to shed forth the wealth of My love.

J. DANSON SMITH

August 24

Gideon threshed wheat.... And the angel of the LORD ... said unto him, The LORD is with thee. (Judg. 6:11–12)

More courage is required when coming to grips with the commonplace problems of the ordinary day than is required to face batteries of destruction on a field of military conflict.

It is much easier to follow on the track of the heroic than to remain true to Jesus in drab mean streets. Human nature unaided by God cannot do it.

The follower of Jesus is a laborer—but a laborer together with God. He is a man with a hoe—but one who has his part in the harvest whose reapers are the angels.

This is the place where Thou didst bid me stand;
And work and wait;
I thought it was a plot of fertile land,
To tend and cultivate:
Flowers and fruit, I said, are surely there,
In rich earth stored,
And I will make of it a garden fair,
For Thee, my Lord!

Lo! it is set where only bleak skies frown,
With rank weeds sown,
And over it the vagrant thistle-down
Like dust is blown;
Long have I labored, but the barren soil
No crop will yield:
This have I won for all my ceaseless toil—
A bare plowed field!

Nay, even here, where thou didst strive and weep,
Some sunny morn
Others shall come with joyous hearts and reap
The full-eared corn;
Yet is their harvest to thy labor due;
On Me 'twas spent—
Are not the furrows driven straight and true?
Be thou content!

A TILLER OF THE SOIL

August 25

Only believe. (Mark 5:36)

An old woman with an halo of silvered hair—the hot tears flowing down her furrowed cheeks—her worn hands busy over a washboard in a room of poverty—praying—for her son John—John who ran away from home in his teens to become a sailor—John, of whom it was now reported that he had become a very wicked man—*praying, praying always,* that her son might be of service to God.

What a marvelous subject for an artist's brush!

The mother believed in two things, the power of prayer and the reformation of her son. So while she scrubbed she continued to pray. God answered the prayer by working a miracle in the heart of *John Newton*. The black stains of sin were washed white in the blood of the Lamb. *"Though your sins be as scarlet, they shall be as white as snow."*

The washtub prayers were heard as are all prayers when asked in His name. John Newton, the drunken sailor, became John Newton, the sailor-preacher. Among the thousands of men and women he brought to Christ was *Thomas Scott,* cultured, selfish, and self-satisfied. Because of the washtub prayers another miracle was worked and Thomas Scott used both his pen and voice to lead thousands of unbelieving hearts to Christ—among them, a dyspeptic, melancholic young man, *William Cowper* by name.

He, too, was washed by the cleansing Blood and in a moment of inspiration wrote:

> *There is a fountain filled with blood*
> *Drawn from Immanuel's veins,*
> *And sinners, plunged beneath that flood,*
> *Lose all their guilty stains.*

And this song has brought countless thousands to the Man who died on Calvary. Among the thousands was *William Wilberforce,* who became a great Christian statesman, and unfastened the shackles from the feet of thousands of British slaves. Among those whom he led to the Lord was *Leigh Richmond,* a clergyman of the Established Church in one of the Channel Islands. He wrote a book, *The Dairyman's Daughter,* which was translated into forty languages and with the intensity of leaping flame burned the love of Christ into the hearts of thousands.

All this resulted because a mother *took God at His Word* and prayed that her son's heart might become as white as the soapsuds in the washtub.

August 26

And I will betroth thee unto me for ever. (Hos. 2:19)

"Rise up, My love, My fair one, and come away!" He calls. Away from Egypt's bondage—away ... *but with Him!* Divinely betrothed!

"My Beloved!" are the words. No other voice would have so aroused her. To *His* voice her heart responds. *Expectation quickens the hearing;* and

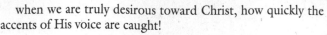

when we are truly desirous toward Christ, how quickly the accents of His voice are caught!

He said: "Wilt thou go with Me
Where shadows eclipse the light?"
And she answered: "My Lord, I will follow Thee
Far, under the stars at night."
But He said: "No starlight pierces the gloom
Of the valley thy feet must tread;
But it leads thee on to a cross and tomb—"
"But I go with Thee," she said.

"Count the cost; canst thou pay the price—
Be a dumb thing led;
Laid on an altar of sacrifice?"
"Bind me there, my Lord," she said.
"Bind me that I may not fail—
Or hold with Thy wounded hand;
For I fear the knife and the piercing nail,
And I shrink from the burning brand.
Yet whither Thou goest I will go,
Though the way be lone and dread—"
His voice was tender, and sweet, and low—
"Thou shalt go with Me," He said.

And none knew the anguish sore
Or the night of the way she came;
Alone, alone with the cross she bore,
Alone in her grief and shame.
Brought to the altar of sacrifice,
There as a dumb thing slain:
Was the guerdon more than the bitter price?
Was it worth the loss and pain?

Ask the seed-corn, when the grain
Ripples its ripened gold;
Ask the sower when, after toil and pain,
He garners the hundredfold.
He said (and His voice was glad and sweet):
"Was it worth the cost, My own?"
And she answered, low at His pierced feet,
"I found at the end of the pathway lone
NOT DEATH, BUT LIFE ON A THRONE!"

ANNIE CLARKE

253

August 27

Joseph said unto them ... Ye thought evil against me; but God meant it unto good, to bring to pass, as it is this day, to save much people alive. (Gen. 50:19–20)

It had been a long road for Joseph; it had been a desperately rough road, too. There was the slimy pit, the brothers' treachery, the slave chains, the terrible palace temptation, and the prison cell. But what a different ending this story has: "And Pharaoh said unto Joseph, See, I have set thee over all the land of Egypt. . . . only in the throne will I *be* greater than thou." And can you not hear Joseph speaking to his brethren: "God meant it unto good . . . to save much people alive."

A whole life committed to God in unswerving loyalty is held as a most sacred trust. The processes used in building a great soul are varied and consume much time. Many a long road seems to have no turning. Frequently "The night is dark and we seem to be far from home," but patience cries out, "Lead Thou me on," "Keep Thou my feet; I do not ask to see the distant scene—one step enough for me." *Faith, courage, and patience* are tremendous qualities in a great life, but *the time element* is the factor which is absolutely necessary to work all these out.

Blessed is that life which is so thoroughly rooted down into the life of God that it can feel and know that, though time moves slowly in long drawn-out tests and trials. God's tides move steadily on in accomplishing His glorious purposes. QUESTS AND CONQUESTS 🖝

> *O tarry thou His leisure,*
> *Praise when He seems to pause,*
> *Nor think that the Eternal One*
> *Will set His clock by yours;*
> *But wait His time, and trust His date,*
> *It cannot be too soon, or late!*

The turn on the long road comes at last!

August 28

Now Jesus loved Martha, and her sister, and Lazarus. (John 11:5)

Jesus does not want all His loved ones to be of one mold or color. He does not seek uniformity. He will not remove our individuality; He only seeks to glorify it. He loved *"Martha, and her sister, and Lazarus."*

"Jesus loved Martha." Martha is our biblical example of a practical woman; *"Martha served."* In that place is enshrined her character.

"And her sister." Mary was contemplative, *spending long hours in deep communion with the unseen.* We need the Marys as well as the Marthas— the deep contemplative souls, whose spirits shed a fragrant restfulness over the hard and busy streets. We need the souls who sit at Jesus' feet and listen to His Word, and then interpret the sweet Gospels to a tired and weary world.

"And Lazarus." What do we know about him? Nothing! *Lazarus seems to have been undistinguished and commonplace.* Yet Jesus loved him. What a huge multitude come under the category of "nobodies"! Their names are on the register of births, and on the register of deaths, and the space between is a great obscurity. Thank God for the commonplace people! They turn our houses into homes; they make life restful and sweet. Jesus loves the commonplace. Here then is a great, comforting thought: we are all loved—the brilliant and the commonplace, the dreamy and the practical.

"Jesus loved Martha, and her sister, and Lazarus." J. H. JOWETT

"Does the wildflower bloom less carefully and are the tints less perfect because it rises beside the fallen tree in the thick woods where mankind never enters? Let us not bemoan the fact that we are not great, and that the eyes of the world are not upon us."

> *Loved! then the way will not be drear,*
> *For One we know is ever near,*
> *Proving it to our hearts so clear*
> *That we are loved.*
>
> *Loved when we sing the glad new song*
> *To Christ, for whom we've waited long,*
> *With all the happy ransomed throng—*
> *Forever loved.*

August 29

Is not this the carpenter? (Mark 6:3)

This is my beloved Son, in whom I am well pleased. (Matt. 3:17)

Yes, yes, a carpenter, same trade as mine!
How it warms my heart as I read that line.
I can stand the hard work, I can stand the poor pay,
For I'll see that Carpenter at no distant day.
MALTBIE D. BABCOCK

It suits our best sense that the One who spoke of "putting the hand to the plow," and "taking the yoke upon us," should have made plows and yokes, Himself, and people do not think His words less heavenly for not smelling of books and lamps. Let us not make the mistake of those Nazarenes: *that Jesus was a carpenter* was to them poor credentials of divinity, but it has been *Divine credentials to the poor* ever since. Let us not be deceived by social ratings and badges of the schools.

Carey was a cobbler, but he had a map of the world on his shop wall, and outdid Alexander the Great in dreaming and doing.

What thoughts were in the mind of Jesus at His workbench? One of them was that the kingdoms of this world should become the kingdoms of God—*at any cost!* SELECTED

"What is that in thine *hand?"*

Is it a hoe, a needle, a broom? A pen or a sword? A ledger or a schoolbook? A typewriter or a telegraph instrument? Is it an anvil or a printer's rule? Is it a carpenter's plane or a plasterer's trowel? Is it a throttle or a helm? Is it a scalpel or a yardstick? Is it a musical instrument or the gift of song?

Whatever it is, give it to God in loving service.

Many a tinker and weaver and stonecutter and hard worker has had open windows and a sky, and a mind with wings!

August 30

Not disobedient. (Acts 26:19)

Whither, O Christ? The *vision did not say; nor did Paul ask, but started on the way.* If Paul had asked, and if the Lord had said; if Paul had known the long hard road ahead; if with the heavenly vision Paul had seen stark poverty with cold and hungry mien, black fetid prisons with their chains and stocks, fierce robbers lurking amid tumbled rocks, the raging of the mob, the crashing stones, the aching eyes, hot fever in the bones, perils of mountain passes wild and steep, perils of tempest in the angry deep, the drag of loneliness, the curse of lies, mad bigotry's suspicious peering eyes, the bitter foe, the weakly, blundering friend, the whirling sword of Caesar at the end—would Paul have turned his back with shuddering moan and settled down at Tarsus, had he known? No! and a thousand times the thundering No! *Where Jesus went, there Paul rejoiced to go.* Prisons were palaces where Jesus stayed; with Jesus near, he asked no other aid; the love of Jesus kept him glad and warm, bold before kings and safe in any storm. *Whither, O Christ? The vision did not say. Paul did not care. He started on the way.* AMOS R. WELLS

"A great *Must* dominated the life of the Son of Man. That *must* will dominate ours if we follow in His footsteps. The Son of Man *must*, and so His followers *must*."

> *Lord, I would follow, but—*
> *First I would see what means that wondrous call*
> *That peals so sweetly through life's rainbow hall,*
> *That thrills my heart with quivering golden chords,*
> *And fills my soul with joys seraphical.*
>
> *Lord, I would follow, but—*
> *First I would leave things straight before I go—*
> *Collect my dues, and pay the debts I owe:*
> *Lest when I'm gone, and none is here to tend,*
> *Time's ruthless hand my garnering o'erthrow.*
>
> *Lord, I would follow, but—*
> *First I would see the end of this high road*
> *That stretches straight before me fair and broad;*
> *So clear the way I cannot go astray,*
> *It surely leads me equally to God.*
>
> *Who answers Christ's insistent call*
> *Must give himself, his life, his all,*
> *Without one backward look.*
> *Who sets his hand upon the plow,*
> *And glances back with anxious brow,*
> *His calling hath mistook;*
> *Christ claims him wholly for His own;*
> *He must be Christ's and Christ's alone.*

SELECTED

The Spirit of God does not come with a voice like thunder (that may come ultimately) but as a gentle zephyr, yet it can only be described as an imperative compulsion—*This thing must be done!*

August 31

Thou shalt be above only, and thou shalt not be beneath. (Deut. 28:13)

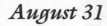

This verse came to me first as a very real message from God in a time of great pressure. We had fourteen guests in the Mission house and were almost without domestic help. I had, perforce, to lay aside correspondence and other duties and give my time and attention to cooking and housework, and was feeling the strain.

Then God's Word spoke to me with power: *"Thou shalt be above only, and thou shalt not be beneath,"* and in a moment I saw there was no need to go under—no need to be overwhelmed by my circumstances. No need to trouble because it seemed as if I could not get through and my ordinary work was getting in arrears—somehow, I could be above it all! *"Above only, and not beneath."* How often I used to say as I went about my kitchen, "I refuse to go down," and how the lesson I learned in those difficult days has been an inspiration ever since. Do you wonder that Deuteronomy 28:13 is one of my favorite verses in the Bible?

I see in it the possibility of a life of constant victory—not up today in heights of blessedness, and down in the depths tomorrow. This is a *steady* life. It is the life that has been established and settled by the God of all grace.

"Above only" is a *position* of victory, too. It is that position which is ours in Christ Jesus. "Quickened us together . . . in heavenly places in Christ Jesus" (Eph. 2:5–6). "Your life is hid with Christ in God" (Col. 3:3).

When we lived in Alexandria, Egypt, we used to see some fierce squalls of wind and rain, which lashed the sea into fury. The great buoys in the harbor would be covered with spray and foam, but when the wind died down again they were still there in their places, unmoved and steady. "Above only" for they had that within them which kept them on the top. And have we not *power* within us, too, which should insure our *triumph?*

Let us absolutely refuse to come down to live and work on a lower level. A MISSIONARY'S TESTIMONY

"Far above all."

September 1

The steps of a good man are ordered by the LORD. (Ps. 37:23)

We often make a great mistake thinking that God is not guiding us at all, because we cannot see far ahead. But He only undertakes that *the steps* of a good man should be ordered by the Lord; not next year, but tomorrow; not for the next mile, but the next yard: *as you will acknowledge when you review it from the hilltops of Glory.*

"The *stops* of a good man, as well as his *steps,* are ordered by the Lord," says George Müller. Naturally an opened door seems more like guidance to us than a closed one. *Yet God may guide by the latter as definitely as by the former.* His guidance of the children of Israel by the pillar of cloud and of fire is a clear case in point. When the cloud was lifted the Israelites took up their march: it was the guidance of God to move onward. But when the cloud tarried and abode upon the tabernacle, then the people rested in their tents. Both the tarrying and the journeying were guidance from the Lord— the one as much as the other.

I shall never be able to go too fast, if the Lord is in front of me; and I can never go too slowly, if I follow Him always, everywhere.

It is just as dark in advance of God's glorious leading as it is away behind Him.

You may be trying to go faster than He is moving. Wait till He comes up and then the way will no longer lie in darkness. He has left footprints for us to follow. *Make no footprints of thine own!*

> *Not so in haste, my heart!*
> *Have faith in God and wait:*
> *Although He linger long*
> *He never comes too late.*
>
> *Until He cometh, rest,*
> *Nor grudge the hours that roll,*
> *The feet that wait for God*
> *Are soonest at the goal*
>
> *Are soonest at the goal*
> *That is not gained by speed.*
> *Then hold thee still, my heart,*
> *For I shall wait His lead.*

BAYARD TAYLOR

Let the great Master's steps be thine!

September 2

When thou walkest through the fire, thou shalt not be burned.
(Isa. 43:2)

In giving a lecture on flame a scientist once made a most interesting experiment. He wanted to show that in the center of each flame there is a hollow—a place of entire stillness—around which its fire is a mere wall. To prove this he introduced into the midst of the flame a minute and carefully shielded charge of explosive powder. The protection was then carefully removed and no explosion followed. A second time the experiment was tried, and by a slight agitation of the hand the central security was lost and an immediate explosion was the result.

Our safety, then, is only in *stillness of soul.* If we are affrighted and exchange the principle of faith for that of fear, or if we are rebellious and restless, we shall be hurt by the flames and anguish and disappointment will be the result.

Moreover, God will be disappointed in us if we break down. Testing is the proof of His love and confidence, and who can tell what pleasure our steadfastness and stillness give to Him? If He allowed us to go without testing it would not be complimentary to our spiritual experience. Much trial and suffering mean, therefore, that God has confidence in us; that He believes we are strong enough to endure; that we shall be true to Him even when He has left us without outward evidence of His care and seemingly at the mercy of His adversaries. If He increase the trials instead of diminishing them it is an expression of confidence in us up to the present, and a further proof that He is looking to us to glorify Him in yet hotter fires through which He is calling us to pass. *Let us not be afraid! We shall be delivered from the transitory and the outward and drawn into closer fellowship with God Himself!*

O God, make us children of quietness! AN ANCIENT LITURGY

September 3

Employed to sing day and night. (1 Chron. 9:33, Trans.)

There is a legend of a man who found the barn where Satan kept his seeds ready to be sown in the human heart, and on finding the seeds of discouragement more numerous than others, learned that those seeds could be made to grow almost anywhere. When Satan was questioned he reluctantly admitted that there was one place in which he could never get them to thrive. "And where is that?" asked the man. Satan replied sadly, *"In the heart of a grateful man."*

The Psalmist realized that *gratitude* plays an essential part in true worship. He sang praises to God at all times; often, in his darkest moments. When in his despair he called on God, his praises soon mingled with his cries of anguish, showing the victory accomplished by his habitual thankfulness.

> Sometimes a light surprises
> The Christian while he sings.

Is it midnight in your experience? Is it an interminable time since the gold and crimson hope died out in the west—and a seemingly longer interval before the hoped-for dawning of day? *Midnight! Still, dark, and eerie! It is time to pray! and it is time to sing! Strange how prayer and singing open prison doors—but they do!*

Do *you* need doors to be opened? *Try prayer and singing; they go together! They work wonders!*

When the heaven is black with wind, the thunder crackling over our heads, then we may join in the paean of the Storm-spirits to Him whose pageant of power passes over the earth and harms us not in its march.

The choir of small birds, and night crickets, and all happy things, praise Him all the night long.

Not somehow *but* triumphantly!

September 4

He cometh forth like a flower. (Job 14:2)

The lotus flower (the spiritual symbol of the East) is rooted in the mud. It is quite as much indebted to the mud and water for its beauty as to the air and sunshine in which it blooms.

We must not scorn the study of root culture, nor neglect it in enthusiasm for the beauties of the orchid; for though that exquisite flower is an air plant, it needs to attach itself to a sturdier growth that is rooted in the ground and draws its nourishment from the soil to feed both itself and its parasite. *The tree will outlive many seasons of orchids!*

"Some time ago in the late autumn," says a writer, "I was in the hothouse of one of our florists. We were in the cellar, and in the dimly lighted place one could see arranged in regular file long rows of flowerpots. The florist explained that in these pots had been planted the bulbs for their winter flowers. It was best for them, he said, that they be rooted in the dark." Not in the glaring sunlight, but in the subdued shadows their life-giving roots were putting forth. They would be ready for the open day a little later. Then their gay colors would cheer many hearts; then their sweet perfume would laden the winter air.

Rooted in the shadows to bloom in the light!
Roots, then roses.

September 5

Then the fire of the LORD fell, and consumed the burnt sacrifice, and the wood, and the stones, and the dust, and licked up the water that was in the trench. (1 Kings 18:38)

Prayer is one of the most sacred and precious privileges vouchsafed to mortals. The following is a scene from the life of that mighty *Elijah in prayer,* Charles G. Finney.

The summer of 1853 was unusually hot and dry; pastures were scorched. There seemed likely to be a total crop failure. At the church in Oberlin the great congregation had gathered as usual. Though the sky was clear the burden of Finney's prayer was for rain.

"We do not presume, O Lord, to dictate to Thee what is best for us; yet Thou didst invite us to come to Thee as children to an earthly father and tell Thee all our wants. *We want rain.* Our pastures are dry. The earth is gaping open for rain. The cows are wandering about and lowing in search of water. Even the squirrels are suffering from thirst. Unless Thou givest us rain our cattle will die, and our harvest will come to naught. O Lord, *send us rain, and send it now!* This is an easy thing for Thee to do. *Send it now,* Lord, for Christ's sake."

In a few minutes he had to cease preaching; his voice could not be heard because of the roar and rattle of the rain! LIFE OF FINNEY

Life has outgrown
Faith's childish way,
The proud and scoffing

Folk insist;
And so they laugh
At all who say
God's miracles exist.

Well, let them laugh!
The trusting heart
Has joys which they
Know naught thereof.
And, daily, miracles are wrought
For us who hold
To faith and love!
MIRACLES, BY JOHN RICHARD MORELAND

The world wants something that has God in it!

September 6

Christ in you. (Col. 1:27)

It is a great secret I tell you today, nay, I can give you—if you will take it from *Him,* not from me—a secret which has been to me, oh, so wonderful! Many years ago I came to Him burdened with guilt and fear; I took that simple secret, and it took away my fear and sin. Years passed on, and I found sin overcame me, and my temptations were too strong for me. I came to Him a second time, and He whispered to me, *"Christ in you."* And I have had victory, rest and sweet blessing ever since. . . . I look back with unutterable gratitude to the lonely and sorrowful night, when, mistaken in many things, and imperfect in all, and not knowing but that it would be death in the most literal sense before the morning light, my heart's first full consecration was made, and, with unreserved surrender, I first could say,

Jesus, I my cross have taken,
All to leave and follow Thee:
Destitute, despised, forsaken,
Thou from hence my all shall be.

Never, perhaps, has my heart known such a thrill of joy as when, the following Sunday morning, I gave out these lines, and sang them with all my heart. And, if God has been pleased to use me in any fuller measure, it has been because of that hour. And it will be still, in the measure in which that hour is made the keynote of a consecrated, crucified, and Christ-devoted life. This experience of Christ our Sanctifier, marks a definite and distinct crisis in the history of a soul. We do not grow into it, but we cross a definite line of demarcation, as clear as when the hosts of Joshua crossed the Jordan and were over in the Promised Land, and set up a great heap of stones, so that they never could forget that crisis hour. A. B. SIMPSON ☞

September 7

The greatest of these is love. (1 Cor. 13:13 RSV)

❧

"I'll master it!" said the ax; and his blows fell heavily on the iron. And every blow made his edge more blunt till he ceased to strike.

"Leave it to me!" said the saw; and with his relentless teeth he worked backward and forward on its surface till his teeth were worn down and broken, and he fell aside.

"Ha, ha!" said the hammer. "I knew you wouldn't succeed! I'll show you the way!" But at the first fierce stroke off flew his head, and the iron remained as before.

"Shall I try?" asked the still, small flame.

They all despised the flame, but he curled gently around the iron and embraced it, and never left it till it melted under his irresistible influence.

Hard indeed is the heart that can resist love.

"And now abideth faith, hope, love ... the greatest of these is love."

September 8

I will not go away from thee. (Deut. 15:16)

Thy bondman forever. (Deut. 15:17 RSV, margin)

❧

No man ever makes *Him* supreme and suffers loss; for Jehovah will not be left in any man's debt. When a man holds on, God takes away; when a man lets go, He gives, and that liberally.

Make me a captive, Lord,
And then I shall be free.

Force me to render up my sword,
And I shall conqueror be.
I sink in life's alarm
When by myself I stand;
Imprison with Thy mighty arm,
Then strong shall be my hand.

My heart is weak and poor,
Until it Master finds;
It has no spring of action sure,
It varies with the wind.
It cannot freely move
Till Thou hast wrought its chain;
Enslave it with Thy mighty love,
Then deathless I shall reign.

My power is faint and low
Till I have learned to serve:
It wants the needed fire to glow,
It wants the breeze to nerve;
It cannot drive the world
Until itself be driven;
Its flag can only be unfurled
When Thou shalt breathe from heaven.

My will is not my own
Till Thou hast made it Thine;
If it would reach the monarch's throne
It must its crown resign.
It only stands unbent
Amid the clashing strife,
Till on Thy bosom it has leant,
And found in Thee its life.

GEORGE MATHESON

O Master, show me this morning how to yield myself up to Thee completely, and then how to ask of Thee things great enough to be *worthy of a King's giving.* Make me equal in my requests to Thy infinite eagerness to give.

Touch with Thy Pierced Hand the hidden springs that will cause every part of my being to fly wide open to Thee, my Lord and my God!

September 9

I know WHOM *I have trusted.* (2 Tim. 1:12, Trans.)

God loves an *uttermost confidence in Himself*—to be *wholly trusted*. This is the sublimest of all the characteristics of a true Christian—the basis of all character.

Is there anything that pleases you more than to be trusted—to have even a little child look up into your face, and put out its hand to meet yours, and come to you confidingly? By so much as God is better than you are, by so much more does He love to be trusted.

There is a Hand stretched out to you; a Hand with a wound in the palm of it. Reach out the hand of your faith to clasp it, and cling to it, for "without faith it is impossible to please God." HENRY VAN DYKE

Reach up as far as you can, and God will reach down all the rest of the way. BISHOP VINCENT

> *Not what, but WHOM I do believe!*
> *That, in my darkest hour of need,*
> *Hath comfort that no mortal creed*
> *To mortal man may give.*
> *Not what, but WHOM!*
> *For Christ is more than all the creeds,*
> *And His full life of gentle deeds*
> *Shall all the creeds outlive.*
> *Not what I do believe, but WHOM!*
> *WHO walks beside me in the gloom?*
> *WHO shares the burden wearisome?*
> *WHO all the dim way doth illume,*
> *And bids me look beyond the tomb*
> *The larger life to live?*
> *Not what I do believe, BUT WHOM!*
> *Not what,*
> *But WHOM!*

JOHN OXENHAM

September 10

Spread the sail. (Isa. 33:23)

Picture a vessel lying becalmed on a glassy sea—not a breath of air stirs a sail. But, presently, the little pennant far up on the masthead begins to stir and lift! There is not a ripple on the water; not the slightest movement of the air on deck, but there is a current stirring *in the upper air!* At once the sails are spread to catch it!

"So in life," says Dr. Miller, "there are higher and lower currents. Too many of us use only the lower sails, and catch only the winds blowing along earthly levels. It would be an unspeakable gain to us all were we to let our life fall under the influence of these upper currents."

Far out to sea, at close of day,
A lonely albatross flew by.
We watched him as he soared away—
A speck against the glowing sky!
Thought I: This lordly feathered one
Is trusting in the faithfulness
Of wind and tide, of star and sun;
And shall I trust the Maker less?

O soul of mine, spread wide thy wings:
Mount up; push out with courage strong!
And—like a bird which, soaring, sings—
Let heaven vibrate with thy song!
SPREAD WIDE THY WINGS, O SOUL OF MINE,
For God will ever faithful be:
His love shall guide thee; winds Divine
Shall waft thee o'er this troubled sea.

Though dangers threaten in the night,
Though tides of death below thee roll,
Though storms attend thy homeward flight,
SPREAD WIDE THY PINIONS, O MY SOUL!
Though shadows veil the verdant shore,
And distant seems the hallowed dawn,
Spread wide thy pinions—evermore
Spread wide thy pinions, and press on.

ROBERT CRUMLY

Spread your sails to catch the upper currents!

September 11

I do not fight with merely human weapons. No, the weapons with which I war are not weapons of mere flesh and blood, but, in the strength of the Lord, they are mighty enough to raze all strong-holds of our foes. I can batter down bulwarks of human reason; I can scale every crag-fortress that towers up bidding defiance

to the true knowledge of God. I can make each rebel purpose
my prisoner of war and bow it into submission to Messiah.
(2 Cor. 10:4–5, Way's trans.)

*He said not,
"Thou shalt not be
Tempested;
Thou shalt not be
Travailed;
Thou shalt not be
Afflicted":
But he said,
"Thou shalt not be
Overcome!"*

JULIAN OF NORWICK, a.d. 1373

We are not here to be overcome, but we are to rise unvanquished after
every knockout blow, *and laugh the laugh of faith—not fear.*

*Tempested on the sea of life;
Travailed sore, amid earth's strife;
Afflicted often, and sore dismayed;
Look up, faint heart, be not afraid,
Thou shalt not be overcome!*

*God's ways are far beyond our ken;
His thoughts are not the thoughts of men;
And He knoweth what is best for you.
Hope on, my friend, He will bear you through.
Thou shalt not be overcome!*

*Though "The reason why" we cannot see,
Our Father knows—'tis enough that we
But trust His love, when our eyes are dim.
Look up! Hold fast! though the fight is grim.
We shall not be overcome!*

MARY E. THOMPSON

September 12

*As he was going on his way, there ran one to him . . . and asked
him . . . What shall I do that I may inherit eternal life? . . . And*

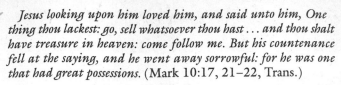

Jesus looking upon him loved him, and said unto him, One thing thou lackest: go, sell whatsoever thou hast . . . and thou shalt have treasure in heaven: come follow me. But his countenance fell at the saying, and he went away sorrowful: for he was one that had great possessions. (Mark 10:17, 21–22, Trans.)

Such was the preparation necessary before this admirable soul could become a disciple of Jesus Christ. To use the language of Dr. Donald Davidson:

"Strip yourself of every possession, cut away every affection, disengage yourself from all *things,* be as if you were a naked soul, alone in the world; be a mere man merely, and then be God's. *'Sell all that thou hast and follow Me!'* Reduce yourself down, if I may say so, till nothing remains but your consciousness of yourself, and then cast the self-consciousness at the feet of God in Christ.

"The only way to Jesus is ALONE. Will you strip yourself and separate yourself and take that lonely road, or will you too 'go away sorrowful'?"

> *We are not told his name—this "rich young ruler"*
> *Who sought the Lord that day;*
> *We only know that he had great possessions*
> *And that—he went away.*
>
> *He went away; he kept his earthly treasure*
> *But oh, at what a cost!*
> *Afraid to take the cross and lose his riches—*
> *And God and Heaven were lost.*
>
> *So for the tinsel bonds that held and drew him*
> *What honor he let slip—*
> *Comrade of John and Paul and friend of Jesus—*
> *What glorious fellowship!*
>
> *For they who left their all to follow Jesus*
> *Have found a deathless fame,*
> *On his immortal scroll of saints and martyrs*
> *God wrote each shining name.*
>
> *We should have read his there—the rich young ruler—*
> *If he had stayed that day;*
> *Nameless—though Jesus loved him—ever nameless*
> *Because—he went away.*

SELECTED

September 13

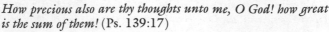

How precious also are thy thoughts unto me, O God! how great is the sum of them! (Ps. 139:17)

Nothing is more beautiful than our Lord's foresight!

There never was anyone so faithful or considerate or farseeing as Jesus. He had great commendation to give a woman, because she came "beforehand" with her ministry. It was His own manner to anticipate events. He was always thinking ahead of the disciples. When He sent His disciples to prepare the Passover, there was found an upper room furnished and prepared. He had thought it all out. His plans were not made only for that day. *He was always in advance of time.* When the disciples came back from fishing, Jesus was on the seashore with a fire of coals and fish laid thereon. He thinks of the morning duties before you are astir; He is there before you. He is waiting long before you are awake. His anticipations are all along the way of life before you.

After the Resurrection, the disciples were bewildered, and the way looked black. But the angel said, "Behold, he goeth *before you* into Galilee." He is always ahead, thinking ahead, preparing ahead. Take this text with you into the future, take it into today's experience: "Let not your heart be troubled, neither let it be afraid. . . . I go to prepare a place for you." He is out in the world doing it. *He* will be there *before* you. He will bring you to your appointed place, and you will find *your appointed resources.* You will discover *His insight, His oversight, and His foresight.* You may not always see Him, but you can walk by faith in the dark if you know that He sees you, and you can sing as you journey, even through the night. JOHN MACBEATH

We mean a lot to Someone;
And 'tis everything to me
That to God His wayward children
Were worth a Calvary.
It's the meaning of my Sunday,
And to Saturday from Monday
It is my hope that one day
My Savior I shall see.
Though the day be dark and dreary,
Here's comfort for the weary—

We mean a lot to Someone
Who died for you and me.
VALUE AND OTHER POEMS

September 14

Surely he shall deliver thee from the snare of the fowler. (Ps. 91:3)

The noblest souls are the most tempted. The devil is a sportsman and likes big game. He makes the deadliest assaults on the richest natures, the finest minds, the noblest spirits. JOHN L. LAWRENCE

> *Lord!—the fowler lays his net*
> *In Thine evening hour;*
> *When our souls are full of sleep—*
> *Void of full power . . .*
> *Look! The wild fowl sees him not*
> *As he lays it lower!*
>
> *Creeping round the water's edge*
> *In the dusk of day;*
> *Drops his net, just out of sight,*
> *Weighted lightly!—Stay!*
> *You can see him at his work . . .*
> *Fly to God!—And pray!*
>
> *Like the wild birds; knowing not*
> *Nets lie underneath!*
> *Gliding near the water's edge—*
> *"Fowler's snare" beneath—*
> *Little feet, caught in the net:*
> *Souls lie, near to death.*
>
> *But the promise still rings clear:*
> *"He delivers thee,"*
> *From the snare, however great*
> *He will set thee free.*
> *"Pluck my feet out of the net!"*
> *He delivers me.*
>
> *When Thou dost deliver, Lord,*
> *From the fowler's snare,*
> *Then—the glory is all Thine,*

Thou madest us aware,
And though it was stealthy-laid,
We saw it was there!

L. M. WARNER

Those who have the gale of Holy Spirit go forward even in sleep.
BROTHER LAWRENCE

September 15

I count all things but loss for the excellency of the knowledge of
Christ Jesus my Lord. (Phil. 3:8)

The Swedish Nightingale, Jennie Lind, won great success as an oper-
atic singer, and money poured into her purse. Yet she left the stage while
she was singing her best, and never returned to it. She must have missed
the money, the fame, and the applause of thousands, but she was content
to live in privacy.

Once an English friend found her sitting on the steps of a bathing
machine on the sea sands with a Bible on her knee, looking out into the
glory of a sunset. They talked, and the conversation drew near to the
inevitable question: "Oh, Madame Goldschmidt, how is it that you came
to abandon the stage at the very height of your success?"

"When every day," was the quiet answer, "it made me think less of this
(laying a finger on the Bible) and nothing at all of that (pointing to the sunset), what else could I do?"

May I not covet the world's greatness! It will cost me the crown
of life!

September 16

Having loved his own ... he loved them unto the end. (John
13:1)

Sadhu Sundar Singh passed a crowd of people putting out a jungle fire
at the foot of the Himalayas. Several men, however, were standing gazing
at a tree, the branches of which were already alight.

"What are you looking at?" he asked. They pointed to a nest of young birds in the tree. Above it a bird was flying wildly to and fro in great distress. The men said, "We wish we could save that tree, but the fire prevents us from getting near to it."

A few minutes later the nest caught fire. The Sadhu thought the mother bird would fly away. But no! she flew down, spread her wings over the young ones, and in a few minutes was burned to ashes with them.

> *Such love, such wondrous love,*
> *Such love, such wondrous love,*
> *That God should love a sinner such as I,*
> *How wonderful is love like this!*

Let us have love heated to the point of sacrifice.

September 17

Even as Christ forgave you, so also do ye. (Col. 3:13)

A custom way out in the African bush which has no equivalent in this part of the world is *"Forgiveness Week."* Fixed in the dry season, when the weather itself is smiling, this is a week when every man and woman pledges himself or herself to forgive any neighbor any wrong, real or fancied, that may be a cause for misunderstanding, coldness, or quarrel between the parties.

It is, of course, a part of our religion that a man should forgive his brother. But among recent converts, and even older brethren, this great tenet is, perhaps naturally, apt to be forgotten or overlooked in the heat and burden of work. *"Forgiveness Week"* brings it forcibly to mind. The week itself terminates with a festival of happiness and rejoicing among the native Christians.

Is it too much to suggest that in this *supposedly more civilized portion of the world* a similar week might be instituted?

> *Nothing between, Lord—nothing between;*
> *Shine with unclouded ray,*
> *Chasing each mist away,*
> *O'er my whole heart hold sway—*
> *Nothing between.*

Let grudges die "like cloudspots in the dawn!"

When God forgives, He forgets!

September 18

Nevertheless, afterward. (Heb. 12:11)

It is not a bit of good struggling for the premature unfolding of the Divine mystery. The revelation awaits our arrival at a certain place in the road, and when *Time* brings us to that place, and we enter into its experiences, we shall find, to our delighted surprise, that it has become luminous.

And so the only thing we need to be concerned about is to be on the King's high road, stepping out in accordance with His most holy will.

"Light is sown for the righteous."

It is the end which justifies all and explains all. It is to the ultimate goal that God's eye is ever turning. At the right moment the shining harvest will appear! What though the seed may seem to perish in the dark cold ground! What will that matter when the blade bursts forth, and the ear unfolds, and the full corn waves over the golden harvest field?

Luther was once in earnest prayer over some matter of great moment, desiring to know the mind of God in it; and it seemed as though he heard God say to him, "I am not to be traced."

If God is not to be traced, He is to be trusted.

"After these things Jesus manifested Himself."

However dark the *nows* may be in your experience, the *afters* of God are worth waiting for!

As we think of God's dealings with His children we are impressed with *His leisureliness.* God's ways may be hidden, but

Wait for God's Afters!

September 19

Them that are quiet in the land. (Ps. 35:20)

We are to enter into God's chamber, and hide there, and *be still.* Then God will call us the *"quiet in the land."* Have this stamp upon you. Be quiet outside—you will then be quiet inside. Be quiet in spirit. Beware of soul activities. The dross must be burned out to have the mountain vision. We

274

must get back to *God only,* and cease to see the human instruments. Hide deeper in God. *He* must be *real*—more and more real!

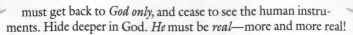

> *Hide with Christ in God at the Throne;*
> *Be at the Spring of things!*

"In quietness and in confidence *shall be* your strength." Set yourself to move everything through God, not man. *Go direct to Him. Every step with God* "in quietness and in confidence" *gives you absolute Victory over everything!*

> *Keep in step with God.*

Get quiet, beloved soul; tell out thy sorrow and complaint to God. Let not the greatest pressure of business divert thee from God. When men rage about thee, go and tell Jesus. Hide thee in His secret place when storms are high.

Get into thy closet, shut thy door, and quiet thyself as a weaned babe. But if thy voice is quiet *to* man, let it never cease to speak loudly and mightily *for* man.

We need to be quiet to get the ear of God!

> *'Mid all the traffic of the ways,*
> *Turmoils without, within,*
> *Make in my heart a quiet place,*
> *And come and dwell therein!*

> *A little shrine of quietness,*
> *All sacred to Thyself,*
> *Where Thou shalt all my soul possess,*
> *And I may find myself!*

> JOHN OXENHAM

Pascal said: "One-half of the ills of life come because men are unwilling to sit down quietly for thirty minutes to think through all the possible consequences of their acts."

September 20

Shall the thing formed say to him that formed it, Why hast thou made me thus? (Rom. 9:20)

A piece of wood once bitterly complained because it was being cut and filled with rifts and holes; but he who held the wood and whose knife was cutting into it so remorselessly did not listen to the sore complaining. He was making a flute out of the wood he held, and was too wise to desist when entreated to do so. He said:

"Oh, thou foolish piece of wood, without these rifts and holes thou wouldst be only a mere stick forever—a bit of hard black ebony with no power to make music or to be of any use. These rifts that I am making, which seem to be destroying thee, will change thee into a flute, and thy sweet music then shall charm the souls of men. My cutting thee is the making of thee, for then thou shalt be precious and valuable, and a blessing in the world."

David could never have sung his sweetest songs had he not been sorely afflicted. His afflictions made his life an instrument on which God could breathe the music of His love to charm and soothe the hearts of men.

We are but organs mute till a Master touches the keys—
Verily, vessels of earth into which God poureth the wine;
Harps are we—silent harps that have hung in the willow trees,
Dumb till our heartstrings swell and break with a pulse Divine.

Not till the life is broken is it ready for the Master's use.

September 21

That ye present your bodies. (Rom. 12:1)

Lend Me *thy body,* our Lord says. For a few brief years, in the body that was prepared for Me I delighted to do My Father's will. By means of that body I came into contact with the children of men—diseased, weary, sinsick, heavy-laden ones. Those feet carried Me to the homes where sorrow and death had entered; those hands touched leprous bodies, palsied limbs, sightless eyes; those lips told of My Father's remedy for sin, His love for a prodigal world. In that body I bore the world's sin upon the tree, and through its offering once for all My followers are sanctified.

But I need a body still; *wilt thou not lend Me thine? Millions of hearts are longing,* with an indescribable hunger, *for Me.* On that far-off shore are men, women, and little children sitting in darkness and in the shadow of death—men who have never yet heard of My love. *Wilt thou not lend Me thy body,* that I may cross the ocean and tell them that the light after which they are groping has at last reached them; that the bread for which they have so often hungered is now at their very door?

I want a heart, that I may fill it with Divine compassion;
and lips, purged from all uncleanness, wherewith to tell the story
that brings hope to the despairing, freedom to the bound, healing to the
diseased, and life to the dead. *Wilt thou lend Me thine?*
Wilt thou not lend Me thy body? J. GREGORY MANTLE

All that we own is Thine alone,
A trust, O Lord, from Thee.

September 22

Himself took our infirmities. (Matt. 8:17)

I think perhaps the greatest of all hindrances in our getting hold of
God for our bodies is the lack of *knowing Him,* for after all, in its *deepest
essence* Divine healing is not a *thing;* it is not an *experience;* it is not an *"it."*
It is the *revelation of Jesus Christ* as a living, almighty *Person,* and then the
union of this living Christ with your *body,* so that there becomes a tie, a
bond, *a living link* by which His life keeps flowing into yours, and because
He lives you shall *live* also. This is so very real to me that I groan in spirit
for those who do not know Him in this blessed union, and I wonder sometimes why He has let me know Him in this gracious manner. There is not
an hour of the day or night that I am not conscious of *Someone* who is
closer to me than my heart or my brain. I know that *He is living in me,* and
it is the continual inflowing of *the life of Another.* If I had not that I could
not live. My old constitutional strength gave out long, long ago, but Someone breathed in me gently, with no violence, no strange thrills, but just His
wholesome *life.* A. B. SIMPSON

I remember how once I was taken suddenly and seriously ill alone in
my study. I dropped upon my knees and cried to God for help. Instantly
all pain left me and I was perfectly well. It seems as if God stood right there,
and had put out His hand and touched me. The joy of healing was not so
great as the joy of meeting God. R. A. TORREY

She only touched the hem of His garment,
As to His side she stole,
Amid the throng that had gathered around Him
And straightway she was whole.

Oh, touch the hem of His garment,
And thou, too, shall be free;

His healing power this very hour,
Will bring new life to thee.

"Jesus . . . the same yesterday, and today, and for ever."

September 23

Job . . . perfect and upright, and one that feared God, and eschewed evil. (Job 1:1)

Such was Job's character as given by God. He asked Satan, "Hast thou considered my servant Job, that there is none like him in the earth?" Satan, in reply, says in effect, "Strip him, and he will curse Thee to Thy face." Satan sought Job's fall; God sought his blessing. Satan gets leave from God to strip Job. With malignant energy he sets to work, and in one day he brings the greatest man in all the East into abject poverty and visits him with sore bereavement. Blow after blow of such a crushing nature and with such rapidity falls upon Job, that one marvels at the testimony of the Holy Ghost that: "In all this did not Job sin with his lips." *What a triumph for God! What a defeat for Satan!*

"But these strange ashes, Lord? This nothingness,
This baffling sense of loss?"
"Son, was the anguish of My stripping less
Upon the torturing Cross?

"Was I not brought into the dust of death,
A worm, and no man I;
Yea, turned to ashes by the vehement breath
Of fire, on Calvary?

"O Son beloved, this is thy heart's desire:
This and no other thing
Follows the fall of the consuming fire
On the burnt offering.

"Go on and taste the joy set high afar,
No joy like that for thee;
See how it lights thy way like some great star!
Come now, and follow Me!"

A. W. C.

September 24

Every branch in me that beareth not fruit he taketh away: and every branch that beareth fruit, he purgeth it, that it may bring forth more fruit. (John 15:2)

"Only a little more cutting." How strange the words sounded; and then I heard the ring of the gardener's ax as he cut away at the lilac bushes. They were very close to the windows and kept out the sunlight and air; more, they obstructed the view. We watched the process and as one bush after another fell, one remarked: "Only a little more cutting and we shall get it. These lilac bushes actually shut out the view of the White Mountains!"

I was glad the gardener did the cutting that day, for so much was brought out by the absence of the bushes and suggested by the exclamations that followed: "How lovely that little tree is! I did not see it before!" "What a beautiful evergreen that is! I never noticed it until now!" Have we not heard similar exclamations after severe cuttings and removals in our lives? Have we not said: "I never loved God so much as I have since He took my little one!" "I never saw the beauty of such and such a Scripture until now!"

Ah, He knows! Only trust Him. We shall see it all in the clear light sometime.

> *God is a zealous Pruner,*
> *For He knows*
> *Who, falsely tender, spares the knife*
> *But spoils the rose.*
> THE PRUNER, BY JOHN OXENHAM 🍃

Give me the courage to submit to the surgery of Thy Spirit. Give me the bravery to part with what I hold most dear if it separates me from Thee. Through Christ, I pray!

September 25

My glory was fresh in me. (Job 29:20)

It was when Job's glory was fresh in him that his "bow was renewed" in his hand. Freshness and glory! And yet, the brilliant music of these words is brought down to *a minor strain* by the little touch "it *was*"—not it *is.*

"All my fresh springs are *in Thee.*"

If our glory is to be fresh in us, it all depends upon what the glory in us *is!* There is only one unfailing source—*Christ Himself!* He is "*in you,* the hope of glory," if you have admitted Him; and He *is* your glory. Then you may sing, "My glory *is* fresh in me."

Jesus Christ is *always fresh!*

And so is the oil with which He anoints us. "I *shall be* anointed with *fresh oil.*" Fresh oil of joy! Fresh oil of consecration! Fresh oil upon the sacrifice as we offer to God continually "*the fruit of our lips* giving thanks to his name."

> *My heart is parched by unbelief,*
> *My spirit sere from inward strife;*
> *The heavens above are turned to brass,*
> *Arid and fruitless is my life.*
>
> *Then falls Thy rain, O Holy One;*
> *Fresh is the earth, and young once more;*
> *Then falls Thy Spirit on my heart;*
> *My life is green; the drought is o'er!*
>
> DROUGHT, BY BETTY BRUECHERT

A desert road? when the Christian has ever at his command

> *Fresh springs! Fresh oil! Fresh glory!*

September 26

And the famine was sore.... They had eaten up the corn which they had.... Except we had lingered, surely now we had returned.... And they took double money in their hand, and Benjamin; and rose up, and went. (Gen. 43:1–2, 10, 15)

Praise God for the famine in our life, that drives us in utter helplessness back to Him! Praise Him that what we have gets eaten up, and we must turn to Him for more! But how like unto the faltering, fearful family of Israel we act! We could find absolute relief, sufficiency, satisfaction in Jesus Christ;

yet we delay, debate, wonder, waste time, and *stay hungry.*
When finally in desperation we are driven to Him we think we must
do some great thing to meet His terms, and we try to carry "double
money" in all sorts of ways, to make sure of *what He is yearningly waiting
to give us.* He *does ask* us for one thing, and one only: and that is the dearest possession of our lives. With Israel's family the dearest possession was
Benjamin. When we lay down our dearest possession, then the treasures
of the kingdom are flung open to us and lavished into our life. MESSAGES
FOR THE MORNING WATCH 🐚

*A drying well will often lead the spirit to the river that flows from
the throne of God.*

September 27

Will give you . . . as he hath promised. (Ex. 12:25)

God is to be trusted for *what He is,* and not for *what He is not.* We may
confidently expect Him to act according to His nature, but never contrary
to it. To *dream* that God will do this and that because we wish that He
would *is not faith, but fanaticism. Faith can only stand upon truth.* We may
be sure that God will so act as to honor His own justice, mercy, wisdom,
power—in a word, so as to be Himself. Beyond all doubt He will fulfill His
promises; and *when faith grasps a promise she is on sure ground.* To believe
that God will give us *what He has never promised to give is mere dreaming.
Faith without a promise revealed or implied is folly.* Yea, though our trust
should cry itself hoarse in prayer, it should be nonetheless a vain dotard if
it had no word of God to warrant it. Happily, the promises and unveilings
of Scripture are ample for every real emergency; but when unrestrained cre-
dence catches at every whim of its own crazy imagination and thinks to see
it realized, the disappointment is not to be wondered at.
It is ours to believe the sure things of God's revelation, but we are not to
waste a grain of precious reliance upon anything outside of that circle.
CHARLES H. SPURGEON 🐚
"Faith does not mean that we are trying to believe something that is
not so; *it just means that we are taking God at His Word.*"

> *Faith is a thread*
> *Slender and frail,*
> *Easy to tear;*

Yet it can lift
The weight of a soul
Up from despair.

MATTHEW BILLER

September 28

Keep thyself pure. (1 Tim. 5:22)

Does the judge know the story of the spotless fur that lines his robes of State? Does the society leader realize the sacrifice which makes possible the lovely ermine wrap which lies so gracefully about her shoulders? Do they know that the little animal whose coat they now wear, as he roamed the forest of Asia was as proud as they—aye, inordinately proud of his beautiful snowy coat? And we do not wonder, for it is the most beautiful fur to be found in all the markets of the world!

Such pride does the little carnivore take in his spotless coat, that nothing is permitted to soil it in the slightest degree. Hunters are well acquainted with this fact and take very unsportsmanlike advantage of this knowledge. No traps are set for him. No, indeed! Instead, they seek out his home—a tree stump, or rocky cleft, and then—be it said to their everlasting shame, they daub filth within and around the entrance. As the dogs are loosed and the chase begins the little animal naturally turns to his one place of refuge. Reaching it, rather than enter such a place of uncleanness, he turns to face the yelping dogs.

Better to be stained by blood than sully his white coat!

Only a white *coat*, little ermine, but how your act condemns *us! "Made in the image and likeness of God," with minds and immortal spirits;* and yet, how often in order to obtain something we desire, our character is sacrificed on the altars of worldly pleasure, greed, selfishness!

Everything is lost when purity is gone—purity, which has been called *the soul of character.* Keep thyself pure: *every thought, every word, every deed, even the motive behind the deed*—all, ermine-pure.

I ask this gift of thee—
A life all lily fair,
And fragrant as the garden be
Where seraphs are.

September 29

And they shall be mine ... in that day when I make up my jewels. (Mal. 3:17)

Christ died that He might make us a "peculiar people." A great many Christians are afraid that they *will* be peculiar. A few weeks before Enoch was translated his acquaintances would probably have said that he was a little peculiar; they would have told you that when they had a Bridge Party and the whole countryside were invited, you would not find Enoch or one of his family present. He was very peculiar, very.

We are not told that he was a great warrior or a great scientist or a great scholar. In fact, we are not told that he was anything that the world would call great, but he walked with God three hundred and sixty-five years, and he is the brightest star that shone in that dispensation.

If he could walk with God, cannot you and I? He took a long walk one day, and has not come back as yet. The Lord liked his company so well that He said, "Enoch, come up higher."

I suppose that if we asked the men in Elijah's time what kind of a man he was, they would have said, *"He is very peculiar."* The King would have said, "I hate him." Jezebel did not like him; the whole royal court did not like him and a great number of the nominal Christians did not like him; he was too radical.

I am glad that the Lord had seven thousand that had not bowed the knee to Baal; but I would rather have Elijah's little finger than the whole seven thousand. I would not give much for seven thousand Christians in hiding. They will just barely get into heaven; they will not have crowns.

See that *"no man take thy crown."* Be willing to be one of Christ's peculiar people, no matter what men may say of you! D. L. MOODY

September 30

Why art thou cast down, O my soul? (Ps. 43:5)

The other evening I found myself staggering alone under a load that was heavy enough to crush half a dozen strong men. Out of sheer exhaustion I put it down and had a good look at it. I found that it was all borrowed; part of it belonged to the following day; part of it belonged to the following week—and here was I borrowing it that it might crush me *now!* It is a very stupid, but a very ancient blunder. F. W. BOREHAM ☞

You and I are to take our trials, our black Fridays, our lone and long nights, and we are to come to Him and say, "Manage these, Thou Wondrous Friend who canst turn the very night into the morning; *manage these for me!*"

> *Sparrow, He guardeth thee;*
> *Never a flight but thy wings He upholdeth;*
> *Never a night but thy nest He enfoldeth;*
> *Safely He guardeth thee.*
>
> *Lily, He robeth thee;*
> *Though thou must fade, by the Summer bemoaned,*
> *Thou art arrayed fair as monarch enthroned;*
> *Spotless He robeth thee.*
>
> *Hear, thou of little faith;*
> *Sparrow and lily are soulless and dying;*
> *Deathless art thou; will He slight thy faint crying?*
> *Trust, thou of little faith!*

R. G. W. ☞

October 1

Lest I should be exalted above measure . . . there was given to me a thorn. (2 Cor. 12:7)

Flowers there are all along life's way; but the thorns are rife also.
"When the thorns of life have pierced us till we bleed,"
where but to heaven shall we look? To whom shall we go but to Him—the Christ who cures? He was crowned with thorns. He alone can transform our testing, torturing thorns into triumphal experiences of grace and glory. B. McCALL BARBOUR ☞

Your path is thorny and rough? Tramp it! You will find wherever you set your foot upon a thorn, *Another Foot* has been there before and taken off the sharpness. THE MORNING MESSAGE ☞

> *Strange gift indeed!—a thorn to prick,*
> *To pierce into the very quick;*
> *To cause perpetual sense of pain;*
> *Strange gift!—and yet, 'twas given for gain.*

Unwelcome, yet it came to stay;
Nor could it e'en be prayed away.
It came to fill its God-planned place,
A life-enriching means of grace.

God's grace-thorns—ah, what forms they take;
What piercing, smarting pain they make!
And yet, each one in love is sent,
And always just for blessing meant.

And so, whate'er thy thorn may be,
From God accept it willingly;
But reckon Christ—His life—the power
To keep, in thy most trying hour.

And sure—thy life will richer grow;
He grace sufficient will bestow;
And in Heav'n's morn thy joy 'twill be
That, by His thorn, He strengthened thee.

J. DANSON SMITH

October 2

They shall not be ashamed that wait for me. (Isa. 49:23)

"They shall not be ashamed that wait for me." Such is the veritable record of the living God—a record made good in the experience of all those who have been enabled, through grace, to exercise a living faith. We must remember how much is involved in these three words— *"wait for me."* The waiting must be a real thing. It will not do to *say* we are waiting on God, when in reality, our eye is askance upon some human prop. We must absolutely be "shut up" to God. We must be brought to *the end of self* and to *the bottom of circumstance,* in order fully to prove what *God's resources* are. "My soul, wait thou only upon God."

Thus it was with Jehoshaphat, in that scene recorded in 2 Chronicles 20. *He was wholly wrecked upon God; it* was either *God or nothing.* "We have no might." But what then? "Our eyes are upon thee." This was enough. Jehoshaphat was in the very best attitude and condition to prove what God was. To have been possessed of creature strength or creature wisdom would only have proved a hindrance to him in leaning exclusively upon the arm and the counsel of the Almighty God. THINGS NEW AND OLD

*When you feel at the end of your tether, remember
God is at the other end!*

October 3

*And we know that all things work together for good to them that
love God, to them who are the called according to his purpose.*
(Rom. 8:28)

The poet Cowper was subject to fits of depression. One day he ordered
a cab, and told the driver to take him to London Bridge. Soon a dense fog
settled down upon the city. The cabby wandered about for two hours, and
then admitted he was lost. Cowper asked him if he thought he could find
the way home. The cabby thought that he could, and in another hour
landed him at his door. When Cowper asked what the fare would be the
driver felt that he should not take anything since he had not gotten his fare
to his destination. Cowper insisted, saying, *"Never mind that, you have
saved my life. I was on my way to throw myself off London Bridge."* He then
went into the house and wrote:

> *God moves in a mysterious way*
> *His wonders to perform;*
> *He plants His footsteps on the sea,*
> *And rides upon the storm.*

The plans at the chapel went wrong; the minister was snowed up. The
plans of the boy under the gallery went wrong; the snowstorm shut him
off from the church of his choice. *Those two wrongs together made a tremendous right, for out of those shattered plans and programs came an event that
has incalculably enriched mankind—Spurgeon's conversion.*

An old Chinese, a very old man named Sai, had only one son and one
horse. Once the horse ran away and Sai was very worried. Only one horse
and lost! Someone said, *"Don't suffer, wait a little."* The horse came back.
Not long after this the only son went out to the field riding the horse.
Returning home he fell from the horse and broke his leg. What a sorrow
had poor Sai then! He could not eat; he could not sleep; he could not even
attend well to the wants of his son. Only one son and crippled! But someone said, *"More patience, Sai!"* Soon after the accident a war broke out.
All the young men went to the war; none of them returned. *Only Sai's son,
the cripple, stayed at home, and remained to live long to his father's joy.* CHI-
NESE LEGEND

October 4

God hath chosen the weak things of the world ... to bring to nought things that are: That no flesh should glory in his presence. (1 Cor. 1:27–29)

Only a blast of rams' horns and a shout—and God made the walls of proud Jericho crumble to their foundations, and the key of all Canaan was in the hand of Israel! (Josh. 6)

Only two women—one, Deborah, inspired courage in the fainting hearts of Israel's men—the other, Jael, with a hammer and nail laid Israel's master low; thus the end came to twenty years of mighty oppression! (Judg. 4 and 5)

Only an ox goad—but with it six hundred Philistines were slain, and Israel delivered by Shamgar's God! (Judg. 3:31)

Only a trumpet blast, the smash of a lighted pitcher, a shout—but by these, and Gideon, God delivered Israel from the seven-year yoke of the Midianites! (Judg. 6, 7, 8)

Only the jawbone of an ass—yet heaps of Philistines fell before it, because God strengthened the arm that wielded it! (Judg. 15)

Only a sling, and a stone sent with unerring precision and directed by Almighty God—and that day Israel's mighty men were put to shame: the giant Philistine was slain, and God's honor was vindicated! (1 Sam. 17)

Only a few ignorant, yet wholehearted and consecrated men and women; but by the power of God they were to put men in possession of that Eternal Salvation which would transform its possessors into the likeness of the Son Himself, and ultimately land them in Eternal Glory!

If you are one of the base, foolish, weak ciphers of this world, *then the very same power, from the very same Lord, for the very same purpose, will be yours!* W. T.

Under the control of God ordinary instruments become extraordinary.

October 5

Not hidden from the Almighty. (Job 24:1)

Thy Savior is near thee, suffering, lonely, tempted friend! *Thou art not the plaything of wild chance. There is a purpose in thy life which Jesus is working out.* Let thy spirit flee for rest to Christ, and to His pierced hand which opens the book of thy life! Rest thee there! Be patient and trustful! All will work out right. Someday thou wilt understand. In the meantime, trust Him "though sun and moon fail, and the stars drop into the dark."

What though the way may be lonely,
And dark the shadows fall;
I know where'er it leadeth,
My Father planned it all.

The sun may shine tomorrow,
The shadows break and flee;
'Twill be the way He chooses,
The Father's plan for me.

He guides my halting footsteps
Along the weary way,
For well He knows the pathway
Will lead to endless day.

A day of light and gladness,
On which no shade will fall,
'Tis this at last awaits me—
My Father planned it all.

I sing through shade and sunshine,
And trust what'er befall;
His way is best—it leads to rest;
My Father planned it all.

"God is working out His purpose."

October 6

He that loseth his life for my sake shall find it. (Matt. 10:39)

In my early life I entered into a partnership with a friend in the whole-sale ice business. For two seasons in succession our ice was swept away by winter freshets. In the winter of which I speak, things had come to a serious pass and it seemed very necessary that we should have ice. The weather became very cold; the ice formed and grew thicker and thicker until it was

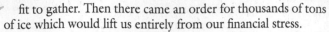

fit to gather. Then there came an order for thousands of tons of ice which would lift us entirely from our financial stress.

Not long before this, God had showed me that it was His will that I should commit my business to Him and trust Him with it absolutely. I never dreamed what testing was coming. At midnight there came an ominous sound—that of rain. By noon the storm was raging in all its violence; by afternoon I had come into a great spiritual crisis in my life.

I have learned this: *a matter may be seemingly trivial, but the crisis that turns upon a small matter may be a profound and far-reaching one in our lives.*

By midafternoon of that day I had come face to face with the tremendous fact that *down deep in my heart was a spirit of rebellion against God.* And that rebelliousness seemed to develop in a suggestion to my heart like this: "You gave all to God. This is the way He requites you." Then another voice: "My child, *did you mean it when you said you would trust Me? Would I suffer anything to come into your life which will not work out for good for you?"* And then the other voice: "But it is hard! Why should He take your business when it is clean and honest?"

At the end of two hours (during which waged one of the greatest spiritual battles of my life) by the grace of God I was able to cry out, "Take the business; take the ice; take everything; only give me the supreme blessing of a will absolutely submitted to Thee." *And then came peace!*

By midnight there came another sound—that of wind. By morning the mercury had fallen to zero, and in a few days we were harvesting the finest ice we ever had. He gave back the ice; He blessed the business; and He led me on and out, until He guided me from it entirely into the place He had for me from the beginning—that of a teacher of His Word. JAMES H. McCONKEY ☙

Give your life to God, and God will give you back your life!

October 7

The LORD is my shepherd. (Ps. 23:1)

The great Father above is a Shepherd Chief. I am His and with Him. I want not. He throws out to me a rope, and the name of the rope is love, and He draws me to where the grass is green and the water is not dangerous.

Sometimes my heart is very weak, and falls down, but He lifts it up again and draws me into a good road.

Sometime, it may be very soon, it may be longer, it may be a long, long time, He will draw me into a place between mountains. It is dark there, but I'll draw back not. I'll be afraid not, for it is in there between the mountains that the Shepherd Chief will meet me, and the hunger I have felt in my heart all through this life will be satisfied. Sometimes He makes the love rope into a whip, but afterwards He gives me a staff to lean on.

He spreads a table before me with all kinds of food. He puts His hands upon my head, and all the "tired" is gone.

My cup He fills, till it runs over.

What I tell you is true, I lie not. The roads that are "away ahead" will stay with me through this life, and afterwards I will go to live in the "Big Tepee" and sit down with the Shepherd Chief forever. AN AMERICAN INDIAN'S VERSION OF THE TWENTY-THIRD PSALM ✍

Fear not, little flock, He goeth ahead,
Your Shepherd selecteth the path you must tread;
The water of Marah He'll sweeten for thee,
He drank all the bitter in Gethsemane.

Fear not, little flock, whatever your lot,
He enters all rooms, "The doors being shut";
He never forsakes; He never is gone,
So count on His presence in darkness and dawn.

PAUL RADER ✍

October 8

Restore such an one in the spirit of meekness . . . lest thou also be tempted. (Gal. 6:1)

From the converts in Uganda
Comes to us a story grander,
In the lesson that it teaches,
Than a sermon often preaches.
For they tell what sore temptations
Come to them; what need of patience,
And a need, all else outweighing,
Of a place for private praying.
So each convert chose a corner

Far away from eye of scorner,
In the jungle, where he could
Pray to God in solitude.
And so often went he thither,
That the grass would fade and wither
Where he trod and you could trace
By the paths, each prayer place.

If they hear the evil tiding
That a brother is backsliding,
And that some are even saying,
"He no longer cares for praying,"
Then they say to one another,
Very soft and gently, "Brother,
You'll forgive us now for showing,
On your path the grass is growing."
And the erring one, relenting,
Soon is bitterly repenting:
"Ah, how sad I am at knowing
On my path the grass is growing.
But it shall be so no longer;
Prayer I need to make me stronger;
On my path so oft I'm going,
Soon no grass will there be growing."

GRASS ON THE PRAYER PATH 🦋

Have a trysting place with God!
And keep a little path open!

October 9

And Abraham built an altar there ... and took the knife to slay
his son. And the angel of the LORD called unto him ... Lay not
thine hand upon the lad. (Gen. 22:9–12)

Our hardest sacrifices are never so hard as we thought they were going to be, *if we go on with them to the uttermost that God asks.* A sacrifice of self to God's will made halfway, *or even nine-tenths, is a grinding, cruel experience.* When it is made the *whole* way, with the altar built and self laid upon the altar, God always *comes with an unexpected blessing that so overwhelms us with love and joy that the hardship of the sacrifice sinks out of sight.* "Now

I know that thou fearest God, seeing thou hast not withheld."
Can He say that to *us* today? No one ever knows the full joy of hearing the word from God until the altar has been built, and the knife is laid to the sacrifice. Messages for the Morning Watch ☞

Is your all on the altar of sacrifice laid?
Your heart, does the Spirit control?
You can only be blest and have peace and sweet rest
As you yield Him your body and soul.

October 10

They held their lives cheap. (Rev. 12:11 WEYMOUTH)

The persecution of the Christians during the reign of Marcus Aurelius was very bitter. The Emperor himself decreed the punishment of forty of the men who had refused to bow down to his image.

"Strip to the skin!" he commanded. They did so. "Now, go and stand on that frozen lake," he commanded, "until you are prepared to abandon your Nazarene-God!"

And forty naked men marched out into that howling storm on a winter's night. As they took their places on the ice they lifted up their voices and sang:

"Christ, forty wrestlers have come out to wrestle for Thee; to win for Thee the victory; to win from Thee the crown."

After a while, those standing by and watching noticed a disturbance among the men. One man had edged away, broken into a run, entered the temple and prostrated himself before the image of the Emperor.

The Captain of the Guard, who had witnessed the bravery of the men and whose heart had been touched by their teaching, tore off his helmet, threw down his spear, and disrobing himself, took up the cry as he took the place of the man who had weakened. The compensation was not slow in coming, for as the dawn broke there were forty corpses on the ice.

Who shall dream of shrinking,
By our Captain led?

At least a thousand of God's saints served as living torches to illuminate the darkness of Nero's gardens, wrapped in garments steeped in pitch. *"Every finger was a candle."*

"Who follows in their train?"

I'm standing, Lord.
There is a mist that blinds my sight.
Steep jagged rocks, front, left, and right,
Lower, dim, gigantic, in the night.
Where is the way?

I'm standing, Lord.
The black rock hems me in behind.
Above my head a moaning wind
Chills and oppresses heart and mind.
I am afraid!

I'm standing, Lord.
The rock is hard beneath my feet.
I nearly slipped, Lord, on the sleet.
So weary, Lord, and where a seat?
Still must I stand?

He answered me, and on His face
A look ineffable of grace,
Of perfect, understanding love,
Which all my murmuring did remove.

I'm standing, Lord.
Since Thou hast spoken, Lord, I see
Thou hast beset; these rocks are Thee;
And since Thy love encloses me,
I stand and sing!

BETTY STAM, MARTYRED IN CHINA

October 11

Until he come whose right it is. (Ezek. 21:27)

Years ago in Cincinnati Handel's *Messiah* was rendered by perhaps the greatest chorus on earth: Patti, then in her prime, was the leading soprano; Whitney, the bass; Theodore Toedt, the tenor; Carey, the alto; and this quartet was supported by more than four thousand voices.

Just before the "Hallelujah Chorus" a deathlike stillness brooded over that vast assemblage. Suddenly the bass sang, "For He shall reign for ever and ever," the alto lifted it a little higher—"For ever and ever," and the tenor lifted it still higher—"For ever and ever," then Patti broke in as though inspired—"King of Kings, and Lord of Lords." As she broke off, paused, and lifted her eyes, a voice seemed to float down from above as the voice of an Angel flinging out through the great hall the question, "How long shall He reign?"—and the thousand sopranos in unison responded, "For ever and ever." Then the four thousand of the chorus broke forth like the shout of an angelic host, "Hallelujah! Hallelujah! Hallelujah!"

What a day for this poor sin-ruined, storm-torn, heartbroken, groping-in-the-blind world, when He shall take His rightful throne and reign in all hearts and over all lives for ever and ever! ELMER ELLSWORTH HELMS

> Hail, universal Lord!
> Messiah—David's Son!
> Take Thou the scepter of the world,
> And reign supreme, alone!

Oh, it seems to me like a prophecy of the glad day when every knee shall bow, and all the nations of the earth shall confess that Jesus Christ is Lord, to the glory of God the Father. And from the teeming millions of Asia shall sound the anthem, "King of Kings, and Lord of Lords"; the shout from Europe will give it power; and the deep undertone of Africa's redeemed will lend it volume; and America, and faraway Australia, and the islands of the sea will join the refrain and pour their matchless music into the ear of Christ; and together, from the uttermost parts of the earth, breaking out in triumphant voice, the whole world shall sing, "King of Kings, and Lord of Lords; the Lord God Omnipotent reigneth!"

Come back! Come back! Take the scepter of our lives! Mount the throne of our hearts! All hail the King! My King! *And thine?*

October 12

My meditation of him shall be sweet. (Ps. 104:34)

Isaac went into the fields *to meditate. Jacob* lingered on the eastern bank of the brook Jabbok after all his company had passed over; there he wrestled with the angel and prevailed. *Moses,* hidden in the clefts of Horeb, beheld the vanishing glory which marked the way by which Jehovah had gone. *Elijah* sent Ahab down to eat and drink while he himself withdrew to the lonely crest of Carmel. *Daniel* spent weeks in ecstasy of intercession on the banks of Hiddakel, which once had watered Paradise. And *Paul,* no doubt in order that he might have an opportunity for undisturbed meditation and prayer, was minded to go afoot from Troas to Assos.

Have you learned to understand the truths of these great paradoxes: the blessing of a curse, the voice of silence, the companionship of solitude?

> *I walk down the Valley of Silence,*
> *Down the dim voiceless valley alone,*
> *And I hear not the sound of a footstep*
> *Around me, but God's and my own;*
> *And the hush of my heart is as holy*
> *As the bowers whence angels have flown.*
>
> *In the hush of the Valley of Silence*
> *I hear all the songs that I sing,*
> *And the notes float down the dim Valley*
> *Till each finds a word for a wing,*
> *That to men, like the dove of the deluge*
> *The message of peace they may bring.*
>
> *But far on the deep there are billows*
> *That never shall break on the beach;*
> *And I have heard songs in the silence*
> *That never shall float into speech;*
> *And I have had dreams in the Valley*
> *Too lofty for language to reach.*
>
> *Do you ask me the place of the Valley?*
> *To hearts that are harrowed by care*
> *It lieth afar, between mountains,*
> *And God and His angels are there—*
> *One is the dark mountain of sorrow,*
> *And one the bright mountain of prayer.*

THE SONG OF A MYSTIC

October 13

If ye shall ask . . . I will do. (John 14:14)

Who is it here who offers to do for us *if we will only ask?*
It is *God Himself!* It is the mightiest doer in the universe who says, "I will do, if you ask."

Think a moment *who* it is that promises: the God who holds the sea in the hollow of His hand; the God who swings this ponderous globe of earth in its orbit; the God who marshals the stars and guides the planets in their blazing paths with undeviating accuracy; the heaven-creating, devil-conquering, dead-raising God. It is this very God who says: *"If ye ask ... I will do!"*

Unrivaled wisdom, boundless skill, limitless power, infinite resources are His.

Wouldst thou not rather call forth *Mine omnipotent doing* by thine asking, if to this I have called thee, than even to be busy with thine own doing? JAMES H. MCCONKEY

"I will do *marvels!"*

October 14

When he had heard therefore that he was sick, he abode two days still in the same place where he was. (John 11:6)

And so the silence of God was itself an answer. It is not merely said that there was no audible response to the cry from Bethany; it is distinctly stated that the absence of an audible response was itself the answer to the cry—it was *when* the Lord heard that Lazarus was sick that *therefore* He abode two days still in the same place which He was. I have often heard the outward silence. A hundred times have I sent up aspirations whose only answer has seemed to be the echo of my own voice, and I have cried out in the night of my despair, *"Why art Thou so far from helping me?"* But I never thought that the seeming farness was itself the nearness of God—that the very silence was an answer.

It was a very grand answer to the household of Bethany. They had asked *not too much,* but *too little.* They had asked only the life of Lazarus. They were to get the life of Lazarus and a revelation of eternal life as well.

There are some prayers that are followed by a Divine silence *because we are not yet ripe for all we have asked;* there are others which are so followed *because we are ripe for more. We do not always know the full strength of our own capacity; we have to be prepared for receiving greater blessings than we have ever dreamed of.* We come to the door of the sepulcher and beg with tears the dead body of Jesus; we are answered by silence *because we are to get something better—a living Lord.*

My soul, be not afraid of God's silence; it is another form of His voice. God's silence is more than man's speech. God's negative is better than the world's affirmative. Have thy prayers been followed by a calm stillness? Well! Is not that God's voice—a voice that will suffice thee in the meantime till the full disclosure comes? Has He moved not from His place to help thee? Well, but His stillness makes *thee* still, and He has something better than help to give thee.

Wait for Him in the silence, and ere long it shall become vocal; death shall be swallowed up in victory! GEORGE MATHESON

All God's dealings are slow!

Think not that God's silence is coldness or indifference. When birds are on the nest preparing to bring forth life, they never sing. *God's stillness is full of brooding. Be not impatient of God!*

When the Lord is to lead a soul to *great faith,* He for a time leaves his prayer unanswered.

October 15

We have an assured confidence that whenever we ask anything in accordance with his will, he listens to us: And since we know that he listens to us, then whatever we ask, we know that we have the things which we have asked from him. (1 John 5:14– 15 WEYMOUTH)

Prayer can obtain everything: it can open the windows of heaven, and shut the gates of hell; it can put a holy constraint upon God, and detain an angel until he leave a blessing; it can open the treasures of rain, and soften the iron ribs of rocks till they melt into tears and a flowing river; prayer can unclasp the girdles of the north—saying to a mountain of ice, "Be thou removed hence, and cast into the bottom of the sea"; it can arrest the sun in the midst of his course, and send the swift-winged winds upon our errands; and to all these strange things and secret decrees, add unrevealed transactions which are above the stars.

When Hudson Taylor was asked if he ever prayed *without any consciousness of joy,* he replied: "Often: sometimes I pray on with my heart feeling like wood; often, too, the most wonderful answers have come when prayer has been a real effort of faith without any joy whatever."

I never prayed sincerely and earnestly for anything but it came; at some time—no matter how distant the day—somehow, in some shape, probably the last I should have devised, *it came.* ADONIRAM JUDSON

For years I've prayed, and yet I see no change.
The mountain stands exactly where it stood;
The shadows that it casts are just as deep;
The pathway to its summit e'en more steep.
Shall I pray on?

Shall I pray on with ne'er a hopeful sign?
Not only does the mountain still remain,
But, while I watch to see it disappear,
Becomes the more appalling year by year.
Shall I pray on?

I shall pray on. Though distant as it seems
The answer may be almost at my door,
Or just around the corner on its way,
But, whether near or far, yes, I shall pray—
I shall pray on.

EDITH MAPES

If thou wilt keep the incense burning there, His glory thou shalt see—sometime, somewhere!

October 16

If ... God command thee ... thou shalt be able. (Ex. 18:23)

Charles G. Finney once said: "When God commands you to do a thing, it is the highest possible evidence, equal to an oath, that we can do it."

The thing that taxes Almightiness is the very thing that you as a disciple of Jesus Christ ought to believe He would do. Sometimes we must be shipwrecked upon the supernatural; we must be thrown upon God; we must lose the temporal—that we may find the Eternal.

"It is God who worketh." Men work like men and nothing more is expected of man than what man can do. But God worketh like a God, and with Him nothing is impossible.

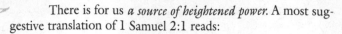

There is for us *a source of heightened power.* A most suggestive translation of 1 Samuel 2:1 reads:

> *My heart thrills over the Eternal;*
> *my powers are heightened by my God.*

Amos was just a herdsman from Tekoa, but *his powers were heightened* by his God. It happened to Peter. It happened to Paul. Abraham Lincoln faced the impossible when he set out to uproot the slave trade.

We are all in need of more power, more courage, more wisdom than we actually possess. This *"plus extra"* comes to him whose heart thrills over the Eternal; who daily waits for Divine resources.

"Difficulty" is a relative term. It all depends upon the power you have available. Difficulty diminishes as the power increases; and altogether vanishes when the power rises to Omnipotence. "Our sufficiency is of God." All God's biddings are enablings. *Always provided that we are on the line of God's written Word, in the current of His revealed purpose, there is nothing you may not trust Him for.*

> *As one of a thousand you may just fail;*
> *But as "ONE, PLUS GOD," you are bound to win.*

October 17

For he commandeth, and raiseth the stormy wind, which lifteth up the waves thereof. (Ps. 107:25)

Stormy wind fulfilling His word. *By the time the wind blows upon us it is His wind for us.* We have nothing to do with what first of all stirred up that wind. It could not ruffle a leaf on the smallest tree in the forest had He not opened the way for it to blow through the fields of air. He commandeth even the winds, and they obey Him. To the winds as to His servants He saith to one, "Go," and it goeth; and to another, "Come," and it cometh; and to another, "Do this," and it doeth it. So, whatever wind blows on us it is His wind for us, *His wind fulfilling His word.*

God's winds do effectual work. *They shake loose from us the things that can be shaken, that those things which cannot be shaken may remain, those eternal things which belong to the Kingdom which cannot be moved.* They have their part to play in stripping us and strengthening us so that we may be the more ready for the uses of Eternal Love. Then can we refuse to welcome them?

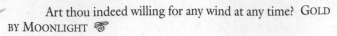
Be like the pine on the hilltop,
Alone in the wind for God.

There is a curious comfort in remembering that the Father depends upon His child not to give way. *It is inspiring to be trusted with a hard thing.* You never asked for summer breezes to blow upon your tree. It is enough that you are not alone upon the hill.

And let the storm that does Thy work
Deal with me as it may.

October 18

And it came to pass after a while, that the brook dried up.
(1 Kings 17:7)

God sent Elijah to the brook and it dried up. It did not prove equal to the need of the prophet. It failed; God knew it would; He made it to fail. *"The brook dried up."* This is an aspect of the Divine providence that sorely perplexes our minds and tries our faith. God knows that there are heavenly whispers that men cannot hear till the drought of trouble and perhaps weariness has silenced the babbling brooks of joy. And He is not satisfied until we have learned to depend, *not upon His gifts, but upon Himself.* PERCY AINSWORTH

His camp was pitched where Cherith's stream was flowing—
The man of God! 'Twas God's appointed spot!
When it might fail, he knew not; only knowing
That God cared for his lot.

Full many days on Cherith's bank he camped him,
And from its cool refreshing, drew his share;
And foolish fears of failing streams ne'er damped him;
Was he not God's own care?

Yet, lo, at length, the prospect strangely altered;
The drought e'en Cherith's fountain had assailed;
Slowly but sure, the flowing waters faltered
Until, at last, they failed!

Then came the word from One whose eye beholding
Saw that the stream, the living stream had dried,
Sending him forth, to find by new unfolding,
None of his needs denied.

Perchance thou, too, hath camped by such sweet waters.
And quenched with joy thy weary, parched soul's thirst;
To find, as time goes on, thy streamlet alters
From what it was at first.

Hearts that have cheered, or soothed, or blest, or strengthened,
Loves that have lavished so unstintedly,
Joys, treasured joys—have passed, as time hath lengthened,
Into obscurity.

If thus, ah soul, the brook thy heart hath cherished
Doth fail thee now—no more thy thirst assuage—
If its once glad, refreshing streams have perished,
Let Him thy heart engage.

He will not fail, nor mock, nor disappoint thee;
His consolations change not with the years;
With oil of joy He surely will anoint thee,
And wipe away thy tears.

J. DANSON SMITH

October 19

Except a corn of wheat fall into the ground and die, it abideth alone. (John 12:24)

A peasant once came to Tauler to confess; but in place of the peasant confessing to Tauler, Tauler confessed to the peasant. The great preacher said, "I am not satisfied." The peasant replied, "Tauler has to die before he can be satisfied."

That great man, who had thousands listening to him, withdrew to a place of quiet and asked God to work out that death in him.

After he had been there for two years, he came out and assembled his congregation. A great multitude came to hear him, for he had been a wonderful preacher. He began to preach, but he broke down and wept. The audience dispersed saying, "What is the matter with Tauler? He can't preach as he once did. He failed today!"

The next time he preached only a little handful came together—those who had caught a glimpse of something—and he preached to them in a brokenhearted way; *but the power of God came down.* God, by the power of the Spirit, *had put John Tauler to death!* SELECTED

Beloved, are you willing to be crucified with Christ?

> *Higher than the highest heavens,*
> *Deeper than the deepest sea,*
> *Lord, Thy love at last hath conquered:*
> *Grant me now my supplication,*
> *None of self, and all of Thee.*

October 20

And they came to the place which God had told him of. (Gen. 22:9)

There the LORD commanded the blessing. (Ps. 133:3)

> *Up, up the hill, to the whiter than snow-shine,*
> *Help me to climb, and dwell in pardon's light.*
> *I must be pure as Thou, or ever less*
> *Than Thy design of me—therefore incline*
> *My heart to take men's wrongs as Thou tak'st mine.*

Have you come to the *place* God *told you* of? Have you gone through the sacrifice of death? Are you willing to make the moral decision that the thing die out in you which never was in Jesus?

Up to that whiter than snow-shine; up to that place that is as strong and firm as the Throne of God. Do not say, "That pure, white, holy life is never for me!" Let God lift you; let Him take the shrouds away; let Him lift up; up to the hill, *to the whiter than snow-shine.* And when you get to the top what do you find? A great, strong tableland, where your feet are on a rock; your steps enlarged under you; your goings established. OSWALD CHAMBERS

Jesus offers you "life more abundantly." Grasp the offer! Quit the boggy and dark low ground, and let Him lead you up higher! MOUNTAIN TOPS WITH JESUS

Take the supreme climb!

Jesus lead me up the mountain,
Where the whitest robes are seen,
Where the saints can see the fountain,
Where the pure are keeping clean.

Higher up, where light increases,
Rich above all earthly good,
Where the life of sinning ceases,
Where the Spirit comes in floods.

Lead me higher, nothing dreading,
In the race to never stop;
In Thy footsteps keep me treading,
Give me grace to reach the top.

Courage, my soul, and let us journey on!

October 21

Let patience have her perfect work, that ye may be perfect and entire, wanting nothing. (James 1:4)

Look with Edison at his deafness, with Milton at his blindness, with Bunyan at his imprisonment, and see how patience converted these very misfortunes into good fortunes.

Michelangelo went to Rome to carve statues, and found that other artists had taken over all the Carrara marble—all but one crooked and mis-shapen piece. He sat down before this and studied with infinite patience its very limitations, until he found that by bending the head of a statue here, and lifting its arms there, he could create a masterpiece: thus *The Boy David* was produced.

Let us sit down in front of our very limitations, and with the aid of patience dare to produce, with God's help, *a masterpiece!*

"I see the stubborn heights,
The bruising rocks, the straining soul."

"I see the goal!"

"I see the tearing plow,
The crushing drag, the beating rain."

"I see the grain!"

> *"I see compressing walls,*
> *And seething flux, and heats untold."*
>
> *"I see the gold!"*
>
> *"I see the cruel blows,*
> *The chisel sharp, the hammer's mace."*
>
> *"I see My face!"*

OUR VIEW AND HIS,
BY PHILIP WENDELL CRANNELL 🐦

October 22

Understanding what the will of the Lord is. (Eph. 5:17)

It may seem a very terrible thing for the soul to yield itself wholly and unreservedly to the will of Christ. "What is going to happen? What about tomorrow? Will He not put a very heavy burden upon me if I yield; if I take the yoke?" Ah, you have not known my Master; you have not looked into His face; you have not realized His infinite love for you. Why, God's will for you means your fullest happiness! Christ's will and your deepest happiness are synonymous terms. How can you doubt that your Lord has planned for you the very best thing?

The admiral that goes out with his fleet under sealed orders does not know what is in the packet; but he goes out prepared to do the will of the Government of his country. And although it seems to you that you take from Christ the sealed packet of His will and know not *what* is in it, yet knowing *who He is* that has *planned your future* you can step out without realizing all that it means, just as you take His promises. *The value of any promise depends upon the promiser; and so it is with His will. Whose* will is it? *Whose* yoke is it? *"My yoke,"* says the gentle, loving Jesus; "Take *my yoke* upon you." To take His yoke is cheerfully to accept His will for us, not only in the present moment, but for the whole future that He has mapped out.

Surrender your will to God. He will never take advantage of you.
EVAN H. HOPKINS 🐦

> *"I dare not promise, Lord," I cried,*
> *"For future years close-sealed.*
> *Surrender is a fearful thing—*
> *I long—but dare not yield."*

How clear and swift the answer came:
"I only ask of thee
A present of THYSELF for time
And for eternity."

An easy thing to MAKE A GIFT!
My fears found swift release.
I gave myself to Him, and found
Past understanding, peace.

BERTHA GERNEAUX WOODS

October 23

Mending their nets; and he called them. (Matt. 4:21)

Salome! Had you been with me in the boat,
You would not chide and moan because our boys
Have gone with the Beloved from this our home.
Let me, Salome, tell you how it came.
The night was still—the tide was running strong,
Heavy our nets—the strain reached breaking point,
And while 'twas dark we docked, and as we worked
I felt as though new strength and steady joy
Surged through my being, so I sang a Psalm—
As David sang—a song to greet the morn;
And then my heart was filled with quiet calm.

The boat was soon in order, and we turned
To dry and mend our nets. Then Jesus came—
He called the boys, first John, then James, by name,
And they arose and went to follow Him.
I turned and gazed on Jesus standing there—
He seemed to me all clothed in shining light
As He stood in the pathway with the night
Behind Him and the dawn breaking around,
His form so radiant and glad and free.

And when He climbed the hill our sons went too—
James was behind, and John was by His side;
And when they talked, John scarcely seemed our John—
I felt that he had caught a marvelous light.
And all my being seemed to overflow;

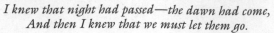

I knew that night had passed—the dawn had come,
And then I knew that we must let them go.

ZEBEDEE'S SONS

"So shall his part be that tarrieth by the stuff: they shall part alike" (1 Sam. 30:24).

To some Christ calls: "Leave boat and bay,
And white-haired Zebedee";
To some the call is harder: "Stay
And mend the nets for Me."

SELECTED

October 24

Return to thy place, and abide with the king. (2 Sam. 15:19)

There is a little fable which says that a primrose growing by itself in a shady corner of the garden became discontented as it saw the other flowers in their gay beds in the sunshine, and begged to be removed to a more conspicuous place. Its prayer was granted. The gardener transplanted it to a more showy and sunny spot. It was greatly pleased, but there came a change over it immediately. Its blossoms lost much of their beauty, and became pale and sickly. The hot sun caused them to faint and wither. So it prayed again to be taken back to its old place in the shade. The wise gardener knew best where to plant each flower.

So God, the Divine Husbandman, knows where His children will best grow into what He would have them to be. Some require the fierce storms; some will only thrive spiritually in the shadow of worldly adversity; and some come to ripeness more sweetly under the soft and gentle influences of prosperity, whose beauty rough experiences would mar.

Humbolt, the great naturalist and traveler, said that the most wonderful sight he had ever seen was a primrose flourishing on the bosom of a glacier.

The brightest souls which glory ever knew
Were rocked in storms and nursed when tempests blew.

October 25

He that goeth aside to sit quietly in the secret place with the Most High, will find him coming over so close that this man shall be lodging under the very shadow of the Almighty. (Ps. 91:1, Free trans.)

It was my practice to rise at midnight for worship. God came to me at that precise time and awoke me from sleep that I might enjoy HIM. He seemed to pervade my being. My soul became more and more attracted to Himself like the waters of a river which pass into the ocean and after a time become one with it. Oh, unutterable happiness! Who could have thought that one should ever find happiness equal to this!

Hours passed like moments, when I could do nothing else but pray. It was a prayer of rejoicing, of possession, when the taste of GOD was so great, so pure, so unblended that it drew and absorbed the soul into a profound state of confiding and affectionate rest in God, without intellectual effort for I had no sight but of Jesus only. MADAME GUYON

A moment in the morning ere the cares of the day begin,
Ere the heart's wide door is open for the world to enter in;
Ah, then, alone with Jesus, in the silence of the morn,
In heavenly sweet communion, let your happy day be born;
In the quietude that blesses with a prelude of repose,
Let your soul be soothed and softened as the dew revives the rose.

Two men were confessing to each other the causes of their failure in the ministry. "I let my hand slip out of God's hand," said one. The other said, "My soul-life raveled at the point where I ceased to pray, because there were things in my life I could not speak to God about." *Prayer is a handclasp with God.*

Take time for prayer if you have to take it by violence. *Take time to behold Him!*

October 26

Because this widow troubleth me, I will avenge her. (Luke 18:5)

We should be careful about what we ask from God; but when once we begin to pray for a thing we should never give up praying for it until we receive it, or until God makes it very clear and definite that it is not His will to grant it. R. A. TORREY ☞

It is said of John Bradford that he had a peculiar art in prayer. When asked his secret, he said: "When I know what I want, I always stop on that prayer until I feel that I have pleaded it with God, and until God and I have had dealings with each other upon it. I never go on to another petition until I have gone through the first."

To the same point Mr. Spurgeon said: "Do not try to put two arrows on the string at once—they will both miss. He that would load his gun with two charges cannot expect to be successful. Plead once with God and prevail, and then plead again. Get the first answer and then go after the second. Do not be satisfied with running the colors of your prayers into one another until there is no picture to look at, but just a huge daub—a smear of colors badly laid on."

Far better would it be to know what our real needs are, and then concentrate our earnest supplications upon those definite objects, taking them thoughtfully one at a time.

"Ask what I shall give thee."

October 27

God spake. (Gen. 46:2)

Any man may hear the voice of God.

When man will listen, God speaks. When God speaks, men are changed. When men are changed, nations are changed.

In the ancient days *God spake,* and the wonderful things which He told Moses on the mountaintop have inspired mankind for centuries.

Down through the years men of God have heard His voice. *God spake* to George Müller, and he became the modern apostle of faith. Hudson Taylor heard Him speak, as he walked by the seashore on a memorable Sabbath morning, and in obedience to that Voice he launched forth into inland China, establishing Mission Stations in every province of that vast country.

God spake to Dr. A. B. Simpson and he stepped aside from a well-beaten path, and like Abraham of old "went forth, not knowing whither he went." Today, *The Christian and Missionary Alliance,* operating in more than twenty

Mission Fields of the world, is the result of his obedience and untold numbers have been blessed through his ministry.

Charles Cowman heard the "soft and gentle Voice," when *God spake* saying, "Get thee out of thy country, and from thy kindred, and from thy father's house, unto a land that I will show thee." The result—The Oriental Missionary Society, with hundreds of Mission Stations dotted all over the Orient! And now its activities embrace the wide world.

> *God is not dumb that He should speak no more.*
> *If thou hast wanderings in the wilderness*
> *And find'st not Sinai, 'tis thy soul is poor:*
> *There towers the mountain of the Voice no less,*
> *Which whoso seeks shall find; but he who bends*
> *Intent on manna still, and mortal ends,*
> *Sees it not, neither hears its thundering lore.*

LOWELL

October 28

Ye have compassed this mountain long enough: turn . . . northward. (Deut. 2:3)

Last summer a party of us lost our way among the lakes of Ontario. A violent storm came up, but we found shelter under a great rock till the storm raged past. Then we resumed our hunt dispiritedly until one said, *"Let us climb this rock; we may spy the trail from the top."* It was a hard climb, but the challenge of the rock restored our courage. As we *conquered the heights* we gained confidence and mastery, and *the hilltop gave us a vision* of our way out.

Get high enough up, you will be above the fog; and while the men down in it are squabbling as to whether there is anything outside the mist, you from your sunny station will see the far-off coasts, and haply catch some whiff of perfume from their shores, or see some glinting of glory upon the shining turrets of "the city that hath foundations."

The soul which hath launched itself forth upon God is in a free place, filled with the fresh air of the hills of God.

> *Oh, there are heavenly heights to reach*
> *In many a fearful place,*
> *While the poor, timid heir of God*

Lies blindly on his face;
Lies languishing for light Divine
That he shall never see
'Till he goes forward at Thy sign,
And trusts himself to Thee.

C. A. FOX

We are continually retreating behind our limitations and saying, "Thus far and no farther can I go." God is ever laying His hand upon us and thrusting us into the open, saying, *"You can be more than you are; you must be more than you are."*

Are the hills of God thine atmosphere?

October 29

We will flee upon horses. (Isa. 30:16)

God is never slow from *His* standpoint, but He is from *ours*, because impetuosity and doing things prematurely are universal weaknesses.

God lives and moves in eternity, and every little detail in His working must be like Himself, and have in it the majesty and measured movement, as well as the accuracy and promptness of infinite wisdom. We are to *let God do the swiftness* and *we do the slowness*.

The Holy Spirit tells us to "be swift to hear, slow to speak, slow to wrath," that is, *swift* to *take in from God*, but *slow* to *give out the opinions, the emotions of the creature*.

We miss a great many things from God by not going slow enough with Him. Who would have God change His perfections to accommodate our whims? Have we not had glimpses into God's perfections, insight into wonderful truths, quiet unfoldings of daily opportunities, gentle checks of the Holy Spirit upon our decisions or words, sweet and secret promptings to do certain things?

There is a time for everything in the universe to get ripe—and *to go slow with God is the heavenly pace that gathers up all things at the time they are ripe.*

What they win, who wait for God, is worth waiting for!

Going slow with God is our greatest safety!

October 30

Not yours, but God's. (2 Chron. 20:15)

There are times when doing nothing is better than doing something. Those are the times when only God can do what is needed. True faith trusts Him then, and Him alone, to do the miracle. Moses and Jehoshaphat knew this secret; they knew the same Lord and the same Divine grace.

As the pursuing Egyptians trapped the helpless Israelites at the Red Sea, Moses said: "Fear ye not, stand still, and see the salvation of the LORD.... The LORD shall fight for you, and ye shall hold your peace" (Ex. 14:13–14).

As the Moabites and the Ammonites, a vast multitude, closed in on Judah, King Jehoshaphat said to the helpless people: "Be not afraid nor dismayed by reason of this great multitude; for *the battle is not yours, but God's*.... Ye shall not need to fight in this battle: set yourselves, stand ye still, and see the salvation of the LORD." (2 Chron. 20:15, 17, emphasis added).

When God alone can win the victory, faith lets God do it all. It is better to trust than to try. SUNDAY SCHOOL TIMES

"Faith is the Victory that Overcomes."

The battle is not yours, but God's;
Therefore why fight?
True faith will cease from struggling,
And rest upon His might:
Each conflict into which you come
Was WON *on Calvary,*
Tis ours to claim what Christ has done,
And "hold" the victory.

H. E. JESSOP

"Hold thee still." "And this," says Saint Jerome, "is the hardest precept that is given to man: inasmuch as the most difficult precept of action sinks into nothingness when compared with this command to inaction."

October 31

And as he lay and slept under a juniper tree, behold, then an angel touched him. (1 Kings 19:5)

God does not chide His tired child when that weariness is a result of toil for Him: "I know thy toil" (Rev. 2:2)—the Greek is *"labor to weariness."* And what happened? "Behold, then an angel touched him." There is no wilderness without its angels. Though Elijah knew it not, angels guarded him round about in his blackest depression and were actually placing bread and water at his head while he was asking for death.

A man may have to cry in the midst of an apostate community, "I, even I only, am left"; *but he is always companied by legions of holy angels.* But more than that. Who is *this* angel? It is the Angel of the LORD, the *Jehovah Angel;* the One who, centuries later in Gethsemane, had to have an angel to strengthen *Him.* He touched His exhausted child. Blessed exhaustion that can bring such a touch!

As the Psalmist has said (Ps. 127:2), "He giveth to His beloved while they sleep" (RSV, margin). And God does not chide His tired child. THE DAWN 🍃

> *Dear child, God does not say today, "Be strong";*
> *He knows your strength is spent; He knows how long*
> *The road has been, how weary you have grown,*
> *For He who walked the earthly roads alone,*
> *Each bogging lowland, and each rugged hill,*
> *Can understand, and so He says, "Be still,*
> *And know that I am God." The hour is late,*
> *And you must rest awhile, and you must wait*
> *Until life's empty reservoirs fill up*
> *As slow rain fills an empty upturned cup.*
> *Hold up your cup, dear child, for God to fill.*
> *He only asks today that you be still.*
>
> GRACE NOLL CROWELL 🍃

November 1

Therefore it is of faith ... to the end the promise might be sure. (Rom. 4:16)

The great devotional teacher of the past century, Dr. Andrew Murray, said, *"When you get a promise from God it is worth just as much as fulfillment.* A promise brings you into direct contact with God. Honor Him by trusting the promise and obeying Him." *Worth just as much as fulfillment.* Do we grasp the truth often? Are we not frequently in the state of *trying* to believe, instead of realizing that these promises bring us into contact with God? *"God's promise is as good as His presence."* To believe and accept the promise of God is not to engage in some mental gymnastics where we reach down into our imaginations and begin a process of auto-suggestion, or produce a notional faith in which we argue with ourselves in an endeavor to believe God. It is absolute confidence in and reliance upon God through His Word.

By a naked faith in a naked promise I do not mean *a bare assent* that God is faithful, and that such a promise in the Book of God *may* be fulfilled in me, but *a bold, hearty, steady venturing* of my soul, body, and spirit upon the truth of the promise with an appropriating act. FLETCHER ☙

"The faith that will shut the mouths of lions must be more than a pious hope that they will not bite."

November 2

Thy way is in the sea, and thy path in the great waters. (Ps. 77:19)

☙

"God's path is in the sea"—just where you would not expect it to be! So when He leads us out by unexpected ways, off the strong solid land, out upon the changing sea, *then* we may expect to see *His ways.* We are with One who finds a path already tracked out, for it makes us perfectly independent of circumstances.

There is an infinite variety in the paths God makes, and He can make them *anywhere!* Think you not that He, who made the spider able to drop anywhere and to spin its own path as it goes, is not able to spin a path for you through every blank, or perplexity, or depression? God is never lost among our mysteries. He sees the road, "the end from the beginning."

Mystery and uncertainty are only to prepare us for deeper discipline. Had we no stormy sea we should remain weaklings to the end of our days. God takes us out into the deeps; but He knows the track! He knows the haven! and we shall arrive.

And with Jesus
Through the trackless deep move on!

C. A. FOX ☙

"O fathomless abyss of God's rich bounty, of His wisdom, of His knowledge! Who can explore His decisions? Who can track out His paths?" *(Rom. 11:33, Way's trans.).*

November 3

The life also of Jesus ... made manifest in our mortal flesh. (2 Cor. 4:11)

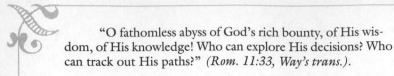

We may have two lives. First, our own life inherited from our parents and given us by our Creator. That life has some value, but how soon it fails and feels the forces of disease, decay, and approaching death!

But we may have another life, or rather the Life of Another—*the life also of Jesus.* How much more valuable and transcendent is this life! It has no weakness nor decay nor limitation. Jesus has a physical life as real as ours, and infinitely greater; He is an actual *man* with a glorified body and a human spirit. And that life belongs to us just as much as the precious blood He shed and the spiritual grace He bestows. He has risen and ascended as our living Head and He is ever saying to us, *"Because I live, ye shall live also."*

Why should we limit Him to what we call the spiritual realm? His resurrection body has in it all the vitality and strength that our mortal frame can ever need. Someday He is to raise us from the dead by virtue of that resurrection life. Why should it be thought *a strange thing* if faith may now *foredate its inheritance* and *claim in advance* part of its physical redemption—a little handful of the soil of that better country—just as a seed is to bring forth more glorious fruit?

This was Paul's experience. Why may it not be *ours?* There was a day at Lystra when under a shower of stones Paul's life was ebbing out and he was left for dead outside the city gates. Then it was that *the life also of Jesus* asserted itself, and, calmly rising up in the strength of his Master, he walked back through the streets whose stones were stained by his own blood, and quietly went on his way preaching the Gospel as if nothing had happened.

The secret of this life is to live so close to Jesus that we shall breathe His very breath and ever be in touch with His life and love. So let us live by Him. Healing is in His living body. We *receive* it as we abide in Him. We *keep* it only as we abide in Him. A. B. SIMPSON

There are miraculous possibilities for the one who depends on God.

November 4

Break forth into singing. (Isa. 49:13)

There is a beautiful story which tells of songbirds being brought over the sea. There were thirty-six thousand, mostly canaries. The sea was very calm when the ship first sailed, and the little birds were silent. They kept their little heads under their wings and not a note was heard. But the third day out at sea, the ship struck a furious gale. The passengers were terrified. Children wept. Then a strange thing happened. As the tempest reached its height, the birds began to sing, first one, then another, until the thirty-six thousand were singing as if their little throats would burst.

When the storm rises in its fury, do we then begin to sing? Should not our song break forth in tenfold joy when the tempest begins?

> *I can hear the songbirds singing their refrain*
> *It is morning in my heart;*
> *And I know that life for me begins again,*
> *It is morning in my heart.*
>
> *It is morning, it is morning in my heart,*
> *Jesus made the gloomy shadows all depart;*
> *Songs of gladness now I sing,*
> *For since Jesus is my King,*
> *It is morning, it is morning in my heart.*

O God, wilt Thou teach us to begin the music of heaven! Grant us grace to have many rehearsals of eternal Hallelujahs! "Bless the LORD, O my soul: and all that is within me, bless his holy name!"

Try singing! Singing in the storm!

November 5

And when Joseph saw Benjamin with them, he said to the steward of his house, Bring the men into the house, and slay, and make ready; for the men shall dine with me at noon. (Gen. 43:16 RSV)

When their brother, who was to be their savior, saw that they had brought with them the dearest treasure of their family, there went forth the instant word for a king's feast to be prepared for them.

That is all that my Savior is waiting for that He may lavish the fullness of His bounty upon me: my bringing to Him the dearest possession of my life—myself—in unconditional surrender to His mastery, confessing my helplessness and awful need. Then He gives the word that *I may come into His own house and eat at His table the best food of which He Himself partakes.*

The surrender of Benjamin, their dearest possession, was the key to all the treasures of the kingdom—yes, even to the recognition of Joseph by the brothers and Jacob. The surrender of the costliest possession of *my life* is the key to the treasures of the Kingdom for me—yes, even to the full recognition and appropriation of *Christ as my whole and only life.*

Oh, Lord Jesus, show me more that I may give up, that I may have more of Thee! MESSAGES FOR THE MORNING WATCH ☙

My friend, beware of me
Lest I should do
The very thing I'd sooner die than do,
In some way crucify the Christ in you.

If you are called to some great sacrifice,
And I should come to you with frightened eyes
And cry, "Take care, take care, be wise, be wise!"
See through my softness then a fiend's attack,
And bid me get me straight behind your back;
To your own conscience and your God be true,
Lest I play Satan to the Christ in you.

And I would humbly ask of you in turn
That if someday in me Love's fires should burn
To whiteness, and a Voice should call
Bidding me leave my little for God's all,
If need be, you would thrust me from your side—
So keep love loyal to the Crucified.

November 6

I speak of my severe labors for the Gospel. I am ready even to die in the same cause. If I am required to pour out my life-blood as a liba-tion over the sacrificial offering of your faith, I rejoice myself and

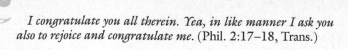

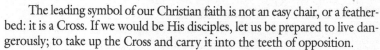

*I congratulate you all therein. Yea, in like manner I ask you
also to rejoice and congratulate me.* (Phil. 2:17–18, Trans.)

The leading symbol of our Christian faith is not an easy chair, or a feather-bed: it is a Cross. If we would be His disciples, let us be prepared to live dangerously; to take up the Cross and carry it into the teeth of opposition.

God is at perfect liberty to waste us if He chooses.

When the fight seems fierce, and you are tempted to be weary and disconsolate, remember that in the interest of His cause your Leader expects you to turn a glad face to the world—*to rejoice and be exceeding glad!*

> *I have shamed Thee; craven-hearted*
> *I have been Thy recreant knight;*
> *Own me yet, O Lord, albeit*
> *Weeping whilst I fight!*
>
> *"Nay," He said, "Wilt thou yet shame Me?*
> *Wilt thou shame thy knightly guise?*
> *I would have my angels wonder*
> *At thy gladsome eyes."*
>
> *Need'st thou pity, knight of Jesus?*
> *Pity for thy glorious hest?*
> *Oh, let God and men and angels*
> *See that thou are blest!*

SUSO

November 7

*Every place that the sole of your foot shall tread upon, that have
I given unto you.* (Josh. 1:3)

This blessed inspiring word greeted Israel as they faced the Promised Land. They had the *promise* of it before; *now* they must go forward into it and place their feet upon it. The promise is in the perfect tense and denotes an act just now completed—*"That have I given unto you."*

Our Joshua gives us the same incentive for conquest: *every promise in the New Testament that we put our feet upon is ours!* The upland of spiritual power is yours though Anak may live there! It is yours if you will but go

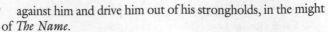

against him and drive him out of his strongholds, in the might of *The Name.*

If we dare to place our foot on anything God has promised *He makes it real to us.* So take Him as the supply for all your need: believe He is yours and never doubt it from this moment.

It may be your need is for spiritual cleansing. His promise covers this: *"Now ye are clean through the word which I have spoken unto you."* If you can believe this you shall be sanctified and kept.

Take the promise that suits your need, and step out on it; not touching it timidly on tiptoe, *but placing your foot flat down upon it.* Do not be afraid it will not hold your weight. *Put your whole need on the Word of the eternal* God for your soul, for your body, for your work, for the dear ones for whom you are praying, for any crisis in your life: *then stand upon it forever!*

All the blessed promises of the Old Book are yours, and *why are you so slack to go up and possess your land?* The size of your inheritance depends upon *how much land you have trodden underfoot, really stood on or walked over.* Between you and your possessions that huge mountain looms up. March up to it and make it yours! Go in this thy might and God will get glory; and you, victory. A. B. SIMPSON

Footprints mean possession, but it must be *your own footprints.*

November 8

At that day, saith the LORD *. . . thou shalt call me Ishi [my husband].* (Hos. 2:16)

The coming of the Comforter is a holy thing, a solemn act, and must be preceded by an intelligent and solemn covenant between the soul and God. It is the marriage of the soul to the Redeemer, and it is not a "trial marriage." No true marriage is rushed into carelessly. It is carefully considered, and it is based upon complete separation and consecration and the most solemn pledges and vows. So, if the Comforter is come to abide, to be with us and in us evermore, we must come out and be separate for Him, we must consecrate ourselves to Jesus fully and forever, and we must covenant to be the Lord's "for better or for worse," and we must trust Him. The soul that thus truly and solemnly dedicates itself to Him becomes

His, and He will come to that soul to abide forever, to be its "shield and exceeding great reward."

Take not back the gift you have voluntarily laid on the altar.

Jesus, Thy life is mine!
Dwell evermore in me;
And let me see
That nothing can untwine
Thy life from mine.

Thy life in me be shown!
Lord, I would henceforth seek
To think and speak
Thy thoughts, Thy words alone,
No more my own.

Thy fullest gift, O Lord,
Now at Thy word I claim,
Through Thy dear Name,
And touch the rapturous chord
Of praise forth-poured.

Jesus, my life is Thine,
And evermore shall be
Hidden in Thee!
For nothing can untwine
Thy life from mine.

FRANCES RIDLEY HAVERGAL

"Thou shalt abide [live] for me many days . . . thou shalt not be for another man: so will I also be for thee" *(Hos. 3:3).*

November 9

God also hath set the one [thing] over against the other. (Eccl. 7:14)

Too often we see life's prose, but not its poetry. Too often we miss the inspiration of the songs. How manifold are our sorrows, but how manifold are His gifts!

Sin is here, but so is boundless grace; the devil is here, but so is Christ; the sword of judgment is crossed by Mercy's scepter.

"Judgment and Mercy," according to a lovely Jewish legend, "were sent forth together after the Fall to minister to the sinning but redeemed race," *and together they still act.* One afflicts, the other heals; where one rends, the other plants a flower; one carves a wrinkle, the other kindles a smile; the rainbow succeeds the storm; the succoring wing covers our naked head from the glittering sword.

Gethsemane had its strengthening Angel!

God everlastingly sets Mercies over against Miseries! His interventions are never mistimed. He never comes at the wrong season. *God has the affairs of the world in His hands.* In your blackest crises the angel presences are doubtless in your neighborhood!

God never strikes the wrong note; never sings the wrong song. If God makes music, the music will prove medicinal. JOSEPH PEARCE ☙

> *With mercy and with judgment*
> *My web of time He wove.*
> *And aye the dews of sorrow*
> *Were lustered with His love,*
> *I'll bless the Hand that guided,*
> *I'll bless the Heart that planned,*
> *When throned where glory dwelleth,*
> *In Immanuel's land.*
>
> *Deep waters crossed life's pathway,*
> *The hedge of thorns was sharp;*
> *Now, these lie all behind me—*
> *Oh! For a well-tuned harp!*
> *Oh! to join Hallelujahs*
> *With your triumphant band,*
> *Who sing, where glory dwelleth*
> *In Immanuel's land.*
>
> SAMUEL RUTHERFORD ☙

Listen for the Night-songs of God!

November 10

Righteousness shall go before him; and shall set us in the way of his steps. (Ps. 85:13)

How I ascertain the will of God:
I seek at the beginning to get my heart into such a state that it has no will of its own in regard to a given matter.

Nine-tenths of the trouble with people is right here. Nine-tenths of the difficulties are overcome when our hearts are *ready to do the Lord's will,* whatever it may be. When one is truly in this state it is usually but a little way to the knowledge of what His will is.

Having surrendered my own will, I do not leave the result to feeling or simply impressions. If I do so, I make myself liable to great delusions.

I seek the will of the Spirit of God through, or in connection with *the Word of God.* The Spirit and the Word must be combined. If the Holy Ghost guides us at all, He will do it according to the Scriptures, and never contrary to them.

Next I take into account *providential circumstances.* These often plainly indicate God's will in connection with His Word and Spirit.

I ask God in prayer to reveal His will to me aright.

Thus, through prayer to God, the study of His Word, and reflection, I come to a deliberate judgment, and if my mind is thus at peace, and continues so after two or three more petitions, I proceed accordingly. In *trivial matters,* and in transactions involving *most important issues,* I have found this method *always effective.* GEORGE MÜLLER 🐦

November 11

He was wounded for our transgressions, he was bruised for our iniquities: the chastisement of our peace was upon him; and with his stripes we are healed. (Isa. 53:5)

He is brought as a lamb to the slaughter. (Isa. 53:7)

Yet it pleased the LORD *to bruise him.* (Isa. 53:10)

I came alone to my Calvary,
And the load I bore was too great for me;
The stones were sharp and pierced my feet,
And my temples throbbed with the withering heat.

But my heart was faint with the toil that day,
So I sat down to think of an easy way;
Loomed sharply before me that tortuous trail—
No use to try—I would only fail.

I turned back in sorrow, clothed with defeat,
For my load was too heavy; I would retreat

To easier highways, with scenery more fair—
Yet a moment I lingered watching there.

As I held my gaze on that flinty side,
A man came up to be crucified;
He toiled all the way of that painful road,
And the cross that he bore far surpassed my load:

His brow with thorns was pierced and torn;
His face had a look of pain and was worn;
He stopped for a moment and looked on me—
And I followed in rapture to Calvary!

My Calvary, by Matthew Biller

Haunt the place called Calvary.

November 12

Though it be tried with fire. (1 Peter 1:7)

"What makes this set of china so much more expensive than that?" asked the customer.

"It has more work on it. It has been put through the fire twice. See, in this one the flowers are in a yellow band; in that one they are on the white background. This had to be put *through the fire a second time* to get the design on it."

"Why is the pattern on this vessel so blurred and marred—the design not brought out clearly?"

"That one was *not burned enough.* Had it remained in the furnace longer *the dark background would have become gold*—dazzling gold, and the pattern would have stood out clear and distinct."

Perhaps some of those who seem to have more than their share of suffering and disappointment are, like the costly china, being *doubly tried* in the fire, that they may be more valuable in the Master's service.

The potter never sees his clay take on rich shades of silver, or red, or cream, or brown, or yellow, until after the darkness and the burning of the furnace. These colors come—*after the burning and darkness.* The clay is beautiful—after the burning and darkness. The vase is made possible—after the burning and darkness.

How universal is this law of life! Where did the bravest man and the purest woman you know get their whitened characters? Did they not get them as the clay gets its beauty—after the darkness and the burning of the furnace? Where did Savonarola get his eloquence? In the darkness and burning of the furnace wherein God discovered deep things to him. Where did Stradivari get his violins? Where did Titian get his color? Where did Angelo get his marble? Where did Mozart get his music, and Chatterton his poetry, and Jeremiah his sermons? They got them where the clay gets its glory and its shimmer—in the darkness and the burning of the furnace. ROBERT G. LEE

Thou who didst fashion man on earth, to be
Strong in Thy strength, and with Thy freedom free,
Complete at last Thy great design in me.

Cost what it may of sorrow and distress,
Of empty hands, of utter loneliness,
I dare not, Lord, be satisfied with less.

So, Lord, reclaim Thy great design in me,
Give or reclaim Thy gifts, but let me be
Strong in Thy strength, and with Thy freedom free.

Let us not rebel at the second breath of the flame if He sends it.

November 13

Now unto him that is able to keep you from falling, and to present you faultless before the presence of his glory with exceeding joy. (Jude 24)

Take that word *keep* and hold it close to your heart tonight and tomorrow. It is one of the great and magnificent messages of the Gospel—"He is able to *keep* you from falling." Put into the word *you* all the weakness, all the unworthiness, all the sinfulness which belongs to man since the Fall; yet, He is able to keep *you*. He does not underrate the disadvantage of its being *you* when *He* bids His messengers say He is "able to keep you from falling." It would be impossible, utterly impossible, were it not undertaken by Infinite love. Look out, and up, then. Look *up* "from the depth"—the vast depth of your weakness, perhaps of your mysteriously inherited weakness. Look *out* of your failure under some temptation, inward or outward, inherited so to speak from yourself, from your own unfaithfulness in the past. Look up, out of your ruined purposes—unto Himself.

Being what He is, Keeper of Israel, God of the promises, Lord of the Sacrifice, Prince of life, present Savior, indwelling Power, He is able to keep *you*, that *your* feet shall not totter. They shall stand "in a large room"; they shall hold on straight, until at last they enter, step by step—for it is one step at a time even then—"through the gates into the city."

"He shall never give thy feet to tottering." H. C. G. MOULE

We may step firmly down upon the temptation which Another has crushed for us, and we are conquerors in Him.

> *Behind the dim unknown*
> *Standeth God within the shadows*
> *Keeping watch above His own.*

November 14

Enoch walked with God. (Gen. 5:22)

A day's walk with God will do more to awaken awe, wonder, and amazement in your soul than would a century of travel through the sights of the earth. He chooses for you a way you know not, that you may be compelled into a thousand intercourses with Him, which will make the journey ever memorable with glory to Him and blessing to you.

> *Jesus, these eyes have never seen*
> *That radiant form of Thine;*
> *The veil of sense hangs dark between*
> *Thy blessed face and mine.*
>
> *I see Thee not, I hear Thee not,*
> *Yet art Thou oft with me;*
> *And earth hath ne'er so dear a spot*
> *As where I meet with Thee.*
>
> *Like some bright dream that comes unsought*
> *When slumbers o'er me roll,*
> *Thine image ever fills my thought*
> *And charms my ravished soul.*
>
> *Yet though I have not seen, and still*
> *Must rest in faith alone,*

I love Thee, dearest Lord, and will,
Unseen but not unknown.

November 15

Abide ye here and keep awake with me. (Matt. 26:38, Trans.)

When He needed God most in the greatest crisis of His life, Jesus sought a garden. Under the olive trees, with the Passover moon shining down upon Him, He prayed in agony for strength to do God's will. Only those who have been through such agony can realize even in part what that bleak hour of renunciation, for the sake of you and me, meant to Christ.

Are we willing that He should suffer Gethsemane and the Cross for us *in vain?*

> *"I go to pray," He said to the eight,*
> *"Rest here at the gate."*
> *But He spake to the three entreatingly,*
> *"Will you watch with me as I pray*
> *A stone's throw away?*
> *I suffer tonight exceedingly."*
> *The eight slept well at the garden gate*
> *(As tired men will);*
> *The three tossed fitfully within,*
> *(Twice half-roused by His need of them)*
> *But they slept—*
> *Till the black in the East turned gray,*
> *Till their garments were drenched with the*
> *tears of the day:*
>
> *Slept*
> *Till He called them—each one by his name—*
> *The three within, and the eight at the gate.*
>
> *The ground was hard where the eight had slept*
> *(As hard as the road the soldiers stepped);*
> *The grass was bent where the three had dreamt,*
> *But red where the Lord had wept.*

MIRIAM LeFEVRE CROUSE

"What, could ye not keep awake with me one hour?" (Matt. 26:40).

November 16

The love of Christ, which passeth knowledge. (Eph. 3:19)

We do not really see the ocean. To do that is beyond our power. Through that vista we glimpse a bit of blue water as though God has painted a picture and framed it with hills and trees. But southward and northward on distance-hidden shores stretches water we have never seen. Bays lie placid by sunlit rocks, and long surges roll in soothing rhythm on smoothly sloping sands. Inlets ripple under tropic moons, and warming currents bear springtime's promise to frozen arctic reefs. Beyond that curved blue line that limits our sight, there rolls an open plain of waters to realms where we have never been, leaving the strands of palmy islands of which we do not know. And this is but the surface! Beneath are miles of depth, fathomless with mysteries beyond the thoughts of men.

God's measureless love is like the ocean. Through the windows of earthly life we catch a gleam. From the valleys of trouble we glimpse it near the shore. On the sands of hope we see it, wave on wave. From the headlands of faith we view a broader tide to the line that blends eternity with time. Our happiest days are islands set in its boundless breadth. Yet, as with the ocean, we have never seen it *all!* Even eternity cannot reveal its greatness to the wondering hosts of heaven, nor all the universe exhaust the fountains whence it flows.

We can only see a little of the ocean,
Just a few miles distant from the rocky shore,
But out there—far beyond our eyes' horizon,
There's more—immeasurably more.

We can only see a little of God's loving—
A few rich treasures from His mighty store;
But out there—far beyond our eyes' horizon,
There's more—immeasurably more.

November 17

LORD, *I am oppressed; undertake for me.* (Isa. 38:14)

Are you feeling that life for you has become a tangled skein; tangled with problems that seem to be desperately hard to unravel? If so, examine them and see whether it be not true that somewhere in the tangle there is the golden thread of an obvious present duty. Commence with that thread: *what ought you to do next? Now! Never mind tomorrow!*

> *Father, my life is in tangle,*
> *Thread after thread appears*
> *Twisted and broken and knotted,*
> *Viewed through the lapse of years.*
>
> *I cannot straighten them, Father;*
> *Oh, it is very hard;*
> *Somehow or other it seemeth,*
> *All I have done is marred.*
>
> *I did not see they were getting*
> *Into this tangled state;*
> *How it has happened I know not—*
> *Is it too late, too late?*
>
> *Is it? "Ah, no!" Thou dost whisper,*
> *"Out of this life of thine*
> *Yet may come wonderful beauty*
> *Wrought by My Power Divine."*
>
> *Take then, the threads, O my Father,*
> *Let them Thy mind fulfill,*
> *Work out in love a pattern*
> *After Thy holy will!*
>
> CHARLOTTE MURRAY

The case looks utterly hopeless. Hope is dead—yea, buried, and the bones are lying scattered at the grave's mouth. *But the eye fixed on the living God can bring a resurrection.* Hope may yet flourish again. The net of terrible entanglement may be broken *by a Father's hand,* and liberty and life abundant may yet be mine!

> *The Savior can solve every problem,*
> *The tangles of life can undo,*
> *There is nothing too hard for Jesus,*
> *There is nothing that He cannot do.*
>
> OSWALD J. SMITH

November 18

But be of good cheer! (John 16:33)

Jesus said, "Ye shall have tribulation"—not difficulties, but *tribulation*. But "tribulation worketh *patience*."

Millstones are used to grind the corn to powder, and typify the sacredness of the discipline of life.

"No man shall take the nether or the upper millstone to pledge: *for he taketh a man's life to pledge*" (Deut. 24:6, emphasis added).

You have been having a snug time in the granary; then God brings you out and puts you under the millstones, and the first thing that happens is the grinding separation of which our Lord spoke: *"Blessed are ye, when men shall . . . cast out your name as evil, for the Son of man's sake."* Crushed forever is any resemblance to the other crowd.

Hands off! when God is putting His saints through the experience of the millstones. We are apt to want to interfere in the discipline of another saint. *Do not hinder the production of the bread that is to feed the world!*

In the East the women sing as they grind the corn between the millstones. *"The sound of the millstones is music in the ears of God."* It is not music to the worldling, but the saint understands that His Father has a purpose in it all.

Ill-tempered persons, hard circumstances, poverty, willful misunderstandings and estrangements are all millstones. Had Jesus any of these things in His life? Had He not! He had a devil in His company for three years! He was continually thwarted and misunderstood by the Pharisees. And *is the disciple above His Master?*

When these experiences come, *remember that God has His eye on every detail.*

But beware! lest the *tiniest element of self-pity keeps God from putting us anywhere near the millstones.* OSWALD CHAMBERS 🖎

November 19

If a son shall ask. (Luke 11:11)

Henry Gibbud was a mission worker in the city of New York. He was a man of great devotion and wonderful power in prayer. On one occasion he had been working all night in the slums of the great city.

Tired and sleepy at the end of his toil, he made his way in the dark of the morning to the Brooklyn ferry dock. He put his hand in his pocket to pay his fare homeward, but to his dismay he discovered that he did not have the three pennies needed. His heart sank in deep discouragement, but he closed his eyes and began to pray. "Lord, I have been toiling all night in Thy service, trying to bring lost men and women to Thee. I am hungry and sleepy and wish to go home, but I do not have even three pennies for my fare. Will You not help me?"

As he closed his simple prayer, he opened his eyes. They fell upon something shining in the dust at his feet. He reached down and picked up the glittering object and found it was a fifty-cent piece. He paid his fare and went on his way rejoicing.

What was the joy that flooded his heart? It was the fulfillment of the precious promise: *"If a son shall ask."*

Have you taken your place in God's presence, not as a stranger, but as a son?

"If a son, then an heir."

Heir of a mighty King, heir to a throne,
Why art thou wandering sad and alone?
Heir to the love of God, heir to His grace,
Rise to thy privilege, claiming thy place.

Heir of a Conqueror, why dost thou fear?
Foes cannot trouble thee when He is near.
Child of the promises, be not oppressed,
Claim what belongs to thee, find sweetest rest.

Heir by inheritance! child of thy God!
Right to thy sonship is found in His Word;
Walk with the noble ones, never alone;
Prince of the Royal Blood, come to thy throne.

Heirs! we are joint-heirs with Jesus our Lord!
Heirs of the Covenant, found in His Word!
Rise to thy privilege, heir to His grace!
Heir to the love of God, rise, claim thy place!

SELECTED

November 20

O LORD, I know that the way of man is not in himself: it is not in man ... to direct his steps. (Jer. 10:23)

We were at the foot of Mont Blanc in the village of Chamouni. A sad thing had happened the day before. A young physician had determined to reach the heights of Mont Blanc. He accomplished the feat and the little village was illuminated in his honor; on the mountainside a flag was floating that told of his victory.

After they had ascended, and descended as far as the hut, he wanted to be released from his guide; he wanted to be free from the rope, and insisted on going on alone.

The guide remonstrated with him, telling him it was not safe; *but he tired of the rope,* and declared that he would be free. The guide was compelled to yield. The young man had gone only a short distance when his foot slipped on the ice and he could not stop himself from sliding down the icy steeps. The rope was gone, so the guide could not hold him nor pull him back. Out on the shelving ice lay the body of the young physician.

The bells had been rung, the village had been illumined in honor of his success; but alas, in a fatal moment he refused to be guided; *he was tired of the rope.*

Do *you* get tired of the rope? God's providences hold us, restrain us, and we get tired sometimes. *We need a guide,* and shall *until* the dangerous paths are over. *Never get disengaged from your Guide.* Let your prayer be "Lead Thou me on," and sometime the bells of heaven will ring that you are safe at home! CHARLES H. SPURGEON

> *Oh, tame me, Lord! rebellious nature calm.*
> *Oh, tame me, Lord!*
> *This heart so tossed and filled with wild alarm;*
> *Oh, tame me, Lord!*
>
> *These human longings, let them end in Thee,*
> *And let me be Thy bond-slave—*
> *Even me.*

THE MARECHAL

November 21

I was left alone, and saw this great vision. (Dan. 10:8)

What lonely men were the great prophets of Israel! John the Baptist stood alone from the crowd! Paul had to say, *"all men forsook me."* And, who was ever more alone than the Lord Jesus?

Victory for God is never won by the multitude. The man who dares to go where others hold back will find himself alone, but he will see the glory of God, and enter into the secrets of eternity. GORDON WATT

I go alone
Upon the narrow way that leads
Through shadowed valleys, over rocky heights,
To glorious plains beyond;
And sometimes when the way is very lone
I cry out for companionship, and long
For fellow-travelers on the toilsome path,
Until a Voice of sweetest music whispers,
"My grace sufficient is, no other guide thou needst
But Me." And then the path grows brighter as
I go alone.

My Savior knows
The way I take. Himself has trod
The selfsame road. He knows each stone,
Temptations, pitfalls hid by blossoms fair,
The hour of darkness that my life must share,
The wilderness of sorrow, doubt, and fear,
Renunciation's agony, and every pang
Of loneliness and labor's wear; enough for me
That He has known it all, that now He stays
To strengthen, guide and help me. I am glad
My Savior knows.

Thy will be done
Whether on pleasant paths I walk along,
Or crouch amid the lightnings of the storm,
Whether for me the larks of springtime sing,
Or winter's icy blasts my being sting;
Whatever Thou dost send is best for me,
With joyful heart I take it all from Thee,
Rejoicing in Thy sovereignty, and pray
That Thou wilt lead me on my upward way;

The road grows smoother as I travel on.
Thy will be done.

AMY L. PERSON

The lone wolf travels a lonely path, *but he beats the pack to the kill!*

November 22

Lo, all these things worketh God ... with man. (Job 33:29)

In a certain old town was a great cathedral. And in that cathedral was a wondrous stained-glass window. Its fame had gone abroad over the land. From miles around people pilgrimaged to gaze upon the splendor of this masterpiece of art. One day there came a great storm. The violence of the tempest forced in the window, and it crashed to the marble floor, shattered into a hundred pieces. Great was the grief of the people at the catastrophe which had suddenly bereft the town of its proudest work of art. They gathered up the fragments, huddled them in a box, and carried them to the cellar of the church. One day there came along a stranger and craved permission to see the beautiful window. They told him of its fate. He asked what they had done with the fragments; and they took him to the vault and showed him the broken morsels of glass. "Would you mind giving these to me?" said the stranger. "Take them along," was the reply, "they are no longer of any use to us." The visitor carefully lifted the box and carried it away in his arms. Weeks passed by; then one day came an invitation to the custodians of the cathedral. It was from a famous artist, noted for his master-skill in glass-craft. It summoned them to his study to inspect a stained-glass window, the work of his genius. Ushering them into his studio he stood them before a great veil of canvas. At the touch of his hand upon a cord the canvas dropped. And there before their astonished gaze shone a stained-glass window surpassing in beauty all their eyes had ever beheld. As they gazed entranced upon its rich tints, wondrous patterns, and cunning workmanship the artist turned and said: "This window I have wrought from the fragments of your shattered one, and it is now ready to be replaced."

Once more a great window shed its beauteous light into the dim aisles of the old cathedral, but the splendor of the new far surpassed the glory of the old, and the fame of its strange fashioning filled the land.

Do you say that your plans have been crushed? Then know this: Jesus Christ is a matchless life-mender. *Try Him!* JAMES H. McCONKEY

November 23

These are they which follow the Lamb whithersoever he goeth.
(Rev. 14:4)

There are three classes in the Christian life; the men *of the wing,* the men *of the couch,* and the men *of the road.*

The *first* are those who fly before; they are the pioneers of progress; they are in advance of their fellows.

The *second* are those who stand still, or rather lie still; they are the invalids of the human race—they come not to minister, but to be ministered unto.

The *third* are those who follow; they are *the ambulance corps of humanity;* they are the sacrificial souls that come on behind. I think with John that these last are the most beautiful souls of all. They are lovely in their unobtrusiveness; they do not wish to lead, choosing rather to be in the rear; they come forward only when others are driven backward. They want no glory from the battle, no wreath for the victory, no honorable mention among the heroes. They seek the wounded, the dying, the dead; they anoint for life's burial; they bring spices for the crucified; they give the cup of cold water; they wash the soiled feet. They break the fall of Adam; of Magdalene. They take in Saul of Tarsus after he becomes blind. They are attracted by defects; they are lured by every form of helplessness.

> *They come out to meet the shadows:*
> *They go in the track, not of the lark,*
> *but of the nightingale;*
> *They follow the* LAMB.

Give me the trouble without the glitter, O Lord! Let others lead! I am content to follow. Help me to serve Thee in the background! Is it not written *they that tarry at home divide the spoil?* I cannot fight Thy battles, but I can nurse Thy wounded. I cannot repel Thy foes, but I can repair Thy fortress. I cannot conduct Thy marches, but I can succor those who have fainted by the way.

Write my name amongst those *who follow Thee!*

O Captain of my Salvation, *put me with the ambulance corps!* GEORGE MATHESON

> *What though the hindmost place is thine,*
> *And thou art in the rear?*

This need not cause thy heart a pang,
Nor cost thine eye a tear.
The post of duty is the place
Where oft the Captain shows His face.

All cannot charge or lead the van,
All can be brave and true;
And where the Captain's standards wave
There's work for all to do;
And work from which thou may'st not flee,
Which must be done, and done by thee.

Among the stragglers, faint and few,
Thou dost thy march pursue;
This need not make thy heart to droop,
The weak may yet be true;
Through many a dark and stormy day
The Captain thus holds on His way.

SELECTED

"They shall go hindmost with their standards" *(Num. 2:31).*

November 24

I know the plans which I am planning for you, plans of welfare and not of calamity, to give you a future and a hope. (Jer. 29:11, Rotherham)

The love of God a perfect plan
Is planning now for thee,
It holds "a future and a hope,"
Which yet thou canst not see.

Though for a season, in the dark,
He asks thy perfect trust,
E'en that thou in surrender "lay
Thy treasure in the dust,"

Yet He is planning all the while,
Unerringly He guides
The life of him, who holds His will
More dear than all besides.

Trust were not trust if thou couldst see
The ending of the way,
Nor couldst thou learn His songs by night,
Were life one radiant day.

Amid the shadows here He works
The plan designed above,
"A future and a hope" for thee
In His exceeding love.

"A future"—abiding fruit,
With loving kindness crowned;
"A hope"—which shall thine own transcend,
As Heaven the earth around.

Though veiled as yet, one day thine eyes
Shall see His plan unfold,
And clouds that darkened once the path
Shall shine with Heaven's gold.

Enriched to all eternity
The steadfast soul shall stand,
That, "unoffended," trusted Him
Who all life's pathway planned.

I have an heritage of bliss,
Which yet I may not see;
The Hand that bled to make it mine,
Is keeping it for me.

FREDA HANBURY ALLEN

November 25

Take now thy son . . . whom thou lovest. (Gen. 22:2)

God's command is "Take *now*" not presently. To go to the height God shows can never be done *presently*. It must be done *now*.

"*And offer him there for a burnt offering upon one of the mountains which I will tell thee of.*" The mount of the Lord is the very height of the trial into which God brings His servant. There is no indication of the cost to Abraham; his implicit understanding of God so far outreaches his explicit knowledge that he trusts God utterly and climbs the highest height on which God can ever prove him, and remains unutterably true to Him.

There was not conflict; *that was over.* Abraham's confidence was fixed; he did not consult with flesh and blood—his own or anyone else's; he *instantly* obeyed. The point is, that though all other voices should proclaim differently, obedience to the dictates of the Spirit of God at all costs is to be the attitude of the faithful soul.

Always beware when you want to confer with your own flesh and blood—i.e., your own sympathies, your own insight. When our Lord is bringing us into personal relationship with Himself, it is always the individual relationship He breaks down.

If God has given the command, He will look after everything; your business is to *get up and go!* OSWALD CHAMBERS ❦

"The Holy Ghost saith, *Today*" (Heb. 3:7, emphasis added).

> *Not of the sunlight,*
> *Not of the moonlight,*
> *Not of the starlight!*
> *O young Mariner,*
> *Down to the haven*
> *Call your companions,*
> *Launch your vessel*
> *and crowd your canvas,*
> *And, ere it vanishes*
> *Over the margin,*
> *After it, follow it,*
> *Follow the Gleam.*

TENNYSON ❦

November 26

Come apart with me, and rest awhile. (Mark 6:31, Trans.)

There is one pause in music of which the untrained singer does not know the value—the pause: it is not the cessation of the music; it is a part of it.

Before the tide ebbs or flows there is always a time of poise when it is neither ebbing nor flowing.

In a Christian life that is to be effective, there will always be the *pause* and the *poise*.

The desert has been God's training school for many of His prophets—Abraham, Moses, Elijah, Paul. But not all who come from Arabia are prophets; and God has other schools. Before the years of witness, there were the years of stillness. Every witness with a great message has these years. Let not the saints shrink from the discipline and training! The sightless days will mean a grander vision; the silent years, the sweeter song. If the Lord puts you in the dark, it is but to strengthen your eyes to bear the glory that He is preparing for you; if He bids you be silent, it is but to tune your tongue to His praise. Remember that the *pause* is part of the music.

The great Composer writes the theme
And gives us each a part to play;
To some a sweet and flowing air,
Smooth and unbroken all the way;

They pour their full heart's gladness out
In notes of joy and service blent;
But some He gives long bars of "rests,"
With idle voice and instrument.

He who directs the singing spheres,
The music of the morning stars,
Needs, for His full creation's hymn,
The quiet of the soundless bars.

Be silent unto God, my soul,
If this the score He writes for thee,
And "hold the rest," play no false note
To mar His perfect harmony.

Yet be thou watchful for thy turn,
Strike on the instant, true and clear,
Lest from the grand, melodious whole
Thy note be missing to His ear.

ANNIE JOHNSON FLINT

November 27

Spikenard, very costly. (John 12:3)

Love's reckoning will always be *unusual.* It was by no means the *ordinary* thing to do for the homeless Savior; *that* breaking of the alabaster and *that* lavish anointing were quite out of the *usual way.*

Did Mary's heart beat painfully as she glided in with her hoarded treasure? Did she intuitively hide her purpose from all eyes but His, who read its irrepressible meaning? Perhaps she thought only of Him who was her ALL.

Apparently she obtained her spikenard *for the very purpose* that she might anoint the Lord's body in burial. Possibly it was only an impulse which made her decide to anoint Him *beforehand*. Let us rejoice that she made the Master's heart glad before it was too late.

One tiny violet of encouragement will mean more to those with whom we live today than will acres of orchids when their pulses are stilled in death.

There were *four women* who set out later with their spices, only to find the empty tomb.

The opportunity for anointing had passed.

It is passing today! Not in realms of glory will we be able to share in His sufferings, to help in bearing the Cross. *Here, and here alone* such service may be ours.

O soul of mine, be extravagant in love of Jesus!

There is no fragrance like that of my alabaster box—the box I break for Him!

I shall not pass this way again,
But far beyond earth's "where and when,"
May I look back along the road
Where on both sides good seed I sowed.

I shall not pass this way again;
May wisdom guide my tongue and pen,
And love be mine, that so I may
Plant roses all along the way.

I shall not pass this way again;
Grant me to soothe the hearts of men,
Faithful to friends, true to my God;
A fragrance on the path I trod.

November 28

Who keepeth His promise forever. (Ps. 146:6, Trans.)

God never forgets His Word. Long ago He promised a Redeemer; and although *He waited four thousand years*, the promise at last was most surely fulfilled.

He promised Abraham a son; and although a quarter of a century of testing intervened, the promise at last came literally true. He promised Abraham the Land of Promise as an inheritance; and although *four hundred years* of trial intervened, at last the land was possessed. *He promised Jeremiah* that after *seventy years* the captives should return from Babylon; and on the very hour, the action answered to the Word. *He promised Daniel* that at a definite time Messiah should appear; and the most extraordinary evidence that we have to offer to the doubting Hebrew today that Jesus is his Messiah, is the literal fulfillment of the prophecy of Daniel.

Just as true are God's promises to the believer. They are all "Yea and Amen" in Christ Jesus. He has guaranteed them. The promises of God form a great checkbook. Every one is endorsed by the Mediator, and His word and honor are pledged to their fulfillment. To make them "Yea and Amen" *you must sign your name* upon the back of the promise and then *personally appropriate it.*

"No one who believes in Him shall be disappointed" *(Rom. 10:11, Way's trans.).*

November 29

From this day will I bless you. (Hag. 2:19)

꩜

God has certain dates from which He begins to bless us. On the day of consecration (Gen. 22:16–17), the day when our all is surrendered to Him—on that day untold blessing begins.

Have we come to *that date?*

"It was on the 22nd of July, 1690, that happy day," says Madame Guyon, "that my soul was delivered from all its pains. On that day I was restored, as it were, to perfect liberty. I was *no longer depressed,* no longer borne down under the burden of sorrow. I had thought God lost, and lost forever; but I found Him again. And He returned to me with unspeakable magnificence and purity. In a wonderful manner difficult to explain, *all that which had been taken from me was not only restored, but restored with increase and new advantages. In Thee, O my God, I found it all, and more than all!* The peace which I now possessed was all holy, heavenly, inexpressible. What I had possessed some years before, in the period of my spiritual enjoyment, was consolation, peace—the *gifts* of God, but now that I was fully yielded

to the will of God, whether that will was consoling or otherwise, I might now be said to possess not merely consolation, but the
God of consolation; not merely peace, but the God of peace.

*"One day of this happiness, which consisted in simple rest or harmony with
God's will, whatever that will might be, was sufficient to counterbalance years
of suffering.* Certainly it was not I, myself, who had fastened my soul to the
Cross and, under the operations of a providence just but inexorable, had
drained, if I may so express it, the blood of the life of nature to the last
drop. I did not understand it then; but I understand it *now.* It was the Lord
who did it. *It was God that destroyed me, that He might give me true life."*

> *Oh, the Spirit-filled life may be thine, may be thine,*
> *In thy soul evermore the Shechinah may shine;*
> *It is thine to live with the tempests all stilled,*
> *It is thine with the blest Holy Ghost to be filled;*
> *It is thine, even thine, for thy Lord has so willed.*

November 30

The battle is the LORD's! (1 Sam. 17:47)

How prone we are to lose sight of this, and to imagine, because we see
only our little corner in the conflict, that the battle is ours!

*If the battle is the Lord's, then the responsibilities for planning belong to
Him.* Everything connected with the line of attack, the method of defense,
must belong to Him. We need not be anxious as to the enemy's subtlety,
activity, or power.

"As captain of the host of the LORD am I now come."

He has a full view of the enemy's movements, and a perfect knowledge
of the enemy's devices. He has anticipated all the enemy's wiles. It is impossible for Him to be deceived, or to be taken by surprise. It is His glory that
is at stake; the honor of His name that is being assailed. *He is able to withstand the mightiest foe!*

If the battle is the Lord's the supplies will be all-sufficient. No one knows
how much is wanted in the day of battle like that General who has been
through many campaigns. *We shall lack nothing to make us victorious warriors.*

The Victory is certain! The Captain on whose side we are has never
known defeat. He goes forth conquering and to conquer. The enemy may
apparently gain temporary advantage at different points of the battle, but
victory over Christ by Satan is simply impossible!

But He expects us to *rest* in His wisdom. In the thick of the fight, in the midst of the smoke and din of battle, we may fail to see the wisdom of all God's ways. When we cannot see, it is then that we must *rest in His wisdom.* Let us have confidence in His power, and be obedient to His commands.

> *I will not fear the battle,*
> *If Thou art by my side.*

"Now thanks be to God who leads us on in the train of his triumph" (2 Cor. 2:14, Conybeare & Howson).

Queen Victoria said, "We are not interested in the possibilities of defeat. They do not exist!"

December 1

They saw no man, save Jesus only. (Matt. 17:8)

When Samuel Rutherford lay in Aberdeen prison, we are told he used to write at the top of his letters, *"God's Palace, Aberdeen."*

When Madame Guyon was imprisoned in the castle at Vincennes, she said: "It seems as though I were a little bird whom the Lord has placed in a cage, and that I have nothing now to do but sing."

> *And prisons shall palaces prove*
> *If Jesus abides with me there.*

I never had in all my life so great an inlet into the Word of God as now; those Scriptures that I saw nothing in before, are in this place and state [in Bedford Jail] made to shine upon me; Jesus Christ also was never more real and apparent than now; here I have seen and felt Him indeed! JOHN BUNYAN

The New Testament tells of no regret on the part of those who sacrificed themselves for Christ. The apostles never pathetically recite the story of what they gave up for the Christian ministry. The ancient martyrs sometimes kissed the stake at which they suffered so cruelly.

This is the spirit in which *we* should lose, suffer, and die for Christ's sake.

By thus renouncing all, we gain all. Nothing yields higher interest than loving self-denials for the highest claims.

"I have seen the headlight of a giant engine rushing onward through the darkness, heedless of opposition and fearless of danger. I have seen the lightning at midnight leap athwart a storm-swept sky, splintering chaotic darkness with beams of light until the heavens glittered like midday sun. I knew this was grand, but the grandest thing this side of the light that flows from God Almighty's throne, is the blessed benediction of a human life that spends itself in forgetful service for a brokenhearted world and finds its home at last in the bosom of the everlasting God."

I walk alone, and I am sore afraid;
My way is dark, my path with thorns o'erlaid;
Draw near me, Lord, and take my trembling hand
And make me brave to join Thy pilgrim band.

Thou hast a band which fears not dark nor death,
Which suffers agony at every breath,
Yet sings with joy e'en in the midst of pain,
With whom the greatest loss is greatest gain.

Who would not walk with such a company?
Who would not sing with such an ecstasy?
Did I say lone and fear? May God forgive
And teach me, e'en through sorrow, how to live.

Life is not life which knows no shrinking fears;
Life is not life which sheds no bitter tears;
This is true life when, through dark suffering,
One learns from Christ and men brave conquering.

Then lead me on thou martyr-host of God!
Then lead me on, O Christ, to Thine abode;
There with Thy holy ones I shall find rest
And learn that death, in life, was God's great best.

HENRY W. FROST

December 2

He is altogether lovely! (Song 5:16)

What a glorious fact it is that there is one life that can be held up before the eyes of humanity as *a perfect pattern!* There were lips that never spoke unkindness, that never uttered an untruth; there were eyes that never looked aught but love and purity and bliss; there were arms that never closed against wretchedness or penitence; there was a bosom which never throbbed with sin, nor ever was excited by unholy impulse; there was a man free from all undue selfishness, and whose life was spent in going about doing good.

There was One who loved all mankind, and who loved them more than Himself, and who gave Himself to die that they might live; there was One who went into the gates of death, that the gates of death might never hold us in; there was One who lay in the grave, with its dampness, its coldness, its chill, and its horror, and taught humanity how it might ascend above the grave; there was One who, though He walked on earth, had His conversation in heaven, who took away the curtain that hid immortality from view, and presented to us the Father God in all His glory and in all His love.

Such an One is the standard held up in the Church of Christ. The Church rallies round the Cross and gathers around Jesus; and it is because He is so attractive, and lovely, and glorious, that they are coming from the ends of the earth to see the salvation of God. BISHOP MATTHEW SIMPSON 🐝

> *Less than Thyself, Oh do not give.*
> *In might Thyself within me live;*
> *Come all Thou hast and art.*

Oh, there is nothing so admirable, nothing which seems to us in our best moods so worthy of our seeking, and so rich in its possession as that holiness which is the summit of true perfection; not a holiness which is distant and frigid, but a holiness which makes the eyes more tender in their softened light, and the lips more affluent of genial speech, and the hand more helpful in its ready service; which makes an end in the human heart of its passions and selfishness, its moroseness and its meanness; which lifts man up to God, and brings God down to man; and which, should it become pervasive and universal, would make every soul a miniature heaven, and change our woeful earth into a Paradise regained.

"We . . . beholding . . . the glory of the Lord, are changed into the same image . . . even as by the Spirit of the Lord" (2 Cor. 3:18). BISHOP NINDE 🐝

> *The honeysuckle blossoms drenched with rain*
> *That lend enchantment to a summer night;*
> *The purple violet hidden from the sight*

Beside the border of a country lane;
The jasmine vine, which hangs its golden chain
Within the forest like a twinkling light,
Have flourished for a time and taken flight—
Their ashes have returned to earth again.
But what of one whose life was like a flower
Which scatters gentle perfume everywhere,
Whose face had caught the radiance of the sky
From looking ever upward till that hour
When the Great Gardener stripped the branches bare?
God smells such fragrance from His throne on high.

FRAGRANCE, BY THOMAS KIMBER

December 3

That they may have life . . . more abundantly. (John 10:10)

What a contrast there is between a barren desert and the luxuriant oasis with its waving palms and its glorious verdure! between gaunt and hungry flocks and the herds that lie down in green pastures and beside the still waters; between the viewless plain and the mountain height with its "land of far distances."

What a difference there is between the aridity of an artificial, irrigated, stinted existence—a desert existence, and a life of abundant rains, crowding vegetation, and harvests that come almost of themselves—*the abundant life!*

The former is like the *shallow stream* where your boat every moment touches bottom or strikes some hidden rock; the latter is where your deep keel never touches ground and you ride *the ocean's wildest swells!*

There are some Christians who always seem to be kept on scant measure. Their spiritual garments are threadbare, their whole bearing that of people who are poverty-stricken and kept on short allowance—hard up, and on the ragged edge of want and bankruptcy. They come through "by the skin of their teeth" and are "saved so as by fire."

There are other souls who *"have life . . . more abundantly."* Their love "beareth all things, believeth all things, hopeth all things, endureth all things," and "never faileth." Their patience has "all long-suffering with joyfulness." Their peace "passeth all understanding." Their joy is "joy unspeakable and full of glory." Their service is so free and glad that duty is a delight. In a word, this life reaches out into the infinite as well as the eternal, sailing on the shoreless and fathomless seas of God and His infinite grace.

Oh, *where* is such a life to be found? How can the desert place be made to bring forth *abundant life*?

> *"Oh, where is the sea?" the fishes cried,*
> *As they swam the crystal waters through*
> *"We have heard from of old of the ocean tide,*
> *And we long to look on the waters blue.*
> *The wise ones speak of the infinite sea—*
> *Oh, who can tell us if such there be?"*

Are we who live in the sea of the infinite to imitate those silly fishes, and ask, "*Where* is the God who is 'not far from everyone of us,' who may be in our inmost hearts by faith, and in whom 'we live, and move, and have our being'?" DEAN FARRAR

"Hast thou entered into the fountains of the sea?" (*Job 38:16, Trans.*).

The Psalmist said: "O God, with Thee is the fountain of life." "All my fresh springing fountains are in Thee!"

Gushing Fountains!

December 4

Tender-hearted. (Eph. 4:32)

It is much easier to convince a human soul of its natural impurity, than to convince it of its natural hardness and utter destitution of heavenly and Divine tenderness. *The very essence of the Gospel is Divinely imparted tenderness and sweetness of spirit.* Even among intensely religious people, nothing is rarer to find than a continuous and all-pervading spirit of tenderness.

Tenderness of spirit is not the tenderness of mind and manner which results from high culture and a beautiful social training, though these are very valuable in life. No, *it is a supernatural work throughout the whole spiritual being. It is an exquisitely interior fountain of God's own sweetness and tenderness of nature, opened up in the inner spirit to such a degree that it completely inundates the soul, overflowing all the mental faculties and saturating with its sweet waters the manners, expressions, words, and tones of the voice; mellowing the will, softening the judgment, melting the affections, refining*

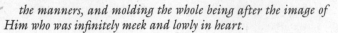

the manners, and molding the whole being after the image of Him who was infinitely meek and lowly in heart.

Tenderness of spirit cannot be borrowed or put on for special occasions; it is emphatically supernatural, and must flow out incessantly from the inner fountains of the life.

Deep tenderness of spirit is the very soul and marrow of the Christ life. What specific gravity is to the planet, what beauty is to the rainbow, what perfume is to the rose, what marrow is to the bone, what rhythm is to poetry, what the pulse is to the heart, what harmony is to music, what heat is to the human body—all this, and much more, is tenderness of spirit to religion. It is possible to be very religious, and staunch, and persevering in all Christian duties; possible, even, to be sanctified, to be a brave defender and preacher of holiness, to be mathematically orthodox and blameless in outward life, and very zealous in good works, and yet to be greatly lacking in tenderness of spirit—that all-subduing, all-melting love, which is the very cream and quintessence of Heaven, and which incessantly streamed out from the voice and eyes of the blessed Jesus.

I would that I could be
A wound-dresser
Of souls—
Reaching the aching heart,
The tortured mind,
Calming them as the night
Calms tired bodies
When she drops the mantle of sleep
Over the world.
As each cold, glittering star
So might I stand in mine,
But with the warmth of a smile
On my face,
And in my eyes
An image of the Soul Divine.

December 5

Do not be over-anxious about anything. (Phil. 4:6 WEYMOUTH)

"I recall an experience in my own Christian life," wrote James H. McConkey. "My father was dying of a disease *brought on by worriment*. A great physician had been summoned from the city. He was closeted with my father for a long time. Then he came out of the sick chamber soberly shaking his head. There was no hope. My father's earthly race was run. My dear mother asked the great doctor to take me aside for a conference; for I myself was breaking in body, and from the same dread enemy which overthrows so many Christian people—*anxious care*.

"The kind physician took me into another room and we sat down for a heart-to-heart talk. Very searchingly, and with all the skill of an expert, did he draw from me the humiliating fact that I was a prey of worriment and suffering from its dread results. In a few keen, incisive sentences, with no attempt at concealment he told me that I had fallen a victim of the same habit that had been my father's undoing, and that unless I overcame it there was no hope for me even as there was none for him.

"I went upstairs. I threw myself upon my knees in my bedchamber. I cried out in my agony of soul: 'O Christ! He says I must overcome worriment, and Thou alone knowest how I have *tried* to do so. I have fought; I have struggled; I have wept bitter tears. And *I have failed*. Oh, Lord Jesus, unless Thou dost undertake for me now it is all over with me.'

"Then and there I threw myself in utter helplessness upon Christ. Somehow, where before I had been struggling, I now found myself trusting as I had never quite done before. From that time onward Jesus Christ began to give me the beauty of victory for the somber ashes of defeat."

> *It is God's will that I should cast*
> *On Him my care each day;*
> *He also bids me not to cast*
> *My confidence away.*
> *But, Oh! I am so stupid, that*
> *When taken unawares,*
> *I cast away my confidence,*
> *And carry all my cares.*

December 6

He shall deliver the needy when he crieth. (Ps. 72:12)

Bending down to us in infinite love God says: "My child, *how needy are you?* What heavy burden is upon *you?* What grievous sorrow is darkening your faith? What fear of future ill is shadowing your pathway? What spiritual thirst do you want slaked? What barrenness of soul enriched? What do you need this hour? For I will deliver the needy."

To miss a need may be to miss a miracle!

You are just the one God is looking for—just the one who is ripe for deliverance—just the special individual to whom His promise is made. The human incompleteness meets the Divine completeness and the want is filled. The deepest yearning in every soul finds in Him the longed-for satisfaction.

Do not be too anxious to be free from needs, unless you want to be free from prayer-power.

We need our needs!

O God, I need Thee!
When morning crowds the night away
And the tasks of waking seize my mind,
I need Thy Poise.

O God, I need Thee!
When clashes come with those
Who walk the way with me,
I need Thy Smile.

O God, I need Thee!
When the path to take before me lies,
I see it—courage flees—
I need Thy Faith.

O God, I need Thee!
When the day's work is done,
Tired, discouraged, wasted;
I need Thy Rest.

December 7

Of thine own have we given thee. (1 Chron. 29:14)

❧

Who gives himself with his gifts feeds three—
Himself, his hungering neighbor, and Me.

LOWELL

"Andrew, I have only five barley loaves left and a couple of fish, but the Master shall have most of it. Here are three loaves, four—but one loaf

I should like to keep. You know, Andrew, it is a long way home, but the four loaves and the fishes I will give to Him."

As Andrew explains that the Master would like to have *all*, a struggle goes on in the boy's heart. He looks repeatedly, first at the fifth loaf, then at the Master. "Andrew, take all," he exclaims joyously as the light breaks. "Take all five, and the fishes, too."

What is the fifth loaf that you have not yet surrendered? Let me plead with you to let Him have ALL. PASTOR DOLMAN 🐝

Was it the "widow's mite," or "all her living" that caught our Lord's attention?

It was Martin Luther who wrote: "I have had many things in my hands, and I have lost them all; but whatever I have been able to place in God's hands I still possess."

There is a Divine law in connection with our giving. Christ with a few loaves and fishes, feeds thousands.

> *Give! as the morning that flows out of heaven;*
> *Give! as the waves when their channel is riven;*
> *Give! as the free air and sunshine are given!*
> *Lavishly, utterly, joyfully give!*
> *Not the waste drops of thy cup overflowing;*
> *Not the faith sparks of thy hearth ever glowing;*
> *Not a pale bud from the June roses blowing:*
> *Give as He gave thee who gave thee to live.*
> *Almost the day of thy giving is over;*
> *Ere from the grass dies the bee-haunted clover*
> *Thou wilt have vanished from friend and from lover:*
> *What shall thy longing avail in the grave?*
> *Give as the heart gives whose fetters are breaking—*
> *Life, love, and hope, all thy dreams and thy waking;*
> *Soon, heaven's river thy soul-fever slaking,*
> *Thou shalt know God and the gift that He gave.*
>
> ROSE TERRY COOKE 🐝

December 8

For a great door and effectual is opened unto me, and there are many adversaries. (1 Cor. 16:9)

Another expedition of Englishmen is trying to conquer Mt. Everest, the highest peak in the world.

Bitter cold, raging winds, a rarefied atmosphere, blinding blizzards, engulfing avalanches of snow and rock—all these dangers stand between brave men and the top of that towering mountain.

The last expedition came the nearest to success. A little more than two thousand feet below the peak the main body of the party pitched their highest camp. From that base two men, Mallory and Irvine, equipped with oxygen tanks, attempted a final dash to the top. They hoped to climb to the peak and return in about sixteen hours. They never came back. Of them the official record of the expedition said in simple words, "When last seen, *they were heading toward the summit.*"

> *Press on! Surmount the rocky steeps,*
> *Climb boldly o'er the torrent's arch;*
> *He fails alone who feeble creeps,*
> *He wins who dares the hero's march.*
> *Be thou a hero! Let thy might*
> *Tramp on eternal snows its way*
> *And through the ebon walls of night*
> *Hew down a passage unto day.*
>
> PARK BENJAMIN

The Kingdom of God will be brought in by Christians who, when last seen, *were heading toward the summit;* Christians who, with Paul, can accept the challenge of the "many adversaries" that guard the open door, even though they go down to defeat in their generation.

December 9

I am doing a great work, so that I cannot come down. (Neh. 6:3)

One of Satan's favorite employees is the "switchman." He likes nothing better than to sidetrack one of God's express trains, sent on some blessed mission and filled with the fire of a holy purpose.

Something will come up in the pathway of an earnest soul, to attract its attention, and occupy its strength and thought. Sometimes it is a little irritation and provocation. Sometimes it is some petty grievance we stop to pursue or adjust.

Very often, and *before we are aware of it,* we are absorbed in a lot of distracting cares and interests that quite turn us aside from *the great purpose of our life.*

We may not do much harm, but we have missed our connection. We have gotten off the main line.

Let these things alone. Let distractions come and go, but press forward steadily and irresistibly with your God-given task. The eagle flying in the upper air pays but little or no attention to what is going on in the earth below him. As children of God we are to occupy our rightful place, "in the heavenlies," "far above all" these petty things. God would have us to be "eagle saints." *Let us not stoop from our position!* A. B. SIMPSON ✥

An eagle does not catch flies!

December 10

For we walk by faith, not by sight. (2 Cor. 5:7)

Faith is taking God at His word. Faith is not belief without evidence. It is belief on the very best of evidence—the Word of Him "that cannot lie" (Titus 1:2). Faith is so rational that it asks no other evidence than this all-sufficient evidence. To ask other than the Word of Him who cannot lie is not *rationalism,* but consummate *irrationalism.* R. A. TORREY ✥

When we can *see,* it is *not faith but reasoning.*

Look at the faith of the master mariner! He looses his cable, he steams away from the land. For days, weeks, or even months, he sees neither sail nor shore; yet on he goes day and night without fear, till one morning he finds himself exactly opposite the desired haven toward which he had been steering.

How had he found his way over the trackless deep? He has trusted in his compass, his nautical almanac, his glass, and the heavenly bodies; and obeying their guidance, without sighting land, he has steered so accurately that he has not changed a point to enter port.

It is a wonderful thing—that sailing or steaming without sight. Spiritually it is a blessed thing to leave altogether the shores of sight and feeling; to say "Good-bye" to inward feelings, cheering providences, signs, tokens, and so forth. It is glorious to be far out on the ocean of Divine love, believing in God, and steering for Heaven straightaway, by the direction of the Word of God. CHARLES H. SPURGEON ✥

December 11

The Lord *bindeth up the breach of his people, and healeth the stroke of their wound.* (Isa. 30:26)

When some friend has proved untrue—betrayed your simple trust; used you for his selfish end, and trampled in the dust the Past, with all its memories, and all its sacred ties, the light is blotted from the sky—for something in you dies.

Bless your false and faithless friend, just smile and pass along—God must be the judge of it: He knows the right and wrong.... Life is short—don't waste the hours by brooding on the past; His great laws are good and just; Truth conquers at the last.

Red and deep our wounds may be—but after all the pain—God's own finger touches us, and we are healed again.... With faith restored, and trust renewed—we look toward the stars—the world will see the smiles we have—but God will see the scars. Scars, by Patience Strong

> *Love grows stronger when assailed;*
> *Love conquers where all else has failed.*
> *Love ever blesses those who curse;*
> *Love gives the better for the worse.*
> *Love unbinds others by its bonds;*
> *Love pours forgiveness from its wounds.*

> *Lord, let me love like Thee!*

December 12

He is faithful that promised. (Heb. 10:23)

God's power will keep God's promises! Promises for the soul, promises for the body, promises for others, promises for our work, promises for our business, promises for time and for eternity: *these are all ours!* It is not your weakness that can defeat God's promise, nor your strength that can fulfill the promise: He that spoke the Word will Himself make it good. *It is neither your business nor mine to keep God's promises:* that is His grace.

The signed check is given us. How foolish if we fear to present it! *Never yet has one single check been dishonored!* "*He is faithful* that promised."

I take; He undertakes!

We may pray much over a promise, and yet never obtain it. *Asking* is not *taking*. *Beseeching* is not *claiming*.

> *I clasp the hand of Love Divine,*
> *I claim the gracious promise mine,*
> *And add to His my countersign.*
> *I take, He undertakes.*
>
> *I simply take Him at His Word;*
> *I praise Him that my prayer is heard*
> *And claim my answer from the Lord.*
> *I take, He undertakes.*

A. B. SIMPSON

Remember what you take *is all you will* ever get.

December 13

The peace of God, which passeth all understanding, shall keep your hearts and minds through Christ Jesus. (Phil. 4:7)

There are depths in the ocean, I am told, which no tempest ever stirs— beyond the reach of all storms that sweep and agitate the surface of the sea. And there are heights in the blue sky above, to which no cloud ever ascends; where no tempest ever rages; where all is perpetual sunshine; where naught exists to disturb the deep serenity. Even *at the center of the cyclone there is rest.*

Each of these is an emblem of the soul which Jesus visits, to whom He speaks peace, whose fear He dispels, whose lamps of hope He trims.

During the test of a submarine it remained submerged for many hours. When it had returned to the harbor, the commander was asked: "Well, how did the storm affect you last night?" The Commander looked at him in surprise and said: "Storm? We knew nothing of any storm!"

> *Dwell deep. When doubts assail and stealthy shadows creep*
> *Across your sky, and fill you with a sense of doom,*
> *And thunders roar, and lightnings frighten with their glare,*
> *And old foundations seem to crumble 'neath your feet,*
> *Dwell deep and rest your soul amid eternal things.*
> *Upon the surface storms may rage, and billows break*
> *On every beach of life, and fling disaster*

*Far and wide; but if your soul is dwelling quiet
In the depths, naught can harm you evermore. Therefore
Dwell deep, and rest your head upon the heart of God.*

"When he giveth quietness, who then can make trouble?"
(Job 34:29).

December 14

They shall be abundantly satisfied. (Ps. 36:8)

Ask the eagle that splashes in the glory of the sun if it ever longs for its cage away down among the dim, distant earth scenes. If it ever stops to look at the old cage of former days, it is to sing its doxology of deliverance and soar away to its home near the sun.

The life of the Spirit-filled heart is *the winged life.* The unsurrendered life is the life of the cage. The best that the cage can give is a momentary thrill that soon gives place to a pitiful beating against the bars.

Our precious Savior, by His death on the Cross, proclaims "liberty to the captives," and you may be *set free;* free, not to take refuge on the branches of a nearby tree, but to "rise and walk in heaven's own light, above the world and sin, with heart made pure, and garments white, and Christ enthroned within!"

"They shall be abundantly satisfied." The song in your heart will daily be:

> *Thou, O Christ, art all I want;*
> *More than all in Thee I find.*

Forget the past, throw off your last fear, and leap boldly forward to *complete emancipation!*

> *O Christ, in Thee my soul hath found,*
> *And found in Thee alone,*
> *The peace, the joy I sought so long;*
> *The bliss till now unknown.*
>
> *I sighed for rest and happiness,*
> *I yearned for them, not Thee;*
> *But while I passed my Savior by,*
> *His love laid hold on me.*

I tried the broken cisterns, Lord,
But ah! the waters failed.
E'en as I stooped to drink they'd fled,
And mocked me as I wailed.

Now none but Christ can satisfy,
None other name for me;
There's love, and life, and lasting joy,
Lord Jesus, found in Thee!

December 15

If any man will come after me, let him deny himself, and take
up his cross, and follow me. (Matt. 16:24)

In the light of eternity, who are those who shall stand before the throne arrayed in white robes? Are they those who have come out of ease and pleasure, out of untroubled calm and unbroken human relationships? Nay, rather they are those who have come out of great tribulation. Had Milton not been blind, neither he nor we could have seen so clearly, and he could never have written,

> *My vision Thou hast dimmed,*
> *That I may see Thyself, Thyself alone.*

Out of blindness he learned the lesson so needed today by those cut off from an active life, that "They also serve who only stand and wait."

If Tennyson had not lost his friend Hallam, we should never have had his "In Memoriam."

One cannot have a victory without a battle! Character without
conflict! Perfect love without suffering!

As we visit the pearl fisheries, we find that life without pain leaves no pearl; that the life lived in sluggish ease, unwounded, without suffering or long-continued friction, forms no jewel.

As we pass the dwellings of men we find that without suffering *the pearl of great price,* the highest human character, is not formed.

Suffering is linked with joy for those who take it aright. *If you suffer without succeeding, it is that someone else may succeed. If you succeed without suffering, it is because someone else has suffered.*

> *"Is there no other way, O God,*
> *Except through sorrow, pain and loss,*

To stamp Christ's image on my soul?
No other way except the Cross?"

And then a voice stills all my soul,
As stilled the waves on Galilee:
"Canst thou not bear the furnace heat,
If 'mid the flames I walk with thee?

"I bore the Cross, I know its weight,
I drank the cup I hold for thee;
Canst thou not follow where I lead?
I'll give the strength—lean thou on me."

SELECTED 🍃

December 16

I am come that they might have life, and that they might have it more abundantly. (John 10:10)

What a breathtaking truth! "I am come." Just another way of saying, *"Before Abraham was, I AM."* All others began to be; our Lord is *pretemporal,* definitely coming out of the eternities for a definite purpose: "That they might have life." This quality of life which the Biologist from Eternity gives, increases in *quantity* forever— *"Abundantly!"*

The abundant life which Christ offers is the possession alone of those whom He designates "my sheep." It is not an entering into material blessedness. It is a spiritual fullness conditional altogether upon likeness to the Lord, and walking in that obedience toward God wherein He walked. Its first condition is the acceptance of the Cross whereby the world is crucified unto the believer and the believer unto the world. But, as this separation is recognized and accepted, and the life is wholly yielded and kept subject to the will of the Father, the Master's incoming and indwelling meets every longing and every need. Then alone will be understood the meaning of the promise of our text: "I am come that they might have life, and that they might have it more abundantly."

Have *we* come to the fountain of life? Are *we* drinking of its fullness? Are *we* living in His love? This is *the life of our spirit; the health of our body; the secret of our joy!*

May we seek this overflowing life, and become *"channels only,"* with *"all His wondrous power flowing through us"* so that He can use us every day and every hour! EVAN H. HOPKINS 🍃

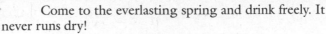

Come to the everlasting spring and drink freely. It never runs dry!

Though millions their thirst are now slaking,
It never runs dry,
And millions may still come partaking,
It never runs dry!

December 17

I will restore to you the years that the locust hath eaten. (Joel 2:25)

How many years we are not told; only this: *"I will restore the years."*

Human lives are often laid bare—barren patches produced by our own failures; a wilderness stretching across our life. But what comfort in these words: *"I will RESTORE to you the years that the locust hath eaten."*

Have you been brooding over some sorrow? Has it darkened your life as a swarm of locusts might darken the sun at midday? And have you cried out in your anguish, "The sun will never shine again"? But read the word He has promised:

"I will restore to you the years that the locust hath eaten."

Turn to Him, dear reader—turn to the One whom you may have been inclined to forget when you lived in the larger house. He is waiting; and if He does not see fit to give you back the earthly possession once so highly prized by you, remember this: *in a higher and better way He will restore those years.*

The years that the locust hath eaten sometimes take another form: years spent away from God in pursuit of worldly pleasure and self-gratification! How many have tried this! No wonder the fields are bare! *Can* God restore these years? Did He not restore the years for Naomi?

GOD CAN!

The blue water lily abounds in several of the canals in Alexandria, Egypt, which at certain seasons become dry; and the beds of these canals, which quickly become burnt as hard as bricks by the action of the sun, are then used as carriage roads. When, however, the water is admitted again, the lily resumes its growth with redoubled vigor and splendor.

December 18

Thou thyself art . . . a light of them which are in darkness. (Rom. 2:19)

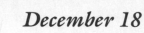

We are kindled that we might kindle others. I would like, if I might have my choice, to burn steadily down, with no guttering waste, and as I do so to communicate God's fire to as many unlit candles as possible, and to burn on steadily until the socket comes in view; then to light in the last flicker, twenty, thirty, or a hundred candles at once, so that as one expires they may begin burning and spreading light which shall shine until Jesus comes.

> *Let me burn out for Thee, dear Lord,*
> *Burn and wear out for Thee;*
> *Don't let me rust, or my life be*
> *A failure, my God, to Thee.*
> *Use me, and all I have, dear Lord,*
> *And get me so close to Thee*
> *That I feel the throb of the great heart of God,*
> *Until I burn out for Thee.*
>
> BESSIE F. HATCHER

December 19

Though he was rich, yet for your sakes he became poor. (2 Cor. 8:9)

The poorest man that ever walked the dirt roads of earth! Born in poverty, reared in obscurity, *yet He enriched all mankind!*

For twenty years He worked as a carpenter in that village which bore the scorn of men: "Can there any good thing come out of Nazareth?"

As far as we know He never possessed the value of one penny. In the wilderness without food, by Jacob's well without water, in the crowded city without a home—thus *He lived, and loved, and died!*

> *The foxes find rest,*
> *And the birds have their nests*
> *In the shade of the forest tree,*

But Thy couch was the sod,
O Thou Son of God,
In the desert of Galilee.

He preached without price, and wrought miracles without money. His parish was the world. He sought breakfast from a leafing fig tree. He ate grain as He walked through the field of corn. *Without money,* did I say? He sent Peter to the sea for the fish that they might have money for the tax! He had no cornfields or fisheries, yet He could spread a table for five thousand and have bread and fish to spare! No beautiful carpets to walk on, yet the waters supported Him!

So poor was He that He must needs bear His own cross through the city, till fainting He fell. His value was thirty pieces of silver—the price of a slave, the lowest estimate of human life. But, on God's side, *no lower price than His infinite agony* could have made possible our Redemption! When He died, few men mourned; but a black crepe was hung over the sun. *His crucifixion was the crime of crimes!*

IT WAS NOT MERELY HUMAN BLOOD THAT WAS SPILLED ON CALVARY'S HILL!

He did not have a house where He could go
When it was night—when other men went down
Small streets where children watched with eager eyes,
Each one assured of shelter in the town,
The Christ sought refuge anywhere at all:
A house, an inn, the roadside, or a stall!

He borrowed the boat in which He rode that day,
He talked to throngs along the Eastern lake;
It was a rented room to which He called
The chosen twelve the night He bade them break
The loaf with Him, and He rode, unafraid,
Another's colt in that triumph-parade.

A man from Arimathea had a tomb
Where Christ was placed when nails had done their deed.
Not ever in the crowded days He knew,
Did He have coins to satisfy a need.
They should not matter, these small things I crave.
Make me forget them, Father, and be brave!

THE TRANSIENT, BY HELEN WELSHIMER

December 20

Behold your God! (Isa. 40:9)

He became the Son of Man that *we* might become the sons of God. Here is a man who was born in an obscure village, child of a peasant woman. He had neither wealth nor influence, neither training nor education; yet in infancy he startled a king; in boyhood He puzzled the doctors. In manhood He walked upon the billows and hushed the sea to sleep. He healed the multitudes without medicine and made no charge for His services. He never wrote a book, *yet all the libraries of the world could not hold the books that could be written about Him.* He never wrote a song, *yet He has furnished the theme of more songs than all songwriters combined.* He never founded a college, *yet all the colleges together cannot boast of as many students as He.*

"*He was rich, yet for your sakes he became poor.*"

How poor? Ask Mary! Ask the Wise Men! He slept in another's manger. He cruised the lake in another's boat. He rode on another man's ass. He was buried in another man's tomb.

While still a young man the tide of popular opinion turned against Him. His friends ran away from Him. One of them denied Him; another betrayed Him and turned Him over to His enemies. He went through the mockery of a trial. He was nailed upon the Cross between two thieves. His executioners gambled for His coat.

Yet, *all the armies that ever marched, all the navies that were ever built, all the parliaments that ever sat, all the kings that ever reigned, put together,* have not affected the life of man as powerfully as has *this one solitary life!*

Great men have come and gone, *yet He lives on!* Death could not destroy Him! The grave could not hold Him!

"Behold, the world is gone after him!" *(John 12:19).*

"Let us also go" *(John 11:16).*

"If thou seek him, he will be found of thee" *(1 Chron. 28:9).*

FIND HIM!

December 21

Save thyself. (Matt. 27:40)

Save thyself! These words have a familiar ring in the Master's ears. He had heard them in all their variations throughout the whole period of His public ministry. When a messenger came to Peraea carrying tidings of the passing of Lazarus, His disciples tried to dissuade Him from going to Bethany, *to save Himself.*

An anxious family waited on Him in Capernaum and begged Him to return to Nazareth *to save Himself.*

Certain Greeks approached Him during the Last Passover and evidently afforded Him an opportunity to slip out of the picture gracefully, *to save Himself.*

In Gethsemane His final decision was made, quite in accord with all of His previous decisions. He would *not* save Himself. Now, agonizing on the cross, He heard the malefactors suggesting that He save Himself—and them. His critics and crucifiers joined the chorus and cried, "Come down from the cross—*save thyself.*"

But He who taught His disciples to deny themselves and to save their lives by losing them had definitely determined to give Himself. THE UPPER ROOM ☞

When a Roman soldier was told by his guide that if he insisted on taking a certain journey it would probably be fatal, he answered, "It is necessary for me to go; it is not necessary for me to live."

That was depth. When we have convictions like that we shall come to something worthy of our name Christian.

> *More than half beaten, but fearless,*
> *Facing the storm and the night,*
> *Reeling and breathless, but fearless,*
> *Here in the lull of the fight.*
> *I who bow not but before Thee,*
> *God of the fighting clan,*
> *Lifting my fists I implore Thee,*
> *Give me the heart of a man!*
>
> *What though I stand with the winners,*
> *Or perish with those that fall?*
> *Only the cowards are sinners;*

Fighting the fight, that is all.
Strong is my foe, who advances,
Snapped is my blade, O Lord;
See their proud banners and lances,
But spare me the stub of a sword!

December 22

He endured, as seeing him who is invisible. (Heb. 11:27)

The life of Moses was a much-enduring one. He endured the banishment from palatial surroundings and the most brilliant court then in existence; he endured the forfeiture of privilege, and the renunciation of splendid prospects; he endured the flight from Egypt, and the wrath of the king; he endured the lonely exile in Midian, where for years he was buried alive; he endured the long trudge through the wilderness at the head of a slave people, whom he sought to consolidate into a nation; he endured the ill manners and the countless provocations of a froward and perverse generation; he endured the lonely death on Nebo, and the nameless grave that angels dug for him there! And here we have the secret of his wondrous fortitude disclosed to us:

"He endured, as seeing him who is invisible."

He realized the presence of God. He lived in the consciousness, "Thou God seest me." He looked up, and had an habitual regard to the heavenly and eternal. In the upper chambers of his soul there was a window that opened skyward, and commanded a view of things unseen. As an old author puts it, "He had a greater view than Pharaoh in his eye, and this kept him right." Yes, and this will keep any of us right: to live under the sense that God is overlooking us—to walk by faith and not by sight. "There is nothing," says a great modern preacher, "that enables a man so well to carry on things that are terraqueous and material, as to have in ascendancy every day that part of his nature which dwells with the invisible." S. Law Wilson

December 23

What lack I yet? (Matt. 19:20)

When Jesus answered the rich young ruler's question, the young man said: "All these things have I kept ... what lack I yet?" Then Jesus told him what his lack was and "he went away sorrowful." The interview was over; Jesus asked for *the Master Key* and the young man refused to give it.

Has Jesus the keys to your life? Has He the key to the *Library* of your life, or do you just read what you please? Has He the key to the *Dining room* of your life—do you feed your soul on His Word? Has He the key to the *Recreation* compartment, or do you just go where you please? Have you given Christ the Master Key to *your* life?

We may have *all* of the Holy Ghost, but has He *all* of us? Are there spaces yet to be filled with the Holy Ghost—spaces, places, rooms, and closets in our spiritual house into which He has not *"fully come,"* because we have not yet given up *all* the keys from cellar to attic of our spiritual homestead?

The House of the Lord has many chambers,
Large and lofty, or low and small;
And some who turn from the world's broad highways
And find the door to the ENTRANCE HALL,
Are satisfied with its shade and coolness,
To know they have come to the House of a Friend,
And, resting there in the peace and quiet,
They think they have fared to their journey's end.

And some are content with the ANTECHAMBER,
That opens out of the entrance hall,
With the winds that blow from the spicy gardens,
The musical splash of the fountain's fall;
They feast on the fruits of the Spirit's giving
And muse on the thought of the joys to come,
And resting there in the peace and quiet,
Are glad that the Lord has brought them home.

But those who have heeded His invitation
To come up higher and enter in
To the UPPER ROOM *of the Master's dwelling,*
To stores of treasures their way shall win.
What eye hath seen them? What mind conceived them?
What heart hath dreamed of the things concealed,
The joys prepared for the Lord's beloved,
To those who seek them alone revealed?

Clothed with His glory they leave His presence,
Girt with His power they walk abroad
Who find the door to the INNER CHAMBER,
The secret place of the Most High God.

THE INNER CHAMBER,
BY ANNIE JOHNSON FLINT 🖋

December 24

Buried with him . . . that . . . even so we also should walk in new-
ness of life. (Rom. 6:4)

No one enters into the experience of entire sanctification without going through a "white funeral," i.e., the burial of the old life. If there has never been this crisis of death, sanctification is nothing more than a vision. There must be a "white funeral," the death that has only one resurrection—a resurrection into the life of Jesus. Nothing can upset this life; it is one with God, for one purpose, to be a witness to Him.

Have I come to my last days really? I have come to them in sentiment, but have I come to them *really?* You cannot go to your funeral in excitement, nor die in excitement. Death means stopping being. Do I agree with God that I stop being the striving earnest kind of Christian I have been? We skirt the cemetery and all the time refuse to go to death. It is not striving to go to death, it is dying—"baptized into his death."

Have I had a "white funeral," or am I sacredly playing with my soul? Is there a place marked in my life as the last day, a place that the memory goes back to with a chastened and extraordinary grateful remembrance—Yes, it was then, that I made an agreement with God. "This is the will of God, even your sanctification." When you realize what the will of God is, you will enter into sanctification as naturally as can be. Are you willing to go through the "white funeral" now?

Do you agree with Him that this is your last day on earth? That moment depends on you. MY UTMOST FOR HIS HIGHEST, BY OSWALD CHAMBERS 🖋

December 25

GOOD TIDINGS OF GREAT JOY! (Luke 2:10)

Tidings of glory! all the sky aflame, all Heaven hymning one imperial Name! radiant glimpses of a Throne, a Crown, all splendor focused on one little town! Tidings of joy, good tidings of great joy! ~~Supernal ecstasy without alloy!~~ The death of sorrow and the end of pain, the bliss, bliss, bliss eternally to reign! News of Salvation! Jesus, Savior, Christ, bearer of mercy ample, and unpriced herald of freedom from the chains of sin, come to our hearts, Lord Jesus, enter in! Tidings to all the people, yea, to all! to kings and shepherds, to the great and small, to rich and poor, to ignorant and wise, to each his blessing from the liberal skies! Oh, for the ready eye and quickened ear, the Advent light to see, and song to hear! To every man and woman, girl and boy, in all the world, *GOOD TIDINGS OF GREAT JOY!*
AMOS R. WELLS 🖎

HE GAVE US THE BEST THAT HE HAD!

To Bethlehem they went to be enrolled;
And there, in Caesar's census book of old,
His name was written 'mong the sons of men
As Caesar's subject: "Jesus"—followed then
By "Son of Mary, born in David's Town,
Of David's line"—the record thus set down.
In a world's book of life, a place they gave
To "Jesus" who was born a world to save.
They numbered Him with sinful men and poor,
Though He was Son of God, Divine and pure.

A heavenly census book His name alone
Bears, on the title page; for 'tis His own,
That Book of Life; and there, writ clear and plain
Are names of those born in that King's domain;
All who alive forevermore shall be
Are there enrolled for all eternity.
Since He was numbered once with sinful men,
We may be numbered as God's own again.
Though Caesar's book has long since passed away,
The Lamb's blest Book of Life shall stand for aye.
THE CENSUS BOOKS, BY KAY McCULLOUGH 🖎

Was it merely the son of Joseph and Mary who crossed the world's horizon nineteen hundred years ago? Your own heart must answer—
"My Lord and my God!"

December 26

And now shall mine head be lifted up above mine enemies round about me. (Ps. 27:6)

There is an old Scottish mansion quite close to where I have a little summer home in the north of Scotland, which has in it a room noted for the sketches and pictures that from time to time have been drawn upon the walls by visiting artists. It is a room to which people came from the ends of the world, and it all began in this way.

That room had been redecorated. Its plaster walls had been repainted. There was an accident in that room with a syphon of soda water which burst and covered the newly decorated plaster wall with stain. The woman of the house was, of course, not unnaturally irritated at such an accident to her newly decorated room, and she was not slow to express her irritation.

There was a great artist staying in the house, no less than Sir Edwin Landseer. He did not say anything to her, but when even the next day her irritation had not altogether abated—for the stain had dried, and it looked even worse then, and was seen to be permanent—he stayed at home when the rest of the party in the house went out on the moors. He took a piece of charcoal, and with a few deft touches and strokes he transformed that disfigurement into a thing of priceless beauty. He made it the background of a waterfall, and he put in the surrounding crags and one or two fir trees, a noble stag.

It is regarded, indeed, that sketch upon the wall, as one of Landseer's most successful sketches of Highland life. The point is this. That which was a disfigurement has become a thing of permanent beauty and priceless-ness. . . .

I do not care where you have failed. I do not care if it is in the deepest motive of your being. I do not care how far you have fallen. I do not care how deeply you have disfigured and defaced the image of God—the great Craftsman, the great Master and Lord of us all, can turn your soul from that very failure into a positive endowment for future service. J. STU-ART HOLDEN

Let God do it for you!

December 27

In returning and rest shall ye be saved; in quietness and in con-
fidence shall be your strength. (Isa. 30:15)

"Desert sweetened." It was only a sign in a wayside fruit stand. But the golden grapefruit that it advertised took on new value! So will any life that follows the formula given by the Master: "Come ye yourselves apart into a desert place, and rest a while." It was in the loneliness of desert reaches that some of the mightiest of the Old Testament prophets received their message: "Thus saith the Lord." In the desert Jesus met and mastered temptation. Out of a three-year desert retreat came Paul to be the greatest missionary of all time!

"Desert sweetened!" A quiet place at the beginning and the close of day. A "little chapel of silence"—"where, though the feet may join the throng, the soul may enter in and pray." Sunshine and silence—synonyms for the desert. May they bring special gifts of calm and courage and confidence—because we have kept our appointment with Christ in these moments of devotion! SELECTED

The road to the Promised Land of spiritual power always leads through desert places where "the still small voice" has a chance to be heard. GLENN RANDALL PHILLIPS

> *In the secret of His presence how my soul delights to hide!*
> *Oh, how precious are the lessons which I learn at Jesus' side!*
> *Earthly cares can never vex me, neither trials lay me low;*
> *For when Satan comes to tempt me, to the secret place I go.*
> *When my soul is faint and thirsty, 'neath the shadow of His wing*
> *There is cool and pleasant shelter and a fresh and crystal spring;*
> *And my Savior rests beside me, as we hold communion sweet:*
> *If I tried I could not utter what He says when thus we meet.*
> *Only this I know: I tell Him all my doubts, my griefs, and fears.*
> *Oh, how patiently He listens! and my drooping soul He cheers.*
> *Do you think He ne'er reproves me? What a false friend He would be*
> *If He never, never told me of the sins which He must see!*
> *Would you like to know the sweetness of the secret of the Lord?*
> *Go and hide beneath His shadow; this shall then be your reward.*
> *And whene'er you leave the silence of that happy meeting-place,*
> *You must mind and bear the image of the Master in your face.*
> ELLEN LAKSHMI GOREH

December 28

Thy love to me was wonderful. (2 Sam. 1:26)

Is it too much to hope that when we see our blessed Lord in the glory, when the trials and the toils and the sacrifices are all at an end—Is it too much to desire that He should say something like this to us: *"Thy love to me was wonderful"?* I tell you it will make the toils of the road and all the renunciations and willing sacrifices of life seem as nothing to have some such words of commendation from the lips of our Savior, and to hear Him say to the one who has sought to be faithful at all cost: "Well done. You were never popular on earth, and nobody knew much about you. The life you lived to My glory in the uninspiring sphere of duty seemed to be wasted and its sacrifice to be worthless by those who knew it; *but your love to Me was wonderful!* Men said you made mistakes and were narrow-minded and did not catch the spirit of the age. Men thought you were a fanatic and a fool and called you so; men crucified you as they crucified Me, but *your love to Me was wonderful!"*

> *Savior, Thy dying love Thou gavest me,*
> *Nor should I ought withhold,*
> *Dear Lord, from Thee:*
> *In love my soul would bow,*
> *My heart fulfill its vow,*
> *Some offering bring Thee now,*
> *Something for Thee.*

"He is altogether lovely."

December 29

Behold, there ariseth a little cloud out of the sea, like a man's hand. (1 Kings 18:44)

The fields were parched for lack of rain. The foliage of the green bay tree wilted in the sun. The earth was dry like powder, and gray dust covered leaf and blade. There was no freshness anywhere. As far as eye could see nature seemed to have dressed herself in sackcloth and ashes. We have never seen such drought as that which had fallen upon Israel in the days of Elijah the Tishbite. There had been no rain for three and a half years. The fields had not yielded their increase, and little children cried for food.

Elijah was on Mount Carmel praying for rain. "Go," he said to his servant, "and look out toward the sea and tell me if any sign of rain appears." Seven times he went and surveyed the western horizon, where the sky seemed to drop into the glittering Mediterranean. The seventh time he returned and said, "Behold, there ariseth *a little cloud* out of the sea, like a man's hand."

A very little cloud it was, but sufficient to assure Elijah that God was answering prayer and that the day of refreshment had come for all the land of Israel.

It is not always so with men. When we cry to God we are impatient to see God's finished answer all at once. We rise from our knees, and because the heavens do not hang heavily with clouds we are too quick to think that God is withholding His showers of blessing. *But God usually gives us by slow degrees the things we need.*

We grow impatient because we have not the sensibility of soul to detect *the faint beginnings* of God's mercies. The first gray tints that touch the eastern skies are a promise of the coming day. The first flickering ray of light that steals across our soul when we cry to God is the beginning of His answer. The first indefinable feeling of comfort that slips into the distressed soul is *a little cloud* bearing promise of refreshing showers.

"I knelt and prayed," said a young woman, "and it seemed that I saw a light across my way, and *then I was sure* that the thing perplexing me would come out all right." The light that shone for a moment in the heart's secret places was the harbinger of great happiness and blessing.

Broken heart, crying to God for comfort, take courage from moments which come like respites when the weight of sorrow is for a little while lightened! How delicately God deals with us! These are intimations of the peace which in the process of God's providence shall at last come.

Perplexed heart, crying to God for guidance, be assured by the events that seem to turn your life in a particular direction and by the light that every now and then falls on your problems—be assured that *God is beginning* to answer your prayer!

O Guilty heart, crying to God for forgiveness, let your desires for purity, your bitterness of soul, the faint whisperings of Divine love heard only by the spirit's ear—let all of these tell you that God is already hearing and answering. Our skies are dotted with *little clouds, faint beginnings* of God's mercies. *They assure the waiting heart of greater clouds just beyond* the horizon, laden with His blessings. COSTEN J. HARRELL ☙

Watch for God's faint beginnings!

December 30

He . . . sat down under a juniper tree. (1 Kings 19:4)

This is Elijah! One is startled, perplexed, disappointed. A while ago we saw him on Mount Carmel surrounded by the thronging thousands of Israel, undismayed by the bold audacity of the worshipers of Baal, and confidently appealing to God to vindicate His own honor, and confound Baalim. Here he is, the prey of deep depression, forgetful of the past, giving all up, wanting God to take away his life. God has not once failed him. Not to any extent at all has one single foe prevailed against him. He should not have lost heart, should not have fled, should not have asked God to take away his life; all this was wrong. He should have remembered how God had wonderfully stood by him in the past, and have firmly trusted Him still. Is not his privilege ours also? May not God's people trust Him fully, firmly, and under all circumstances, and at all times? God is not "afar off," neither has He forgotten to be gracious; and that which He has promised He will unfailingly remember, and do. Are we not always in His hands and under His care? Should we ever have a single fear? Why should we be cast down, or disquieted? J. T. W. ☙

Have faith in God, the sun will shine,
Though dark the cloud may be today!

HAVE FAITH IN GOD!

December 31

For here have we no continuing city, but we seek one to come. (Heb. 13:14)

A great world conqueror was leading his victorious army back to Italy—and home. Onward they marched over rivers and plains, and through wooded forests until they reached the foothills of the towering Alps. Here the thinning ranks of the worn and tired soldiers began to falter as they trudged on over the rocky defiles of the mighty mountain passes. As they climbed higher and still higher, the blinding snow and storms well-nigh discouraged the stoutest hearts. Stopping on an eminence where he could overlook all his men and be heard by them, and pointing upward across the mighty barrier, the great general shouted, "Men, beyond those Alps lies Italy!"

Italy! Waving fields, beautiful orchards, sparkling fountains! Mothers and fathers, wives and children, sweethearts! Home! Ah, sweet home!

Fainting hearts revived. Tired muscles found new strength. Onward and upward that brave army pressed against every obstacle—and won! They reached home.

Another scene. All over the world are members of Prince Emmanuel's army. Many have won decisive battles with the enemy, great victories over sin. They have struggled along life's rugged highway, and many have become worn and weary in the conflict. Long have they marched, homeward bound. But now they have reached great mountains of difficulties, strifes, wars, threatened dissolution of all social and moral standards—the mighty Alps on the stream of time. To this vast army their Captain shouts, "Christian soldiers, beyond these mountains of difficulty lies Home!"

Heaven! Waving fields of living green, kingly forests with never-fading foliage, sparkling fountains! The Tree of Life, and the River of Life! Long-lost friends, mothers and fathers, brothers and sisters, husbands, wives, children, loved ones! Thank God, we are nearing our heavenly home!

> *I've been to the rim of the world, and beyond,*
> *But I'm headin' home tonight.*
>
> E. W. PATTEN

HOMING!

Acknowledgments

The compiler takes pleasure in acknowledging the kindness of authors and publishers who, very generously, have granted permission to use extracts from their copyrighted publications.

Among those to whom such acknowledgments are due are the following: Fleming H. Revell Company for selections from the writings of F. B. Meyer; Dr. C. G. Trumbull for extracts from *Messages for the Morning Watch* and the *Sunday School Times;* Christian Publications, Inc. for quotations from *Days of Heaven upon Earth*, also excerpts from sermons and tracts by Dr. A. B. Simpson; the American Tract Society for selections from John Oxenham's book *Bees in Amber;* the Yale University Press for the poem by Karle Wilson Baker, taken from their anthology *The World's Greatest Religious Poetry;* Mr. Thomas Kimber for several of his poems; Evangelical Publishers, Toronto, Canada, for the use of the poems of Miss Annie Johnson Flint; the Cokesbury Press for extracts from *Walking with God* by Costen J. Harrel; Mr. Matthew Biller for his *My Calvary* and other poems; Mr. J. Danson Smith for his poems.

An earnest endeavor has been made to locate the authors of all copyrighted selections; indulgence is begged where this endeavor has failed. Should we succeed in locating any further copyright owners, acknowledgment will be given.

"A Handbook of Strength and Comfort"

—Barbara Johnson

Just as he did for *My Utmost for His Highest,* editor Jim Reimann has created this new edition of *Streams in the Desert,* which will surely offer support and encouragement for those desolate, dry paths in your life. 366 daily devotional selections crafted by L.B. Cowman are especially designed for people experiencing the challenges of daily life and any type of grief or loss. *Streams in the Desert* now offers a message that is made even more relevant, spiritually motivating, and comforting because it's written in today's language with the Scripture references drawn from the NIV.

Pick up your copy of *Streams in the Desert* at local Christian bookstores and gain a greater appreciation for the oasis of spiritual refreshment provided by our Lord!

Streams in the Desert—Updated Edition
Hardcover: 0-310-21006-2

ZondervanPublishingHouse

Grand Rapids, Michigan
http://www.zondervan.com
AOL keyword ZON
A Division of HarperCollinsPublishers

An anthology of faith, hope, and timeless wisdom

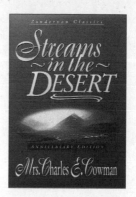

Few books ever attain such widespread recognition and perennial appeal as *Streams in the Desert*. Now over seventy years since its first publication, this marvelous devotional by Mrs. Charles E. Cowman has established itself firmly in the ranks of the Christian classics.

Streams in the Desert, Anniversary Edition is a member of the Zondervan Classics collection. Zondervan Classics brings you the finest in the classic Christian literature—works chosen by readers throughout the years for their beauty, ageless insight, and power to inspire and refresh the heart.

Look for *Streams in the Desert* and other members of the Zondervan Classics collection at bookstores everywhere.

Streams in the Desert—Anniversary Edition
Hardcover: 0-310-48400-6

ZondervanPublishingHouse
Grand Rapids, Michigan
http://www.zondervan.com
AOL keyword ZON
A Division of HarperCollins*Publishers*

NIV Classics Devotional Bible

Devotional and spiritual writings from over one-hundred heroes and heroines of the faith are integrated with the complete Bible text in this inspiring devotional Bible. Insights from the hearts and minds of Christians through the centuries, including C. S. Lewis, John Calvin, Hannah Whithall Smith, Brother Lawrence, Charles Wesley, Corrie ten Boom, and others will help readers reflectively meditate on God's Word. A full year of weekday and weekend devotions in the form of stories, reflections, poetry, and hymns are with the Bible text. Summary descriptions of the characteristics, special concerns, and unique contributions of each major period in church history are included, as well as reading plans, author biographies, subject index, and more.

NIV Version

Hardcover   ISBN 0-310-91962-2
                           ISBN 0-310-91963-0 Indexed
Softcover   ISBN 0-310-91964-9
Burgundy Bonded Leather ISBN 0-310-91965-7
                           ISBN 0-310-91966-5 Indexed
Navy Bonded Leather   ISBN 0-310-91967-3
                           ISBN 0-310-91968-1 Indexed

NRSV Version

Hardcover   ISBN 0-310-91971-1
                           ISBN 0-310-91972-X Indexed
Softcover   ISBN 0-310-91973-8
Black Bonded Leather   ISBN 0-310-91974-6
                           ISBN 0-310-91975-4 Indexed

ZondervanPublishingHouse
Grand Rapids, Michigan
http://www.zondervan.com
AOL keyword ZON
A Division of HarperCollins*Publishers*

NIV Men's Devotional Bible, Classic Hardcover Edition

Devotions for men, from other men they know and trust: that's the distinctive of the *Men's Devotional Bible*. And now the devotional insights of writers like Charles Swindoll, A. W. Tozer, Ben Carson, C. S. Lewis, Dietrich Bonhoeffer, and Philip Yancey come with a marbled green cover design that fits like a quality suit: refined, masculine, perfect for the man who appreciates a professional touch.

NIV Women's Devotional Bible 2, Classic Hardcover Edition

No one understands today's woman like other women: women like Joni Eareckson Tada, Gloria Gaither, Rosa Parks, Luci Shaw, and Elisa Morgan, who know from experience how the truths of Scripture are fleshed out in marriage, at work, at home, at church, among friends ... in all of life. Now these and other writers from the *Women's Devotional Bible 2* present their devotional wisdom in a classy, marbled red cover design. This Bible is designed to complement a woman's unique style—and help her beautify the woman within.

NIV Men's Hardcover Classic ISBN 0-310-91604-6
NIV Women's 2 Hardcover Classic ISBN 0-310-91636-4

AVAILABLE SEPTEMBER 1997

ZondervanPublishingHouse
Grand Rapids, Michigan
http://www.zondervan.com
AOL keyword ZON
A Division of HarperCollinsPublishers

We want to hear from you. Please send your comments about this
book to us in care of the address below. Thank you.

ZondervanPublishingHouse
Grand Rapids, Michigan 49530
http://www.zondervan.com